Marie-Claire Foblets | Luc Leboeuf (eds.)

Humanitarian Admission to Europe

The Law between Promises and Constraints

HART PUBLISHING

Nomos

The Deutsche Nationalbibliothek lists this publication in the Deutsche Nationalbibliografie; detailed bibliographic data are available on the Internet at http://dnb.d-nb.de

ISBN:	HB (Nomos)	978-3-8487-5730-5
	ePDF (Nomos)	978-3-8452-9860-3

British Library Cataloguing-in-Publication Data
A catalogue record for this book is available from the British Library.

ISBN: HB (Hart) 978-1-509939-671

Library of Congress Cataloging-in-Publication Data
Foblets, Marie-Claire / Leboeuf, Luc
Humanitarian Admission to Europe
The Law between Promises and Constraints
Marie-Claire Foblets / Luc Leboeuf (eds.)
371 pp.
Includes bibliographic references.

ISBN 978-1-509939-671 (hardcover Hart)

Onlineversion
Nomos eLibrary

1st Edition 2020

Foreword

Winfried Kluth[1]

Scientific research on migration law is not possible without a close link to reality. For courts and judges the situation is not very different. This was made clear in the opinion of Advocate General *Mengozzi*, presented on 7 February 2018, in the case *X. and X.* involving a Syrian family that had already been subjected to torture and which applied for humanitarian visas at the Belgian embassy in Beirut.

Advocate General Mengozzi argued with respect to the responsibility of the EU and the Member States: "It is, in my view, crucial that, at a time when borders are closing and walls are being built, the Member States do not escape their responsibilities, as they follow from EU law or, if you will allow me the expression, *their* EU law and *our* EU law."

The impulse given by Advocate General Mengozzi's opinion was answered by organizing an international conference focusing on the legal framework of persecution and the genuine dangers that refugees face on their way to "safe harbours". The formidable scientific network of *Marie-Claire Foblets* and the excellent coordination by *Luc Leboeuf* made it possible to invite outstanding experts from several countries to discuss the legal aspects of humanitarian visas and other instruments that can be used to facilitate safe escape paths.

The conference organizers took the very compelling approach of focusing on the topic from different legal and institutional points of view, and this volume likewise follows that logic. The first part starts with an analysis of humanitarian admission in international and EU law, with *Dirk Hanschel*, *Stephanie Law* and *Sylvie Sarolea* presenting their sophisticated observations. The second part adds three national perspectives. The contributions of *Katia Bianchini (Italy)*, *Pauline Endres de Oliveira (Germany)* and *Serge Bodart (Belgium)* vividly illustrate how different nation-states deal with the same problem. The great difficulties inherent in claiming and actually being granted humanitarian admission in reality are demonstrated by *Sophie Nakueira (with reference to Uganda)* and *Tristan Wibault*, who represented the plaintiffs before the European Court of Justice in the case *X*

1 Professor in the Faculty of Law, Martin Luther University Halle-Wittenberg.

and X. Finally, some future prospects on humanitarian admission to Europe are presented by *Catharina Ziebritzki*, *Eugenia Relano Pastor* and *Jean-Yves Carlier*.

This collection of inspiring and dense articles is the result of two days of intensive discussions. The contributions touch on all relevant legal aspects that should be taken into account by the Member States and the EU when they are searching for a "value-based" response to the problems observed in the Mediterranean Sea region.

Recently, the first steps towards such a response were taken with the Malta Declaration of 23 September 2019, but the political agreement on burden sharing between Germany, France and some other countries is only a first step and is not legally binding. The scientific considerations in this book are sure to prove very useful as further political and legal solutions are sought.

Table of contents

Introduction: Humanitarian Admission to Europe. From Policy Developments to Legal Controversies and Litigation

Luc Leboeuf and Marie-Claire Foblets[1]

Contents

Introduction

On 7 March 2017, the CJEU adopted its much-discussed ruling in the *X. and X.* case,[2] by which it decided that the EU Visa Code does not regulate

---

1 Luc Leboeuf is a Head of Research Group in the Department of Law & Anthropology of the Max Planck Institute for Social Anthropology. Marie-Claire Foblets is Director of the Department of Law & Anthropology of the Max Planck Institute for Social Anthropology and Professor in the Law Faculty of the Catholic University of Leuven (KUL).

2 Case C-638/16 PPU *X and X* [2017] EU:C:2017:173. The case has been widely commented by legal scholars, including by some of the contributors to this volume. See, among others: Y Al Tamimi, E Brouwer, and R Coene, 'Verplicht de Visum-

the issuing of humanitarian visas to asylum seekers.[3] The *X. and X.* ruling was adopted at a time of heated controversies in Europe over migration, as the 2015 'refugee crisis' created major divisions among European societies and public opinion, which still continue to this day.[4] For that reason, the

---

code tot afgifte van humanitaire visa aan Syriërs?' (2017) *Asiel en Migrantenrecht* 327-333; M Berger and G Maderbacher, 'Erteilung eines Visums zur Ermöglichung der Asylantragstellung im Inland unterliegt allein nationalem Recht' (2017) *Österreichische Juristenzeitung* 480-481; E Brouwer, 'Een gemiste kans voor een uniforme en mensenrechtelijke uitleg van de Visumcode wat betreft de afgifte van een humanitair visum' (2017) *Nederlands Tijdschrift voor Europees Recht* 69-78; J-Y Carlier and L Leboeuf, 'Droit européen des migrations' (2018) 26 *Journal de droit européen* 247 95-110, 97; R Colavitti, 'Ouvrir la jarre de Pandore ou trancher le nœud gordien ? La Cour face aux conditions d'application du Code des visas aux demandes déposées pour raison humanitaire' (2017) *Revue des affaires européennes* 139-147; J De Coninck and M Chamon, 'Geen recht op tijdelijke visums voor Syrische vluchtelingen' (2017) *Tijdschrift voor Europees en economisch recht* 382-387; B Delzangles and A Louvaris, 'Visas humanitaires et Charte des droits fondamentaux : la confrontation n'a pas eu lieu' (2017) 239 *Journal de droit européen* 170-176; P Endres de Oliveira, 'Antrag syrischer Flüchtlinge auf humanitäres Visum bei belgischer Botschaft im Libanon' (2017) *Neue Zeitschrift für Verwaltungsrecht* 611-615; F Gazin, 'Motifs humanitaires' (2017) 5 *Europe* 18-19; S-P Hwang, 'Humanitäre Visa für Flüchtlinge: Einfallstor für ein unbeschränktes Asylrecht?' (2018) *Europarecht* 269-288; W Kluth, 'Das humanitäre Visum als Instrument der sicheren Fluchtmigration' (2017) *Zeitschrift für Ausländerrecht und Ausländerpolitik* 105-109; H Labayle, 'Visas dits « humanitaires » : la régulation a minima du droit d'asile par la Cour de justice de l'Union' (2017) 18 *La Semaine Juridique* 869-873; V Moreno-Lax, 'Asylum Visas as an Obligation under EU Law: Case PPU C-638/16, X, X v État belge' (2017) *EU Immigration and Asylum Law and Policy* <http://eumigrationlawblog.eu/asylum-visas-as-an-obligation-under-eu-law-case-ppu-c-63816-x-x-v-etat-belge/> (accessed on 17 October 2019); K Müller, 'Kein legaler Zugangsweg in die EU durch humanitäre Visa: Einordnung des Verfahrens "X und X gegen Belgien" in die Europäische Migrations- und Flüchtlingspolitik' (2017) *Zeitschrift für Europarechtliche Studien* 161-184; S Sarolea, J-Y Carlier and L Leboeuf, 'Délivrer un visa humanitaire visant à obtenir une protection internationale au titre de l'asile ne relève pas du droit de l'Union : *X. et X.*, ou quand le silence est signe de faiblesse' (2017) *Cahiers de l'EDEM* <https://uclouvain.be/fr/instituts-recherche/juri/cedie/actualites/c-j-u-e-c-638-16-ppu-arret-du-7-mars-2017-x-et-x-ecli-eu-c-2017-173.html> (accessed on 17 October 2019); H-P Welte, '(Kein) Anspruch auf humanitäres Visum, Visakodex' (2017) *Zeitschrift für Ausländerrecht und Ausländerpolitik* 220-221.

3 Regulation No 810/2009 of the European Parliament and of the Council of 13 July 2009 establishing a Community Code on Visas (Visa Code) [2009] OJ L 243.

4 On these divisions, see among others S Holmes and H Castaneda, 'Representing the "European Refugee Crisis" in Germany and Beyond: Deservingness and Difference, Life and Death' (2016) 43 *American Ethnologist* 12-24; D Thym, 'The "Refugee Crisis" as a Challenge of Legal Design and Institutional Legitimacy' (2016) 53 *CMLRev* 1545-1574.

ruling offers an interesting case study of how the CJEU deals with the social tensions that accompanied the events of 2015. It illustrates the limitations of the current international, EU and domestic legal frameworks in dealing with societal controversies in the field of migration, when such controversies concern migrants who are outside European territory, and how attempts to bring about evolution in these frameworks through court litigation have been received by the judiciary to date.

Building upon that ruling, a workshop was held at the Max Planck Institute for Social Anthropology in May 2018, organised by its Department of Law & Anthropology and the Law Faculty of the Martin Luther University of Halle-Wittenberg. It gathered legal scholars, practitioners and anthropologists with the objective of engaging in a broader reflection on the extent to which these social controversies are channelled and managed through the positivist legal frameworks, starting from the specific case study of legal and safe access to European territory for those in search of protection. This book contains some of the proceedings of this workshop. It aims to offer a reflection on how and to what extent the existing legal frameworks guide the policy debates and controversies on humanitarian admission to Europe, as well as to engage in a broader critical reflection on the role which 'the law' can play in these policy debates.[5]

This introductory chapter sets the scene of the discussions that follow. It gives an overview of the current state of legal and policy debates on so-called 'legal avenues' and 'safe pathways' to Europe, and further questions whether and to what extent the law in its current form is adequately equipped to deal with these challenges. The first Section presents an overview of the main relevant policy developments of the past 10 years at EU level, culminating in the proposal by the EU Commission to establish a Union Resettlement Framework ('URF'). The second Section addresses how policy discussions and controversies on humanitarian admission to Europe have been accompanied by attempts to open up such access to European territory through litigation. The third Section discusses the approach developed by the CJEU in response to these attempts, departing from the *X. and X.* ruling. It identifies and discusses the reasons why the CJEU opposed the judicialisation of policy discussions on humanitarian admission to European territory through EU law. The fourth Section questions the role of the law in supporting policy claims towards humanitarian

5 This chapter constantly refers to the 'law' in its positivist sense, as a set of State-produced norms that have been formally adopted following the applicable legislative and administrative procedures.

admission to Europe for selected refugees. It argues that, despite their strong limitations, the current legal frameworks may still be an adequate tool to indirectly foster policy developments in the field. The last Section presents the way that the chapters of the volume seek to contribute to a better understanding of the relevant legal frameworks and the challenges raised in their implementation, as well as to a critical reflection on current legal paradoxes and limitations.

1 Policy Developments Towards Humanitarian Admission to Europe

Controversies on humanitarian visas, as they ultimately emerged before the CJEU in the *X. and X.* ruling, fit within broader policy debates on humanitarian admission to European territory for refugees. These debates are long-standing and are often connected to discussions on 'burden-sharing' and 'responsibility sharing', i.e., on how to allocate the responsibility to protect refugees fairly among the international community.[6] They led to several kind of policy initiatives at international, EU and domestic levels, in which some States have been involved on a voluntary and discretionary basis. These initiatives have been developed around various policy models, which the first sub-Section classifies broadly in an attempt to clarify the terms of the discussion that will follow in the next chapter of the volume. The second sub-Section then focuses on the developments at EU level, and shows that the main results they yielded so far are in the field of resettlement.

1.1 From 'Legal Avenues' and 'Safe Pathways', to 'Humanitarian Visas' and other 'Protected Entry Procedures'

Humanitarian visas as addressed by the CJEU in the *X. and X.* ruling are but a specific means of granting humanitarian admission to European territory for refugees. A humanitarian visa is generally understood as an authorisation to access the territory of a State, and which is granted by derogation from the applicable rules because of specific humanitarian reasons. The humanitarian visa has been defined in the IOM Glossary as:

6 M Gottwald, 'Burden Sharing and Refugee Protection' in E Fiddian-Qasmiyeh, G Loescher, K Long and N Sigona (eds), *The Oxford Handbook of Refugee and Forced Migration Studies* (Oxford, OUP, 2014).

> A visa granting access to and temporary stay in the issuing State for a variable duration to a person on humanitarian grounds as specified in the applicable national or regional law, often aimed at complying with relevant human rights and refugee law.[7]

Legal and policy issues surrounding the issuing of humanitarian visas are the subject of controversy in the context of a broader debate on so-called 'legal avenues' and 'safe pathways' for refugees. 'Legal avenue' is a term that has been used in various policy documents at EU level to broadly qualify initiatives aimed at offering humanitarian admission to Europe for refugees, such as resettlement programmes, humanitarian visas, humanitarian corridors and other humanitarian admission schemes.[8] The term 'safe pathway' is used in a similarly broad understanding at UN level, for example, in the 2016 New York Declaration for Refugees and Migrants[9] and in the 2018 Global Compact on Refugees.[10] The terms 'avenues' and 'regular pathways' are sometimes used in an even broader sense, to refer to any kind of legal entry procedure, such as labour and education mobility schemes, whose initial aim is not to offer safe access to protection for asylum seekers, but which some asylum seekers may incidentally be eligible for.[11] In its Resolution 2015/2095, for example, the European Parliament called for a 'holistic' approach to migration that goes beyond a focus on satisfying some protection needs through specific protection tools, to include a broader reflection on migration in all its aspects, including other

7 IOM, *Glossary on Migration* (Geneva, IOM, 2019) 95.

8 See, for example, the 2016 European Commission proposal to reform the Common European Asylum System (CEAS): COM (2016) 197 final, Communication from the Commission to the European Parliament and the Council towards a reform of the common European asylum system and enhancing legal avenues to Europe.

9 New York Declaration for Refugees and Migrants, UNGA Res 70/1 (19 September 2016).

10 Global Compact for Safe, Orderly and Regular Migration (adopted at Marrakech on 19 December 2018).

11 S Carrera, A Geddes, E Guild and M Stefan (eds), *Pathways Towards Legal Migration into the EU. Reappraising Concepts, Trajectories and Policies* (Brussels, Centre for European Policy Studies, 2017); E Collett, P Clewett and S Fratzke, *No Way Out for Refugees? Making Additional Migration Channels Work for Refugees* (Brussels, Migration Policy Institute, 2016); UNHCR, *Complementary Pathways for Admission of Refugees to Third Countries: Key Considerations* (Geneva, UNHCR, 2019); UNHCR and OECD, *Safe Pathways for Refugees. OECD-UNHCR Study on Third Country Solutions for Refugees: Family Reunification, Study Programmes and Labour Mobility* (Paris, OECD and Geneva, UNHCR, 2018); UNHCR, *Legal Avenues to Safety and Protection Through Other Forms of Admission* (Geneva, UNHCR, 2014).

legal entry procedures such as labour migration schemes and family reunification, fighting the root causes of forced migration, and integration in the host country.[12]

In policy documents, a variety of policy initiatives, each with its own specific features, have since been described as 'legal avenues' or 'safe pathways'. The exact meaning of these terms varies considerably, however, depending on the context. The vocabulary that is being used is not always consistent and very much depends on the policy *jargon* developed within the institution concerned. It is, however, possible to identify some broad categories of 'legal avenues' and 'safe pathways' from current State practices. In the next paragraphs we venture to identify some of these, with a focus on admission schemes that have been developed with the humanitarian objective of offering humanitarian admission to asylum seekers.

First, resettlement programmes are a long-standing form of humanitarian admission that has been developed specifically for those who have been formally recognized as refugees. They are defined in the IOM Glossary as:

> The transfer of refugees from the country in which they have sought protection to another State that has agreed to admit them – as refugees – with permanent residence status.[13]

Resettlement programmes rest on a collaboration with local authorities and often involve the UNHCR as intermediary. The overall objective of resettlement programmes is to engage in some form of burden-sharing by transferring the duty to offer protection from countries facing a large number of refugees to other countries with higher hosting capacities. The selection of the refugees who will be resettled is made by the receiving country, among a pool of refugees who have been preselected by the UNHCR and other local partners. The preselection by the UNHCR results from a vulnerability assessment, with the objective of identifying specific protection needs that cannot be addressed in the host country, such as health-related issues and gender-related persecutions.[14] While common, resettlement programmes usually concern a limited number of refugees. In 2018, for example, 55,680 refugees were resettled worldwide through UNHCR sponsored

---

12 EP Res of 12 April 2016 on the situation in the Mediterranean and the need for a holistic EU approach to migration.

13 IOM (n 7) 181.

14 UNHCR, *Resettlement Handbook* (Geneva, UNHCR, 2011).

resettlement programmes, of a total of 81,337 refugees preselected by the UNHCR for resettlement.[15]

Second, 'evacuation programmes' are aimed at bringing civilians to safety following a humanitarian emergency caused by a disaster and/or armed conflict. These are large-scale responses and, contrary to resettlement programmes, their implementation does not presuppose an individual assessment nor impose any requirement that a person have specific vulnerabilities. As noted by the UNHCR, 'humanitarian evacuation does not focus, as does resettlement, on addressing individual protection needs, rather it focuses on the protection requirements of the group'.[16] Evacuation programmes usually take place close to the conflict (or disaster) zone. Humanitarian evacuation programmes were implemented during the Yugoslavian conflict, for example, as civilians were allowed to cross the border between Kosovo and Macedonia, where they were hosted in refugee camps managed by the UNHCR in cooperation with local authorities.[17] More recently, 'evacuation' programmes have been set up by the IOM and the UNHCR with EU support to the benefit of refugees detained in horrendous conditions in Libya, some of whom were removed to refugee camps in Niger. These programmes were set up on a much smaller scale, however, and developed together with 'assisted voluntary return' programmes encouraging voluntary returns from Libya to the home country.[18] They are also to be distinguished from earlier understandings of 'evacuation' programmes. The aim is not to organise the flight of a civilian population away from a war zone, but rather to offer an alternate solution to selected refugees with vulnerable profiles.

Third, some States provide for 'protected entry procedures' (PEPs), which are formalised procedures that allow foreigners to individually and directly petition the State to obtain humanitarian admission to their terri-

15 UNHCR, *Resettlement Data*, <https://www.unhcr.org/resettlement-data.html> (accessed 10 August 2019).

16 UNHCR, *Updated UNHCR Guidelines for the Humanitarian Evacuation Programme of Kosovar Refugees in the Former Yugoslav Republic of Macedonia* (Geneva, UNHCR, 1999).

17 M Barutciski and A Suhrke, 'Lessons from the Kosovo Refugee Crisis: Innovations in Protection and Burden-sharing' (2001) 14 *Journal of Refugee Studies* 95–134.

18 C Loschi, L Raineri and F Strazzari, 'The Implementation of EU Crisis Response in Libya: Bridging Theory and Practice' (2018) *EUNPACK Working Paper* <http://www.eunpack.eu> (accessed 4 August 2019); J Brachet, 'Policing the Desert: The IOM in Libya Beyond War and Peace' (2016) 48 *Antipode* 2 272-292.

tory.[19] In such procedures, 'the individual is directly engaging the potential host State in a procedure aiming at securing his or her physical transfer and legal protection [...] In this mechanism, [his/her] individual autonomy ... is accorded a central role'.[20] Protected entry procedures differ from other humanitarian admission schemes, such as resettlement, in that a more active role is bestowed upon the applicants, who engage directly with the receiving State authorities. They give rise to direct contact between the State and the foreigner seeking protection, without requiring the intervention of a local intermediary or of the UNHCR.

Humanitarian visas can be seen both as a PEP and as a tool that helps to implement other humanitarian admission schemes. Humanitarian visas are a PEP where they are issued in a particular situation, where the State was petitioned by an individual because of specific humanitarian considerations and following a procedure established under national law. Such visas are issued on a discretionary basis and under very specific circumstances as shown by the practices of the three EU Member States under investigation in this volume in the contributions of Serge Bodart, Pauline Endres de Oliveira and Katia Bianchini (Belgium, Germany and Italy).[21] Humanitarian visas may also be issued to implement a broader humanitarian admission scheme, for example, to grant administrative authorisation to cross the border to those selected for resettlement. This is the case notably for some of the resettlement programmes implemented in Belgium,[22] as well as for the 'humanitarian corridors' set up by Italy.[23]

These various policy models for humanitarian admission have been discussed at EU level, where developments intensified with the growing externalisation of EU border policies. Policy discussions culminated as the 2015

---

19 G Noll, J Fagerlund and S Liebaut, *Study on the Feasibility of Processing Asylum Claims Outside the EU Against the Background of the Common European Asylum System and the Goal of a Common Asylum Procedure* (Danish Centre for Human Rights, Copenhagen, 2002); G Noll, 'From "Protective Passports" to Protected Entry Procedures? The Legacy of Raoul Wallenberg in the Contemporary Asylum Debate' in J Grimheden and R Ring (eds), *Human Rights Law: From Dissemination to Application. Essays in Honour of Göran Melander* (Leiden, Martinus Nijhoff, 2006) 237-249.

20 G Noll, J Fagerlund and S Liebaut (n 19) 20.

21 See also the conclusions of a study commissioned by the European Parliament, which identified provisions on humanitarian visas within the legislation of 16 Member States: U I Jensen, *Humanitarian Visas: Option or Obligation?* (Brussels, European Parliament, Study for the LIBE Committee, 2014).

22 See the contribution of Serge Bodart to this volume.

23 See the contribution of Katia Bianchini to this volume.

'European refugee crisis' increased policy interest in novel approaches to the management of migration movements. The policy developments at EU level are presented and discussed in the second sub-Section.

1.2 Policy Developments at EU Level. A Focus on Resettlement

In the EU, policy debates on humanitarian admission to Europe took a new turn in the 2000s as European countries started engaging more intensively in the 'externalisation' of their borders through so-called 'remote control' practices. The objective of such practices is to prevent irregular migration to Europe by 'policing at a distance' through legal and policy instruments allowing control of migrants before they reach European territory and preventing irregular migration to Europe.[24] The trend towards the externalisation of EU borders is leading to mounting criticisms from a human rights perspective, because one of its indirect effects is to prevent refugees from seeking safety in flight, whereas they often have no other practical alternative than to cross borders irregularly.[25] It has been criticised for being mainly driven by security considerations (increasing State control over migration movements) at the expense of humanitarian ones (guaranteeing access to safety for refugees). According to that critique, the strengthening of European border controls through externalisation has not been sufficiently counterbalanced by policy innovations that protect the fundamental rights of those subject to external border controls. In its 2013

24 E Guild and D Bigo, 'The Transformation of European Border Controls' in B Ryan and V Mitsilegas (eds), *Extraterritorial Immigration Control* (Martinus Nijhoff, Leiden, 2010) 257-278; R Zaiotti, 'Mapping Remote Control: The Externalisation of Migration Management in the 21st Century' in R Zaiotti (ed) *Externalizing Migration Management. Europe, North America and the spread of 'remote control' practices* (London, Routledge, 2016). The externalisation of EU border policies has the effect of generating numerous forms of international cooperation of a varying nature. For an overall presentation of these instruments, see: M Maes, D Vanheule, J Wouters and M-C Foblets, 'The International Dimensions of EU Asylum and Migration Policy: Framing the Issues' in M Maes, M-C Foblets and P De Bruycker, *External Dimensions of European Migration and Asylum Law and Policy / Dimensions Externes du Droit et de la Politique d'Immigration et d'Asile de l'UE* (Brussels, Bruylant, 2011) 11-60.

25 See, for example, a report by the Red Cross EU Office, *Shifting Borders - Externalising Migrant Vulnerabilities and Rights?* (Brussels, Red Cross EU Office, 2013). See also D S Fitzgerald, *Refuge beyond Reach. How Rich Democracies Repel Asylum Seekers* (Oxford, OUP, 2019).

report on *The Management of the External Borders of the European Union and its Impact on the Human Rights of Migrants*, for example, the UN Special Rapporteur for the Human Rights of Migrants, François Crépeau, concluded his comprehensive study of EU border management practices by emphasising that:

> Despite the existence of a number of important policy and institutional achievements in practice, the European Union has largely focused its attention on stopping irregular migration through the strengthening of external border controls.[26]

These concerns have also been echoed at global level, where there is a broader policy trend towards incentivising developed countries to organise some humanitarian admission schemes for selected refugees. In the New York Declaration, the UN General Assembly expressed its will 'to expand the number and range of legal pathways available for refugees to be admitted to or resettled in third countries'.[27] The Global Compact on Refugees similarly calls for the establishment of 'complementary pathways' to resettlement, including 'humanitarian visas, humanitarian corridors and other humanitarian admission programmes'.[28]

In reaction to these concerns, a variety of policy initiatives have been developed by the EU institutions with the aim of adopting some measures intended to offer humanitarian admission to Europe to some preselected refugees. These initiatives have been intensifying in the past years, notably following the proposal for a regulation establishing a Union Resettlement Framework ('URF'). While they are often criticised for having yielded little concrete result so far, they are far from new.[29] Already on the occasion of the June 2003 Thessaloniki meeting, the European Council had invited the European Commission 'to explore all parameters in order to ensure more orderly and managed entry in the EU of persons in need of international

---

26 Report of the Special Rapporteur on the human rights of migrants, François Crépeau, *Regional Study: Management of the External Borders of the European Union and its Impact on the Human Rights of Migrants*, A/HRC/23/46 (24 April 2913) at para 75.

27 UN GA Res 71/1 adopted on 19 September 2016, at para. 77.

28 Global Compact on Refugees A/73/12 (Part II) at para. 95. The Global Compact also refers to regular pathways other than humanitarian admission, including educational opportunities and labour mobility.

29 On this criticism, see: F Gatta, 'Legal Avenues to Access International Protection in the European Union: Past Actions and Future Perspectives' (2018) *Journal européen des droits de l'homme/European Journal of Human Rights* 163.

protection'.[30] Taking into consideration that the EU Member States were already individually engaged in the resettlement of refugees without overall coordination at EU level,[31] the EU Commission suggested the organisation of an EU-wide resettlement scheme to be implemented in close cooperation with the UNHCR.[32] The objective was to enhance reception capacities in first countries of asylum by transferring the most vulnerable refugees to Europe, where their specific protection needs (such as health care or education) could be addressed in a way that would ultimately allow them to achieve self-reliance.

Further EU policy documents connect the involvement of the EU in the field of humanitarian admission to Europe with the broader policy objective of preventing disordered secondary movements of refugees to Europe. Resettlement has been privileged in an attempt to reconcile humanitarian considerations with security ones and it is consistently viewed by the EU not only as a humanitarian policy tool, but also as a border management tool. The objective of the involvement of the EU in resettlement programmes is to guarantee the dignity of the refugees stranded in third countries that lack the capacity to host them, in a way that offers them a 'durable solution', i.e., a 'means by which the situation of refugees can be satisfactorily and permanently resolved to enable them to lead normal lives'[33], in line with the goals pursued by the UNHCR. It is also to prevent disordered movements of refugees to Europe by enhancing the hosting capacities in countries of first asylum, relieving them from the duty to offer protection to the most vulnerable refugees who have specific protection needs requiring additional assistance.

At first, various initiatives in support of resettlement were financially steered by the EU in the context of 'Regional Protection Programmes' (RPPs). RPPs are policy programmes pursuing the overall objective to 'en-

---

30 D/03/3, Presidency Conclusions of the Thessaloniki European Council of 19 and 20 June 2003, Conclusion 26.

31 K Duken, R Sales and J Gregory, 'Refugee Resettlement in Europe' in A Bloch and C Levy (eds), *Refugees, Citizenship and Social Policy in Europe* (Basingstoke, Palgrave Macmillan, 1999) 105-131.

32 COM (2004) 410 final, Communication from the Commission to the Council and the European Parliament on the managed entry in the EU of persons in need of international protection and the enhancement of the protection capacity of the regions of origin "improving access to durable solutions".

33 IOM Glossary (n 7) 57.

hance the capacity of areas close to regions of origin to protect refugees'.[34] More concretely, RPPs are to be seen as a tool for financing projects in third countries that improve refugee protection. These projects are often led by the UNHCR in cooperation with local NGOs.[35] Projects with a resettlement component obtained EU funding under the RPP framework.[36] Over time, however, the EU started also supporting resettlement initiatives led by its Member States outside the RPP framework. As noted in a ECRE study, 'while EU support for resettlement started in the framework of the RPP, progressively it developed somewhat independently'.[37] For example, the involvement of EU Member States in UNHCR-sponsored resettlement programmes has also been financed through the European Refugee Fund (ERF), whose main objective was to support domestic initiatives in the field of refugee protection.[38]

These policy developments led the EU Commission to suggest, in 2009, the establishment of a 'Joint EU resettlement Programme' with a view to coordinating at EU level a more consistent involvement of the Member

---

34 COM (2005) 388 final, Communication from the Commission to the Council and the European Parliament on regional protection programmes. RPPs were subsequently integrated into the EU Global Approach on Migration and Mobility (GAMM), of which they constitute one of the main components; see P Garcia Andrade, I Martin with the contribution of V Vita and S Mananashvili, *EU Cooperation With Third Countries in the field of Migration* (Brussels, European Parliament, Study for the LIBE Committee, 2018) 42; M Garlick, 'EU Regional Protection Programmes: development and prospects' in M Maes, M-C Foblets and P De Bruycker (n 24) 371-386.

35 L Tsourdi and P De Bruycker, *EU Asylum Policy: In Search of Solidarity and Access to Protection* (Florence, Migration Policy Centre, Policy Brief, 2015) 6.

36 For example, an independent evaluation of the RPPs, led at the request of the EU Commission, mentions a project in Tanzania that 'helped to develop a sophisticated method for the screening and profiling of persons with disabilities for the purpose of resettlement'. <http://ec.europa.eu/smart-regulation/evaluation/search/download.do;jsessionid=1Q2GTTWJ1m0pM7kSWQ90hlv 1CBzxjvJpV2-CLp0BgQxQv 8zyGqQ3j!1601440011?documentId=3725> (accessed on 17 October 2019). The evaluation is mentioned in ECRE, *Regional Protection Programmes: An Effective Policy Tool?* (Brussels, Discussion Paper, 2015).

37 Ibid. 7. The European Council on Refugees and Exiles (ECRE) is a civil society organisation gathering European NGOs advocating for refugee rights.

38 The third ERF (2008-2013) explicitly provided for the financing of resettlement programmes; see Decision No 573/2007/EC of the European Parliament and of the Council of 23 May 2007 establishing the European Refugee Fund for the period 2008 to 2013 as part of the General programme Solidarity and Management of Migration Flows and repealing Council Decision 2004/904/EC OJ L 144, 6.6.2007, p. 1–21, recital 18.

States in resettlement programmes, for example by setting annual priorities regarding the profile and the number of asylum seekers to be resettled.[39] The Joint EU Resettlement Programme was adopted in 2012. It is financed through the 'Asylum, Migration and Asylum Fund' (AMIF) that is the successor to the ERF, and that now provides for a lump sum per refugee resettled.[40] The administrative implementation of the Joint EU Resettlement Programme is supported by the 'European Asylum Support Office' (EASO), an EU agency founded in 2010 to encourage and strengthen administrative cooperation among EU Member States in the field of asylum.[41]

In 2013, the sinking of a boat off the coast of Lampedusa and the drowning of around 500 migrants attracted major attention and led to an intensification of policy discussions on 'legal avenues' to Europe beyond resettlement. An expert group set up by the EU Commission following a meeting of the Council, the 'Task Force Mediterranean' (TFM), identified various areas of action to prevent further loss of life at sea.[42] The organisa-

39 COM (2009) 447 final, Communication from the Commission to the European Parliament and the Council on the establishment of a joint EU resettlement programme.

40 Regulation (EU) No 516/2014 of the European Parliament and of the Council of 16 April 2014 establishing the Asylum, Migration and Integration Fund, amending Council Decision 2008/381/EC and repealing Decisions No 573/2007/EC and No 575/2007/EC of the European Parliament and of the Council and Council Decision 2007/435/EC, OJ L 150, 20.5.2014, p. 168–194, recital 40. The lump sum varies between EUR 6,000 and 10,000.

41 Article 7 of Regulation (EU) No 439/2010 of the European Parliament and of the Council of 19 May 2010 establishing a European Asylum Support Office, OJ L 132, 29.5.2010, p. 11–28. On the role of EASO-supported forms of administrative cooperation in deepening the EU harmonisation process in the field of asylum, see L Tsourdi, 'Bottom-up Salvation? From Practical Cooperation Towards Joint Implementation Through the European Asylum Support Office' (2016) 1 *European Papers* 3, 997-1031. The Commission proposed to reform the EASO into a European Agency for Asylum (COM, 2018, 633 final), see C Hruschka, 'Perspektiven der Europäischen Asylpolitik' in S Beichel-Benedetti and C Janda (eds.), *Hohenheimer Horizonte. Festschrift für Klaus Barwig* (Baden-Baden, Nomos-Verlag, 2016) 382-400 393.

42 EU Council of 7 and 8 October 2013, Press Release 14149/13. The move was also welcomed by the European Parliament, which insisted in being involved in the works of the TFM; see: EP Res of 23 October 2013 on migratory flows in the Mediterranean, with particular attention to the tragic events off Lampedusa (2013/2827(RSP)) OJ C 208, 10.6.2016, 148–152, point J.5.

tion of 'legal avenues' to Europe is one of the actions it identified.[43] The conclusions of the Task Force urge the EU institutions and the Member States 'to increase their current commitment on resettlement'. The TFM also calls for them 'to explore further possibilities for protected entry in the EU (and) (…) to open legal channels which give an opportunity for migrants to reach Europe in a regular manner.'[44] These suggestions of the TFM were followed in part in the 2015 European Agenda on Migration. It announced the setting-up of an EU-wide resettlement scheme with the objective to enable 20,000 refugees to take up residence in Europe between 2015 and 2017.[45] However, no specific action at EU level followed the conclusions of the TFM regarding the development of legal channels other than resettlement. The European Agenda on Migration simply encouraged EU Member States 'to use to the full the other legal avenues available to persons in need of protection, including private/non-governmental sponsorships and humanitarian permits, and family reunification clauses'.[46]

The EU resettlement scheme was adopted by the European Council on June 2015, at which European Heads of State or Government pledged to resettle 22,504 refugees from the Middle East, the Horn of Africa and North Africa.[47] It was implemented beyond expectations as, in the end, up to 27,800 refugees were resettled.[48] The success of that first EU resettlement scheme led to another one, which is still ongoing and at the time of writing set a target of 50,000 refugees to be resettled by 2019.[49] In addition to these schemes, which are of a general nature as they may apply to refugees of any nationality from a great variety of countries, another EU resettlement scheme was set up specifically to benefit Syrian refugees staying

43 COM (2013) 869 final, Communication from the Commission to the European Parliament and the Council on the Work of the Task Force Mediterranean. Other actions include security measures such as increased border surveillance, and additional support to the Member States facing higher migratory pressure.

44 Ibid. point 2.2, 2.4 and 2.5.

45 COM (2015) 240 final, Communication from the Commission to the European Parliament, the Council, the European Economic and Social Committee and the Committee of the Regions. A European Agenda on Migration.

46 Ibid. 5.

47 EUCO 22/15, Conclusions of the European Council meeting of 25 and 26 June 2015; decision adopted following the Commission Recommendation (EU) 2015/914 of 8 June 2015 on a European resettlement scheme C/2015/3560 OJ L 148, 13.6.2015, 32–37.

48 COM (2018) 798 final, Managing migration in all its aspects: Progress under the European agenda on migration, 4.

49 C (2017) 6504, Commission Recommendation of 27.9.2017 on enhancing legal pathways for persons in need of international protection.

in Turkey. It was part of the 'EU-Turkey Statement' and provides for the resettlement in the EU of one Syrian refugee staying in Turkey for every one being returned to Turkey from the Greek Islands (the '1:1 scheme').[50] This resettlement programme reflects a different policy approach. Resettlement in this case is used to the strict extent necessary to support and facilitate the adoption and implementation of a border control arrangement.

The success of these EU resettlement programmes led the EU Commission to propose the adoption of a regulation establishing a 'Union Resettlement Framework' (URF) as part of the ongoing reform of the Common European Asylum System (CEAS). The objective of the URF is to establish a comprehensive and permanent resettlement framework, that would consistently guide EU-supported resettlement initiatives to be launched in the future.[51] The underlying idea is to move from ad hoc EU initiatives on resettlement to a consistent overarching approach at EU level. The proposal for a URF includes eligibility criteria that broadly correspond to the criteria set up by the UNHCR and that are based on the identification of specific needs induced by additional factors of vulnerabilities. The proposal also establishes exclusion grounds founded on public order and national security considerations. It organises standardised procedures that leave to the Member States the task of identifying the refugees who will be resettled and may be expedited in case of a humanitarian emergency. An annual Union Resettlement Plan will be established by the Council, and the Commission may establish more targeted resettlement schemes in line with that plan. The implementation of the HURF will be supervised by a High-

---

50 C (2015) 9490, Commission Recommendation of 15.12.2015 for a voluntary humanitarian admission scheme with Turkey.

51 COM (2016) 468 final, Proposal for a Regulation of the European Parliament and of the Council establishing a Union Resettlement Framework. For a detailed analysis of the proposal, see A Radjenovic, *Resettlement of Refugees: EU Framework* (Brussels, Briefing of the European Parliamentary Research Service, 2019). The proposal has generated some criticisms among civil society organisations for linking resettlement to migration management considerations; see: K Bamberg, *The EU Resettlement Framework: From a Humanitarian Pathway to a Migration Management Tool?* (Brussels, EPC Discussion Paper, 2018); ECRE, *Untying the EU Resettlement Framework* (Brussels, Policy Note, 2016); S Carrera and R Cortinovis, *The EU's Role in Implementing the UN Global Compact on Refugees. Contained Mobility vs. International Protection* (Brussels, CEPS Paper on Liberty and Security in Europe, 2019) 14; M Tissier-Raffin, 'Réinstallation – Admission humanitaire : solutions d'avenir pour protéger les réfugiés ou cheval de Troie du droit international des réfugiés ?' (2017) 13 *La Revue des droits de l'homme* <https://journals.openedition.org/revdh/3405> (accessed on 10 August 2019). On that debate, see the contribution of Catharina Ziebritski to this volume.

Level Resettlement Committee, which will be chaired by the Commission and composed of representatives of the Council, the European Parliament, the High Representative of the Union for Foreign Affairs and Security Policy, and representatives of the Member States. The European Union Agency for Asylum (which is expected to succeed to the EASO once the recast of the CEAS is adopted), the UNHCR and the IOM may be invited to attend the meetings of the committee.

The main principles of the URF proposal reflect an approach already developed in past EU resettlement initiatives. *First*, EU-sponsored resettlement programmes are intended to function on a voluntary basis. The URF provides a general framework in which Member States are invited to participate (and thus benefit from EU funding). But it does not in and of itself create a legal obligation to resettle refugees on account of EU Member States. *Second*, EU resettlement programmes are to be developed and implemented in cooperation with the UNHCR. The URF proposal explicitly recognises the 'key role' of the UNHCR in identifying resettlement priorities and executing resettlement programmes. *Third*, there is a strong tie between resettlement and the enhancement of hosting capacities in third countries that are facing the arrival of a large number of refugees. The URF proposal connects EU resettlement programmes to the proposal of a 'new Partnership Framework with third countries under the European Agenda on Migration' that strives to support countries of origin and of transit in dealing with large refugee flows.[52] It states that the objective of EU resettlement is also to support 'partnerships with key third countries of origin and transit through a coherent and tailored engagement where the Union and its Member States act in a coordinated manner'.[53] From a policy perspective, resettlement remains conceived at EU level as both a humanitarian tool and a tool for migration management: the intent is to prevent disordered movements of asylum seekers to Europe by supporting hosting capacities in transit countries and countries of origin. As argued by Catharina Ziebritski in her contribution to this volume, policy developments towards increasing involvement of the EU in resettlement are slowly but surely leading to legal developments and a 'EU resettlement law' that has the potential of enhancing refugee protection, in so far as it remains

52 COM (2016) 385 final, Communication from the Commission to the European Parliament, the European Council, the Council and the European Investment Bank on establishing a new Partnership Framework with third countries under the European Agenda on Migration.

53 COM (2016) 468 final (n 51) 5.

aligned on the fundamental rationale and legal dynamics of the Common European Asylum System.

So far, the increasing involvement of the EU in resettlement programmes has not, however, ended the debates regarding the opening and securing of humanitarian admission to Europe for refugees, for a variety of reasons. *First*, the EU resettlement policy remains of an essentially intergovernmental nature. The involvement of the Member States is strictly voluntary. They set the target numbers through the Council, and they freely decide on their own contribution.[54] *Second*, the scope of existing EU resettlement programmes remains relatively limited. They concern people in the thousands – an extremely low figure compared to the flows of people forcibly displaced worldwide, which numbers in the tens of millions.[55] A large number of them is thus likely to search for alternative solutions in order to reach safety. *Third*, and perhaps more importantly, EU resettlement programmes do not allow individuals to directly petition European authorities to obtain humanitarian admission to Europe on grounds relating to protection. Some of those who were not eligible for resettlement have therefore engaged in alternative procedures in an attempt to reach Europe safely and legally. Litigation is one of these. The next Section sets out the main developments that have taken place within the realm of the judiciary, and more specifically before European courts.

2 *Litigation for Humanitarian Admission to Europe*

In law, the intensification of policy debates on humanitarian admission to European territory for refugees is reflected in a number of vivid doctrinal as well as judicial debates. Those advocating the opening of 'safe pathways' and 'legal avenues' often ground their claims in international law. The arguments rely mainly on fundamental rights, such as the principle of *non-refoulement* and the right to leave one's country. The legal issues raised are intricate, as they relate not only to the content of migrants' rights (is there a violation?), but also to the allocation of responsibility for internationally wrongful acts (which State is responsible for the violation?). These arguments are discussed extensively among legal scholars, who highlight the

54 Some Member States have consistently refused to contribute; see: COM (2015) 240 final (n 45) 4.

55 In 2018, the UNHCR estimated the global population of those forcefully displaced worldwide as being comprised of 70.8 million individuals; see: UNHCR, *Global Trends. Forced Displacement in 2018* (Geneva, UNHCR, 2019).

tensions between the right to asylum and external border control practices that can have the effect of preventing access to asylum.[56]

These legal claims and doctrinal debates are, in their own way, shaping policy debates on humanitarian admission to Europe, and increasingly so in the wake of attempts to involve the judiciary through litigation. Such attempts could be qualified as 'cause lawyering' by reference to the relevant socio-legal literature.[57] 'Cause lawyering' is a concept that has been used to qualify attempts to obtain and foster social and policy changes through the courts. It refers to the way legal professionals mobilise the legal system to campaign for a cause they actively support.[58] Using the concept of "cause lawyering" to qualify the increasing attempts to channel policy debates on legal avenues to Europe through the legal system indicates that policy and legal debates on safe pathways to Europe are deeply intertwined: Legal arguments have from the outset been used in the policy debate, and understandably so, since the internationally recognised right of refugees to seek protection lies at its core. It is therefore not surprising that over the past few years various attempts have been made to advancing arguments before the courts in support of the better organisation and securing of humanitarian admission to Europe for refugees. The contribution of Tristan Wibault to this volume offers a testimony of the high degree of personal involvement of some lawyers, who invest a lot of time and effort in searching for all the available legal means to defend the interests of their clients and ease their sufferings.

The first attempts at involving the judiciary in the debate were submitted to the ECtHR, in cases concerning contentious (and therefore vividly debated) external border control practices.[59] In the leading case *Hirsi Jamaa v Italy*, the ECtHR held Italy responsible for the violations of migrants' rights on the occasion of an external border control operation. Italy was

---

56 See among others: E Guild and V Stoyanova, 'The Human Right to Leave Any Country: A Right to Be Delivered' (2018) *European Yearbook on Human Rights* 373-394; N Markard, 'The Right to Leave By Sea: Legal Limits on EU Migration Control By Third Countries' (2016) 27 *IJRL* 591-616; V Moreno Lax, *Accessing Asylum in Europe. Extraterritorial Border Controls and Refugee Rights under EU Law* (Oxford, OUP, 2017).

57 A Sarat and S Scheingold (eds), *Cause Lawyering and the State in a Global Era* (Oxford, OUP, 2001).

58 L Israël, 'Cause Lawyering' in O Fillieule, L Mathieu and Cécile Péchu (eds), *Dictionnaire des mouvements sociaux* (Paris, Presses de Sciences Po, 2019) 94-100.

59 Various attempts were also made before domestic courts; see: J Hathaway and T Gammeltoft-Hansen, 'Non-Refoulement in a World of Cooperative Deterrence' (2015) 53 *Colombia Journal of Transnational Law* 2 235-84.

condemned for the so-called 'push-back' to Libya of asylum seekers who had been intercepted by Italian coastguards in the Mediterranean Sea before reaching European territory.[60] To reach its conclusion, the ECtHR ruled that migrants brought on board the vessels of European coastguards fall under the 'jurisdiction' of European States as, under the Law of the Sea, the jurisdiction of a State extends to vessels carrying their flags in international waters. The mere circumstance that migrants are intercepted on the high seas, outside of European territorial waters, does not dispense States from their responsibilities under the ECHR.

By reaching that conclusion, the ECtHR opened the door to some kind of international responsibility towards refugees in extraterritorial situations. The ruling in *Hirsi Jamaa v Italy* had the concrete effect of partially lifting one of the main legal obstacles to litigation for humanitarian admission to Europe, which is the limitation of the scope of the ECHR to the 'jurisdiction' of the State parties.[61] Through an important body of case law initially developed in the context of military interventions outside of European territory, the ECtHR interpreted the requirement of 'jurisdiction' as going beyond the national territory to include every situation that falls under the 'effective control' of the State.[62] The requirement of 'effective control' is a complex one that has been widely discussed among legal scholars.[63] It depends on numerous factors and requires an in-depth assessment of all relevant circumstances. With the *Hirsi Jamaa* ruling, the ECtHR clarified that these principles are also applicable to cases concerning migrants. What is important here is that this jurisprudential move allows

60 The ECtHR ruled that sending migrants back immediately, without prior examination of their individual situation and without offering them any opportunity to apply for asylum, violates various provisions of the ECHR, including the prohibition against collective expulsion; *Hirsi Jamaa v Italy* (App No 27765/09) ECHR 23 February 2012. For a detailed comment on this case, see: M Den Heijer, 'Reflections on Refoulement and Collective Expulsion in the *Hirsi* Case' (2013) 25 *IJRL* 265-290; M Giuffré, 'Watered-down Rights on the High Seas: *Hirsi Jamaa and others v Italy*' (2012) 61 *ICLQ* 728-750; V Moreno-Lax, '*Hirsi Jamaa and others v Italy* or the Strasbourg Court versus Extraterritorial Migration Control?' (2012) 12 *HRLR* 3 574-598.

61 European Convention on Human Rights (adopted 4 November 1950; entered into force 3 September 1953) (ECHR) art 1.

62 *Al Skeini v the United Kingdom* (App No 55721/07) ECHR 7 July 2011.

63 For the main terms of the debate, see M Milanovic, *Extraterritorial Application of Human Rights Treaties: Law, Principles and Policy* (Oxford, OUP, 2011); B Miltner, 'Revisiting Extraterritoriality after Al-Skeini: The ECHR and Its Lessons' (2012) 33 *Michigan Journal of International Law* 4 693-745.

for some judicial review of external border control practices and hence litigation by individuals.

That 'opening' on the part of the ECtHR is in itself insufficient, however, to pave the way to litigation for refugees seeking humanitarian admission to Europe. The ruling in *Hirsi Jamaa* safeguards the overall coherence of the case law of the ECtHR regarding the scope of the ECHR, but it does not mean that from now on every migrant who is subjected to external border control measures would be entitled to invoke the ECHR. Despite the interpretation of State jurisdiction as including extraterritorial situations that are subject to the 'effective control' of the State, the competence of the ECtHR in dealing with external border controls remains limited. It is debatable, to say the least, whether it also covers forms of so-called 'contactless controls'[64] which are performed through the intermediary of third countries. As Dirk Hanschel shows in his chapter, the position of the ECtHR corresponds to a broader trend in the field of international human rights law, where criteria for allocating responsibility for international wrongful acts remain primarily territorial in nature. In her contribution to this volume, Sylvie Sarolea further highlights what she labels 'the paradox of the foot in the door': only those refugees who somehow managed to reach the jurisdiction of a State, even if irregularly and at the risk of their lives, are in the position to make a protection claim on that State.

That is not to say that future changes in international law and in the interpretation of the ECHR must be ruled out.[65] On the contrary, the ECtHR has always emphasised that the ECHR is a 'living instrument', whose

---

64 V Moreno-Lax and M Giuffré, 'The Rise of Consensual Containment: From "Contactless Control" to "Contactless Responsibility" for Forced Migration Flows' in S Juss (ed), *Research Handbook on International Refugee Law* (Cheltenham, Edward Elgar, 2019) 82-108. For example, Italy entered into an administrative cooperation agreement with Libyan authorities (a so-called 'Memorandum of Understanding') so that migrants are being intercepted by the Libyan coast guard; see D Nakache and J Losier, 'The European Union Immigration Agreement with Libya: Out of Sight, Out of Mind?' (2017) *E-International Relations* <https://www.e-ir.info/2017/07/25/the-european-union-immigration-agreement-with-libya-out-of-sight-out-of-mind/> (accessed 23 July 2019). Attempts are being made at involving the legal responsibility of Italy for the actions of Libyan coast guard through litigation before the ECtHR; see A Pijnenburg, 'From Italian Pushbacks to Libyan Pullbacks: Is Hirsi 2.0 in the Making in Strasbourg?' (2018) 20 *EJML* 4 396-426.

65 For example, in the *M.N. v Belgium* case (App 3599/18) that is currently pending before the Grand Chamber of the ECtHR, a Syrian family applied to the ECtHR following the rejection of their application for a humanitarian visa by Belgian authorities. One of the arguments invoked in the course of the proceedings to justi-

interpretation may evolve to account for social change.[66] It cannot be excluded that the interpretation of the ECHR by the ECtHR regarding external border controls might evolve in the future to guarantee that the increasingly sophisticated forms of border control do not lead to serious human rights violations. Some legal scholars have called for such an evolution. To them, there should not be a fragmented reading of international law. Other rights should also be considered in the interpretation, such as the right to leave one's country and the duty to rescue as established by the Law of the Sea.[67]

The current state of ECHR law, and its focus on responsibility for acts that are primarily territorial in nature, explains the search for other ways of judicialising the debate on humanitarian admission to Europe. EU law appeared as one such way. As demonstrated by Stephanie Law in her contribution to this volume, the scope of the EU Charter of Fundamental Rights ('EUCFR') has not been limited to the territory of EU Member States. It covers any act implementing EU law in line with the *Akerberg Fransson* doctrine, without explicit restriction to acts committed on European territory.[68] Drawing on this reasoning, the mere fact that migrants are subject to the application of EU law implies that they can call upon the EUCFR. The EU Visa Code explicitly provides for the issuing of humanitarian visas

---

fy the competence of the ECtHR is the one of 'optional jurisdiction', so to speak: because it made the sovereign choice to establish a provision to apply for humanitarian visas, Belgium is bound to implement that provision in a way that respects the ECHR (pleading by Frédéric Krenc, who represented the Bar Council of French- and German-Speaking lawyers in Belgium that intervened before the ECtHR in favour of the applicants; see the video transmission of the hearing available on <https://www.echr.coe.int/Pages/home.aspx?p=hearings&w=359918_24042019&language=lang&c=&py=2019>, accessed 23 July 2019). On that case, see D Schmalz, 'Will the ECtHR Shake up the European Asylum System?' (2018) *Verfassungsblog* <https://verfassungsblog.de/will-the-ecthr-shake-up-the-european-asylum-system/> (accessed 23 July 2019).

66 G Letsas, 'The ECHR as a Living Instrument: Its Meaning and Legitimacy' in A Føllesdal, B Peters and G Ulfstein (eds), *Constituting Europe. The European Court of Human Rights in a National, European and Global Context* (Cambridge, CUP, 2013) 106-141.

67 V Moreno-Lax, 'Seeking Asylum in the Mediterranean: Against a Fragmentary Reading of EU Member States' Obligations Accruing at Sea' (2011) 23 *IJRL* 2 174-220; N Markard, 'The Right to Leave by Sea: Legal Limits on EU Migration Control by Third Countries' (2016) 27 *EJIL* 3 591-616; E Guild and V Stoyanova, 'The Human Right to Leave Any Country: A Right to Be Delivered' in W Benedek, P Czech, L Heschl, K Lukas and M Nowak, *European Yearbook on Human Rights 2018* (Antwerp, Intersentia, 2019) 373-394.

68 Case C-617/10 *Akerberg Fransson* [2013] EU:C:2013:105.

by EU Member States in exceptional cases, namely when they 'consider it necessary on humanitarian grounds'.[69] Litigation thus ultimately found its way to the CJEU, as we will examine in the next Section.

3 A Cautious and Reserved Judicial Intervention

So far, litigation before the CJEU in an attempt to securing humanitarian admission to Europe for refugees has stumbled over the limits of the competence of the Court. In the *X. and X.* ruling, the CJEU ruled that these controversies fall outside the scope of EU law. The jurisprudential approach adopted by the Court is presented in sub-Section 1. In response to the question why the CJEU opted for a cautious and reserved stance, we argue in sub-Section 2 that the refusal of the Court to engage in debates on humanitarian admission to Europe reflects the shortcomings of the current EU legal framework. This in turn is to be seen in connection to a broader constitutional deficit, which the Court may not have the legitimacy to address in the current political social context characterised by strong divisions on migration that have amplified as a result of the 2015 'European refugee crisis'. We argue that not only these divisions, but also the constitutional deficit EU law is suffering from more generally speaking, help explain why attempts at involving the CJEU in the policy debate on humanitarian admission to Europe through litigation have failed so far.

3.1 The CJEU Invoking the Limits to its Competence of Judicial Review

In the *X. and X.* case, a Belgian court called on the CJEU to interpret the provision of the EU Visa Code on humanitarian visas. The Court of Justice was asked whether EU law may impose, under some exceptional circumstances, an obligation to issue such a visa. The position taken by the CJEU has been extensively discussed in the legal literature.[70] In a nutshell, the Court declined to address the merits of the case. It noted that the EU Visa Code covers short stays of less than three months only (the so-called 'tourist stay') and argued that it is not applicable to humanitarian visas requested by asylum seekers, who intend to apply for asylum and, thus, to

69 EU Visa Code (n 3), art 25.
70 See n 2.

stay longer than three months.[71] The Court supported that interpretation by citing the Dublin Regulation and the territorial scope of the CEAS. The Dublin Regulation allocates the responsibility to examine asylum applications to the various EU Member States on the basis of a variety of criteria, including the State of first entry to European territory.[72] The Dublin Regulation does not apply to humanitarian visa applications; such applications are to be submitted to the consular representation of the migrant's choice. Moreover, allowing asylum seekers to apply for humanitarian visas on the basis of the EU Visa Code would run counter the territorial nature of the CEAS. The scope of the CEAS is indeed limited to EU territory.[73] As underlined by the Court:

> to conclude otherwise [that is, to conclude that the EU Visa Code applies to applications for a humanitarian visa introduced by asylum seekers] [...] would mean that Member States are required, on the basis of the Visa Code, de facto to allow third-country nationals to submit applications for international protection to the representations of Member States that are within the territory of a third country.[74]

The position of the CJEU met with criticism among legal scholars,[75] some of whom expressed reservations about a strict distinction between the common visa policy and the CEAS. It is true that these policies have a different legal basis in the Treaty but, in practice, it is common for aliens to apply for a long-term residence status, including asylum, only after having en-

---

71 In his Opinion, Advocate General Mengozzi considered, on the contrary, that 'the intention of the applicants in the main proceedings to apply for refugee status once they had entered Belgium *cannot alter the nature or purpose of their applications*'. He also considered that, as a consequence, there is an obligation to issue a humanitarian visa if refusal would mean that the applicant would suffer from serious human rights violations (Case C-638/16 PPU *X and X* [2017] EU:C:2017:93 Opinion of AG Mengozzi).

72 Regulation (EU) No 604/2013 of the European Parliament and of the Council of 26 June 2013 establishing the criteria and mechanisms for determining the Member State responsible for examining an application for international protection lodged in one of the Member States by a third-country national or a stateless person [2013] OJ L180/31.

73 Directive 2013/32/EU of the European Parliament and of the Council of 26 June 2013 on common procedures for granting and withdrawing international protection [2013] OJ L180/60, art 3; Directive 2013/33/EU of the European Parliament and of the Council of 26 June 2013 laying down standards for the reception of applicants for international protection [2013] OJ L 180/96, art 3.

74 *X. and X.* (n 2) at 48.

75 See the comments cited in n 2.

tered European territory on the basis of a tourist visa. There is a 'grey area'[76] between the common visa policy and the CEAS, which is well illustrated by the practices of some Member States, such as Belgium and Italy, where humanitarian visas are issued to refugees who are granted the benefit of resettlement programmes (Belgium) and in the case of the 'humanitarian corridors' (Italy).[77] In the *X. and X.* case, neither the Belgian court nor the administration initially contested the application of the EU Visa Code. That argument only came up later on, during the proceedings before the CJEU.[78]

In essence, these doctrinal criticisms are directed at the way the Court is fulfilling its constitutional role of guaranteeing the overall consistency of EU law and respect for primary law, including the EUCFR. What is regretted is the refusal of the Court to engage with ongoing legal and policy debates on humanitarian visas, and its decision to limit (or refuse to expand) the scope of EU law to addressing the issue of humanitarian admission to Europe. These criticisms are very similar to the ones targeting the approach adopted by the CJEU in the three cases *NF, NG and NM v European Council*, which concerns annulment proceedings brought against the 'EU-Turkey Statement' on the ground that, in violation of EU law, it prevents access to effective protection.[79] In an order adopted in that case a few months before the *X. and X.* ruling, the General Court of the CJEU declared that it did not have jurisdiction to rule on that legal challenge. It considered that the 'EU-Turkey Statement' was not adopted by the European Council, but by all the EU Member States acting in their individual capacity, and that it can therefore not been considered as a legal act of EU law falling under its competence of judicial review.

The *X. and X.* ruling thus seems to fit within a broader jurisprudential trend, showing that the CJEU prefers not to intervene in policy debates on humanitarian admission to Europe on account of the norms limiting its

76 R Colavitti (n 2).

77 See the contributions of S Bodart and K Bianchini to this volume.

78 S Sarolea, J-Y Carlier and L Leboeuf (n 2).

79 Cases T-192/6 *N.F. v European Council* [2017] EU:T:2017:128; T-193/16 *N.G. v European Council* [2017] EU:T:2017:129 and T-257/16 *N.M. v European Council* [2017] EU:T:2017:130. Appeals introduced against these rulings before the Court of Justice were ruled to be inadmissible for formal reasons relating (Cases C-208 to C-210/17 P *NF, NG and NM v European Council* [2018] ECLI:EU:2018:705), see: M H Zoeteweij and O Turhan, 'Above the Law – Beneath Contempt: the End of the EU-Turkey Deal?' (2017) 27 *Swiss Review of International and European Law* 2 151.

competence of judicial review.[80] Such a jurisprudential approach stands in stark contrast with the one adopted in other areas of EU law, where the CJEU has at times been accused of 'judicial activism' for expanding the scope of EU law in a way that overtly supports the harmonisation process.[81] This raises the question why the Court adopts such a 'cautious'[82] and reserved approach when it comes to issues regarding humanitarian admission to European territory. In our view, this approach cannot be disconnected from the broader European social context, marked as it is by extremely sensitive divisions and contrasting views on migration, and from some fundamental shortcomings in the current EU legal framework which the Court of Justice may not have the legitimacy to address. These factors are further identified and discussed in the next sub-Section.

3.2. *Some Limits to the Intervention of Courts in Policy Debates on Humanitarian admission to Europe*

It is the essence of the role of courts, and in particular of the higher courts entrusted with the constitutional function of safeguarding the overall coherence and integrity of the legal framework, such as the CJEU, to adapt

---

80 T Spijkerboer, 'Bifurcation of People, Bifurcation of Law: Externalization of Migration Policy Before the EU Court of Justice' (2018) 31 *JRS* 2 216-239.

81 I Goldner Lang, 'Towards "Judicial Passivism" in EU Migration and Asylum Law? Preliminary Thoughts for the Final Plenary Session of the 2018 Odysseus Conference' (2018) *EU Immigration and Asylum Law and Policy* <https://eumigrationlawblog.eu/towards-judicial-passivism-in-eu-migration-and-asylum-law-preliminary-thoughts-for-the-final-plenary-session-of-the-2018-odysseus-conference/> (accessed 20 July 2019). In *Zambrano*, for example, the CJEU expanded the scope of EU law to guarantee the effective protection of the rights of EU citizens. It referred to the 'substance of the rights' of EU citizens as protected by the Treaties, holding that these rights may be invoked in purely internal situations that have no connections with the EU legal order, for example because EU citizens have not exercised their freedom of movement. Calls for the Court to apply a similar reasoning to determine the extent of the scope of EU law in situations arising outside of EU territory, allowing for its application in the case of a violation of 'the substance of the rights' established in the EU Charter, such as the right to asylum, have not been followed so far (J-Y Carlier and L Leboeuf, 'The *X. and X.* case: Humanitarian visas and the genuine enjoyment of the substance of the rights, towards a middle way?' (2017) *EU Immigration and Asylum Law and Policy* <https://eumigrationlawblog.eu/the-x-and-x-case-humanitarian-visas-and-the-genuine-enjoyment-of-the-substance-of-rights-towards-a-middle-way/>, accessed 20 July 2019).

82 J-Y Carlier and L Leboeuf (n 2) 96.

the law to evolving social realities. The law is not fixed, but in constant evolution depending on court interpretations. However, the fact that the CJEU did not start engaging with policy debates on safe and legal access to Europe for refugees also points to the limits of the role which the judiciary can play in steering the development of the law. These limits pertain to both legal and social conditions, which are deeply intertwined.

The jurisprudential stance of the CJEU regarding litigation in the field of humanitarian admission to the CEAS reveals a broader 'constitutional deficit' when it comes to regulating the external dimensions of EU asylum and migration policy.[83] The reason why the Court is reluctant to review legal acts concerning migrants who are outside European territory, and to address the controversies on humanitarian admission to EU territory, arise from broader legal uncertainties pertaining to the content of the norms which guide its judicial review.[84] EU institutional rules and the EU fundamental rights framework turn out to be inadequate, in their current form, to govern in an efficient, coherent and transparent way issues surrounding access to European territory. Rules on the division of competence between the EU and the Member States are intricate[85] and the extent of fundamental rights obligations towards migrants who are (still) outside EU territory is unclear, to say the least.

Moreover, little guidance is available from the ECtHR, which is itself facing the limits of the 'jurisdiction' requirement as outlined above. It may further be questionable whether the (relatively) strong human rights guar-

83 On the 'constitutional deficit' of the external dimensions of EU asylum and migration law, see S Carrera, J Santos Vara and T Strik (eds), *Constitutionalising the External Dimensions of EU Migration Policies in Times of Crisis. Legality, Rule of Law and Fundamental Rights Reconsidered* (Cheltenham, Edward Elgar, 2019); L Leboeuf, 'La Cour de justice face aux dimensions externes de la politique commune de l'asile et de l'immigration: un défaut de constitutionnalisation?' (2019) 55 *Revue trimestrielle de droit européen* 1 55-66.

84 By 'EU constitutional framework', we refer to the fundamental rules as established by the EU Treaties to govern EU actions. These fundamental rules pursue two main objectives. *First*, they organise the institutional framework by establishing norms and principles on the division of competence between EU institutions and the Member States, and among EU institutions. *Second*, they set out the general objectives governing EU action, including the values to be respected while fulfilling these objectives. These values include respect for the fundamental rights established in the EUCFR.

85 P Garcia Andrade, 'EU External Competences in the Field of Migration: How to Act Externally When Thinking Internally' (2018) 55 *CMLRev* 1, 157–200; E Neframi, *Division of Competences Between the European Union and its Member States Concerning Immigration* (Brussels, Study for the European Parliament, 2011).

antees established for the benefit of those who are found on the territory of a State, can be extended as such to external situations with a view to embracing access to Europe as well. The evolution of international human rights law has led to a body of guarantees that include protection against removal and some residence and minimal rights, such as adequate reception conditions for asylum seekers and access to the social assistance system for refugees.[86] One may wonder whether the extension of these guarantees to every migrant risking a violation of Article 3 ECHR or other forms of persecution, would be a realistic move, given the potentially unlimited number of persons concerned. As noted by the ECtHR in the inadmissibility decision it adopted in the *Abdul Wahab Khan v the UK* case concerning the refusal of a visa application grounded on a risk of ill-treatment in the home country, another interpretation 'would, in effect, create an unlimited obligation on Contracting States to allow entry to an individual who might be at real risk of ill-treatment contrary to Article 3, regardless of where in the world that individual might find himself'.[87] It is thus most likely that any move towards the establishment of some kind of humanitarian admission to Europe for refugees will also require the establishment of additional criteria, such as a focus on some particular vulnerabilities similar to the one developed in UNHCR-sponsored resettlement programmes, or, as indirectly suggested in the question addressed by the Belgian court to the CJEU in the *X. and X.* case, the requirement of a special connection with EU territory, for example, because family members are already living in Europe. These are major legal innovations, which go far beyond the mere extension of existing rules to situations that they were not initially designed to cover.

For these reasons, engaging in the debate on humanitarian admission to Europe would have required the development of innovative legal interpretations without a stable and clear constitutional foundation. It would have required engaging in the interpretation not only of the scope of the law, but also of its substance, in a new and groundbreaking way. The overall social context within which the CJEU is currently operating may not support such evolution. There does not seem to be an overall consensus for increasing judicial intervention in debates on 'legal avenues' and 'safe pathways' to Europe for refugees. The high legitimacy cost that may result

86 On that evolution, see among others: M Gil-Bazo, 'Refugee Protection under International Human Rights Law: From Non-Refoulement to Residence and Citizenship' (2015) 34 *RSQ* 1, 11-42.

87 *Abdul Wahab Khan v the UK* (App No 11987/11) ECHR (dec.) 28 January 2014, para 27.

from intervening in that debate was apparent in the *X. and X.* case, which can also be regarded as an attempt, by domestic judges, to safeguard their own legitimacy in the face of heavy internal criticism.[88] The request for a preliminary reference was addressed to the CJEU in a context of significant internal tensions concerning humanitarian visas. A previous ruling by the Belgian courts ordering the issuance of a humanitarian visa provoked outcry and an intense public debate in which some argued on the basis of fundamental rights considerations whilst others accused judges of exceeding their constitutional prerogatives and engaging in a 'government of judges'.[89] The proceedings before the CJEU in *X. and X.* thus fit into a broader judicial strategy to make up a legitimacy deficit at national level.[90]

Lastly, other social and policy factors, at EU level, may help explain why the CJEU declined to delve into the controversy and avoided dealing with the (major) shortcomings of the current EU constitutional framework. In other recent cases in the field of asylum and migration, the CJEU was confronted with social and policy controversies that resulted from concurring pressures aimed at questioning the fundamental principles of the EU *acquis* in the field of asylum and migration. For example, attempts have been made to circumvent the prohibition of systematic internal border controls, as clearly established by the Schengen Border Code. In the *Touring Tours und Travel and Sociedad de Transportes* case, in particular, the CJEU opposed the externalisation of internal border controls by Germany, which required private companies to systematically check passengers embarking on the territory of other Member States before transporting them to German territory.[91] The court's ruling referred to the useful effect of the

88 L Leboeuf, 'Visa humanitaire et recours en suspension d'extrême urgence. Le Conseil du contentieux des étrangers interroge la Cour constitutionnelle et la Cour de justice de l'Union européenne' (2016) *Cahiers de l'EDEM* <https://uclouvain.be/fr/instituts-recherche/juri/cedie/actualites/c-c-e-assemblee-generale-8-decembre-2016-n-179-108.html> (accessed on 17 July 2019).

89 On that controversy, see De Standaard, 'Heeft de rechter de scheiding der machten geschonden?' (9 December 2016) <https://www.standaard.be/cnt/dmf20161209_02617185> (accessed on 17 July 2019).

90 Running parallel to the case before the CJEU, the Belgian court addressed a preliminary reference to the Belgian Constitutional Court, asking it to specify the extent of the power of judicial review on the part of lower courts. The Constitutional Court declined to address the issue. See: Belgian Constitutional Court, Judgement of 18 October 2018 in the case 141/2018. See also the contribution of S Bodart to this volume.

91 Joined Cases C-412/17 and C-474/17 *Bundesrepublik Deutschland v Touring Tours and Travel GmbH and Sociedad de Transportes s.a.* [2018] EU:C:2018:1005.

prohibition against systematic internal border controls, which it re-affirmed in the same social context of heavy divisions at play.[92]

There thus seems to be some 'legitimacy trade-off' at play, so to speak. The CJEU fulfils its role of enforcing the EU constitutional framework where its content is (relatively) clear, but it avoids engaging actively in further developing that framework where its content is controversial and would require that the judiciary develop particularly innovative interpretations to help it be attuned to the situation at hand. Such effort would necessitate a wide social consensus, which is clearly not present in the area of migration today. Jurisprudential innovation risks being met with strong opposition and may ultimately affect the legitimacy of the CJEU, as experienced by Belgian domestic courts. Our understanding of the Court's position is that it is anxious to prevent aggravating existing divisions within European societies, and therefore exercises its power of judicial review in an extremely cautious way when it concerns laws or actions in fields that are highly controversial from a political point of view and still unclear in terms of EU constitutional framework. While, on the one hand, it does not hesitate to enforce norms that are of sufficient quality and offer certainty, on the other it refrains from developing major jurisprudential innovations that might enhance the quality of the existing legal framework but would also be met with severe opposition.

Does this stance mean that any attempt at bringing the debate about humanitarian admission to Europe and, more broadly, about external border control practices before the judiciary is doomed to fail? As we will show in the next Section, that is not necessarily the case: in our societies governed by the rule of law, the law aspires to govern every action of the executive. Further litigation attempts are therefore highly likely.

4 *The Revolving Doors of the Rule of Law*

In societies governed by the rule of law, legal arguments usually keep reappearing in policy debates and the law will somehow keep reappearing through the back door. Actors will seek to develop further innovative interpretations of the legal framework in an attempt to support their policy arguments. This is well illustrated by the pending litigation before the EC-

92 J J Rijpma, 'A Rose by Any Other Name: het Hof van Justitie stelt grenzen aan controles binnen het Schengengebied' (2019) *Nederlands Tijdschrift voor Europees Recht* 5-6 129-136, 136.

tHR in the *MN v Belgium* case, where it has been argued that any State which made the policy choice of adopting provisions on humanitarian visas should implement them in line with the requirements set out in the ECHR, including the requirements of due process.[93] It is also worth noting that, from a strictly legal perspective, the ruling of the CJEU in *X. and X.* does not definitely close the door to future litigation attempts. On the contrary, the legal reasoning of the Court in *X. and X.* bears the seeds for further litigation. For example, the criteria of the intent of the applicants used by the CJEU to establish a strict distinction between the CEAS and the common visa policy may lead to further issues and litigation in the future. In *X. and X.* and as mentioned above, the CJEU relied on the declared intent of the applicants to apply for asylum once on Belgian territory in order to rule out the application of the EU Visa Code. But what if applicants were to conceal such intent in the future? Is there a duty on the part of the Member States to engage in a thorough study of short stay visa applications on humanitarian grounds to determine whether the 'true intent' of the parties is to apply for asylum? And to justify their decision accordingly and in line with the EUCFR, including with the principle of good administration?

The European Parliament, too, might not be entirely willing to leave free rein to the executives of EU Member States. As shown by Eugenia Relano Pastor in her contribution to this volume, the ongoing recast of the EU Visa Code was seized by some members of the European Parliament (MEPs) as an opportunity to move forward the introduction of a specific provision on humanitarian visas that would clearly regulate access to EU territory for refugees. This attempt failed to yield concrete results. But it shows that the debate remains alive within the European Parliament, and reminds us that future legislative interventions cannot be entirely excluded.

These prospects for the future evolution of the legal frameworks on humanitarian admission to Europe should not, however, ignore the strong opposition to the involvement of the judiciary into the debate. The language of the judges is the one of subjective rights, for there is often no litigation without individual rights to be litigated. It can reasonably be feared that, if refugees are entitled to some kind of subjective right to access European territory, the EU Member States' administrations will be overwhelmed by applications. By contrast, other forms of humanitarian admission, such as resettlement programmes that rest on a collaboration be-

93 App No 3599/18 and pleading by Frédéric Krenc (n 65).

tween the receiving and the hosting State, offer a higher degree of flexibility. For that reason, it is likely that European Governments will keep systematically opposing the emergence of concrete legal commitments and will do everything possible to prevent their responsibility from being engaged under the law because of some claims for international protection made outside their territory. Further attempts at litigating towards humanitarian admission in individual cases are likely, but they might also be doomed to fail in any predictable future.

Such litigation attempts contribute, however, to creating the overall conditions that incentivise States to participate in resettlement programmes and, more broadly, to open up a broader debate on the evolution of EU border policies, and the way these should be encapsulated by the rule of law. Commenting on the inflation of legal arguments and court cases concerning remote border control practices, Hathaway and Gammeltoft-Hansen noted that:

> law will thus be in a position to serve a critical role in provoking a frank conversation about how to replace the duplicitous politics of non-entrée with a system predicated on the meaningful sharing of the burdens and responsibilities of refugee protection around the world.[94]

Interestingly enough, the ruling in the *X. and X.* case has not prevented the emergence of such 'frank conversation'. It sends a clear message that one should not expect the CJEU to delve into policy debates on humanitarian admission to European territory. But, by declining to reply on the merits, the CJEU did also avoid that, by so doing, it would exclude any future application of the EUCFR to extraterritorial border control measures. Only a few months after the ruling in *X. and X.*, the position adopted in *El Hassani* seems to confirm that the EUCFR must be respected while implementing EU law outside European territory.[95] In *El Hassani*, the Court held that the EUCFR is applicable to decisions implementing the EU Visa Code and that concern migrants who are outside European territory.[96] Future developments in the case law of the CJEU to impose the respect of some human

94 J Hathaway and T Gammeltoft-Hansen (n 59).

95 Case C-403/16 *El Hassani* [2017] EU:C:2017:960. See also the Case C-680/17 *Vethanayagam* [2019] EU:C:2019:627.

96 The case concerned the refusal of a visa application submitted by the family members of a Polish citizen they wished to visit in Poland. What the ruling makes clear is that there is a right to an effective remedy against the refusal of such visa applications.

rights obligations when applying external border control mechanisms established by EU law cannot be ruled out.

Such debate is still likely to generate strong legal and policy controversies for the years to come, as it requires calling into question the legal understanding of the State as a territorial entity that extends over a fixed and well-defined physical space.[97] The development of the external dimensions of EU asylum and migration policies has profoundly modified the realities of border control, through the latter's externalisation and the multiplication of remote control practices. As a result, the border is no longer exclusively a fixed control point located at the edge of the territory of a State. It has become a complex and evolving social and policy process, which rests on intricate legal and policy mechanisms involving multiple actors.[98] There is no 'border' anymore, but rather numerous 'bordering processes'[99] leading to a 'shifting border' which 'relies on law's admission gates rather than a specific frontier location'.[100] Subjecting 'shifting' border practices to the rule of law requires major legal innovations, since the human rights framework was developed from a traditional Westphalian perspective, focusing on migrants who reside within a State's territory.

There is no consensus on how that fundamental challenge to the way the legal system has been conceived needs to be addressed. Legal uncertainties and controversies are thus likely to persist, alongside divisions and policy disagreements on how to address migratory movements. Irrespective of the opposition and failures that have been met so far, the legal debates show that ultimately, recourse to the law still functions as an appropriate tool to manage social divisions on migration and foster social change. Litigation on humanitarian admission to Europe fosters a much-needed conversation which this volume aims to further support by means of a thorough analysis of the current international, EU and domestic legal frameworks of the selected countries, as well as of their mobilisation by

---

97 The existence of 'a defined territory' is among the constitutive elements of the State as an actor of international law, see the Montevideo Convention on the Rights and Duties of States (adopted on 26 December 1933; entered into force 26 December 1934) art 1(b).

98 D Duez and D Simonneau, 'Repenser la notion de frontière aujourd'hui. Du droit à la sociologie' (2018) 98 *Droit et Société* 1 37-52.

99 V Kolossov and J Scott, 'Selected conceptual issues in border studies' (2013) *Belgeo* 1; D Newman, 'The Lines that Continue to Separate Us: Borders in Our "Borderless" World' (2006) 30 *Progress in Human* Geography 2, 143-161.

100 A Shachar, 'Bordering Migration/Migrating Borders' (2019) 37 *Berkeley Journal of International Law* 1 93-147, 96.

the actors and the concrete difficulties that have arisen in its implementation. The content of the volume is briefly presented in the next Section.

5 The Law Between Promises and Constraints

The contributions to the collective volume address four main questions: *First,* which international and European legal obligations are binding both on the EU and on the Member States, and what constraints do they place – potentially and actually – on the international dimensions of EU migration and asylum policy? *Second,* does the law in the selected Member States (Belgium, Germany and Italy) provide for humanitarian admission procedures and, if so, what are the practices? *Third,* how do lawyers make use of existing provisions to obtain humanitarian admission, and how do refugees experience the functioning of current resettlement programs? *Fourth,* what are the prospects for future evolutions of the EU legal framework?

In the first part, several papers reflect on the limits of the current international and EU legal frameworks in regulating the situation of migrants who are outside European territory. Fundamental questions of human rights law and EU law are addressed, such as the extent of the jurisdiction of states and the scope of the EU Charter of Fundamental Rights. The paradoxes of the right to asylum are highlighted and questioned. Dirk Hanschel discusses the controversies surrounding the extent of the jurisdiction of the State under international human rights law. Drawing on the case law of the ECtHR and focusing on instruments such as the International Covenant on Civil and Political Rights and the International Covenant on Economic, Social and Cultural Rights, the author raises intricate questions of territory and jurisdiction that require nuanced answers. Stephanie Law discusses controversies surrounding the scope of EU law and of the EUCFR. She examines the relevant case law of the CJEU concerning the scope and implementation of EU law and analyses whether the application of the EUCFR is contingent on a territorial connection. The author advances the argument that territoriality is of no relevance to the application of the EUCFR. Sylvie Sarolea discusses the deficiencies in the current international and EU legal frameworks when it comes to dealing with the protection of migrants who are outside EU territory. She addresses the topic from a critical perspective and connects it with the broader issue of how to access justice.

In the second part, the national legal framework and practices regarding humanitarian admission are addressed in three selected Member States

(Germany, Belgium and Italy). A concrete understanding of the everyday practices of these States regarding humanitarian admission and of the corresponding legal issues is provided. Katia Bianchini explores Italian legislation and practices regarding humanitarian admission, while devoting particular attention to the implementation of 'humanitarian corridors'. After explaining what the humanitarian corridors are, their legal basis, essential elements, and the potential for their replicability, she discusses their strengths and shortcomings. Pauline Endres de Oliveira analyses the conditions and procedures of the various humanitarian admissions programmes at the federal and regional (Länder) levels in Germany. She highlights the differences in procedure and in residence statuses. Serge Bodart analyses the Belgian legal framework on humanitarian admission and the limits on the judicial review performed by Belgian courts. He discusses the *X. and X.* ruling from the viewpoint of the domestic administrative tribunal over which he is now presiding and which requested a preliminary ruling from the CJEU.

In the third part, the concrete difficulties that have arisen in the implementation of existing provisions for humanitarian admission are highlighted. Tristan Wibault, the lawyer acting for the Syrian family in the *X. and X.* case, shares his experience of mobilising the law to obtain a humanitarian visa. He reflects critically on his own work by showing how, in practice and contrary to what the notion of 'strategic litigation' may suggest, lawyers tend to accompany as closely as possible the developments of a case, but are rarely in a position to develop, beforehand, a proactive and comprehensive strategy aimed at obtaining modifications of the legal framework. Sophie Nakueira, on the basis of the qualitative empirical data she collected during her extensive fieldwork in a refugee camp in Uganda, provides an account of the concrete difficulties vulnerable refugees face when trying to access resettlement programmes. She highlights and discusses the shortcomings and difficulties inherent in the implementation of the vulnerability criteria developed by the UNHCR to select refugees for resettlement, in a context where most of them are confronted with dire living conditions.

In the fourth part, concrete prospects for evolutions of the EU legal framework are being discussed. Catharina Ziebritski shows the emergence of an 'EU resettlement law' which, she argues, bears the promise of enhancing refugee protection if it remains aligned with the constitutional rationale of the CEAS. Eugenia Relano Pastor analyses the initiatives taken by the European Parliament to introduce a provision on humanitarian visas within the EU Visa Code, and the subsequent developments which ultimately led to the withdrawal of that proposal. She shows how the legal tensions which have emerged before the CJEU and the ECtHR also had an impact on the debates within the European Parliament and among the EU institutions.

Jean-Yves Carlier concludes the volume by calling for renewed forms of global migration governance that would move beyond the strict dichotomy between open and closed borders. He makes the proposal of launching a broader reflection on how visas may be abolished in the long run, and to start admitting some kind of limited judicial review in those instances where the 'substance of the rights' of migrants is being threatened, for example, when the very essence of their fundamental rights is at stake.

Part 1.
Humanitarian Admission Under International and EU Law. The Right to Asylum and its Paradoxes

Chapter 1: Humanitarian Admission Under Universal Human Rights Law: Some Observations Regarding the International Covenants

Dirk Hanschel[1]

Contents

Introduction

The topic of humanitarian admission can be approached from multiple angles, but in many ways it is particularly intriguing from a human rights

---

1 Professor in the Law School of the University of Halle-Wittenberg. The author wishes to thank researchers at his Chair, in particular Jessica Appelmann, Svenja Auerswald and Eva Frenz, for their support in completing this chapter.

perspective.[2] Human rights law is generally contingent to state territory or more broadly state jurisdiction.[3] However, human distress does not stop at borders, and the question arises to what extent human rights law does or should impose duties on states beyond their territory, such as a duty to grant humanitarian visas to refugees either physically appearing in a state ´s embassy abroad or simply filing an application from outside.[4] As Benvenisti has aptly put it:

> 'But a serious look at the idea of human rights will reveal that if these rights precede state sovereignty, they must precede the sovereignty of

---

2 For a general overview of state practice on humanitarian visas see <www.ohchr.org/Documents/Issues/Migration/OHCHR_DLA_Piper_Study.pdf> accessed 29 July 2019.

3 F Coomans, 'The Extraterritorial Scope of the International Covenant on Economic, Social and Cultural Rights in the Work of the United Nations Committee on Economic, Social and Cultural Rights' (2011) 11 *Human Rights Law Review* 1, 2.; generally on jurisdiction see M Den Heijer, *Europe and Extraterritorial Asylum (2012)* (Oxford Heart Publishing) 25 ff; see furthermore F Svensén, '*Humanitarian Visas and Extraterritorial Non-Refoulement Obligations at Embassies*' (2016) Faculty of Law Stockholm University, 38 <www.diva-portal.se/smash/get/diva2:1060800/FULLTEXT01.pdf> accessed 20 July 2019 who claims that jurisdiction has come to be the '[t]hreshold criterion', hence '*non-refoulement* obligations stemming from human rights law apply wherever a state is exercising jurisdiction abroad'.

4 See generally, G Noll, 'Seeking Asylum at Embassies: A Right to Entry under International Law? (2005), 17 *International Journal of Refugee Law*, 542–573; K Ogg, 'Protection Closer to Home? A legal case for claiming asylum and embassies and consulates' (2014) 33(4) *Refugee Survey Quarterly* 81.; Den Heijer (n 3); T Gammeltoft-Hansen, 'The Extraterritorialization of Asylum and the Advent of "Protection Light" (2007) DIIS working paper <www.econstor.eu/dspace/bitstream/10419/84510/1/DIIS2007-02.pdf> accessed 02 August 2019; on the importance of this question see P Endres de Oliveira, 'Legaler Zugang zu internationalem Schutz – zur Gretchenfrage im Flüchtlingsrecht' (2016) 2 *Kritische Justiz*, 167; European Parliamentary Research Service, Humanitarian visas: European Added Value Assessment accompanying the European Parliament's legislative own initiative report (PE 621.823, 2012) <www.europarl.europa.eu/cmsdata/150782/eprs-study-humanitarian-visas.pdf> accessed 30 July 2019; S Morgades-Gil, 'Humanitarian Visas and EU Law: Do States Have Limits to Their Discretionary Power to Issue Humanitarian Visas?' (2017) European Papers <www.europeanpapers.eu/en/europeanforum/humanitarian-visas-and-eu-law-do-states-have-limits-to-their-discretionary-power> accessed 29 July 2019; T Spijkerboer and E Brouwer and Y Al Tamimi, 'Advice in Case C-638/16 PPU on prejudicial questions concerning humanitarian visa' (2017) <thomasspijkerboer.eu/wp-content/uploads/2017/01/Advies-VU-English1.pdf> accessed 29 July 2019; Den Heijer (n 3) 35.

> all states, and therefore all states must consider the human rights of foreigners when they make decisions that affect them.'[5]

This raises the contested issue of extraterritorial jurisdiction.[6] At the same time, even where territorial jurisdiction is triggered, human rights protection is not limitless. Whilst human rights apply to a person under a state's jurisdiction, they do not necessarily entail a state duty to host that person indefinitely in order to guarantee that they can permanently benefit from this high standard. As long as someone does not enjoy citizenship or another right of permanent residence, the only clear limit to sending people back to their country of origin is where this would be contrary to the principle of non-refoulement as established in international refugee law and fortified in international human rights law.[7]

This shows that the promise of universal human rights is in fact a rather contingent one. Not only does effective human rights protection depend on state territory or jurisdiction, but the state can also determine to some extent whom it allows onto the territory or whom it subjects to its jurisdiction.[8] This is, of course, a natural consequence of state sovereignty, borders and the limitations of human rights commitments that states have entered into. Encroachments on sovereignty are limited. In real life, this can lead to inhumane consequences that are at odds with the idea of protection against fundamental experiences of injustice.[9] Human rights, on the one hand, claim to be universal standards that are not negotiable, whilst, on the other hand, they can get stronger or weaker depending on the proximity of a person towards a state's authority, which the state itself can influence. Human rights provide strong and often absolute guarantees, but their applicability may in fact be of a gradual nature. The positivist legal construct of human rights only pierces state sovereignty in a vertical (state-subject within jurisdiction), not in a diagonal way (state-subject within an-

5 E Benvenisti, 'Law as a Barrier, Law as a Bridge? On "Humanitarian Visas" and the Obligations of Distant States' (2017) *Global Trust - Sovereigns as Trustees of Humanity* <globaltrust.tau.ac.il/law-as-a-barrier-law-as-a-bridge-on-humanitarian-visas-and-the-obligations-of-distant-states/> accessed 31 July 2019.

6 See generally Den Heijer (n 3).

7 J Allain, The ius cogens Nature of non-refoulement' *International Journal of Refugee Law* (2001), 534ff.; G Goodwin-Gill, 'The Refugee in International Law' (2007), 232f.

8 Generally on jurisdiction and human rights Den Heijer (n 3) 28 ff.

9 For this understanding of human rights see for instance E Riedel 'Menschenrechte als Gruppenrechte auf der Grundlage kollektiver Unrechtserfahrungen' (1999) in H Reuter (ed): Ethik der Menschenrechte, 295 ff.

other state´s jurisdiction). Hence, to relate once more to Benvenisti´s article, human rights law is sometimes more of a 'barrier' than of a 'bridge'.[10]

Of course, one might argue that the refugees´ countries of origin have usually entered into human rights obligations themselves. Failure to respect them cannot completely be compensated by other governments that are often far away from and little responsible for the actual violations. State sovereignty can only be limited by human rights obligations within the field that sovereignty covers. This may pose limits to the controversial notions of humanitarian intervention or responsibility to protect.[11] However, it does not bar states from relaxing or expanding access to their domestic human rights standards and by interpreting these standards in a way that is less reliant on territory or jurisdiction.

The following analysis will deal with the question to what extent these pleas correspond to existing duties under universal human rights law and to what extent they deserve consideration *de lege ferenda*. The guiding hypothesis is that whilst human rights obligations as such posit strong and sometimes absolute claims that increasingly demand extraterritorial application, states can still control their scope to some extent by regulating the degree of physical and legal proximity (or distance) between them and the potential rights holders. If human rights are, as often claimed, like spotlights, states are the illuminators that decide to some extent upon their direction. This is particularly the case with regard to extraterritorial jurisdiction, which concerns human rights obligations relating to embassies such as in the *X and X v Belgium* case[12] which constitutes the occasion for this volume.

The case of humanitarian visas serves to illustrate this in a paradigmatic fashion as it raises the question under which circumstances states, under existing human rights law, are required to issue humanitarian visas, or at least should be required to do so, if the idea of human rights is to be taken seriously.[13] In order to make that very principled point, this chapter concentrates on the universal dimension of human rights, ie the International

10 E Benvenisti (n 5).

11 I Winkelmann, 'Responsibility to Protect' in Max Planck Encyclopedia of Public International Law (2010), para. 1-3.

12 CJEU *X and X v Belgium* 2017 C-638/16 PPU. For the opinion of Advocate General Mengozzi see <curia.europa.eu/juris/document/document.jsf?text=&docid=187561&pageIndex=0&doclang=EN&mode=lst&dir=&occ=first&part=1&cid=664302> accessed 2 August 2019.

13 See Riedel (n 9) for attempts to underpin human rights from ethical perspectives.

Covenants on Civil and Political Rights (ICCPR) and on Economic, Social and Cultural Rights (ICESCR). These instruments, together with the Universal Declaration on Human Rights (UDHR), constitute the so-called Universal Bill of Rights and underpin the non-refoulement provision (Art 33) in the Geneva Convention. Whilst focusing on these instruments, the author recognizes that other global treaties (such as the Convention against Torture) and regional treaties (such as the European Convention on Human Rights (ECHR)), as well as fundamental rights in Constitutions, provide ample material for further study.[14]

The following analysis is divided into several sections that will display a major discrepancy, several observations and a tentative conclusion together with an outlook.

1 A Major Discrepancy Between Moral Claim and Legal Reality

As the introductory remarks have indicated, human rights suffer from a discrepancy between the moral claim and legal reality. This can be shown in particular where a state acts beyond its territory.[15] The *X and X* case before the Court of Justice of the European Union (CJEU) aptly illustrates that.[16] A Syrian family addressed the Belgian embassy in Lebanon in order to obtain a visa under Art 25 para 1, lit. a of the Visa Code 'with limited territorial validity',[17] which the Member State can grant 'on humanitarian grounds' where it 'considers' this 'necessary'.[18] The applicants aimed to use the visas as a basis to enter Belgium in order to then apply for protection as refugees.

Whilst Advocate General Mengozzi stated that in light of human rights obligations, Belgium was required to grant the visa in this case, the CJEU rejected the claim and reaffirmed that it was at the State's discretion whether such a visa should be granted or not. The question concerned Art 3 of the ECHR, Art 4 of the European Charter of Fundamental Rights and

---

14 For further analysis see Ogg (n 4).

15 M Milanovic, *Extraterritorial Application of Human Rights Treaties: Law, Principles, and Policy* (OUP 2011) 3.

16 *X and X v Belgium* (n 12) 173.

17 Idem 19.

18 Regulation (EC) No 810/2009 of the European Parliament and of the Council of 13 July 2009 establishing a Community Code on Visas (Visa Code) [2009] OJ 2 243/1, Art 25(1)(a).

Art 33 of the Geneva Convention.[19] The Advocate General stated first of all that

> 'The fundamental rights recognized by the Charter, which any authority of the Member States must respect when acting within the framework of EU law, are guaranteed to the addressees of the acts adopted by such an authority *irrespective of any territorial criterion*'.[20]

He claimed that there is a 'parallelism between EU action, whether by its institutions or through its Member States, and application of the Charter'.[21] According to his view, the Charter of Fundamental Rights was therefore triggered as European Union (EU) law (ie the Visa Code) was applied.[22] By contrast, he refused to deal with the question whether the ECHR is applicable which serves to interpret the Charter which has similar guarantees.[23] The Court did not dispute the argument as such, but simply held that the claimants had only applied for the visa to claim asylum in Belgium, and that the latter situation was not covered by the Visa Code, which meant that the Charter was not applicable, either.[24]

To put the consequence of this judgment in a rather blunt, but not exaggerated way: If, for instance, a family wants to seek protection abroad from a civil war it seems that they need to physically reach a safe country or find another way into its jurisdiction. This can lead to enormous additional suffering and entail the exposure to severe risks to their lives, as the example of refugees in the Mediterranean shows. Moreover, many people may not even be able to make such choices, because they are too sick, too weak or too poor. If the family manages to reach their destination – legally or illegally – they may be subjected to the full or at least to some substantial human rights protection. By contrast, if they do not manage to cross the border, they may have risked everything but receive no protection. Is this really compatible with the notion of human rights? At the same time, how far can we stretch human rights without asking states to do the im-

---

19 *X and X v Belgium* (n 12) 28.

20 Idem. [89] (Opinion of AG Mengozzi).

21 Idem [91].

22 Idem [108]; see further on this Endres de Oliveira (n 4); see furthermore M Zoeteweij-Turhan and S Progin-Theuerkauf, 'AG Mengozzi's Opinion On Granting Visas to Syrians From Aleppo: Wishful thinking?' (2017) *European Law Blog.* 71 f, <europeanlawblog.eu/2017/02/14/ag-mengozzis-opinion-on-granting-visa-to-syrians-from-aleppo-wishful-thinking/> accessed 5 August 2019.

23 Zoeteweij-Turhan and Progin-Theuerkauf [71 f].

24 *X and X v Belgium* (n 12) 42-45.

possible or discarding the notion of state sovereignty which international law is built upon?

Essentially, human rights law as stipulated by the ICCPR and ICESCR means that a state is responsible for the protection of its own citizens and for residents on its territory. This does not only apply to countries such as Germany or France that are currently in peace and have a rather solid record of human rights protection. It also applies to countries where some of the worst civil wars and human rights violations are observed, even though comparable standards of human rights protection are in place (Syria, for instance, which ratified both Covenants already in 1969). Hence, the question is to what extent foreign states are legally responsible for what happens in a country where human rights are not safeguarded.

One way in which such responsibility could manifest itself would be through intervention onto the territory of the foreign state. Under certain very limited circumstances such intervention may be mandated by a decision of the UN Security Council under Chapter VII of the UN Charter. Lacking such authorization, concepts such as humanitarian intervention or more recently the responsibility to protect (R2P) might apply.[25] The former concept essentially relies on the emphasis on human rights in the Charter when formulating several conditions to allow interventions without a Security Council mandate in situations of grave human suffering.[26] The latter notion results from an essentially new understanding of sovereignty in the Charter – sovereignty not only as a right but also as a duty, the disregard of which may lead to intervention from outside.[27] Whilst such controversial notions are beyond the scope of this chapter, they do reveal the discrepancy between the idea of human rights as one of universal protection and its limits in light of sovereignty and the lack of will or ability of states to afford adequate protection domestically.

The discrepancy between 'is' and 'ought' becomes even more clearly visible where the issue is not intervention, but domestic responsiveness in the sense that a state is aware of and responds to human rights challenges of

25 See for instance C Gray, *International Law and the Use of Force* (OUP 2008) 51ff; R Thakur, 'Responsibility to Protect' (2016) 92 *International Affairs*, 415ff2; H Rahman Basaran, 'Responsibility to Protect: An Explanation' (2014) 36 *Houston Journal of International Law* 581, 583.

26 See for instance A Cassese, 'Ex inuiria ius oritur: Are We Moving towards International Legitimization of Forcible Humanitarian Countermeasures in the World Community?' (1999) *European Journal of International Law*, 23 ff.

27 V Guiraudon and G Lahav, 'The Reappraisal of the State Sovereignty Debate: The Case of Migration' (2000) 33 *Comparative Political Studies*, 163.

persons who seek shelter within the jurisdiction of another state. This is the case of humanitarian visa, which constitutes the core of this analysis. The fact appears to be that, as the *X and X* case shows, states often undertake a major effort to avoid a situation where they need to provide full protection. Paradoxically, just because the standard of legally guaranteed human rights protection is so high, states may cautiously limit its scope in a way that makes human rights part of the ratio for borders. They may aptly do so under existing international law, but when looking at the notion of human rights as such, it is doubtful whether they should.

2 *Observations*

Keeping this major discrepancy in mind, it is worthwhile examining in more detail where the limits of existing international human rights law are. This in turn will help illustrate the scope of the above-mentioned gap.

2.1 *The Scope of Human Rights - Territory, Jurisdiction and Beyond?*

The first observation concerns the question as to how far human rights are applicable in the domestic realm. Are the limits aptly defined by state territory and jurisdiction or do they reach beyond these confinements?

The notion of territory characterizes statehood in a classical way, as the well-known three-elements- theory by Georg Jellinek expresses, according to whom the state consists of territory, a people that inhabits it and governmental power that is exercised with regard to the former.[28] As to the scope of applicability of the law, jurisdiction is the crucial term as it is connected but not limited to territory. It aptly determines the scope of application for domestic norms, including those that a state has accepted under international law.[29] Jurisdiction undoubtedly exists within the confine-

28 G Jellinek, *Allgemeine Staatslehre* (Verlag v. O Häring 1914), 396 ff; B Schöbener and M Knauff, *Allgemeine Staatslehre* (C.H. Beck, 2019) § 3, 43 ff; M Herdegen, *Völkerrecht* (C.H. Beck 2019) § 8, 4; N Akipinarli, 'The Fragility of the "Failed State" Paradigm' (2010) 2 *Revue belge de droit international*, 6.

29 Generally on the topic of jurisdiction M Akehurst 'Jurisdiction in International Law' (1972-1973) 46 *British Yearbook of International Law*, 145 ff.

ments of territory of a state.[30] Case law and scholarly opinions reveal quite a rich debate as to how far exactly jurisdiction beyond the territory may go.[31] International law partially determines the discussion as treaties define the scope of their application in different ways, as will be shown in the subsequent section.[32]

Irrespective of these aspects, there seems to be a major agreement that jurisdiction cannot merely be established by a legal bond, in particular citizenship (for instance nationals abroad that seek help through their embassy after they lost their passport). Instead, it can also be generated through a factual relationship, e.g. some kind of effective control of a state beyond its borders, which may in turn lead to legal obligations.[33] With regard to the former type of jurisdiction (which may also be described as *de iure* as opposed to *de facto* jurisdiction) it is quite clear that the relation between a state and its citizens (personal jurisdiction) can create jurisdiction beyond territory, which is demonstrated by the instrument of diplomatic protection.[34] It appears more difficult to establish criteria for extraterritorial *de facto* jurisdiction. Authority and effective control seem to be the more accepted criteria in this regard.[35] If a state occupies a country, the state can incur human rights obligations even though it does not possess the territory.[36] The fulfillment of such criteria might stem from military occupation (legally or illegally) or interventions in a foreign country.[37] *De facto* control can also be exercised in relation to persons (and that will usually

30 J Crawford, *Brownlie's Principles of Public International Law* (OUP 2012) 456 f; J Klabbers *International Law* (CUP 2017), 100; B Oxman, 'Jurisdiction of States' in Max Planck Encyclopedia of Public International Law (2007), para 11.

31 Oxman, para 9 ff.

32 On this issue see also F Coomans, *Extraterritorial Application of Human Rights Treaties* (Intersentia 2004), 41ff, 201ff.; Den Heijer (n 3) 24; the scope of the ICCPR and the ICESCR will be discussed properly in the following section.

33 Den Heijer (n 3) 52 with reference to the jurisprudence; for an overview see furthermore Svensén (n 3) 42 ff.

34 Svensén (n 3) 40 ff.

35 Idem, 42 ff.; on effective control see for instance Wilde, EJIL Talk <www.ejiltalk.org/let-them-drown-rescuing-migrants-at-sea-and-the-non-refoulement-obligation-as-a-case-study-of-international-laws-relationship-to-crisis-part-ii/> accessed 5 August 2019; see also www.icj.org/wp-content/uploads/2018/09/Belgium-Nahhas-Intervention-Advocacy-Legal-Submission-2018-ENG.pdf accessed 5 August 2019.

36 See *Legal Consequences of the Construction of a Wall in the Occupied Palestinian Territory* (Advisory Opinion) [2004] ICJ Rep 136, para. 107-112; on jurisdiction resulting from control over territory see for instance Den Heijer (n 3) 35 ff.

37 See Coomans (n 3) 6; furthermore with reference to case law Den Heijer (n 3) 55.

be the case where a part of the territory is controlled).[38] This control overlaps with the *de iure* control of citizens abroad.

These categories of jurisdiction will become relevant in the analysis of human rights obligations in embassies (see 2.3 below), preceded by an examination of the general framework of extraterritorial jurisdiction according to the Covenants.

2.2 *Extraterritorial Jurisdiction According to the ICCPR and the ICESCR*

When it comes to the details of extraterritorial jurisdiction, it is necessary to look generally at the respective human rights instruments, each of which stipulates its own rules. In that vein, the extension of jurisdiction played a major role in cases before the European Court on Human Rights (ECtHR), eg in *Bankovic and Others v Belgium and 16 Other Contracting States* [39] where the Court established and applied the concept of effective control for military missions beyond a state´s territory.[40] Furthermore, the notion of *espace juridique*, ie the juridical space of the Convention, helped illustrate the scope of the Convention and its (limited) applicability beyond the territory of its Member States.[41] As Caflisch points out with regard to Article 1 of the ECHR, "jurisdiction of the Strasbourg court is essentially territorial"[42], but can, apart from being derived from sovereignty, also "flow…from lesser degrees of dominance such as occupation" or certain other types of control. [43] In addition, jurisdiction can emanate from specif-

---

38 See generally Den Heijer (n 3) 41 ff.

39 ECtHR *Bankovic and Others v Belgium and 16 Other Contracting States* 2001 App no 52207/99.

40 On further case law see for instance D Schmalz, 'Will the ECtHR Shake up the European Asylum System?' (Verfassungsblog, 30 November 2018) <www.academia.edu/37884076/Will_the_ECtHR_shake_up_the_European_asylum_system_On_what_to_expect_from_the_case_Nahhas_and_Hadri_v._Belgium> accessed 31 July 2019; on the long list of ECtHR cases regarding extraterritorial jurisdiction see ECtHR, Factsheet – Extra-territorial jurisdiction of States Parties <www.echr.coe.int/Documents/FS_Extra-territorial_jurisdiction_ENG.pdf> accessed 31 July 2019.

41 See for instance R Wilde (2005) The 'Legal Space' or 'Espace Juridique' of the European Convention on Human Rights: Is it Relevant to Extraterritorial State Action?, European Human Rights Law Review, 115-124.

42 L. Caflisch, 'Attribution, Responsibility and Jurisdiction in International Human Rights Law' *Colombian Yearbook of International Law* (2017) 181.

43 Idem, 184.

ic rules of international law, e.g. relating to "flag States of vessels at sea, aircraft in airspace or space vessels in outer space; the jurisdiction arising from the activities of diplomatic and consular officers and other agents abroad; and the jurisdiction resulting from the consent of the territorial sovereign".[44] Hence, whilst certain activities in embassies may incur jurisdiction, this does not entail that jurisdiction is triggered simply by the fact that a refugee enters an embassy. As tempting as it is to engage further with the rich case law in this regard (and the cases of M and others versus Belgium and Nahhas and Hadri v Belgium[45] will shed light on this), this chapter will focus on the international Covenants which, by their number of ratifications, provide a much broader framework of protection. The ICCPR and ICESCR as the two human rights instruments that aspire to universal application provide quite distinct standards in this regard.

2.2.1 The Standard of the ICCPR

The ICCPR states in Art 2 that

> 'Each State Party to the present Covenant undertakes to respect and to ensure to all individuals within its territory and subject to its jurisdiction the rights recognized in the present Covenant.'

This has invited a major discussion as to whether this 'and' is of a cumulative nature.[46] Both criteria will usually be fulfilled in parallel since territory normally entails jurisdiction. The issue becomes more difficult in cases that are beyond the territory but might still incur jurisdiction. Contrary to the narrow, cumulative understanding by some countries (in particular the United States), the Human Rights Committee (HRC) and most scholars

---

44 Caflisch (n 42) 184; for an alternative interpretation of Art. 1 ECHR see S Besson who demands 'i)effective,(ii)overall,and(iii)normative power and control', 'The Extraterritoriality of the European Convention on Human Rights: Why Human Rights Depend on Jurisdiction and What Jurisdiction Amounts to' *Leiden Journal of International Law* (2012), 884.

45 ECtHR *Nahhas and Hadri v Belgium* 2018 App no 3599/18. <www.icj.org/wp-content/uploads/2018/09/Belgium-Nahhas-Intervention-Advocacy-Legal-Submission-2018-ENG.pdf> accessed 5 August 2019.

46 See also Caflisch (n 42) 181; R Wilde, (2013) 'The extraterritorial application of international human rights law on civil and political rights' in S Sheeran and N Rodley (eds), *Routledge Handbook of International Human Rights Law* (Abingdon Rothledge 2013) (635 - 661); see also M Milanovic (n 15) 222 ff.

adhere to a wider interpretation which lets the criterion of jurisdiction suffice as a trigger for the application of the ICCPR.[47]

The HRC established this in principle as early as in the well-known case of *Lopéz/Burgos v Uruguay*[48]. The Committee held that Uruguay had violated the right to be free from torture and it asserted extraterritorial jurisdiction. It emphasized that the fact that Article 2 (1) of the Covenant places an obligation upon a State party to respect and to ensure rights 'to all individuals within its territory and subject to its jurisdiction' does not mean 'that the State party concerned cannot be held accountable for violations of rights under the Covenant which its agents commit upon the territory of another State, whether with the acquiescence of the Government of that State or in opposition to it'.[49]

In an individual opinion, Christian Tomuschat adds a nuanced note to this dictum which he considers too broad. He finds "that it was the intention of the drafters ... to restrict the territorial scope of the Covenant in the view of such situations where enforcing the Covenant would be likely to encounter exceptional obstacles". However, he adds that it was "[n]ever [...] envisaged [...]to grant States parties unfettered discretionary power to carry out wilful and deliberate attacks against the freedom and personal integrity of their citizens living abroad.' [50]

In its General Comment No 31 the Committee later expressed the view: 'States Parties are required by article 2, paragraph 1, to respect and to ensure the Covenant rights to all persons who may be within their territory and to all persons subject to their jurisdiction.' To avoid any misunderstandings it adds:

> 'This means that a State party must respect and ensure the rights laid down in the Covenant to anyone within the power or effective control of that State Party, even if not situated within the territory of the State Party.'[51]

The International Court of Justice (ICJ) has confirmed this view by stating in its advisory opinion on the legal consequences of the wall built by Israel

---

47 D Moeckli (ed), International Human Rights Law (OUP 2014), 133; C Tomuschat, 'International Covenant on Civil and Political Rights (1966)' in Max Planck Encyclopedia of Public International Law 2010, para 22-26; see also Wilde (n 46) 635 ff.

48 *Delia Saldias de Lopez v Uruguay* (1984) UN Doc CCPR/C/OP/1 88.

49 Idem. [12.3].

50 Idem. [Appendix].

51 CCPR/C/21/Rev. 1/Add. 1326 May 2004, General Comment No. 31, [10].

in the occupied Palestine territories that both the ICCPR and the ICESCR are applicable.[52] With regard to the ICCPR it takes note of the divergent interpretations, but, relying inter alia on the practice of the Committee and the *travaux préparatoires* in the end concludes that it is 'applicable in respect of acts done by a State in the exercise of its jurisdiction outside its own territory'.[53] As Ogg points out, this decision 'provides strong authority for the position that the ICCPR applies extraterritorially'.[54] In the case of *Democratic Republic of the Congo v Uganda* the Committee essentially confirmed this view.[55]

It appears that the approach of the HRC is to assert extraterritorial obligations where state action 'exposes an individual to violations of Covenant rights in another jurisdiction'.[56] Most of the jurisprudence on extraterritorial human rights obligations is focused on state action. There is little evidence when it comes to omissions in spite of a duty to act, even though such positive duties of protection are not necessarily weaker than the corresponding duties to refrain from intervention, depending on the particular case.[57] With regard to humanitarian visas, potential positive duties are in fact crucial. Technically, the denial of a visa can be characterized as an action. However, when viewed in relation to the situation of the refugee, it appears more appropriate to qualify it as an omission to help in light of a potential duty to deal with visa applications in the same way that a country would when the applicant has reached the national soil.[58] Without the opportunity to dwell further on this point, it does not appear too difficult to

52 ICJ Rep 136 (n 36) para.107-112.

53 Idem. [111].

54 See K Ogg (n 4) 90.

55 Armed Activities on the Territory of the Congo (Democratic Republic of the Congo v Uganda), Judgment, I.C.J. Reports 2005, 168, [216]-[220]; the Court refers to the Advisory Opinion on the *Legal Consequences of the Construction of a Wall in the Occupied Palestinian Territory* (2004) I.C.J. Reports 136, [106]; see also F Svensén (n 3) 35.

56 F Svensén (n 3) 58, with references to pertinent HRC views.

57 On this issue Den Heijer (n 3) 52ff., for instance on 52: 'Problematic however, is that the nature of duties to protect and to fulfill (or: positive obligations 'not to omit') may make it difficult to identify what specific conduct of the state would engender a "jurisdictional link" between the state and the individual'. The author asserts that 'international courts are at the least receptive for claims relating to positive obligations in an extraterritorial setting'. Instead of effective control what appears to matter is a specific relationship between the state and the individual due to circumstances and the ability to 'positively influence a person's human rights situation.'.

58 G Goodwin-Gill (n 7) 54f.

imagine such a duty, e.g. resulting from the protection of life or prohibition of torture in the ICCPR.[59] The requirement for that is, of course, that a situation falls within the state jurisdiction. With regard to embassies, this is not easy to establish (as section 2.3 will show).

2.2.2 *The Standard of the ICESCR*

In the ICESCR the wording is markedly different from the ICCPR, potentially providing a much broader scope for extraterritorial application. Art 2 states:

> 'Each State Party to the present Covenant undertakes *to take steps*, individually and through international assistance and co-operation, especially economic and technical, *to the maximum of its available resources*, with a view to achieving progressively the full realization of the rights recognized in the present Covenant by all appropriate means, including particularly the adoption of legislative measures.'[60]

The precise scope of this obligation is not clearly determined.[61] However, the absence of a focus on jurisdiction and the stipulation of a positive duty to provide international assistance could indicate that states have to go far beyond domestic measures in realizing their economic, social and cultural rights. The ICJ takes a more cautious view by stating:

> 'The International Covenant on Economic, Social and Cultural Rights contains no provision on its scope of application. This may be explicable by the fact that this Covenant guarantees rights which are essentially territorial. However, it is not to be excluded that it applies both to territories over which a State party has sovereignty and to those over which that State exercises territorial jurisdiction.'[62]

The Committee on Economic, Social and Cultural Rights appears to take a broader perspective by stating in General Comment No 14 that states have

---

59 Article 6 ICCPR (Right to Life), Article 7 ICCPR (Prohibition of Torture).

60 Italics added.

61 See for instance Coomans (n 3) 7; see also E Riedel 'International Covenant on Economic, Social and Cultural Rights (1966)' in Max Planck Encyclopedia of Public International Law (2011), para. 7.

62 See ICJ Rep 136 (n 36) para 112.

> 'to prevent third parties from violating the right in other countries, if they are able to influence these third parties by way of legal or political means, in accordance with the Charter of the United Nations and applicable international law'.[63]

With regard to Israel, the Committee has held that 'the Covenant applies to all areas where Israel maintains geographical, functional or personal jurisdiction'.[64]

A consortium of various actors led by NGOs pushed the agenda and passed the Maastricht Principles on Extraterritorial Obligations in 2011.[65] These principles seem to have been inspired more directly by questions of corporate responsibility than by issues of migration. Nonetheless they entail very relevant statements regarding the overall responsibility of states towards the realization of human rights. The Principles claim to reflect existing international human rights law[66], whilst they go quite far in some respects and have sparked off some discussion.[67] They deal with actions and omissions which may help to tackle the deficiencies described above. The document addresses extraterritorial obligations (ETOs) as 'a missing link in the universal human rights protection system'. It expresses a general obligation of states to 'respect, protect and fulfil human rights...both within their territories and extraterritorially' (I.3).[68]

The Principles distinguish between obligations 'relating to the acts and omissions of a State, within or beyond its territory, that have effects on the enjoyment of human rights outside of that State's territory' (II.8).[69] When looking at the catalogue carefully it becomes clear that jurisdiction is key to the scope of application as well. For this purpose, Principle 9 lists certain situations under the heading 'Scope of Jurisdiction'

---

63 CESCR,/E/C.12/2000/4, 11 August 2000, General Comment No. 14, para 39; see furthermore Den Heijer (n 3) 52.

64 CESCR, E/C.12/1/Add.27, 4 December 1998, Concluding observations of the Committee on Economic, Social and Cultural Rights, para 6; see furthermore Den Heijer (n 3) 56.

65 <www.etoconsortium.org/nc/en/main-navigation/library/maastricht-principles/?tx_drblob_pi1 %5BdownloadUid%5D=23> accessed 5 August 2019.

66 Ibid.

67 See for instance W Vandenhole, 'Beyond Territoriality: The Maastricht Principles on Extra-Territorial Obligations in the Area of Economic, Social and Cultural Rights', *Netherlands Quarterly on Human Rights* (2011), 233.

68 See Introduction Maastricht Principles, 3 <www.etoconsortium.org/nc/en/main-navigation/library/maastricht-principles/?tx_drblob_pi1 %5BdownloadUid %5D=23> accessed 30 July 2019.

69 Ibid.

> 'a) situations over which it exercises authority or effective control [...]; b) situations over which State acts or omissions bring about foreseeable effects on the enjoyment of economic, social and cultural rights [...]; c) situations in which the State [...] is in a position to exercise decisive influence or to take measures to realize economic, social and cultural rights extraterritorially, in accordance with international law.'[70]

Hence, a much wider notion of jurisdiction is employed which might trigger obligations vis-à-vis asylum seekers in many different situations beyond the territory. As much as refugees might benefit from such an expansion of jurisdiction it remains to be seen whether such a reading of the ICESCR will be fully accepted by states or the Committee. It may, however, be used as a blueprint for future consensus raising interesting questions as to how far such duties might actually go when considering that in a given situation several states might be under a duty to protect at the same time. One might assert that the ICESCR is less important for the determination of non-refoulement obligations than the ICCPR, as it rather contains promotional obligations that are hard to determine in an absolute fashion. This argument may be countered by referring to the fact that all human rights are necessarily formulated in abstract fashion, "requiring concretization through court decisions and administrative and legislative measures".[71] When it comes to the question of resources, it is important to keep in mind that "[a]ll human rights involve costs, both procedurally and substantively, and the cost argument boils down to a question of degree, not of substance".[72] Since the 1990ies, the Committee on Economic, Social and Cultural Rights has come to demand progress from states in a rather robust fashion.[73] As part of this approach, the Committee on Economic, Social and Cultural Rights determined that all states need to safeguard the 'survival kit' by way of minimum core obligations.[74] In civil wars, for instance, states will often not meet this standard, which underlines the im-

70 Idem Principle 9.

71 E Riedel, 'Reflections on the UN Human Rights Committee' in *Archiv des Völkerrechts* (2016), 134.

72 Ibid.

73 Idem., 139: "States have to show how they have actually made progress in their social rights protection between two reporting cycles, and States parties have accepted that".

74 CESCR General Comment No. 3 (1990) The Nature of States Parties Obligations, para. 10; see also Riedel (n 71) 138 who asserts that "there are certain elements of rights that take immediate effect and must be safeguarded by States without delay or restrictions".

portance of economic, social and cultural rights in the field of humanitarian visas.

2.3 The Exercise of Jurisdiction and Resulting Human Rights Obligations in Embassies

The preceding analysis sets out the general scope for extraterritorial jurisdiction under the two Covenants which now allows discussing resulting human rights obligations in the operation of embassies. The generic question arising from the *X and X* case is to what extent the establishment and operation of a diplomatic mission abroad may incur human rights obligations not only towards the state´s own citizens but also towards foreigners who are somehow in contact with the embassy or consulate, for instance by appearing inside the building and filing an application for visas.

The operation of embassies and consulates is primarily governed by the theory of functional necessity.[75] Art 3 of the Vienna Convention on Diplomatic Relations describes the functions of the diplomatic mission which involve inter alia 'Representing the sending State in the receiving State' and 'Protecting in the receiving State the interests of the sending State and of its nationals, within the limits permitted by international law'. This entails that for the purpose of setting up an embassy the sending state does not receive a piece of territory in the host state, but merely exercises authority (and its agents enjoy immunity) to the extent that this is necessary for the smooth operation of the mission in light of the powers granted by the Vienna Conventions on Diplomatic and on Consular Relations. These powers do not entail jurisdiction related to territory (as the territory still belongs to the host state), but the embassy will allow a state to exercise personal jurisdiction regarding its own nationals. In that sense, the establishment and entertainment of diplomatic and consular relations including the operation of embassies on foreign ground is in fact one of the most prominent manifestations of extraterritorial jurisdiction.[76]

Beyond that the question (and this is the decisive one here) is whether there is also jurisdiction regarding foreigners that visit the embassy and want to enter the country that operates it. One might argue that de facto jurisdiction depends on 'physical presence' of applicants on the premise of the embassy or 'actions taken by the diplomatic agents' depending on the

75 C Barker, *The Protection of Diplomatic Personnel* (Routledge 2006) 48 ff.
76 See for instance Oxman (n 30) para 11, 18.

'level of engagement and contact'.[77] Some cases may serve to illustrate this.[78] The case of *R (B & Others) v SSFCA* concerned two young Afghans who sought asylum in the British Consulate in Australia.[79] The British court stated:

> 'In summary, international law recognizes that embassy and consular authorities are entitled, in the territory of the receiving State, to exercise the authority of the sending State to a limited extent, particularly over the nationals of the sending State. The premises on which this limited authority is exercised are inviolable. It is not easy to see that the exercise of this limited authority gives much scope for the securing, or the infringing, of Convention rights.'[80]

However, since the asylum seekers were taken care of in the embassy the Court was

> 'content to assume (without reaching a positive conclusion on the point) that while in the Consulate the applicants were sufficiently within the authority of the consular staff to be subject to the jurisdiction of the United Kingdom for the purpose of Article 1.'[81]

In the case *Mohammad Munaf v Romania* a dual Iraqi-US-American citizen the HRC had to determine

> 'whether, by allowing the author to leave the premises of the Romanian Embassy in Baghdad, it exercised jurisdiction over him in a way that exposed him to a real risk of becoming a victim of violations of his rights under articles 6, 7, 9, 10, paragraph 1 and 14 of the Covenant, which it could reasonably have anticipated.'[82]

The HRC starts by 'recall[ing] its jurisprudence that a State party may be responsible for extra-territorial violations of the Covenant, if it is a link in the causal chain that would make possible violations in another jurisdiction'. The Committee concludes that 'the risk of an extra-territorial violation must be a necessary and foreseeable consequence and must be judged

---

77 Svensén (n 3) 51.

78 See also Svensén (n 3) 49 ff.

79 See *The Queen on the Application of 'B' & ORS v Secretary of State for the Foreign & Commonwealth Office* [2004] EWCA Civ 1344; Ogg (n 4) 99.

80 Ogg (n 4) 63.

81 Ibid 66.

82 *Mohammad Munaf v Romania*, CCPR/C/96/D/1539/2006, para 14.2.

on the knowledge the State party had at the time: in this case at the time of the author's departure from the Embassy'.[83]

Looking at recent cases and developments Ogg concludes that 'an obligation to grant protection will exist if:

> 'there is a real risk that a person ... will be subject to torture or cruel, inhuman, or degrading treatment; – the embassy or consulate exercises jurisdiction over the asylum-seeker; and – the asylum-seeker would, as a direct consequence of being expelled from the embassy or consulate premises or being handed over to the agents of the receiving State, be exposed to torture or cruel, inhuman or degrading treatment.'[84]

There are similar cases by the ECtHR, such *W M v Denmark* where the Commission stated that

> 'authorised agents of a State, including diplomatic or consular agents, bring other persons or property within the jurisdiction of that State to the extent that they exercise authority over such persons or property. In so far as they affect such persons or property by their acts or omissions, the responsibility of the State is engaged'.[85]

These cases show that there is an increasing tendency to expand the scope of state jurisdiction regarding embassies, which can trigger human rights obligations. They all entail a concrete physical element; hence it is hard to conceive how simply filing an application from outside might be sufficient. Furthermore, the underlying rationale of all decisions seems to be that the state in one way or another bears a specific responsibility for the person. The question is whether jurisdiction is triggered by the mere fact that a refugee enters a foreign embassy or whether it requires further aggravating circumstances. It appears that de facto jurisdiction requires some special form of protection promised or provided which can then not be removed any more. It may result from permission to enter the premises of an embassy and a corresponding engagement to provide a certain level of protection.[86] The case law is not very clear in this regard. *De iure* jurisdiction might be established by the simple fact that embassies enjoy a certain status under the international law of diplomacy which confers certain rights onto the sending state. However, that jurisdiction mainly relates to the

83 Ibid.

84 Ogg (n 4) 112.

85 See *W.M. v Denmark* App No 17392/90 (Commission Decision 14 October 1992).

86 Ibid.

state's citizens. To what extent the state provides assistance to foreigners is essentially dealt with by domestic law. The *X and X v Belgium*[87] raises this question of jurisdiction. At the same time it is different in such a way that Art 51 of the Charter of Fundamental Rights specifically states that this instrument is only applicable to the Member States 'when they are implementing Union law'. This is less a question of jurisdiction of a state than of the CJEU which depends on the applicability of EU law. Or to put it in another way: It is a question of EU jurisdiction which then incurs Member States obligations through Art 51 of the Charter. The reasoning of the CJEU according to which an application for a short term visa in order to enter the country and file an asylum application is beyond the scope of EU law and therefore of the Charter of Fundamental Rights and its jurisdiction is less than convincing, as it threatens to compartmentalize jurisdiction by distinguishing between aims that fall within and outside of it.[88]

In spite of the difficulty to find a common denominator within the case law, it appears that with regard to visa applications or jurisdiction it might suffice that such an application is processed by the embassy or consulate.[89] Engagement with an asylum seeker in an embassy or the existence of national visa codes that grant a certain right to apply, on the premises of the embassy, for entry and protection in the state, can trigger extraterritorial jurisdiction. Jurisdiction is hence essentially established through domestic legal rules (or in the *X and X* case: EU rules, in particular the Visa Code). This is aptly shown by the fact that states usually restrict applications of asylum-seekers to those that have reached their territory, which may help to control immigration but probably indirectly contributes to the devastating flight of millions of people. Hence, restrictive rules on admissible claims in embassies may exclude a human rights obligation to process an application for asylum. There seems to be no established rule of international law stating that jurisdiction is simply triggered by the filing of an application in an embassy. However, once *de iure* or *de facto* jurisdiction can be ascertained, human rights may dictate that the state processes an application for asylum and allows a foreigner to enter the country in order to file such an application. Furthermore, the principle of non-refoulement will have to be safeguarded.

---

87 *X and X v Belgium* (n 12).

88 For a critical account of the judgment see for instance Zoeteweij-Turhan and Progin-Theuerkauf (n 22) 72.

89 See Svensén (n 3) 53.

More recent developments indicate that there is a tendency to expand the scope of extraterritorial jurisdiction. Probably the best example of that is the ECHR decision in the *Hirsi case*[90] where the Court accepted both *de facto* and *de iure* jurisdiction of Italy. While it emphasized that extraterritorial jurisdiction remains the exception (para 72) it established that the ship was under exclusive Italian jurisdiction (and therefore control) and that the refugees were de facto treated by Italian military staff.[91] Several views by human rights committees and court decisions seem to point in the direction that embassies might increasingly be viewed in a similar light[92], even though one difference is that they are established on another state´s territory. With regard to the latter, probably the strongest pledge can be found by Judge Pinto de Albuquerque who, in his concurring opinion in the *Hirsi case*, emphasizes that whilst there is no duty of providing diplomatic asylum, international human rights law may demand that, under certain circumstances of extreme danger, asylum seekers be granted visa to enter the territory.[93]

> 'For instance, if a person in danger of being tortured in his or her country asks for asylum in an embassy of a State bound by the European Convention on Human Rights, a visa to enter the territory of that State has to be granted, in order to allow the launching of a proper asylum procedure in the receiving State.'[94]

It should be interesting to observe the further dynamic development of case law. In that vein, a major focus is currently placed on the case of *Nahhas and Hadri v Belgium*[95] which is pending before the ECtHR and picks up many of the issues that were pertinent in the *X and X v Belgium* case.[96] Several NGOs have referred to the Court´s case law and argued that "[w]hilst there is no right for a non-national to enter or remain in a State, immigration applications made by individuals outside a Contracting State's territory have been found to trigger the jurisdiction of the relevant Contracting State".[97] However, the authorities inferred are not compelling and so far do not appear to warrant the conclusion that full jurisdiction is

90 ECtHR *Hirsi Jamaa and Others v Italy* 2016 App no 27765/09.
91 Idem, 81.
92 Svensén (n 3) 49.
93 *Hirsi Jamaa and Others v Italy* (n 90) 70.
94 Idem.
95 *Nahhas and Hadri v Belgium* (n 45).
96 *X and X v Belgium* (n 12); see also D Schmalz (n 40).
97 *Nahhas and Hadri v Belgium* (n 45) p. 1.

engaged by merely operating an embassy that allows for the filing of visa applications or by the rejection of such applications. It may be, however, that the ECtHR will use the opportunity of this case to expand the scope of the Convention, in particular with regard to the prohibition of inhuman or degrading treatment (Art 3 ECHR) where positive obligations appear particularly strong. This would have major legal and political consequences.

Even where jurisdiction is established, the level of human rights protection is, however, limited. State duties are essentially circumscribed by the principle of non-refoulement expressed in Art 33 of the 1951 Geneva Convention. This entails that

'[n]o Contracting State shall expel or return ("refouler") a refugee in any manner whatsoever to the frontiers of territories where his life or freedom would be threatened on account of his race, religion, nationality, membership of a particular social group or political opinion'.[98]

Art 14 para 1 of the UDHR states that 'Everyone has the right to seek and enjoy in other countries asylum from persecution'. Whilst that norm never became binding and anyway does not stipulate a state obligation to grant asylum[99], human rights treaties provide duties of protection that have added further substance to the non-refoulement principle.

This principle, which is hence supported and enhanced by international human rights law,[100] is clearly applicable in the case of territorial jurisdiction, ie where an applicant has entered another state's territory. The notion of sending someone back appears to suggest a relation to territory. However, the case law mentioned above seems to indicate that non-refoulement may also concern cases of extraterritorial jurisdiction.[101] The ECtHR concedes that refoulement (or in this case expulsion) is, like jurisdiction, 'principally territorial'; however it adds that,

> '[w]here as in the instant case, the Court has found that a Contracting State has, exceptionally, exercised its jurisdiction outside its national territory, it does not see any obstacle to accepting that the exercise of

98 See P Weis, The Refugee Convention 1951: The Traveaux Preparatoires Analysed With A Commentary <www.unhcr.org/4ca34be29.pdf> accessed 31 July 2019.

99 T Gammeltoft-Hansen 'The Right to Seek – Revisited. On the UN Human Rights Declaration Article 14 and Access to Asylum Procedures in the EU' *European Journal of Migration Law* (2008), 446; Ogg (n 4) 84.

100 See Svensén (n 3) 19.

101 See furthermore Svensén, who speaks about the 'expansion of the extraterritorial scope of the principle of *non-refoulement*' (n 3) 62.

> extraterritorial jurisdiction by that State took the form of collective expulsion'.[102]

One factor that may influence the assessment of a case is whether asylum is sought in an embassy that is situated in the country where the persecution occurs or elsewhere.[103] In the former case the problem is whether this scenario lies within the rationale of the Geneva Convention. In the latter case, where the applicant has already managed to leave the country where he or she was under threat of persecution[104], it may be less likely that the lack of help in the embassy will directly lead to severe suffering, since the responsibility of the embassy's host state will normally have been engaged anyway. Whether that responsibility is in each case effectively discharged is, of course, another question.

The bottom line is that, with some and probably increasing limitations, states can still largely control to what extent operation of their embassies entails subjecting them to the observation of human rights guarantees *vis-à-vis* their foreign visitors. As the X and X case shows, extraterritorial obligations are often triggered where states have accidentally not limited their jurisdiction sufficiently, which is quite unsatisfactory when considering the human distress and suffering that embassies are witnessing. Obviously, the state of origin has human rights obligations as well, and if it lives up to them such disruptive effects do not occur. Failure to do so cannot place all the burden on other states. Extraterritorial human rights obligations may easily overburden states. One should not infer them light-heartedly from existing guarantees which states have largely limited to their own territory. Nevertheless, the resulting double-standard is frustrating. Hence, a stepwise widening of the effective control doctrine by either interpreting it widely or by replacing it with notions such as influence (as stipulated under the Maastricht Principles) might be appropriate. That means that where a state has an influence on the human rights situation on a foreign territory, and be it only by operating an embassy that can provide some relief, it may under certain circumstances be under an obligation to act accordingly.

---

102 *Hirsi Jamaa and Others v Italy* (n 90) 70. See on this matter further the detailed analysis by Ogg (n 4) 106 ff.

103 For this see for example Svensén (n 3) 62 ff.

104 *X and X v Belgium* (n 12) para 20.

2.4 *Inside Jurisdiction and/or Territory, but Outside Full Human Rights Protection*

To the extent that human rights provide an extraterritorial right to file an application for protection in embassies or to enter the territory for that purpose and to not be subjected to treatment that is contrary to the non-refoulement principle, the level of protection appears to be quite the same as under territorial jurisdiction. This seemingly happy conclusion is, of course, subject to a number of major constraints: First, embassies are the rare exception of how states can be addressed outside their territory. Second, their rules will often exclude the filing of asylum applications so that no *de iure* jurisdiction is established. Cases where applications for short term visa are admissible (which might serve to enter the country in order to then apply for asylum) are (as the *X and X v Belgium* case shows) on the borderline and will probably still generate much dispute – they are certainly no reliable basis. In a way one might even be inclined to argue that states use the law as a shield against having to apply human rights standards.

Finally, even where asylum or some other status of (subsidiary) protection is granted, this does not give individuals any guarantee to be protected in the same way that citizens or other inhabitants with a permanent right of residence are. Even if a person enters a country physically or otherwise manages to be subjected to its jurisdiction this does not mean that they are admitted to a 'paradise of human rights protection', because the level of protection is largely dependent on their right to reside in that country. The strongest guarantee of that right of residence is usually citizenship, followed by a multitude of other categories of status that can provide similar or slightly less protection.[105]

As long as refugees do not obtain such a status, their enjoyment of rights may be of a temporary nature only, ending upon lawful termination of their residence, subject to the non-refoulement requirement. The limitations that human rights place on sovereignty do not curtail the sovereign right of nations to decide about whom they should apply to that follows from conferral of rights of residence. As long as individuals do not enjoy an entrenched position as citizens, states can essentially decide to strip them of their human rights protection (again within the limits of the non-refoulement principle) by terminating their residence. This shows the discrepancy between claims for universality and actual limits of access which

105 See for instance G Goodwin-Gill (n 7) 51ff.

make human rights, in some way, a privilege. The inherent limitations of fundamental rights protection certainly help to protect state sovereignty which includes its right to protect the borders and decide who will enter the territory. Even in a globalized world where borders have in many regards been increasingly put in perspective, this right continues to provide an important function. Nevertheless, this sharp dividing line is very unsatisfactory when looking at the idea of human rights *per se*, even though it seems very unrealistic to solve all problems of human suffering through an expansion of human rights law.

The legal reasoning behind restricting the scope of human rights application is to assume an inherent limitation of state responsibility for actions by other states, even where one′s own action or omission is likely to expose the person to situations that by themselves constitute human rights violations. Obviously, it might be an immense overburdening to place a demand on each state to guarantee perfect enjoyment of human rights worldwide to the maximum extent of what domestic resources can afford. It might endanger social cohesion and lead to the opposite, namely an increasing opposition to human rights claims. One should also keep in mind that human rights "are not the cure to all ills", and that there are other means of legal protection such as international humanitarian and criminal law.[106]

That being said, the current doctrines that limit the applicability of human rights rather strictly to domestic situation do not fully live up to the notion of universal protection which the Bill of Rights and its underlying ideas are supposed to afford.

Conclusion and Outlook

There is, *de lege lata*, still no general human rights duty to provide for humanitarian admission through visas, as states, according to their sovereignty, may essentially still limit the extraterritorial scope of their human rights. In addition, even after arrival in a foreign country, there is no guarantee that a person enjoys the same human rights protection as nationals or accepted permanent residents. The human rights idea may ultimately suffer a damage or even make a mockery of itself if it does not offer procedures/mechanisms that allow a broader and more reliable access to enter the human rights regime. Exposure to high physical risks is no appropriate

---

106 Besson (n 44) 884.

limitation of the number of applications that may validly reach a country. This shows that a coordinated international effort is necessary *de lege ferenda* to expand the human rights regime. In light of persisting controversies, e.g. on the Global Compact, such a consensus appears rather unlikely at the moment. If we overstretch the human rights claim we may dilute the existing level of protection and frustrate the effort of states. Still, if no further steps are taken by the states to allow people to enter the human rights regime, the result may be that people will have to risk their life to enter a country. For people who are somehow unable to do so this would just be 'bad luck'. It appears very doubtful that such a rather cynical approach might be a solution. From the perspective of universal human rights law the claim for humanitarian visas in the *X and X v Belgium* case is a paradigmatic example of the rupture that is created by double standards. In that sense human rights might almost be criticized as becoming, to some extent, another way of richer nations to protect their welfare, with attempts to strengthen true universalism of the human rights claim being refuted where they appear. The divergence between the opinion of the Advocate General and the Court in the X and X and the long list of observations by Member States[107] might serve to illustrate this at least to some extent.

Since states have been cautious to limit their international human rights obligations *de lege lata*, the regime on the protection of migrants urgently requires reform. Whilst international practice as shown in decisions by human rights courts and committees has increasingly alleviated some of the pressure by a rather wide or even expansive reading of pertinent provisions, their wording and underlying state consensus poses certain limits to that endeavor. As much as one might wish to expand this scope further, one cannot replace the lack of state consensus by an increasingly expansive construction of treaty provisions. There may well be, as Den Heijer puts it, an 'emerging consensus among international courts and supervisory bodies that human rights constitute a paramount code of conduct for all state activity'[108]. However, the case law to some extent evokes the impression that it does not build upon a coherent doctrine but rather attempts to rem-

---

107 See *X and X v Belgium* (n 12), observations were issued by the Governments of Austria, the Czech Republic, Belgium, Denmark, Estonia, Finland, France, Germany, Hungary, Malta, the Netherlands, Poland, Slovakia and Slovenia and the European Commission.

108 Den Heijer (n 3) 62.

edy very specific situations of injustice.[109] Where the situation is somehow grave enough courts and committees appear to lean towards triggering the non-refoulement obligation. This is, indeed, a very human behavior that deserves respect, and it certainly appeals to the human rights idea as such. But it may also express a certain helplessness resulting from the fact that the law is so far away from effectively protecting human rights in situations of terrible distress. This puts judicial and quasi-judicial bodies in a situation where on the one hand they may want to provide relief, but on the other hand must not stretch the existing provisions too much in order to maintain credibility und to respect the limits of the (existing) law.

Therefore, one needs to think further in the direction of changes *de lege ferenda*, ie to generate a new and stronger consensus in the first place. The Global Compact and the New York Declaration are very important stipulations of that request. The Compact emphasizes human rights in many of its sections, e.g. in para 15 (f):

> 'The Global Compact is based on international human rights law and upholds the principles of non-regression and non-discrimination. By implementing the Global Compact, we ensure effective respect for and protection and fulfilment of the human rights of all migrants, regardless of their migration status, across all stage of the migration cycle.' [110]

This is preceded by various sections in the New York Declaration.[111] One may hope that, in spite of all the criticism that have accompanied them, these documents may pave the way for future regulation which comes to

109 As Den Heijer (n 3) 60 points out: 'Discussions on the extraterritorial application of human rights have been burdened with a substantial amount of conceptual confusion, in particular in respect of the relationship between the meaning and functions of the notions of territory, jurisdiction and sovereignty within the body of human rights law.'.

110 Global Compact for Safe, Orderly and Regular Migration, UN A/Res/73/195.

111 New York Declaration for Refugees and Migrants, UN A/Res/71/1, e.g. para 26, which reads: 'We will continue to protect the human rights and fundamental freedoms of all persons, in transit and after arrival…' or para 41: 'We are committed to protecting the safety, dignity and human rights and fundamental freedoms of all migrants, regardless of their migratory status, at all times'. Similarly in para 42: 'We commit to safeguarding the rights of, protecting the interests of, and assisting our migrant communities abroad, including through consular protection, assistance and cooperation in accordance with relevant international law.' But this also includes 'that each State has the sovereign right to determine whom to admit to its territory, subject to that State's international obligations'. (para 42); 'consider facilitating opportunities for safe, orderly and regular migration…' (para 57); 'We reaffirm that international refugee law, international hu-

grips with the specific vulnerability of migrants resulting from their being on the move and often falling between regulatory frameworks.

man rights law and international humanitarian law provide the legal framework to strengthen the protection of refugees.' (para 66).

Chapter 2: Humanitarian Admission and the Charter of Fundamental Rights

Stephanie Law[1]

Contents

1 Lecturer in Law, University of Southampton; previously, Senior Research Fellow, Max Planck Institute Luxembourg for Procedural Law. As usual, all errors remain those of the author alone. Nevertheless, I would like to thank colleagues at the MPI for Social Anthropology in Halle as well as all other participants for an inspiring conference; particular thanks are due to Professor Marie-Claire Foblets, Professor Burkhard Hess and Dr Luc Leboeuf. Moreover, I would like to express my sincere gratitude to Dr Edoardo Stoppioni and Martina Mantovani at the MPI Luxembourg for consistently inspiring discussions.

Introduction

The examination of humanitarian admission from the perspective of EU law and policy brings to the fore a number of issues underpinning the EU's migration and asylum system. This chapter will examine three dimensions of this regime: the character of the EU visa regime and asylum framework and the challenges to which it gives rise for third-country nationals who wish to travel safely and legally, to seek asylum; the possibility for those individuals, often in dire need of protection, to rely on EU fundamental rights and international human rights; and the significance attached to the sovereignty-sensitive character of allowing access to Member State territory.[2]

This chapter will examine these issues in light of the European Court of Justice (ECJ) case of *X and X*[3] and the EU legal framework that underpins and shapes the discourse on the issuance of visas on a humanitarian basis by the authorities of EU Member States. It proceeds in the following four steps. Firstly, the facts of the *X and X* case are briefly set out, in light of the contours of the EU *acquis* on the application and issuance of visas. This brief outline will facilitate the second step, in which the understanding of the concept of the humanitarian visa as a Protected Entry Procedure is set out. Thereafter, the divergent reasoning of the Advocate General (AG) and Court in *X and X* will be examined, and the protections afforded to individuals seeking asylum under the EU legal framework and its interrelation with international law, assessed in this light.[4] Fourthly, the focus shifts to the scope and application of the fundamental rights dimension of EU legal protections, namely the Charter of Fundamental Rights (hereinafter CFR),[5] in the context of applications for humanitarian visas. Finally, legal and political (that is to say, with some general comments as to which insti-

---

2 See L Ypi, 'Borders of Class: Migration and Citizenship in the Capitalist State' (2018) 32 *Ethics and International Affairs* 141, 144, and highlighting the class dimensions of migration, which are often obscured in discourses on immigration.

3 Case C-638/16 PPU *X and X* EU:C:2017:173.

4 A key issue appears to be one of fragmentation in protections afforded to individuals in light of the objectives of different legal regimes; this characteristic will not be discussed further here however.

5 The CFR codifies fundamental rights protected in the EU in a single document. While proclaimed in 2000, the CFR was attributed the status of primary law in Art 6(1) Treaty on the EU (Treaty of Lisbon amending the Treaty on European Union and the Treaty establishing the European Community (European Union [EU]) [2007] OJ C306/1).

tution should be responsible for such decision-making) conclusions are drawn from the analysis undertaken in light of the reforms in EU law.

Between a Rock and a Hard Place: The Plight of the Syrian Family and the Externalisation of Border Control by the EU

This section sets out the limitations of the framework for making claims for asylum, the fundamental characteristics of the EU visa regime, and the problems these regimes pose in respect of the circumstances of the Syrian family in the case of *X and X*.

The EU Treaties set out that the Union policy on asylum and migration should be governed by the principles of solidarity and fair sharing of responsibility between the Member States in Art 80 TFEU; moreover, as regards the absence of internal border controls, Art 67(2) TFEU provides that the EU should 'frame a common policy on asylum, immigration and border control, based on solidarity between Member States which is fair towards third-country nationals'. The adherence to these principles as well as the notion that the Union should aim to facilitate managed migration as well as provide, where relevant, for safe, legal and controlled migration (both for people in need of protection and to deal with labour market needs)[6], and ensure respect for the right to claim asylum, have increasingly been called into question.[7] These issues have come to the fore in the last decade as increasing numbers of individuals fleeing conflict zones in Africa, Asia and the Middle East, have sought to reach EU Member State territory in order to make claims for asylum. In the absence of finding a safe and legal way to do so, they have turned to irregular means of migration including smuggling, resulting in devastating losses of life at sea. The following section will briefly set out the rules of the EU's Common European Asylum System (CEAS) and its visa regime in order to identify some of the problems faced by third country nationals seeking to make claims for asylum in a Member State of the EU.[8]

Before examining these issues further, it should be noted that the EU, and its Member States, have made considerable efforts in recent years to ex-

6 European Parliament, 'Briefing - Legal Migration to the EU' PE 635.559 (Brussels, 2019).

7 See for example, E Guild, C Costello, M Garlick and V Moreno-Lax, 'Enhancing the CEAS and Alternatives to Dublin' Study for the LIBE-Committee of the European Parliament (Brussels, 2015).

8 It should be noted that this analysis is by no means exhaustive.

ternalise[9] its border controls. Indeed, the case of *X and X* illustrates the relationship between this externalisation and the application of EU law, and especially fundamental rights protections. This externalisation derives *inter alia* from national and EU policies that have an impact outside the borders of territorial Europe and the extension of the EU's 'external' borders far beyond its Member States' territories.[10] The overarching aim of these policies seems to be to ensure that third-country nationals do not leave those third countries through irregular means or, if they do, that they are returned. Notwithstanding that the EU is engaged in active externalisation in this field, the judgment in *X and X* unfortunately ensures that these law and policy actions are kept outside the scope of Union law, with the consequence that third-country nationals cannot access either the EU or the ECJ's jurisdiction.

The Common European Asylum System (CEAS)

The right to asylum was recognised in the 1951 Geneva Convention Relating to the Status of Refugees[11] and is now also established in Art 18 CFR. In the Treaty of Amsterdam,[12] the Member States transferred competences to the EU (then European Community) in the field of asylum, providing foundations basis for the development of rules on asylum from its international law basis to the EU *acquis*. Established initially in 1999, the CEAS has been under an almost constant process of reform. Increasingly, in light of the humanitarian crises surrounding asylum claims made in EU Member States, it has been subject to criticism from a number of perspectives. This chapter does not provide for detailed information on the functioning of the CEAS but rather aims to set out how it operates in line with the EU rules on visas in light of the *X and X* case.

---

9 As well as to privatise and securitise its policy and law; see T Spijkerboer, 'Bifurcation of People, Bifurcation of Law: Externalization of Migration Policy before the EU Court of Justice' (2017) 31 *Journal of Refugee Studies* 216.

10 Including for example, requirements that airlines check visas and travel documentation (and consequent sanctions), requirements on third countries to take back individuals who have attempted to immigrate to Europe, patrols outside of the territorial seas of EU Member States and indeed in third country territorial waters.

11 Convention relating to the Status of Refugees (United Nations [UN]) 189 UNTS 137, UN Reg No I-2545, [1954] ATS 5, Cmnd 9171.

12 Treaty of Amsterdam Amending the Treaty on European Union, the Treaties Establishing the European Communities and Related Acts, OJ 1997 C 340.

The CEAS is made up of a number of pieces of EU legislation.[13] Given that the EU (Schengen area) is a space within which individuals who are on its territory can freely move across open borders, it has long been considered that there is a need for common EU rules to govern it and to ensure the existence of a strong external border. Each piece of legislation thus aims to provide for common rules, harmonising common minimum standards for the making and granting of asylum. The CEAS has the objectives to ensure that asylum seekers are treated fairly, that there is equality of outcome regardless of where the application is made, and that the responsibility for asylum applications is shared between Member States. The EU thus aims to be an area of protection for individuals seeking asylum. Whether these objectives are satisfied has long been called into question. Nevertheless, the CEAS is largely envisaged as providing a framework for the governance and cooperation of interstate relations, and not necessarily for individual protection. The component part most relevant to the issues explored in this chapter is the Dublin III Regulation, the most recent version of which came into force in 2013.[14] The Dublin III Regulation establishes the criteria by which Member States should be allocated the responsibility for the processing of claims for asylum, aims to ensure that problems potentially arising in national asylum systems from migration crises can be managed[15], and aims to ensure the protection of asylum seekers in this process.

The Member State on whose territory an asylum claim is made may not necessarily be responsible for the handling of that claim however. As such, in the first place it is necessary that every Member State is able to assess and

13 Including, amongst others: the revised Asylum Procedures Directive 2013/32/EU; the revised Reception Conditions Directive 2013/33/EU; the revised Qualifications Directive 2011/95/EU; the revised EURODAC Regulation (EU) No 603/2013 and the revised Dublin Regulation (EU) No 604/2013 (Dublin III or Dublin regime).

14 The Dublin III Regulation has been subject to ongoing discussions since its adoption (http://www.europarl.europa.eu/legislative-train/theme-towards-a-new-policy-on-migration/file-jd-revision-of-the-dublin-regulation/12-2016); see also the proposal of 4 May 2016 of the European Commission for a revised Regulation COM(2016) 270 final (https://ec.europa.eu/home-affairs/sites/homeaffairs/files/what-we-do/policies/european-agenda-migration/proposal-implementation-package/docs/20160504/dublin_reform_proposal_en.pdf).

15 To prevent, per recital 22 Dublin III, 'a deterioration in, or the collapse of, asylum systems'. The Dublin III Regulation includes an early warning, preparedness and crisis management system to ensure that problems in national systems can be identified and dealt with, and that Member States dealing with a high number of applications can be provided with assistance.

determine whether it is responsible for the examination of a claim.[16] The Dublin regime is based on the principle that only one State is responsible for examining an asylum claim, and that the responsible State is under an obligation to ensure effective access for individuals to its asylum procedure. As such, it intends to facilitate the operation of an efficient system for dealing with asylum claims, the speedy determination of which dictates that a single and clearly identifiable Member State is responsible for the quick resolution of those applications.[17] It provides that Member States can make transfer decisions by which individuals can be transferred to the Member State that is responsible for processing his or her claim for asylum.

Fundamentally for this chapter, Art 3(1) Dublin III sets out that applications for asylum must be made either at the border of, or on the territory of a Member State by the individual seeking asylum. Per Arts 3 of the Asylum Procedures Directive, governing applications for international protection, the directive applies only to requests made on the territory, at the border, in the territorial waters or in the transit zones of the Member States; it does not apply to requests made at their representations and Member States are not obliged to allow such applications.[18] Under the Dublin regime, third-country nationals, who wish to make a claim for asylum in an EU Member State, cannot do so on the territory of their state of origin, or another third State.[19] Chapter III of the Regulation sets out a hierachical set of criteria for determining which single Member State is responsible, from family members, to recent residence permit or visa possession, to the entry into the Member State of the EU. Asylum seekers should apply for asylum in the first country they enter, i.e. cross the EU's external

16 Member States are entitled and free to examine any asylum claim made on their territory, even if that Member State would not be the one to which the claim would be allocated under the Dublin III Regulation.

17 The Dublin regime sets out the criteria (in hierarchical order) for establishing and allocating responsibility to Member States. The general rule is that asylum seekers should apply for asylum in the first country they enter unless they have family elsewhere or another country has issued a residence permit or a visa. Currently, the criterion most applied is that of illegal entry or stay in a Member State – that is, of the country of first entry into EU territory.

18 Directive 2013/32 on common procedures for granting and withdrawing international protection. The scope Directive 2013/33/EU laying down standards for the reception of applicants for international protection, per Art 3, is similar.

19 Indeed, in line with Art 1(2) 1951 Refugee Convention, the term applies, amongst other criteria, to those persons who are outside of the country of their nationality.

border, unless they have family elsewhere or another Member State can be designated in light of the criteria set out at Chapter III. The rule in Art 3(2) is that, where no Member State can be identified as responsible on the basis of these criteria, the first Member State in which an application is made shall be responsible. Applicants can be transferred to the Member State that has been indicated to be primarily responsible.[20] The Dublin III Regulation may result in different Member States being faced with processing different numbers of asylum applications. In light of this, Relocation Decisions have been introduced to relocate asylum seekers; for example, in 2015, 160,000 asylum seekers were moved from Italy and Greece to other EU Member States.[21] According to Eurostat, in 2017 and 2018, the States with the highest number of first-time applicants were Germany, France, Greece, Spain, and Italy.[22]

Schengen and the EU Legal Framework on Visas

The Schengen area, established on the basis of the Schengen Agreement 1985,[23] covers the territory of 22 Member States, 4 associated States and over 4 million square km of European "territory". The Schengen area is one without internal borders,[24] meaning that those who can enter it (whether citizens or residents of EU Member States, or visitors to the EU)

---

20 Unless, per Art 3(2)(2), 'there are substantial grounds for believing that there are systemic flaws in the asylum procedure and in the reception conditions for applicants in that Member State, resulting in a risk of inhuman or degrading treatment within the meaning of Article 4 of the Charter of Fundamental Rights'.

21 Council Decision (EU) 2015/1601 of 22 September 2015 establishing provisional measures in the area of international protection for the benefit of Italy and Greece and Council Decision (EU) 2016/1754 of 29 September 2016 amending Decision (EU) 2015/1601 establishing provisional measures in the area of international protection for the benefit of Italy and Greece.

22 See Eurostat, 'Main Countries of Destination'; available at: https://ec.europa.eu/eurostat/statistics-explained/index.php?title=File:Number_of_(non-EU)_asylum_seekers_in_the_EU_and_EFTA_Member_States,_2017_and_2018_(thousands_of_first_time_applicants)_YB19.png.

23 Agreement between the Governments of the States of the Benelux Economic Union, the Federal Republic of Germany and the French Republic on the Gradual Abolition of Checks at their Common Borders [2000] OJ L239/13.

24 Under Schengen, the Member States can introduce temporary border controls in the event of a threat to public policy or internal security. It must be exceptional and proportionate, limited in term and be limited to the very minimum required. The Commission can issue an opinion as to the choices of the Member States to

can travel freely therein. This freedom nevertheless depends on the type of visa issued and the restrictions attached to it; visas with a limited territorial validity, including for example, a humanitarian visa issued on the basis of Art 25 Visa Code, allows only for travel to the Member State that issued the visa. As a result, it has been deemed necessary that the external Schengen border is strong and that checks are made on travellers who enter and exit it.[25] These checks and controls are organised and coordinated by the EU's Frontex agency (the European Border and Coast Guard Agency) and the Member States.[26] According to the amended Regulation by which it was established,[27] the Agency should operate in line with 'respect for fundamental rights and international protection'.[28] For the most part, these controls take place at the border of the territory of the EU. However, increasingly they are being externalised. This control might be exercised by the Member States' authorities, or by Frontex together with the authorities of a third State. This externalisation can be identified in Frontex's operation on the territory of a third State, facilitated by Status Agreements; the

---

introduce such controls. The bases on which such controls can be introduced are set out in Arts 26 – 29 of the SBC). This was done, for example, by certain Member States in light of the humanitarian crisis related to immigration from a number of countries.

25 Art 8 Regulation (EU) 2016/399 of the European Parliament and of the Council of 9 March 2016 on a Union Code on the rules governing the movement of persons across borders (Schengen Borders Code) sets out that checks should be undertaken on cross-border movement at the external Schengen borders.

26 FRONTEX aims to secure cooperation between Member States. It primarily coordinates operations to help Member States in managing flows of migration. These include operations coordinated by the Frontex Agency at sea are governed by Regulation 656/2014, which establishes rules on interception, rescue and disembarkation. EUROSUR (European Border Surveillance System) is a mechanism that helps Schengen countries to establish an operational and technical framework, to work against cross-border crime, to prevent unauthorized border crossings and to reduce the deaths of migrants at sea.

27 Regulation (EU) 2016/1624 of the European Parliament and of the Council of 14 September 2016 on the European Border and Coast Guard and amending Regulation (EU) 2016/399 of the European Parliament and of the Council and repealing Regulation (EC) No 863/2007 of the European Parliament and of the Council, Council Regulation (EC) No 2007/2004 and Council Decision 2005/267/EC, OJ L 251, 16.9.2016, p. 1.

28 Art 34 Regulation (EU) 2916/1624 refers to the 1951 Geneva Convention, as well as the CFR and 'relevant international law'; see further, O de Schutter, 'The Implementation of the Charter of Fundamental Rights in the EU Legal Framework' Study for the DG for Internal Policies, Committee on Constitutional Affairs, PE 571.397, 42-46.

first instance of such an exercise derives from the joint operation of Frontex and Albanian border guards on the Greek-Albanian border from May 2019.[29]

The Schengen Border Code[30] and a common visa policy, by which the EU structures its migration regime through its relations with third States, governs the crossing of Schengen's external border, transits through Schengen States and short-term stays in Schengen States. This framework provides for common rules to be applied in governing external border checks, entry requirements and duration of stays in the Schengen area and beyond;[31] it establishes which nationals need a visa and those who do not. The EU Visa Code[32] encompasses a list of those countries whose citizens require a visa to enter Schengen, and those for whom a visa can be waived, on the basis of visa waiver agreements between the EU and non-EU States.[33] Nevertheless, it also aims to ensure that persons with a legitimate interest in entering the EU will be able to access and enter EU territory. The EU Visa Code and the Schengen Border Code[34] establish harmonised conditions and procedures for the issuance of short-stay visas (of less than 90 days in a 180-day period).[35] Visas for long periods and the issuance of residence permits are governed by national rules and remain matters to be determined by the Member States.[36]

---

29 Status Agreement between the European Union and the Republic of Albania on actions carried out by the European Border and Coast Guard Agency in the Republic of Albania 10290/18. See the press release of the European Commission, 'European Border and Coast Guard: Launch of First Ever Joint Operation Outside the EU'; available at: http://europa.eu/rapid/press-release_IP-19-2591_en.htm?utm_source=NEWS&utm_medium=email&utm_content=1st+section+2nd+story+eu&utm_campaign=HQ_EN_therefugeebrief_external_20190522.

30 Regulation (EU) 2016/399 of the European Parliament and of the Council of 9 March 2016 on a Union Code on the rules governing the movement of persons across borders (Schengen Borders Code).

31 The United Kingdom and Ireland have an opt out from EU visa rules and rather apply their own visa policies.

32 EU Visa Code Regulation (EC) 810/2009.

33 Negotiations are generally bilateral; and the EU aims at visa reciprocity with non-EU countries per Regulation 1289/2013.

34 Regulation (EU) 2016/399 of the European Parliament and of the Council of 9 March 2016 on a Union Code on the rules governing the movement of persons across borders (Schengen Borders Code).

35 A short stay for non-EU citizens is defined as a stay of 90 days within a 180-day period; this has been applicable since October 2013.

36 The EU has a legal competence to adopt legislation to regulate the issuance of long-term visas or permits (Art 79(2)(a) TFEU) but has not yet adopted legislation on this basis.

A Schengen Visa is a short-stay visa that allows for travel in and across the 26 Schengen States.[37] It can either be issued for transit through or an intended stay in a Schengen State or transit through a transit area of an airport. Applications for short-term visas have to be made in the embassy or the consulate of the country that the applicant intends to visit.[38] If applicants intend to visit more than one country, the application should be made in the embassy or consulate of their main destination, though visas are generally valid for the entire Schengen area. One exception is the limited territorial visa, of which the visa issued on a humanitarian basis (amongst others bases per Art 25(1) EU Visa Code), to which the chapter turns below, is one example. Without delving further into its operation, it is simply worth noting that the applications of the rules of the CEAS may function so as to generate streams of irregular travel into the EU. That is to say, the EU rules do not facilitate the regulated arrival of asylum seekers to EU territory and only apply once the individuals reach the territory of the EU Member States; rather, individuals seeking asylum usually enter into the territory of an EU Member State without the documentation required, i.e. in most cases without a visa, or using unauthorised points to cross from one State to another. The resulting difficulty is reflected in mixed flows of asylum seekers and irregular migrants.[39]

Protected Entry Procedures and Humanitarian Visas

The EU visa regime is a mobility scheme for short-stay visits.[40] It is not asylum seeker-specific. That is to say, EU law does not provide for a separate

---

37 The Visa Code as well as other pieces of legislation provides for certain conditions that must be satisfied for a visa to be issued.

38 The usual requirements for a visa are set out in the Schengen Borders Code and Art 19(4) of the EU Visa Code.

39 European Parliament, 'EU Legal Framework on Asylum and Irregular Migration 'On Arrival' – State of Play' PE 551.333 (Brussels 2015), 5.

40 It is worth noting that humanitarian visas exist in both EU and States, outside of the EU, including for example Brazil. L Lyra Jubilut, C Sombra Muiños de Andrade and A de Lima Madureira, 'Humanitarian Visas: Building on Brazil's Experience' (2016) 53 Forced Migration Review (https://www.fmreview.org/community-protection/jubilut-andrade-madureira#_edn1). The existence of humanitarian visas in certain EU Member States has been set out in UI Jensen, 'Humanitarian Visas: Option or Obligation?' (2014) Study for the LIBE Committee of the European Parliament, 41. He notes that such visas are issued on a discretionary basis by the national authorities.

procedure to allow refugees who seek to make a claim for asylum in one of its Member States, to travel to its territory legally and safely. Individuals who wish to travel to the EU in order to make a claim for asylum in an EU Member State have to apply for a visa under the grounds set out in the EU Visa Code for the type of visa potentially relevant to individuals of their status. The judgment in *X and X* brings to the fore the question of whether individuals seeking asylum will be able to apply for a visa to travel to the EU. The combination of the EU policy and law on visas, together with the Schengen system, and carrier sanctions requiring individuals travelling to the EU from third States show documentation to their transport operate, give rise to the problem of the 'foot in the door' to the EU.[41] Certain mechanisms are, or have been until the judgment in *X and X*, envisaged in EU law and policy to facilitate safe and legal access to the territory of the EU Member States. Known as Protected Entry Procedures, these aim '[...] from the platform of diplomatic representations, [to allow] a non-national to approach the potential host state outside its territory with a claim for asylum or other form of international protection, and to be granted an entry permit in case of a positive response to that claim, be it preliminary or final'.[42]

Protected Entry Procedures, including visas issued on humanitarian grounds, have a number of aims, one of which is the promotion of safe and legal avenues to access the territory of EU Member States.[43] One example of a Protected Entry Procedure is a visa issued on the basis of Art 25(1) EU Visa Code which provides that Member States can derogate from the usual requirements to be fulfilled for the issuance of such documents. Art 25(1) provides that a short-stay Schengen limited territorial validity (LTV) visa can be 'issued exceptionally...(a) when the Member State concerned considers it necessary on humanitarian grounds, for reasons of national interest or because of international obligations'.

---

41 Moreover, data seems to indicate that the numbers of individuals arriving in the EU from third States by air transport and being denied entry has declined considerably in recent years. See T Spijkerboer, 'Bifurcation of People, Bifurcation of Law: Externalization of Migration Policy before the EU Court of Justice' (2017) 31 *Journal of Refugee Studies* 216, 13. As Spijkerboer notes, it is unclear that there has been a similar decrease in those trying to reach the EU territory irregularly.

42 G Noll *et al*, 'Study on the Feasibility of Processing Asylum Claims Outside the EU' (2002) The Danish Centre for Human Rights: Study for the European Commission, 3.

43 Fundamental Rights Agency, 'Legal Entry Channels to the EU for Persons in Need of International Protection: A Toolbox' (2015) Fundamental Rights Agency - Focus.

Art 25(1) EU Visa Code provides a basis upon which an LTV visa can be issued exceptionally where the concerned Member State considers it necessary – for the above-mentioned reasons – to do so, derogating from 'the principle that the entry conditions laid down in Article 5(1)(a), (c), (d) and (e) of the Schengen Borders Code must be fulfilled',[44] as well as the admissibility requirements for short-term access to the territory in Art 19 EU Visa Code[45]. These admissibility requirements are standards that asylum seekers may not be able to satisfy because they lack the required documents or the resources to obtain them. While Art 25(1) may provide a basis for the relaxation of those standards in certain, limited circumstances,[46] it cannot be said that its purpose is to provide a basis for the issuance of humanitarian visas to asylum seekers.[47] Indeed, as examined below, the Court in *X and X* found that this was not the case. It is worth noting that where a visa is issued on humanitarian grounds, an initial assessment of these grounds is conducted in the embassy or consulate of the Member State; this does not constitute or relate to the application for asylum. Indeed, a separate and distinct assessment is made for asylum; in line with Art 3(1) Dublin III, the asylum procedure can only be conducted in the country in which refuge is sought after the asylum seeker reaches that territory. What is unclear is the determination of the exact criteria of Art 25(1) EU Visa Code, that is, the basis on which an LTV visa might be issued, both as regards humanitarian considerations and the relevant international obligations. It was these questions that came before the ECJ in *X and X*; moreover, following *X and X*, one must now ask in which circumstances such a visa might be issues on humanitarian grounds.

While the EU Visa Code provides the basis in EU law for the issuance of a humanitarian visa, EU law and policy only covers a certain dimension of the access to EU Member State territory for third-state individuals. That is to say, there is a certain set of considerations that should be taken into account as regards the competence for establishing the requirements and conditions for short and long-term access to Member State territory, and moreover, it must be recalled that in all circumstances, the decisions are

44 Art 25(1)(a)(i) EU Visa Code.

45 Art 19(4) EU Visa Code.

46 The humanitarian visa procedures are different from resettlement or other forms of humanitarian admissions to the territory of EU Member States.

47 Although, as found in the report of UI Jensen, 'Humanitarian Visas: Option or Obligation?' (2014) Study for the LIBE Committee of the European Parliament, 43, a number of Member States do engage Art 25(1) Visa Code as a basis for issuing humanitarian visas to individuals in order to afford international protection.

made by the authorities of the Member State. The discourse surrounding obligations to issue short-term visas, including that of the *X and X* case, can be said to be a reflection of the need to balance sovereignty of nation states and the protection under EU and international law of the fundamental rights of refugees.

The Problem of the 'Foot in the Door' to the EU

Before examining further the circumstances of the Syrian family, and the challenges they, and other, in a similar position, face, the problem of the 'foot in the door' to the EU should be unpicked. The problems faced by individuals seeking asylum are manifold and are often exacerbated by EU law and policy. The application of the CEAS rules, which dictate that applications for asylum must be made at the border of or on the territory of an EU Member State, alongside the EU visa policy, may impede the access of individuals to procedures by which they can claim asylum in an EU Member State. By requiring that applications for asylum must be made at the border of or on the territory of an EU Member State, these rules generate risks of irregular migration where a visa is not available to individuals. The operation of these policies may clash with and undermine the fundamental rights of migrants,[48] including the right to claim asylum, protection against non-refoulement as well as access to effective judicial protection, and ultimately result in a loss of human life.

Given that Europe has long been a place in which people have sought refuge, individuals have – as a result of the absence of safe and legal avenues to reach Europe – taken to crossing the Balkans or the Mediterranean illegally. Not only does it mean that individuals have to take considerable risk to reach and enter the territory of EU Member States, it means that even those who have a good basis for an asylum application might not be able to reach the EU to make that claim if they cannot afford to pay a smuggler to get them to Europe or are in an unfit physical state to make such an arduous journey. This system also dictates that the Member States located in the Mediterranean or in the Balkans are the first states that these individuals encounter, with the result that they are obliged to be responsible for more asylum applications than any other Member State. It therefore should be noted that this problem of the 'foot in the door' not only contributes to irregular migration but it also gives rise to a dispropor-

48 Set out at Arts 4, 18, 19 as well as 47 CFR.

tionate number of applications being made in neighbouring third states to those in conflict as well as in those at which refugees might arrive by sea, including notably Greece and Italy.[49] The CEAS, and especially the Dublin regime, which are intended largely to govern the relations between States as regards the management of and exchange of information on applications for entry to the territory of EU Member States[50] and for asylum respectively, have been criticised largely as regards the burden that results on these particular States.

As a result, individuals who wish to claim asylum in an EU Member State are faced with two options. The first, unthinkable, but a forced reality for many: they try to reach the border or territory of a Member State themselves. The second, apparently more palatable but often still dangerous and difficult: they try to make use of mechanisms, established in EU law to facilitate safe and legal access to the territory of an EU Member State.

The Situation of the Syrian Family

Referred to the European Court of Justice for a preliminary ruling by the *Conseil du Contentieux des Étrangers* (the Belgian Council for Asylum and Migration, hereinafter Belgian Council) in December 2016, the case of *X and X*[51] concerned the obligations on the part of EU Member States to facilitate safe and legal access for third-State individuals to their territory in order to allow them to exercise a right to apply for asylum. In particular, and for the purposes of this chapter, it concerned the existence on the part of the Member States of an obligation to issue a visa on humanitarian

---

49 The external dimension of EU asylum law: V Moreno-Lax, Accessing Asylum in Europe: Extraterritorial Border Controls and Refugee Rights under EU Law (Oxford, Oxford University Press, 2017), T. Gammeltoft-Hansen, *Access to Asylum: International Refugee Law and the Globalisation of Migration Control* (Cambridge, Cambridge University Press, 2011); G Noll, *Negotiating Asylum: The EU Acquis, Extraterritorial Protection and the Common Market of Deflection* (The Hague, Kluwer Law International, 2000).

50 The Visa Information System allows Schengen States to exchange information on visas, especially in relation to short-term visas. The Schengen Information System also aims to ensure that data on suspected criminals, as well as individuals who may not have the right to enter or stay in the EU, on missing persons and on lost or stolen property can be exchanged. The EU has developed IT systems to facilitate this. Another important dimension concerns the need to ensure the security of travel documents and avoid the possibility that they might be counterfeited.

51 Case C-638/16 PPU *X and X* EU:C:2017:173.

grounds to individuals (per Art 25(1) EU Visa Code), where the non-issuance of such a visa might otherwise result in the violation of their fundamental rights.

The case concerned an Orthodox Christian family from Aleppo, Syria, who had travelled at great risk to their safety to the Belgian embassy in Beirut, Lebanon, where they applied for a humanitarian visa that would allow them to reach the Belgian territory safely and legally. In support of their application, they provided evidence that in Aleppo they had been subject to abduction, beatings and torture, and remained at further risk of persecution on the basis of their religious beliefs. It was subsequently also impossible for them to apply for asylum or otherwise financially support a stay in Lebanon. When making the application for the visa at the Belgian embassy in Beirut, the family indicated that they intended to apply for asylum as soon as they reached Belgium in line with the CEAS. Their application for the visa, a short-term visa with a limited territorial scope on humanitarian grounds,[52] was rejected by the Belgian Immigration Office on the basis that the family did not meet its short-term criteria; rather, they intended to apply for asylum once they reached Belgium and thus stay there for the long term.[53]

Still in Aleppo and with the assistance of a Brussels-based human rights law firm,[54] the family challenged the decision of the Immigration Office before the Belgian Council for Asylum and Migration, which decided to make a preliminary reference to the ECJ, asking two questions.[55] Firstly, it asked whether the 'international obligations' referred to in Art 25(1) EU Visa Code, included the provisions of the CFR, the ECHR protections and the provisions of the Geneva Convention, creating *de facto* a right of entry for asylum seekers to the territory of a Member State. Secondly, it asked whether Art 25 EU Visa Code should be interpreted as obliging Member States to issue humanitarian visas where there is a risk of the infringement

52 Art 25(1) EU Visa Code envisages the possibility of issuing a short-stay Schengen limited territorial validity visa on humanitarian grounds, grounds of national interest, or because of international obligations.

53 The maximum number of days for which an applicant would be allowed to stay in a Member State on a humanitarian visa.

54 For a testimony from the lawyer in charge of the case, see the contribution of Wibault to this volume.

55 For an explanation, by the First President of the Belgian Council, of the domestic context surrounding that procedure, see the contribution of Bodart to this volume.

of the prohibition of torture, of the right to asylum, of non-refoulement and of any other international obligations.

The two questions referred to the ECJ by the Belgian Council concerned this access as well as the nature of the protections that shape it. Essentially, the family had argued that Arts 4 (prohibition of torture and inhuman or degrading treatment or punishment) and 18 (right to asylum) CFR encompass a positive obligation on Member States to issue short-term visas for humanitarian reasons under Art 25(1) EU Visa Code, so as to avoid that asylum seekers have to undertake considerable sufferance to even have access to procedures affording them international protection, and to avoid the potential violations of Art 3 ECHR and Art 19(2) CFR (prohibition of torture and principle of non-refoulement) that might arise were they to remain in a conflict zone. This argumentation gave rise to the questions referred by the Belgian Council, and in particular, that of whether Member States are obliged to facilitate access for individuals to the territory of the EU territory, in order for them to exercise their right to make a claim for asylum. With the Belgian Council considering that the applicants could rely on Art 3 ECHR only if they were within Belgian territory, the question arose as to whether the exercise of the visa policy could be understood as an exercise of jurisdiction. The facts of the *X and X* case illustrate the problem of the need for individuals to have a 'foot in the door' to the territory of an EU Member State. Access to asylum procedures, and to the legal protection that they offer, is limited to those who have managed to reach EU territory or its borders; as has been well documented, in order to reach this position, many thousands of individuals will travel irregularly, and embark on a perilous journey, subjecting themselves to trafficking and so on, in order to reach this position.

The ECJ's Interpretation of EU Law

This chapter focuses on the responses of the Advocate General and Court to these questions, examines the confrontation between the interpretation of EU law offered by both and evaluates the limits of the Court's judgment. In light of these limits, this section focuses on the second question referred, namely on the scope of the application of the EU legal framework, particularly as regards the existence of an obligation on Member States under EU law and EU fundamental rights law, to issue humanitarian visas. For the moment, it should be noted that the first question referred was left unanswered by both the AG and the Court. This question is one which has subsequently come before the European Court of Human

Rights (ECtHR) in the case of *MN and Others v Belgium*,[56] which has similar facts to the *X and X* case, and is to be heard in April 2019 before the Grand Chamber.[57] Indeed, the case is also an interesting one from an academic perspective as it offers two distinct interpretations of EU law from the AG and the Court, with each drawing opposite conclusions on the scope of EU law and the resultant obligations on the Member States. The second question concerns two key issues: the first relates to whether the determination of whether to issue such visas fell within the scope of EU law so as to trigger the CFR (for the Court, whether the EU's had a legislative competence to regulate access to EU territory via short-and long term visas) and the second to the scope of the discretion held by the Member States to decide whether or not to grant access to migrants to their territory. These two issues arise in light of the absence of a relevant uniform procedure and criteria at the EU and national levels in the determination of the circumstances in which humanitarian visas might be issued.

In his non-binding opinion, the soon-to-retire AG Mengozzi adopted a fundamental rights-based approach to his reasoning. The AG held that the issuance of humanitarian visas fell within the scope of the implementation of EU law, as it was envisaged by the EU Visa Code; moreover, he reasoned that the applicants would stay for no longer than 90 days in Belgium on the basis of that particular visa, as they would subsequently apply for asylum and be resident in Belgium on the basis of that asylum claim. For AG Mengozzi, the issuance of a visa under Art 25(1) EU Visa Code amounted to a decision to issue a document to allow for the crossing of the EU's external border, 'subject to a harmonised set out rules and…therefore in the framework of and pursuant to EU law'.[58] The discretion afforded to the Member States in deciding whether to issue a visa on such a basis did not change this finding.[59] As the EU Visa Code was relevant, the matter fell

---

56 *MN and Others v Belgium*, App. No. 3599/18.

57 Interestingly, in the case of MN, there was a conflict between the Belgian *Office des Étrangers* and the *Conseil du Contentieux des Étrangers*; when the applicants filed for an interim injunction in Belgium, asserting that the process of application for a humanitarian visa had not engaged their fundamental rights concerns, it was the Belgian Council that issued the injunction and requested that the *Office des Étrangers* consider further the possible application of Art 3 ECHR. The Belgian Cour d'Appel then overturned this decision. For an overview of the case, see D Schmalz, 'Will the ECtHR Shake up the European Asylum System?' *VerfBlog*, 2018/11/30, https://verfassungsblog.de/will-the-ecthr-shake-up-the-europe an-asylum-system/.

58 Case C-638/16 PPU *X and X* EU:C:2017:93, para 80.

59 ibid, paras 81-83.

within the scope of the implementation of Union law, thus triggering the application of the CFR per Art 51(1).[60] As a result, he found that where there is a substantial basis to believe that the refusal of a humanitarian visa would result in the infringement of the rights set out therein, the discretion of the Member States could be limited. The AG referred in particular to the potential risk of torture, and of inhuman or degrading treatment (either in the third State or via irregular travel to a country in which asylum might be sought), or the deprivation of the individual to a legal path to be able to exercise his or her right to apply for asylum. Were substantial grounds to exist for such a belief, the Member States would be obliged to issue a visa on a humanitarian basis to that applicant. The AG drew his conclusions to a close with a powerful and oft-quoted statement setting out the humanitarian crises of irregular migration, urging the Grand Chamber of the ECJ to adopt a fundamental rights reasoning, in order to oblige Member States to issue humanitarian visas to facilitate safe and legal access to the EU's territory.[61]

The judgment of the Court – sitting as the Grand Chamber – differed considerably from the Opinion of the AG. It considered that the Syrian family's application was not for a short-term visa, which would fall within the scope of EU competence, but rather for a long-term right to stay on Belgian territory. Visas issued on the basis of Art 25(1) EU Visa Code were considered by the ECJ only to concern visas issued to allow access to the territory of a particular Member States for a limited period of time, 'not exceeding 90 days in a 180 day-period'.[62] As such, it held that the application made by the Syrian family was not covered by the provisions of the EU Visa Code and was not a matter of harmonised EU law;[63] instead, the issuance of such a visa was deemed to be a matter of national law and a determination for the Member States. Fundamentally, as the Court considered that the matter was not one in which EU law was being implemented, it found no trigger for the application of the CFR in line with Art 51(1) CFR. With this reasoning, the Court shaped its judgment in two ways. On the one hand, it found that it had no competence to reply on the merits as there was no issue of EU law at stake. Moreover, the Court avoided a fundamental rights analysis of the case, by finding that the matter was not one by which the Member State was 'implementing Union law' in line with

60 ibid, paras 84 and 88.
61 ibid, para 175.
62 ibid, paras 43-45.
63 ibid, paras 43-45.

Art 51(1) CFR, and therefore found no trigger for the application of the CFR and the rights protection established therein. On the other hand, the Court found that the issuance or refusal to issue visas that might afford entry to a Member States for a period of more than 90 days, even though these visas might be offered on a humanitarian basis, was a matter of national, and not EU law.[64] As such, there could be no EU law obligation on the part of Member States to issue such visas even if the facts of the situation dictated that the individuals making the application might be at risk of the violation of their rights under the CFR. Instead, Member State authorities are free to decide, in line with national law and policy, whether to grant such a visa.

The judgment of the Grand Chamber has been criticised for various reasons[65]. By avoiding a fundamental rights interpretation, the Court instead framed the issue as one of the EU's limited legislative competences as regards long-term access to Member State territory. The Court adopted a strictly formal reasoning, starting from the notion that EU law has not envisaged the possibility for a humanitarian visa to be issued in order to enable an application for asylum to be made. That is to say, the Court highlighted that while the EU Visa Code is based on Art 77(2)(a)(b) TFEU[66] which provides a legislative ground for the issuance of travel documents allowing for a short-term stay, no EU legislation has been adopted on the basis of Art 79(2)(a) TFEU (which provides a legislative competence for harmonised EU rules on travel documents) allowing for a long-term stay on EU Member State territory. As such, the Court seemingly anticipated that were it to have extended Art 25(1) EU Visa Code so as to also encompass

64 ibid, para 51.

65 A number of blogposts and commentaries have been published in reaction to the judgment of the Court. See for example: E Brouwer, 'The European Court of Justice on Humanitarian Visas: Legal Integrity vs Political Opportunism?' CEPS Commentary, 16 March 2017; available at: https://www.ceps.eu/wp-content/uploads/2017/03/Visa%20Code%20CJEU%20E%20Brouwer%20CEPS%20Commentary_0.pdf; J-Y Carlier and L Leboeuf, 'The X and X Case: Humanitarian Visas and the Genuine Enjoyment of the Substance of the Rights, Towards a Middle Way?' EU Immigration and Asylum Law and Policy, 27 February 2017; available at: https://eumigrationlawblog.eu/the-x-and-x-case-humanitarian-visas-and-the-genuine-enjoyment-of-the-substance-of-rights-towards-a-middle-way/; V Moreno-Lax, 'Asylum Visas as an Obligation under EU Law: Case PPU C-638/16 X and X – Parts I and II' EU Immigration and Asylum Law and Policy, 16 and 21 February 2017; available at: http://eumigrationlawblog.eu/asylum-visas-as-an-obligation-under-eu-law-case-ppu-c-63816-x-x-v-etat-belge/.

66 Formerly Art 62(2)(a) and (b) Treaty establishing the EC.

long-term residence, that this would have amounted to an instance of judicial activism that would have been unwelcome by the Member States and the EU institutions. Indeed, the issue is one which has been subject to political discussions in the European Commission, Council and Parliament, with each institution adopting a different approach, and one which was opposed by 13 Member States (and the European Commission) who made submissions to the ECJ in the *X and X* hearing.[67] Moreover, the Court reasoned that had it allowed the Syrian family long-term access via the EU Visa Code, it would have *de facto* obliged Member States to allow for applications for asylum to be made outside Member State territory; this, for the Court, would have created a conflict between the Dublin regime and the Visa Code, where the latter was not intended to harmonise the rules governing applications for international protection.[68]

This would potentially be done in two ways; on the one hand, this decision would allow individuals seeking asylum to decide on the particular Member State in which he or she wants to make a claim for asylum. Per the Dublin regime, this 'choice' might be said to be indirect, to the extent that the Member State at which the individual first arrives is normally responsible for dealing with that application, absent other considerations. The Court then highlighted that the Procedure Directive 2013/32 and the Dublin Regulation exclude explicitly the possibility that individuals can make claims for asylum at the embassies or consulates of Member States in third States. That is to say, the Court anticipated that such a decision would have engendered a harmonised rule arising from the EU Visa Code (which was not intended to harmonise such laws) to require Member States to allow third-State individuals to make claims for asylum in the representation of those Member States in third countries.[69] The Court used the Dublin regime and related legislative provisions to exclude the factual situation in *X and X* from the scope of EU law, notwithstanding that the preliminary reference did not concern the interpretation of this legislation.[70] The Court used the purpose of the visa application, and the time period that results from it, to take the application of the Syrian family outside of the scope of the EU Visa Code[71]. In so doing, it further isolated humanitarian visas from the EU's visa policy notwithstanding that the very

67 On these discussions, see the contribution of Relano Pastor to this volume.

68 Case C-638/16 PPU *X and X* EU:C:2017:173, para 48.

69 ibid, paras 47-49.

70 ibid, para 49.

71 Moreover, it did not delve into the notion that the EU Visa Code itself establishes rules as to when visas might be exceptionally issued or extended in certain cir-

need for such visas often might stem from the application of the rules in the Visa Code and Dublin regime, as discussed above. The case is undoubtedly a reflection of the political difficulties faced by the Court in not undermining existing legislative regimes and ensuring the protection of third-State individuals. Nevertheless, a failure to deal with the 'foot in the door' problem and the related risks of irregular migration can be identified on the part of the ECJ.

The Application of the EU Fundamental Rights Framework to Humanitarian Visas

The *X and X* judgment reflects the conflict that arises between one the one hand, the protection of the rights of third-State individuals and on the other, the EU Member State's preservation of its sovereignty, particularly where the Member State has a discretion to exercise. The doctrine of State sovereignty emerged at the end of the 19th and beginning of the 20th centuries, and has been used to justify the notion that States have a largely unlimited discretion to decide on who can enter their territory.[72] The responsibility of States for human rights protection is typically limited to the jurisdiction of that State. This means that human rights apply only territorially and not beyond the borders of that State; as a result, individuals of third States would not fall within the scope of the human rights responsibilities of EU Member States. As outlined above, the AG and the Court adopted different approaches in responding to these concerns, with the latter adopting a largely formalistic approach that allowed it to reject entirely the reasoning of the former.[73] While the notion of jurisdiction is primarily territorial, it may also extend beyond State borders. As regards the questions referred by the Belgian Council, the issue unanswered by the ECJ is whether the provisions of the ECHR or the CFR might apply outside of the territory of the Member States, and whether the State's implementation of visa policy might amount to an exercise of jurisdiction. Here, several cases of the ECtHR are relevant to determination of the extraterritorial obligations of States.[74]

---

cumstances beyond the usual limitation of 90 days in a 180-day period per Art 25(1)(b) and 33.

72 See *Chae Chan Ping v United States* 130 US 581 (1889).

73 Case C-638/16 PPU *X and X* EU:C:2017:93, para 175.

74 Jurisdiction may also exist extraterritorially where a State exercises effective control over persons there. Relevant cases include *Hirsi Jamaa and Others v Italy* App.

The EU Treaties provide that certain values and protections, including those of human rights, should be placed at the heart of the EU's operation. Via Art 21(1) and 21(3) TEU[75] and Art 3(5) TEU,[76] the EU and its Member States have committed to promote its Art 2 TEU[77] values across all fields of international relations. Nevertheless, the application of these values and fundamental rights in practice to areas which have external consequences, including the EU's migration and asylum as well as visa regime, is unclear. The Treaties make no reference to how the EU should facilitate or attain these objectives.

Does the EU Visa Code attribute to EU Member States the possibility to give a humanitarian visa to those seeking asylum? Were the Member States obliged – under the CFR – to grant such visas where rights set out under the CFR might otherwise be undermined? For AG Mengozzi, both of these questions should be answered in the affirmative. The Court on the other hand interpreted the EU Visa Code narrowly (that is as excluding travel documents that might allow individuals to stay in a Member State in the long term), which led it to avoid answering both questions. By virtue of

---

No. 27765/09, *Al-Skeini and Others v UK* App. No. 55721/07 and *Al Jedda v UK* App. No. 27021/08. In *Al Skeini* and *Al Jedda* the ECtHR set out the possibility that a State need not exercise control over a territory in order to be deemed to have exercised jurisdiction for Convention purposes; instead, the exercise of the authority of an agent of the State or of functional jurisdiction may be sufficient to establish jurisdiction. See also, S Besson, 'The Extraterritoriality of the European Convention on Human Rights: Why Human Rights Depend on Jurisdiction and What Jurisdiction Amounts To' (2012) 25 *Leiden J Int'l L* 857.

75 Art 21(1) TEU: 'The Union's action on the international scene shall be guided by the principles which have inspired its own creation, development and enlargement, and which it seeks to advance in the wider world: democracy, the rule of law, the universality and indivisibility of human rights and fundamental freedoms, respect for human dignity, the principles of equality and solidarity, and respect for the principles of the United Nations Charter and international law.'.

76 Art 3(5) TEU: 'In its relations with the wider world, the Union shall uphold and promote its values and interests and contribute to the protection of its citizens. It shall contribute to peace, security, the sustainable development of the Earth, solidarity and mutual respect among peoples, free and fair trade, eradication of poverty and the protection of human rights, in particular the rights of the child, as well as to the strict observance and the development of international law, including respect for the principles of the United Nations Charter.'.

77 Art 2 TEU: 'The Union is founded on the values of respect for human dignity, freedom, democracy, equality, the rule of law and respect for human rights, including the rights of persons belonging to minorities. These values are common to the Member States in a society in which pluralism, non-discrimination, tolerance, justice, solidarity and equality between women and men prevail.'.

this interpretation, the Court found that EU Visa Code did not attribute the possibility to the Member States to issue a humanitarian visa on the particular facts of the case; instead, this was a matter for national law. Relatedly as to the second question, the ECJ had the possibility in *X and X* to clarify the application of the CFR to its visa regime. It did not do so, rather avoiding the question by finding that the issuance of humanitarian visas did not fall within the scope of Union law. Indeed, by adopting a narrow interpretation of the EU Visa Code, the Court managed to also avoid the second question of the Belgian Council, concerning the extraterritorial application of the CFR and of relevant international obligations. Moreover, the ECJ then avoided the question as to whether the implementation of the visa policy might otherwise amount to an exercise of a State's jurisdiction, so as to engage the need to avoid violations of the ECHR, and relevant international obligations. The key question for both the AG and the Court was whether the matter was one that fell within the scope of EU law. The AG found that it did, by virtue of which he identified no need to examine the first question of the Belgian Council, while the Court reasoned on the basis of a limited EU legislative competence, finding that the matter was not one falling within the scope of Union law. These findings then determined whether the CFR could be triggered to allow for an EU fundamental rights reasoning.

As regards the existence of a territorial requirement, the CFR is silent. The relevant provision on the CFR's application – Art 51(1) CFR – refers to the notion that the 'provisions of this Charter are addressed to the institutions, bodies, offices and agencies of the Union with due regard for the principle of subsidiarity and to the Member States only when they are implementing Union law'. [78] The provision has been included in the CFR in

78 The ECJ has held that the application of EU fundamental rights protection is mainly concerned with ensuring that the level of that protection does not vary across the EU Member States to such an extent that the 'primacy, unity and effectiveness of EU law' is undermined. This is in line with Art 53 CFR, confirmed by the ECJ in *Melloni*. The ECJ provided "It is true that Article 53 of the Charter confirms that, where an EU legal act calls for national implementing measures, national authorities and courts remain free to apply national standards of protection of fundamental rights, provided that the level of protection provided for by the Charter, as interpreted by the Court, and the primacy, unity and effectiveness of EU law are not thereby compromised", Case C-399/11 *Melloni* EU:C:2013:107, para 60. This was further confirmed in Case C-617/10 *Åkerberg Fransson* EU:C:2013:280, para 29. This objective has arguably allowed the ECJ to construct a broad framework as regards the interpretation of what falls within the notion of implementing EU law.

line with Art 6(2) TEU which requires respect for fundamental rights on the part of the Union institutions, and the case law of the ECJ, which requires respect on the part of the Member States when they are acting in the scope of[79] or implementing Union law.[80]

The body of case law on this notion of 'implementing EU law' is expanding, much due to the difficulties in understanding this concept, and the nature of enforcement in the EU legal order.[81]The difficulties in establishing when a national measure amounts to a measure implementing EU law are well known; it is the gatekeeper of the provision of Art 51(1) and delineates the application of the CFR. The CFR in itself does not in itself form the basis for the jurisdiction of the ECJ nor does it extend the field of application of Union law; CFR rights are not self-standing (in comparison to the ECHR) but must be triggered by another provision of EU law.[82]

In *Åkerberg Fransson*, the ECJ held that the notion of implementing EU law should be understood as to coincide with measures that are 'governed by European Union law' and 'fall within the scope of European Union law'.[83] This could be satisfied where a legal concern or dispute is 'connected in part' to an EU law obligation so as to trigger the application of the CFR, where a 'direct link' exists between the CFR and national law.[84] As Ward has stated, '*Åkerberg Fransson* confirms that the Court will undertake

79 Case C-5/88 *Wachauf* EU:C:1989:321, paras 17-19 and Case C-260/89 *ERT* EU:C:1991:254, para 42.

80 Case C-292/97 *Karlsson and Others* EU:C:2000:202, para 37. Further on Art 51 CFR, see A Ward, 'Article 51 - Scope' in S Peers *et al* (eds), *The EU Charter of Fundamental Rights: A Commentary* (London, Hart, 2014), 1413-1454.

81 The implementation, application and enforcement of EU law is for the most part decentralised; that is to say, the Member States are attributed the key role in these tasks. It is necessary therefore that the Member States ensure that the implementation of EU law is made in compliance with the CFR. The basis of the EU fundamental rights regime is Art 6 TEU which sets out the duty of the EU to respect fundamental rights. This duty extends to the national level and measures taken by the Member States given this decentralised system of enforcement, creating an obligation on the Member States (complementary to their international and constitutional obligations).

82 As the President of the CJEU, Judge Lenaerts, has written, 'Metaphorically speaking, the Charter is the "shadow" of EU law. Just as an object defines the contours of its shadow, the scope of EU law determines that of the Charter'; K Lenaerts and JA Gutiérrez–Fons, 'The Place of the Charter in the EU Constitutional Edifice' in S Peers and others (eds), *The EU Charter of Fundamental Rights: A Commentary* (Oxford, Hart, 2014), 1567.

83 Case C-617/10 *Åkerberg Fransson* EU:C:2013:280, paras 17-21.

84 ibid, paras 24-26.

a subject matter analysis. If some part of the subject matter of the dispute concerns substantive laws of EU law, then the Charter will be applicable, subject to the discretion…in the hands of Member States to determine the fundamental rights dispute by reference to national fundamental rights law in mixed subject matter cases…'.[85] The Court in *Fransson* has been considered to have attributed a rather wide scope to the CFR's application,[86] considering that the subject matter of the matter need only b partially related or connected to Union law.[87] Nevertheless, the decision has also faced criticism, including from the Bundesverfassungsgericht[88].

The ECJ then held in *IBV*, that when Member States' decisions are made within a framework established by EU law, this would be sufficient for Art 51(1) CFR.[89] Subsequently, the scope was more narrowly conceived in *Siragusa*, in which the ECJ provided a set of criteria for the interpretation of Art 51(1) CFR, to determine whether national legislation or national measures encompass the implementation of EU law.[90] The ECJ established a test for when it can be said that there is an implementation of EU law via the application of national rules in those circumstances in which the pertinent national law does not give effect to EU law as such but nevertheless applies in a field related to that occupied by EU law. The Court established that: 'In order to determine whether national legislation involves the implementation of EU law for the purposes of Article 51 of the Charter, some of the points to be determined are whether that legislation is intended to implement a provision of EU law; the nature of that legislation and whether it pursues objectives other than those covered by EU law, even if it is capable of indirectly affecting EU law; and also whether there are specific rules of EU law on the matter or capable of affecting it'.[91] For the

---

85 A Ward, 'Article 51 - Scope' in S Peers *et al* (eds), *The EU Charter of Fundamental Rights: A Commentary* (London, Hart, 2014), 1413-1454, 1452.

86 There is general agreement on this in the commentary on the case, and related case law of the ECJ. See M Ovádek, 'The CJEU on Humanitarian Visa: Discovering 'Un-Chartered' Waters of EU Law' VerfBlog, 13 March 2017; available at: https://verfassungsblog.de/the-cjeu-on-humanitarian-visa-discovering-un-chartered-waters-of-eu-law/.

87 Case C-617/10 *Åkerberg Fransson* EU:C:2013:280, paras 17-31.

88 BVerfG, Judgment of the First Senate of 24 April 2013 - 1 BvR 1215/07, para 91; http://www.bverfg.de/e/rs20130424_1bvr121507en.html.

89 Case C-195/12 *IBV* EU:C:2013:598, para 49.

90 Case C-206/13 *Siragusa* EU:C:2014:126, confirmed by Case C-198/13 *Hernández* EU:C:2014:2055, para 37, in which the court highlights that the determination of what falls within the scope of EU law is a question of fact.

91 ibid, para 25.

Court, the CFR would be inapplicable where EU law in that relevant area 'did not impose any obligation on Member States with regard to the situation at issue in the main proceedings'.[92] The danger with this approach is that the purpose of EU fundamental rights law, and the provisions of the CFR in particular, are attributed with a predominant objective; that is, only to ensure the primacy, effectiveness and coherence of Union law and not for protection of individuals who are potentially affected when a Member State acts in the field of, or related to, EU law.

The existence of a margin of discretion for the Member States when implementing EU law generates a significant amount of uncertainty. The key question is whether the existence of this discretion in the implementation precludes a national matter from being deemed to fall within the scope of EU law. Previously this has not been the case. For example, in *NS and Others*, the ECJ has held that the notion of 'implementing EU law' not only encompasses situations where the Member States are implementing EU legislation via national law, ie adopting national law, but also extends to situations where the Member States is exercising a discretion that is found in EU law.[93] In *NS*, the ECJ held that Art 3(2) of Regulation 343/2003 attributed to the UK a discretion to accept (through the Secretary of State) the responsibility for examining an asylum application; the exercise of this discretionary power by the Member State 'forms part of the mechanism for determining the Member State responsible for an asylum application' and must be understood to amount to the implementing of Union law for Art 51(1) CFR purposes.[94] While the cases are of course different, one must simply ask whether they are so distinct so that it can be said that a similar discretion does not exist with regard to *X and X*, where as in *NS*, there was no obligation on the Member State to come to any particular finding. *NS* has been interpreted as meaning that 'the Court found that when deciding whether to exercise discretion, ie whether to process the asylum claim, the UK was still 'implementing' EU law'.[95] The scope of the discretion is unclear – that is whether it applies to the assessment of the humanitarian considerations, or potential violations of international obligations, or to the issuing of the LTV visa itself – but regardless, these two assessments are

---

92 ibid, para 26.

93 Joined Cases C-411/10 and C-493/10 *NS and Others* EU:C:2011:865, para 68.

94 ibid, para 68.

95 E Spaventa, 'The Interpretation of Article 51 of the EU Charter of Fundamental Rights: The Dilemma of Stricter or Broader Application of the Charter to National Measures', Study commissioned by the European Parliament's Policy Department for Citizens' Rights and Constitutional Affairs (Brussels, 2016), 19.

interrelated.[96] It has been suggested that the discretion afforded to Member States under Art 25(1)(a) EU Visa Code 'forms part of the mechanisms' for determining when a visa available under that provision should be issued, so as to fall within the common European visa policy and thus within the scope of EU law.[97] Reference can also be made to the case of *El Hassani*.[98] The ECJ held that as the EU legislature left it to the Member States to decide on the nature and conditions of remedies available following a refusal of a visa in line with their national procedural autonomy, this is limited by the principle of effectiveness and equivalence.[99] Moreover, the ECJ considered that when a Member State adopts a decision refusing to issue a visa under Art 32(1) EU Visa Code, it is a matter falling within the scope of EU law. As such Art 47 CFR applies, so as to require that a decision of an administrative body following that refusal must be subject to a further judicial control; essentially, the CFR requires that the Member States ensure access to a court at one stage of the proceedings.[100] Moreover, the discretion cannot be unlimited; it is at least limited by the case law of the ECtHR.[101]

Before examining the jurisprudence of the Strasbourg Court, it is worth highlighting that the reference in Art 51 CFR is therefore not to its geographical but rather its functional scope. This has led commentators to suggest that it is attributed a wide application, with no territorial condition. For example, Moreno-Lax and Costello have argued that the CFR is triggered simply by virtue of the notion that EU law is being implement-

96 This was seemingly confirmed by the ECJ in Case C-84/12 *Koushkaki* EU:C:2013:862, paras 58-60 which found that the Member States have a wide discretion in the assessment of relevant facts, but could not refuse to issue a visa unless one of the grounds for refusal in the EU Visa Code existed.

97 S Morgades-Gil, 'Humanitarian Visas and EU Law: Do States Have Limits to Their Discretionary Power to Issue Humanitarian Visas?' (2018) (2) *European Papers* 1005, 1013-1014.

98 A case concerning the availability and nature of a judicial appeal under the EU Visa Code and in line with Art 47 CFR, following the refusal of an application of a Schengen visa made at Poland's Consul in Rabat.

99 Case C-403/16 *El Hassani* EU:C:2017:960, paras 25-28.

100 ibid, paras 35-41, particularly in light of the notion that the administrative authority may not satisfy the requirements of independence and impartiality.

101 For AG Mengozzi, 'humanitarian grounds' also consisted a 'concept of EU law', and should also be limited by the ECJ's case law; Case C-638/16 PPU *X and X* EU:C:2017:93, para 130.

ed.[102] The ECJ seemed to find the same in *Fransson*; it held that the 'applicability of European Union law entails applicability of the fundamental rights guaranteed by the Charter', while reiterating that the CFR itself does not provide a basis for the ECJ to exercise its jurisdiction.[103] Nevertheless, this would suggest that the application of the CFR is unhindered by territorial conditions. Moreover, as AG Bobek found in *El Hassani*, following *Fransson*, the CFR – and particularly Art 47 – applies where 'two cumulative conditions' are satisfied; the matter falls within EU law, and there is a concrete right or freedom guaranteed by Union law to trigger the right to an effective remedy before a tribunal; there is no mention of a requirement of territoriality (the application for the visa was made in Rabat).[104] The ECJ in *X and X* nevertheless seemed to depart from the above-mentioned case law, only partially referencing *Fransson* as regards the application of the CFR.[105] AG Mengozzi referred to the notion that the rights established in the CFR 'are guaranteed to the addressees of the acts adopted by such an authority irrespective of any territorial criterion'.[106] The Court made no such finding, instead reasoning that Art 25(1) EU Visa Code falls outside the scope of implementing EU law, such that Member States cannot be required by virtue of the rights established in the CFR to allow, by extension, applications for international protection to be made in their representations outside of their territory. It is worth noting that in the recent *Front Polisario* cases, the General Court[107] and the ECJ[108] have confirmed that the application of the CFR does not rest on a territorial connection; in

---

102 V Moreno-Lax and C Costello, 'The Extraterritorial Application of the Charter: From Territoriality to Facticity, the Effectiveness Model' in S Peers *et al* (eds), *The EU Charter of Fundamental Rights: A Commentary* (London, Hart, 2014), 1657-1684.

103 Case C-617/10 *Åkerberg Fransson* EU:C:2013:280, paras 21-22.

104 Case C-403/16 *El Hassani* EU:C:2017:659, para 74 and 78. Moreover, while AG Bobek considered there to be no 'right to a visa' under EU law, there being no right of entry to EU territory, there is a right to have an application 'fairly and properly processed', paras 102-106.

105 Case C-638/16 PPU *X and X* EU:C:2017:173, para 45.

106 Case C-638/16 PPU *X and X* EU:C:2017:93, para 89.

107 T-512/12 *Front Polisario v Council* EU:T:2015:953, para 143.

108 The ECJ did not deal with the issue in its judgment: Case C-104/16 P *Council v Front Polisario* EU:C:2016:973. However, the Opinion of AG Wathelet illustrates the discussions surrounding the question of the need for a territorial connection for the triggering of the CFR; he held that 'since in this case neither the European Union nor its Member States exercise control over Western Sahara and Western Sahara is not among the territories to which EU law is applicable, there can be no question of applying the Charter of Fundamental Rights there' (Case

both internal and external policies, the EU institutions and Member States will be bound by acting within the scope of the implementation of EU law.[109] This approach establishes that the CFR applies, regardless of territorial connection, to the implementation of EU law by the institutions or the Member States; where the matter falls within the scope of the implementation of EU law, the CFR is applicable to establish that the EU owes human rights obligations towards individuals regardless of where they are located. This understanding is deemed to find further support from Art 52(3) CFR, which establishes that the protections afforded in the CFR can be extended beyond those set out in the ECHR. Art 52(3) CFR sets out the need for 'at least equivalent protection' between it and the ECHR, in line with Art 53 ECHR, while providing that Union law can provide 'more extensive protection'.[110]

To take the analysis of the ECHR slightly further, it is worth noting that a State's jurisdiction under Art 1 ECHR is normally territorial, ie exercised through the State's territory; the State is obliged to ensure that Convention rights of everyone on their territorial jurisdiction are protected[111] The ECtHR has found that States are required to protect the rights of individuals extraterritorially only in exceptional circumstances. These exceptions are to be assessed on the particular facts of the case, and where power or control has actually been exercised over the person of the applicant or on the basis of control actually exercised over the relevant foreign territory.[112] From the paragraphs above, it is submitted that the CFR is not limited by the same territorial conditions as the ECHR but can instead apply extraterritorially.[113] Were a territorial condition to exist, one might consider the following situations. The Syrian applicants have never been on the territory of an

---

C-104/16 P *Council v Front Polisario* EU:C:2016:677, para 177), suggesting that the CFR applies only where EU law is applicable extraterritorially on a limited basis, eg Art 355 TFEU).

109 O de Schutter, 'The Implementation of the Charter of Fundamental Rights in the EU Legal Framework' Study for the DG for Internal Policies, Committee on Constitutional Affairs, PE 571.397, 55-57.

110 See also AG Mengozzi, who rejected the argument of the Belgian State that the need for equivalence between the CFR and ECHR would mean that the territorial or jurisdictional limit in Art 1 ECHR should also apply to the CFR; Case C-638/16 PPU *X and X* EU:C:2017:93, paras 97-101.

111 *Assanidze v Georgia* App. No. 71503/01, para 139.

112 *Al-Skeini and Others v UK* App. No. 55721/07, paras 105 and 132-133, respectively.

113 Case C-638/16 PPU *X and X* EU:C:2017:93, para 94, identifying no need for control or authority as under the ECHR.

EU Member State.[114] The applicants had however been to the Belgian embassy; one might question – however unlikely – that a territorial connection could be drawn on the basis of this visit in line with the ECtHR case law. It remains unclear, even if such a territorial condition applied to the CFR, it would be worth exploring the notion that for Convention purposes, exceptional circumstances might arise from activities of a State's diplomatic or consular agents on the basis of international law where there is an exercise of authority and control over the relevant persons or their property.[115] It would be necessary to examine further whether the decision to issue or deny a visa would satisfy these exceptional circumstances. This becomes even more blurry when one considers that the decision of the EU Member State, here Belgium, to issue or deny a visa might not have been made (giving rise to the notion of exercise or control) at the embassy situated on the third State but instead in Belgium.

This gives rise to a final dimension of this analysis. As Bartels sets out, States and international organisations might violate and be responsible for the human rights of individuals through extraterritorial conduct, and through conduct exercised domestically but which has extraterritorial effect [116] The Belgian Council considered that the applicants could rely on Art 3 ECHR only if they were within Belgian territory; the question that the Council seemed to ask but which was not answered by the Court was whether the implementation of EU visa policy by a Member State could amount to an exercise of Belgium's jurisdiction so to as to engage either the CFR[117] or relevant international obligations, including the ECHR and the principle of non-refoulement. Had the CFR been deemed to apply or had the ECJ assessed the applicability of the ECHR, the application of, and need to respect, these fundamental rights would have given rise to an obligation on the part of the Member States to issue the visa, and to allow en-

---

114 Compare, concerning the ECHR, that in *Soering v UK* App. No. 14038/88, para 91, the individual concerned was already on UK territory and a decision was made to extradite him, which could have given rise to a violation of Convention rights; see S Miller, 'Revisiting Extraterritorial Jurisdiction: A Territorial Justification for Extraterritorial Jurisdiction under the European Convention' (2009) 20 *EJIL* 1223.

115 *Banković and Others v. Belgium and Others* App. No. 52207/99, para 73 and *M v Denmark* App. No. 17392/90.

116 L Bartels, 'The EU's Human Rights Obligations in Relation to Policies with Extraterritorial Effects' (2015) 25 *EJIL* 1071, 1071.

117 Including the right to remain free from torture and degrading or inhuman treatment per Art 4 CFR, the right to claim asylum per Art 18 CFR and the principle of non-refoulement per Art 19 CFR.

try to the territory in order to avoid their potential violation.[118] The ECHR dimension was instead left to the ECtHR.[119] The question that arises is whether there might be another basis on which the possible violation of these rights, which arises through the extraterritorial effects of States' domestic conduct, may generate an obligation on the part of the Member States to take preventative measures to avoid that very violation. Here, we might adopt Ryngaert's discussion of the human rights obligations that might be owed by the EU to third States with which they have concluded trade agreements. Firstly one might ask whether the EU or its Member State, via its decision not to grant a visa actually facilitate human rights violations (as might be the consequences under the trade agreement).[120] In exploring this consideration, Ryngaert suggests that a failure on the part of the EU, its institutions or Member States, to undertake due diligence or pay respect to the existence of a duty of care in making a decision that affects individuals and potential undermines their human rights, might generate consequences on those institutions. In the situation for example of *X and X*, the failure on the part of the EU Member State to exercise such due diligence might not amount to facilitating torture but could facilitate, for example, the denial of the right to asylum. This would amount to a territorial exercise on the part of the Member State, regardless that the consequences, ie the violation of the fundamental rights, are felt elsewhere. For Ryngaert, the decision having been taken on EU territory: '...institutional failures by the EU...to carry out a proper due diligence inquiry can be deemed to occur on EU territory, thus triggering the applicability of territorial human rights obligations'.[121] As Bartels notes, the situation in respect of human rights is less clear than as regards States' trade policies.[122] It is difficult to assert concretely that the above-mentioned Treaty provisions on the EU's promotion of fundamental rights in its external relations (Art 21 and Art 3(5) TEU)[123] or the general principles of Union law or the CFR (Arts 6(1) and 6(3) TEU) apply to (internal) policy which has extraterritori-

118 Including the prohibition of inhuman or degrading treatment in Art 3 ECHR, the right to a fair trial and effective remedy per Arts 6(1) and 13 ECHR, as well as the principle of non-refoulement in Art 33 of the Geneva Convention.

119 *MN and Others v Belgium*, App. No. 3599/18.

120 C Ryngaert, 'EU Trade Agreements and Human Rights: From Extraterritorial Obligations' (2018) 20 *International Community Law Review* 375, 386.

121 ibid, 387.

122 L Bartels, 'The EU's Human Rights Obligations in Relation to Policies with Extraterritorial Effects' (2015) 25 *EJIL* 1071, 1072.

123 See also European Commission and High Representative of the European Union for Foreign Affairs and Security Policy Communication on Human Rights and

al effect? The situation is even more unclear in the context of asylum and migration. What this would require is not necessarily an obligation to issue humanitarian visas but a requirement that procedural obligations on the part of the Union are fully engaged; that 'the EU adopt suitable human rights-sensitive processes, in particular carry out human rights impact assessments [eg] when negotiating international trade agreements' to ensure the 'procedural quality of Brussels-based institutional decision-making processes that may create human rights risks'.[124]

This argument might not be deemed to be fully applicable to the *X and X* case, in light of the fact that the processing of LTV visas is not something that is undertaken by the EU but by the Member States' authorities, which as the Court has held does not fall within the scope of EU law. Nevertheless, there is some indication that the Member States should engage in ensuring that such sensitive approaches are taken in the context of visa applications. While the Court did not touch on the process, AG Bobek in *El Hassani* considered that there exists a right to have one's visa application fairly and properly processed, he also identified a right to an effective judicial remedy if that application is refused, a matter which is deemed not only to a right to be 'treated fairly and correctly stemming from the right to human dignity, but also the particular interest of the EU and its Member States to uphold and control the exercise of public power and (European) legality. That need might be even stronger in geographically distant places.'[125] This finding ultimately depended however on the identification of a matter falling within the scope of Union law, and the triggering of the CFR.[126] Moreover, the Court's reasoning in *X and X* highlights that it en-

Democracy at the Heart of EU External Action – Towards a More Effective Approach, COM(2011)886 final, 12 Dec. 2011, 7, in which it was provided that 'EU external action has to comply with' the CFR and ECHR.

124 C Ryngaert, 'EU Trade Agreements and Human Rights: From Extraterritorial Obligations' (2018) 20 *International Community Law Review* 375,, 388.

125 Case C-403/16 *El Hassani* EU:C:2017:659, paras 103-106 and para 111.

126 The Commission's (non-binding) Handbook also provides, 'The processing of visa applications should be conducted in a professional and respectful manner and fully comply with the prohibition of inhuman and degrading treatments and the prohibition of discrimination enshrined, respectively, in Articles 3 and 14 of the European Convention on Human Rights and in Articles 4 and 21 of the Charter of Fundamental Rights of the European Union.' European Commission, 'ANNEX to the Commission Implementing Decision amending Commission Decision No C(2010) 1620 final of 19 March 2010 establishing the Handbook for the processing of visa applications and the modification of issued visas' C(2019) 3464 final, 2.

gaged in no assessment of the extraterritorial application of the CFR or indeed the extraterritorial consequences of decisions made on the territory of an EU Member State. For AG Mengozzi, such an analysis was unnecessary as the CFR was deemed to apply given that the decision of the Belgian authorities to issue or deny a visa on the basis of Art 25(1) EU Visa Code amounted to the implementation of EU law, regardless of any territorial connection.[127] For the AG, the identification of a territorial condition for the triggering of the CFR would have removed the entire common visa policy from the scope of the CFR and the consequent fundamental rights connection.[128] This does not seem to be what the Court would have intended and yet, it is a potential consequence of its judgment.

The Political Questions: Policy and Legislative Discussions at the EU Level

The Court's approach might be (somewhat) justified on the basis that the questions referred to it were undoubtedly highly-sensitive from a political perspective; this can be seen from the media coverage emerging before the judgment was rendered. Yet, the Court's judgment seems to be one which is both political itself and which aims to avoid the political dimension of the case. That is to say, the Court avoids adopting a fundamental rights approach to the EU and Member States' obligations. Instead, it highlights the need to avoid undermining the 'general structure' of the Dublin regime and a conflict with the Visa Code. At the same time, it bases its judgment on the absence of a legislative basis in the Visa Code for the issuance of a long-term, territorially-limited visa on humanitarian grounds. To this end, the Court seems to suggest that it is not for the Court itself to make this step in order to identify a basis in the existing legislation for the issuance of such visas. As discussed above, it avoids any exercise of judicial activism in a legal and policy field fraught with political difficulties albeit many unjustified.[129]

It should be noted that both the Dublin regime and the Visa Code, which does provide a legislative basis for the issuance of humanitarian

127 Case C-638/16 PPU *X and X* EU:C:2017:93, para 89.

128 ibid, para 93; see also, M Rhimes, 'The Extraterritorial Application of the EU Charter in Syria: To the Union and Beyond?' UK Human Rights Blog (10 March 2017); www.ukhumanrightsblog.com/2017/03/10/the-extraterritorial-application-of-the-eu-charter-in-syria-to-the-union-and-beyond-michael-rhimes/.

129 See again L Ypi, 'Borders of Class: Migration and Citizenship in the Capitalist State' (2018) 32 *Ethics and International Affairs* 141.

visas (with limited territorial validity and on a short-term basis), have been under almost constant review.[130] Avoiding the questions referred by the Belgian Council, the Court instead focused on the EU's (lack of) legislative competence, noting that 'as European law currently stands' the issuance of visas on a humanitarian basis is for the Member States in line with national sovereignty.[131] The Court reasoned on the basis that the Syrian applicants applied for a visa with the purpose of applying for asylum in Belgium. By adopting this approach, the Court looked not at the purpose of

130 In light of the absence of a specific procedure for humanitarian visas in EU law, with the exception of Art 25(1) of the EU Visa Code, there have been discussions since at least 2002 surrounding the introduction of a clear legal basis for the issuance of visas on humanitarian grounds. The main developments have taken place in recent years, reflecting it seems the unfolding of the crisis in North Africa and the Middle East. In 2014, the European Commission released its proposal for a recast of the Visa Code. This proposal did not include a framework for the issuance of humanitarian visas, notwithstanding that repeated calls had been made by the UNHCR, the ECR and the ECRE, for humanitarian visas to be included in any revision of the Visa Code. The European Parliament then launched its own call for a holistic approach to be adopted in relation to migration. This would aim to allow persons seeking international protection to apply for a European humanitarian visa directly at any Member State consulate or embassy in a third country. Once those persons were on the territory of a Member State, they would then be able to apply for international protection, i.e. for asylum. The European Commission announced in its 2018 Work Programme that it would withdraw its 2014 Proposal and advance a new one in March 2018. Similarly to the previous proposal, no provision was made in this proposal for humanitarian visas. The equivalent to Art 25(1) in the current Visa Code has been removed. Against this background, the European Parliament drafted and released its own Working Document on humanitarian visas in April 2018, in which it calls for a separate EU instrument for such visas. In December 2018, the Parliament voted on a resolution calling on the Commission to table a proposal for a Regulation on a European Humanitarian Visa (alongside clear criteria, procedural rules, administrative mechanisms and so on) as a means of accessing asylum procedures in Europe; a right to be heard without risking one's life, to combat human smuggling, and to manage arrivals, reception and processing of asylum claims better. Revisions to the Visa Code were adopted in July 2019 (Regulation EU 2019/1155 amending Regulation (EC) No 810/2009 establishing a Community Code on Visas (Visa Code)). The Regulation introduces certain mechanisms to simplify the process for short-term visa applications, including an extension of the time period in which applications can be made; it also introduces mechanisms, including means of incentivising and 'punishing' (increased fees, lengthier processes) which aim to link visa policy and the EU's external policy, and to encourage third States to cooperate with the EU on readmissions. The reference to humanitarian grounds remains in Art 25(1).

131 Case C-638/16 PPU *X and X* EU:C:2017:173, para 45.

the applicants in applying for the particular visa, i.e. their situation which engaged humanitarian concerns, which it recognised had been 'formally submitted' on the basis of Art 25(1) EU Visa Code, but used this apparent objective of seeking asylum to turn their application into one for a long-term residence application. The application was thus deemed not to adhere to the objectives of the Visa Code itself. The approach can be said to conflict with that adopted by a number of EU Member States, which have issued humanitarian visas via Art 25(1) Visa Code for the purposes of affording individuals international protection.[132] At the same time, the Court's reasoning provides a basis for Member States to avoid the scope for the international obligations – a question that the Court entirely ignored, leaving it for the ECtHR – and fundamental rights obligations that arise from the application of both EU law, ie the Visa Code, and national law. Notwithstanding that the national measure or matter is deemed to fall outside the scope of EU law, so that the CFR is not triggered, relevant international law, Convention rights and national constitutional protections still apply.[133] It is exactly this issue on which the Belgian Council asked for clarification as regards the notion of 'international obligations' in Art 25(1) EU Visa Code. Where usually the Member States have a discretion under Art 25(1) Visa Code as to whether to issue visas with limited territorial scope, the Belgian Council is asking whether this discretion turns into a positive obligation where an absolute right of non-refoulement might otherwise be violated.[134]

The Court's determination can ultimately be deemed to be an 'unconvincing teleological one',[135] whereby it denies the application of the Visa

---

132 UI Jensen, 'Humanitarian Visas: Option or Obligation?' (2014) Study for the LIBE Committee of the European Parliament, 43.

133 K Lenaerts, 'The ECHR and the CJEU: Creating Synergies in the Field of Fundamental Rights Protection', Solemn hearing for the opening of the Judicial Year, 26 January 2018, 3, citing Case C-256/11 *Dereci and Others* EU:C:2011:734, paras 72-73 and Case C-23/12 *Zakaria* EU:C:2013:24, para. 41.

134 Moreover, the Court did not provide for a detailed analysis of fundamental rights and international obligations as forming part of the values underpinning the Union, per Art 2 and 3 TEU. Nor did it examine the provision in Art 78(1) TFEU which sets out that 'The Union shall develop a common policy on asylum, subsidiary protection and temporary protection with a view to offering appropriate status to any third-country national requiring international protection and ensuring compliance with the principle of non-refoulement...[in line with] the Geneva Convention of 28 July 1951.'.

135 E Brouwer, 'The European Court of Justice on Humanitarian Visas: Legal Integrity vs Political Opportunism' CEPS Commentary, 16 March 2017, 4.

Code, and in so doing rejects the possibility to provide clarification as to its objective, in favour of upholding the integrity of the Dublin regime. According to Brouwers, this priority is attributed to the Dublin Regulation, notwithstanding its deficits, and against providing international protection to the rights of third-State individuals.[136] Indeed, as Meloni sets out, the Court's judgment in *X and X* illustrates that security and foreign policy concerns underpin EU visa policy, and that while there may be a turn towards rights-based protections of individuals, visa policy nevertheless remains 'a policy which straddles the sovereignty sensitive areas of internal security and foreign policy'.[137] Moreover, it calls into question whether fundamental rights protections are really 'practical and effective' as opposed to 'theoretical and illusory', at least for individuals of third States.[138]

Conclusion

The question arises as to whether the ECJ's judgment and deferral in this case is satisfactory, especially given the problematics of irregular migration. The Court did not deal with the issue of whether there was any territorial requirement to the CFR but simply found that there was no implementation of Union law on the facts of the case. By finding neither that the facts of the case gave rise to the implementation of EU law, so as to trigger the application of the CFR, and having not considered whether the CFR or international obligations have any other scope, the Court reinforced that the European system of asylum and migration operates as one where, in these circumstances, the Union and its Member States avoid responsibilities and avoid encounters between third-country individuals and Union or national authorities[139]. What was ultimately at stake in the Court's judgment in *X and X* was not the Visa Code but ensuring the coherence of the Dublin regime. To this end, the Court largely avoided an examination of EU

136 ibid, 4.

137 Through the inclusion of rights to appeal the refusal of an application for a visa, to the grounds set out as to when a visa might be refused to the shift away from discretionary rules; see A Meloni, 'EU Visa Policy: What Kind of Solidarity?' (2017) 21 *Maastricht Journal of European and Comparative Law* 1, 7.

138 *Hirsi Jamaa and Others v Italy* App. No. 27765/09, para 175.

139 See I Mann, *Humanity at Sea: Maritime Migration and the Foundations of International Law* (Cambridge, Cambridge University Press, 2016) and D Schmalz, 'Review of I Mann, *Humanity at Sea: Maritime Migration and the Foundations of International Law*' (2017) 28 *EJIL* 649, 653, where the notion of encounter constitutes the basis of rights.

Treaty law and the CFR in favour of a mere analysis of whether the relevant secondary law, namely the Visa Code, was the correct basis on which an individual could apply for a visa to safely and legally access EU Member State territory, thus separating EU visa policy and the humanitarian visa entirely. The *X and X* case illustrates that the focus in visa policy cannot yet be said to be that of individual rights. As above, the question unanswered by the ECJ as to whether Member States might be obliged by virtue of Art 3 ECHR to issue visas on humanitarian grounds where a refusal of a visa might lead to a violation of the rights set out therein, remains an open issue, heard by the ECtHR in April 2019. The Court's deferral of this question illustrates the fragmentation that exists as regards the protection of individuals in the field of asylum and migration. Moreover, this question left unanswered by the Court will undoubtedly come not only before the ECJ in the near future but will also be a matter of legislative and policy-orientated concern. It has been expressed succinctly by Judge Paulo Pinto de Albuquerque in his concurring opinion in *Hirsi Jamaa*; namely, 'how Europe should recognise that refugees have the "right to have rights"'.[140]

140 *Hirsi Jamaa and Others v Italy* App. No. 27765/09 citing Hannah Arendt; H Arendt, 'We Refugees', in *The Menorah Journal*, 1943, republished in M Robinson (ed), *Altogether Elsewhere: Writers on Exile* (Boston, Faber and Faber, 1994).

Chapter 3: Is Access to Asylum the Same as Access to Justice?

Sylvie Sarolea [1]

Contents

---

1 Professor in the Law Faculty of the Catholic University of Louvain (UCL). A first version of this article was presented during the Workshop, entitled 'Humanitarian Visas and the External Dimensions of the EU Migration and Asylum Policy' organised by Pr MC Foblets and Dr L Lebœuf at the Max Planck Institute Halle in May 2018. The article was last updated in March 2019.

Introduction

For those forced to flee, seeking asylum is tantamount to seeking access to justice. Justice, however, requires access to a place where, unlike where the asylum seeker previously resided, human rights could be claimed and guaranteed, at least the most basic human rights. Seeking asylum is a second-rate solution, the better solution is to ensure that asylum seekers will again be able to live in what they consider their own home and fully claim these basic rights there. It follows that if access to such basic rights is impossible or denied, so, too, the access to the right to justice. The universality of human rights remains under question until and unless human rights can be claimed some place else. This 'somewhere' is a State or an inter-State. These rights do not exist independent of an institutional incarnation, and access to that institution in question, namely the State, is central to asylum seekers.

In asylum law, the right of access to 'justice' has increasingly become a highly debated issue, especially in case law. In guaranteeing the principle of *non-refoulement*,[2] the Geneva Convention also relies on several international and regional conventions relating to fundamental rights. The principle is so worded as to safeguard the notion that no one may be returned 'in any way whatsoever' to a country where there is a risk of injury to life or threat of torture.

But in order to avoid being turned or sent back, it is still necessary to have arrived at a place where such a right can and will be upheld and exercised. Availing oneself of this right presupposes an interlocutor, a debtor of this right. This interlocutor is the guardian of the gateway to this 'justice'. The central question then becomes: *Where* is this gateway?

Access to justice depends on the existence of this gateway. But does it really exist? There is no simple or unique answer to that, for the reality is plural. Sometimes the gate to be crossed only exists on maps where borders are very long or in a hostile environment such as when they run across a desert. Its physical non-existence certainly does not necessarily mean an absence of danger but that access may possibly be allowed. The gateway is sometimes a waterway – rivers or seas – separating States. Here, too, it must be navigated, often under perilous conditions. Sometimes, the gateway exists physically, like in the airports, train stations, or where fences are installed (around Ceuta and Melilla, at the eastern borders of European Union).

2 Geneva Convention, article 33.

Europe is surrounded by such gateways. Should they then at least be half-opened when they are already reached, when the asylum seeker is physically in front of the gate, seeking to step in? These metaphors reflect a reality. Everything then rests on accessing roads to this gateway, and knowing how to reach them.

The gates to Europe have been dangerous these past years. Since 1993, the UNITED network has been monitoring the 'deadly results of the building of "Fortress Europe" by making a list of the refugees and migrants, who have died in their attempt of entering the "Fortress" or as a result of Europe's immigration policies'.[3] The number of deaths last documented was 36,570. The list mentions names, and sometimes just the initials of the dead, along with their place of origin and the information source. This list was published in several major newspapers.

The only way to escape this high-level risk is by providing access to legal avenues. Despite being increasingly debated at the EU policy level, as underlined by Francesco Gatta,[4] this issue has only led to very limited implementation and transposition into practical measures and common European actions. This volume reports and analyses a number of initiatives towards opening and making available safe mobility channels (resettlement initiatives, humanitarian admission programmes and so-called humanitarian visas). But those programmes are not compulsory and can grant access to migrants *only if States decide to express their right to open their borders.*

This chapter revisits the premises of the first European case on this subject, namely ECJ's *X & X* ruling on the question of issuing humanitarian visas to asylum seekers at consular and diplomatic representations in third countries. This case has, however, spawned a wide range of reflections on the responsibility of States in regards to asylum, as well to future options. The fundamental issues this topic raises are much larger and complex than *X & X*, which is the focus of this chapter. This is mainly because the current orientations of the EU policy in this field have made it necessary to act more and more outside of its geographical borders. Besides the delicate question of the nature of the acts adopted within the framework of this ex-

---

3 European network against nationalism, racism, fascism and in support of migrants and refugees, www.unitedagainstracism.org/campaigns/refugee-campaign/fortress-europe/#99; http://unitedagainstrefugeedeaths.eu/.

4 F Gatta, 'Legal avenues to access international protection in the European Union: past actions and future perspectives' (2018) 3 *Journal européen des droits de l'homme - European Journal of Human Rights (JEDH)*. See also the contribution of Ziebritzki to this volume.

ternal action, it is essential to view the exercise of its extraterritorial jurisdiction through the prism of fundamental rights.

This raises complex technical questions, or rather questions to which the answers are neither clear nor unambiguous in light of the current legal framework and the point of view ultimately adopted. Beyond a *de lege lata* analysis regarding the current legal framework, the global consistency of the solution adopted must be questioned. The point of view of this paper will be a legal one, not because ethics and law would be in opposition but because it is our point of view. But before that, it is important to mention that the 'other' European Court will pronounce a judgment in the following months on the same subject.

On 24 April 2019, the Grand Chamber of the European Court of Human Rights (ECHR, Strasbourg) held its hearing on humanitarian visas in *MN and others v Belgium*[5]. The applicants are a Syrian family from Aleppo who applied for humanitarian visas for the entire family at the Belgian embassy in Beirut. The refusal to issue visas was suspended by the Council for Aliens Law Litigation (hereinafter: the Belgian Council) under the extreme urgency procedure.[6] Several domestic decisions followed the first one. The first judgment was based on the alleged risk of violation of Article 3 ECHR. Belgium's obligation to issue a visa because of this risk is the central issue on which the Court of Strasbourg will have to decide. The provisions at stake are Article 1 (which define the territorial scope of the Convention), Article 3, Article 6(1) (guaranteeing the right to a fair trial), and Article 13 (protecting the right to an effective remedy).

5 The case was heard but the decision is still pending (as on 11 September 2019).

6 In Belgian law, the extreme urgency procedure is available as a complement to an action for annulment of an administrative decision. The Council for Aliens Law Litigation is the administrative court that is competent to hear appeals lodged against decisions relating to asylum and residence. It reviews the legality of these measures mainly with respect to infringement of essential procedural requirements. Where it is not automatically suspensive, the action for annulment may be accompanied by a request for suspension and/or a request for provisional measures. Those last ones [specify] may be lodged in ordinary procedure or in extreme urgency. Then a decision could be taken at a very short delay (a few days or even hours, if necessary). Since neither the action for annulment, nor the request for suspension is suspensive, the urgent procedure is the only way to benefit for an effective remedy. Otherwise, the applicant could have been removed without a decision of the judge or be subjected to a refusal to access the territory during a long period of time. That is why, here, the applicant used the extreme urgency procedure to obtain a rapid decision in view of the dramatic situation in Aleppo.

The importance of this case in understanding States' obligations in the field of asylum has prompted several interventions from other States[7] but also from NGOs and professional organisations.[8] The former (other States) sided with Belgium while the latter supported the applicants. The stakes in this case justified its referral to the Grand Chamber. At the time of writing this article, it is only possible to make prognostications on the basis of the existing case law and the general principles governing the protection of human rights.

1. *The Setting of the Play: The Right of Asylum, a Right 'of the Foot in the Door'*

International law is grounded on a schizophrenic paradox. Asylum seekers only have the right to leave a country, including their own, but no right to enter a third country, even to ask for protection. This results from the silence of international law on legal avenues and the limited scope of territorial application of the principle of *non-refoulement*.[9]

To apply for asylum, it is necessary to have arrived in a third country and thus to have entered or, to say the least, fallen under the jurisdiction of another sovereign State, which means being on what is legally considered its territory: land, maritime, the border. Indeed, if international law recognises the right to leave any country, including one's own, it guarantees no legal entry to a third country, even in the field of asylum. The principle of *non-refoulement* has territorial limits, for Article 33 of the Geneva Convention guarantees the prohibition of expulsion or return ('*refoulement*') thus:

---

7 Austria, Czech Republic, Croatia, Denmark, France, Germany, Latvia, Netherlands, Slovakia, and United Kingdom.

8 The Human Rights League (LDH), the International Federation of Human Rights Leagues (FIDH), the Centre for Advice on Individual Rights in Europe (the AIRE Centre), the European Council on Refugees and Exiles (ECRE), the International Commission of Jurists, the Dutch Council for Refugees, and the Bar Council of French-speaking and German-speaking Lawyers of Belgium (OBFG).

9 On this subject, see mainly N Frenzen, 'The Practice of Shared Responsibility in Relation to Extraterritorial Refugee Protection' (2016) *University of Southern California Gould School of Law, SHARES Research Paper 80*, www.sharesproject.nl, in: A Nollkaemper and I Plakokefalos (eds), *The Practice of Shared Responsibility in International Law* (Cambridge, Cambridge University Press, 2016); M den Heijer, 'Europe and Extraterritorial Asylum', https://openaccess.leidenuniv.nl/handle/1887/16699.

> No Contracting State shall expel or return (*'refouler'*) a refugee in any manner whatsoever to the frontiers of territories where his life or freedom would be threatened on account of his race, religion, nationality, membership of a particular social group or political opinion.

Even if the expression 'in any manner whatsoever' seems to offer an effective and large degree of protection, in practice, it is limited by its territorial scope of application. Asylum is the right of getting the foot in the door. Asylum seekers are protected by the principle of *non-refoulement* only if they enter the territory or reach the borders. But the applicability of protection in prior areas and zones, or in specific zones, such as the airports and the transit areas, is disputed in case law, and perspectives differ depending on the continent and the geographical area from where access to protection is sought.

Starting with the simplest cases, this chapter will revert to the geographically more complicated ones. Having once, legally or not, entered the territory of a host State, asylum seekers are protected by the principle of *non-refoulement*, which also benefits them at the border insofar as they have access to it. However, questions of interpretation are beginning to arise around the exact definition of the border.

First step: the transit zones of the airport in the host country. In *Amuur v France*,[10] the European Court of Human Rights ruled that those zones are not extraterritorial. Admittedly, even if this judgment did not concern Article 3 but Article 5, it had a direct impact on asylum seekers. France argued that the applicants were free to leave the transit zone to fly back to Syria since they had departed from that country. The Court rejected this alternative, underlining that

> this possibility becomes theoretical if no other country offering protection comparable to the protection they expect to find in the country where they are seeking asylum is inclined or prepared to take them in. Sending the applicants back to Syria only became possible, apart from the practical problems of the journey, following negotiations between the French and Syrian authorities. The assurances of the latter were dependent on the vagaries of diplomatic relations, in view of the fact that Syria was not bound by the Geneva Convention relating to the Status of Refugees (§ 48).

10 ECtHR, *Amuur v France*, 25 June 1996, Appl. No 19776/92.

One step further, at a domestic court: Does the principle of *non-refoulement* protect asylum seekers at an airport in the country of origin? *Roma* stemmed from a 2001 bilateral agreement between the United Kingdom and the Czech Republic, which permits British immigration officers to 'pre-clear' all passengers at the Prague Airport before they board any aircraft bound for the United Kingdom. The UK Appellate Court judged that the principle of *non-refoulement* did not apply to those who had yet to 'leave their country of origin'.[11]

Between those two locations at airports, various other cases occur mostly at sea. Here, one must distinguish between the territorial sea, over which the State has jurisdiction as it is part of the national territory, and the high seas, over which no one nation has jurisdiction and is thus equally accessible to all nations. First, to even establish a precedent, is the famous case of *Sale* of September 1981. The United States and Haiti entered into an agreement to authorise US coastguards to intercept in high seas vessels that were engaged in the illegal transportation of Haitian migrants to US shores. Following the 1992 Executive Order by President H.W. Bush, coastguards started repatriating Haitians, depriving them of any opportunity to establish themselves as refugees. When the case found its way to the US Supreme Court, the Court denied relief to the plaintiffs on the grounds that the *non-refoulement* obligation only applied to those who were 'at the border or within a country, not the high seas'.[12]

This case was the only legal precedent when the European Court of Human Rights was confronted with the application in the *Hirsi* case.[13] While the legal basis was different— the ECHR in the *Hirsi* case and the Geneva Convention in the *Sale* case—the Strasbourg Court offered a contrary ruling. Somali and Eritrean migrants travelling from Libya who had been intercepted at sea by the Italian authorities were sent back to Libya. The Court found that the applicants were within the jurisdiction of Italy for the purposes of Article 1 of the Convention. The criterion of the 'jurisdiction' under this provision was grounded on the notion of effective control. It reiterated the principle of international law, enshrined in the Italian Na-

11 House of Lords, *R (European Roma Rights Centre) v Immigration Officer at Prague Airport* [2004] UKHL 55

12 United States Supreme Court, *Sale v Haitian ctrs. Council, Inc.* (1993) No 92–344, https://caselaw.findlaw.com/us-supreme-court/509/155.html. In disagreement with the Court, read Interam. Comm. H.R., Rapport n° 51/96, case n° 10.675, 13 of March 1997.

13 ECtHR (Grand Chamber—judgment), *Hirsi Jamaa and others v Italy*, 23 February 2012.

vigation Code, that a vessel sailing on the high seas was subject to the exclusive jurisdiction of the State of the flag it was flying. The events had taken place entirely on board the ships of the Italian armed forces with an Italian military crew. In the time between boarding the ships and being handed over to the Libyan authorities, the applicants had been under the continuous and exclusive de jure and de facto control of the Italian authorities.

States have tried to restrict the scope of their control, through fictional notions such as 'the operational border'. In *ND v Spain*,[14] still pending before the Grand Chamber at the time of writing, the first question to be answered by the Court concerned Spain's jurisdiction under the Convention. Could the summary *refoulement* of the applicants be considered an exercise of Spain's jurisdiction within the meaning of Article 1 of the Convention? The Spanish government used the concept of an 'operational border',[15] arguing that the applicants had not 'succeeded in going beyond the protection system at the Melilla border crossing'. According to the Court, the notion of 'operational border' was clarified upstream of the disputed facts, through the operating protocol of 26 February 2014 of the Guardia Civil (Civil Guard), Spain's border surveillance, which contains the following statements:

> With this system of fences, there is an objective need to determine when the illegal entry failed or when it took place. This requires a delimiting line that exists for the sole purpose of defining national territory with respect to the regime governing foreigners: The fence is a physical embodiment of the line of demarcation. Thus, when efforts of law enforcement agencies responsible for border surveillance to contain and repel attempts by migrants to illegally cross this line are successful, no actual illegal entry is said to have taken place. Entry is only considered to have taken place when a migrant has gone beyond the aforementioned internal enclosure, has thus entered the national territory and is therefore subject to the aliens regime.

Citing the *Hirsi* judgment, the applicants and third parties asserted, on the contrary, that

> the removal of aliens, which in their opinion has the effect of preventing migrants from reaching the borders of the State or even returning them to another State, constitutes an exercise of jurisdiction within the

14 ECtHR, *ND and NT v Spain*, 3 October 2017, No 8675/15 and 8697/15.
15 §§ 17 and 44.

> meaning of Article 1 of the Convention, which engages the responsibility of the State in question in the field of Article 4 of Protocol No. 4'.

Some third parties also pointed out that the applicants were already on Spanish territory at the barrier, in view of the territorial delimitations provided for by the international treaties between Morocco and Spain.

The Court opted for the criteria of control exercised by Spain over the applicants. This control made those operations enter into the scope of Spanish jurisdiction rather than a mechanical analysis based on territory. This way the Court avoided the factual dispute about localisation.[16] Rather than ruling on whether or not the applicants were on Spanish territory, the Court stated that 'from the moment the applicants descended from the border fences, they were under the continuous and exclusive control, at least de facto, of the Spanish authorities'.[17] Furthermore, it added that 'no speculation concerning the competences, functions and action of the Spanish police forces on the nature and purpose of their intervention could lead the Court to any other conclusion'. This last clarification defeats the concept of an 'operational border' put forward by the Spanish government. As underlined by Louis Imbert,

> in doing so, the Court further closes the gap between the 'border of controls' (perimeters of the places and contexts in which migration controls are carried out) and the 'border of rights' (perimeters of the places and contexts in which rights are likely to be protected). It therefore confirms once again that the 'border of rights' extends beyond the

16 '53. The Court also observes that the border line between the Kingdom of Morocco and the cities of Ceuta and Melilla has been delimited by the international treaties to which the Kingdoms of Spain and Morocco are parties and that it cannot be modified at the initiative of one of those States for the purposes of a concrete factual situation. It takes note of the statements made by CEAR in its observations on the border perimeter between Spain and Morocco (paragraphs 47 and 33 above) and those of the Commissioner for Human Rights echoing those of the Spanish Ombudsman, according to which Spanish jurisdiction would also be exercised on the land between the fences at the Melilla border crossing and not only beyond the protection system of the post in question (paragraphs 46 and 34 above). 54. In the light of the foregoing and the context of the present applications, the Court refers to the applicable international law and the agreements concluded between the Kingdoms of Morocco and Spain concerning the establishment of land borders between those two States. However, it considers that it is not necessary to establish whether or not the border fence between Morocco and Spain is located on the territory of the latter State.'.

17 § 54.

territorial border to include contemporary border surveillance practises, in particular those that seek to repel attempts to enter the territory of a State Party.[18]

2. *The Need for Legal Avenues*

Those combined rules—no right to legal avenues and limited scope of application of the principle of *non-refoulement*— make all asylum seekers into legal offenders. Do asylum seekers then have no other choice than to resort to irregular means to cross borders and reach safety? They are forced to attempt an irregular entry just to be able to garner the protection guaranteed by international law. When borders are not shared because they are separated by a sea, they must try to cross it.

The solution would be to provide legal avenues. Those that exist are not legally binding. The authorisation to enter legally is governed by the discretionary power of the concerned country. The large-scale loss of life and broader pressures on the EU asylum system have reinvigorated calls for more and better legal avenues of entry into the EU, the 'Protected Entry Procedures' (PEPs). To date, the primary PEP in place in the EU has been resettlement, whereby persons who have been identified as needing international protection are transferred directly to a Member State where they are admitted either on humanitarian grounds or with the refugee status. Figures show us, however, that the percentage of resettlement is very low. Since 2015, EU resettlement programmes have helped over 43,700 people find shelter in the EU. Under the new EU resettlement scheme (December 2017-October 2019), 27,800 persons should be resettled.[19]

Alongside resettlement, humanitarian visas are viewed as an alternative PEP. Humanitarian visas allow asylum seekers to legally access a third country and/or apply for asylum following expedited asylum procedures,

---

18 L Imbert, 'Refoulements sommaires: la CEDH trace la "frontière des droits" à Melilla. Note sous CEDH, 3 octobre 2017, *N.D. et N.T. c. Espagne*, req. n° 8675/15 et 8697/15' (2018) *Revue des droits de l'homme*, https://journals.openedition.org/revdh/3740. See also T Maheshe, 'Expulsions collectives et crises migratoires, note sous Cour eur. D.H., *N.D. et N.T. c. Espagne*, 3 octobre 2017' (October 2017) *Cahiers de l'EDEM*.

19 https://ec.europa.eu/commission/sites/beta-political/files/factsheet_-_union_resettlement_framework.pdf. Read on this subject, K Bamberg, 'The EU Resettlement Framework: From a Humanitarian Pathway to a Migration Management Tool?', www.epc.eu/documents/uploads/pub_8632_euresettlement.pdf?doc_id=2012.

where the merit of their application is examined in situ. Under existing schemes, humanitarian visas are issued at the discretion of individual States and are requested directly by the third country national at the consulate of the State where asylum is sought. The pre-screening process can then be conducted extraterritorially before a humanitarian visa is issued, enabling the asylum seeker to reach the State where they can apply for asylum safely and legally. The decision on the substance of the asylum application is then made on that State's territory. Those humanitarian visas are processed and issued very slowly and a very limited percentage of the arrivals are granted it in reality. It is the legal basis for this answer that was ruled by the ECJ in *X and X*.

3. X & X: Does EU LAW require EU States to Open Legal Avenues for Asylum Seekers?

The applicants were a Syrian family with three children. They were Orthodox Christians from Aleppo. One claimed to have been beaten and tortured by a terrorist group and released for ransom. They sought to claim asylum in Belgium where they had connections. As they wanted to reach Belgium lawfully and safely, without risking life and limb, huddled in dinghies, to the profit of traffickers, they asked Belgium to issue visas and avoid the well-known dangers. Before returning to Syria the following day, they filed the application at the Belgian embassy in Beirut on the basis of Article 25(1)(a) of the Visa Code, which governs applications for visas with limited territorial validity and on humanitarian grounds.

The Belgian authorities' response was that they were not required to grant visas, neither by EU nor by human rights law. The *Office des étrangers* of the Belgian administration held that the family clearly had the intention to stay on in Belgium after the expiry of the visa, since they had specified that they would apply for asylum once in Belgium. The visa application, according to the *Office*, would therefore fall under Belgian national law. It further held that neither Article 3 ECHR nor Article 33 of the Geneva Convention provided for an obligation to admit foreigners on the territory of the States party to the Convention, even if these foreigners lived in 'catastrophic circumstances', but that these articles merely provided for a prohibition of *refoulement*.

According to the principle of *non-refoulement*, States party to the Convention may not remove a person to another State if the person concerned faces a real risk of being persecuted or subjected to torture or to inhuman or degrading treatment in the country to which they are returned. The *Of-*

fice argued that this principle only applied to persons that are already within the Belgian (territorial) jurisdiction. It also argued that Belgian law does not allow its diplomatic posts to accept applications for international protection from third country nationals, and that granting a visa to the applicants in order for them to apply for international protection once on Belgian soil would circumvent the limitation of the competences of the Belgian diplomatic posts.

The urgent domestic administrative procedure (Council for Asylum and Immigration Proceedings) brought to bear against this decision has been suspended to refer the questions to the Court for a preliminary ruling.[20]

There are two principal issues in this case. The first concerns whether the Visa Code *allowed* Belgium to grant Family X the visa they had sought (the Visa issue). The second issue concerned the question of whether fundamental rights under the EU Charter, which include the right to remain free from torture and other degrading treatment in Article 4, positively *required* Belgium to grant it (the Charter issue).

In his opinion, Advocate General Mengozzi stated that the Visa Code not only allowed Belgium to grant a visa to Family X, but that the EU Charter of Fundamental Rights required it in situations where there was a real risk that individuals in question would be exposed to treatment contrary to Article 4, which included the prospect of crossing the Mediterranean sea by boat in perilous conditions.

Article 25 of the Visa Code leaves a certain margin of discretion to the Member States in their assessment of the arguments the applicants brought forward in their appeal to Article 25. However, since the Member States apply EU law for assessing an appeal to Article 25 of the Visa Code, their discretion is limited by EU law.

---

20 '(1) Do the "international obligations" referred to in Article 25(1)(a) of the Visa Code cover all the rights guaranteed by the Charter, including, in particular, those guaranteed by Articles 4 and 18, and do they also cover obligations which bind the Member States, in the light of the ECHR and Article 33 of the Geneva Convention? (2) (a) Depending on the answer given to the first question, must Article 25(1)(a) of the Visa Code be interpreted as meaning that, subject to its discretion with regard to the circumstances of the case, a Member State to which an application for a visa with limited territorial validity has been made is required to issue the visa applied for, where a risk of infringement of Article 4 and/or Article 18 of the Charter or another international obligation by which it is bound is established? (b) Does the existence of links between the applicant and the Member State to which the visa application was made (for example, family connections, host families, guarantors and sponsors) affect the answer to that question?'.

This led the Advocate General to conclude that the Member States are under a positive obligation to take reasonable measures to prevent the risk of torture or inhuman or degrading treatment of which they know or should have known. Therefore, Member States' authorities must inform themselves with regard to the situation in the country of origin of an applicant before deciding to apply one of the reasons for refusal of a visa as listed under Article 32(1).[21]

The Court, however, held that the Visa Code did not govern the situation at hand. In effect, because Family X had intended to stay in Belgium for longer than 90 days, the request was not really for a *short-term visa* within the definition of the Visa Code, but for a *long-term humanitarian visa* which fell outside the scope of EU law. It is apparent from the order for reference and from the material in the file before the Court that the applicants in the main proceedings that had submitted applications for visas on humanitarian grounds based on Article 25 of the Visa Code at the Belgian embassy in Lebanon, did so with a view to applying for asylum in Belgium immediately upon their arrival there and thereafter to being granted a residence permit with a period of validity exceeding 90 days.

As such, it was contended that the Charter point was not relevant, and Belgium was *required to refuse* the visa application under the Visa Code. Even if this question was not included in the preliminary ruling, the Court considers that even a long-term visa would not fall under the scope of EU law as a way to prevent a future action and to 'definitively' close the door on the issue. The Court rules in paragraph 49 that

21 A link could be made with the *NS* case (ECJ, Joined Cases C-411-10 and C-493-10, *NS v United Kingdom and ME v Ireland*): '68. Those factors reinforce the interpretation according to which the discretionary power conferred on the Member States by Article 3(2) of Regulation No 343/2003 forms part of the mechanisms for determining the Member State responsible for an asylum application provided for under that regulation and, therefore, merely an element of the Common European Asylum System. Thus, a Member State which exercises that discretionary power must be considered as implementing European Union law within the meaning of Article 51(1) of the Charter.' '106. Article 4 of the Charter of Fundamental Rights of the European Union must be interpreted as meaning that the Member States, including the national courts, may not transfer an asylum seeker to the "Member State responsible" within the meaning of Regulation No 343/2003 where they cannot be unaware that systemic deficiencies in the asylum procedure and in the reception conditions of asylum seekers in that Member State amount to substantial grounds for believing that the asylum seeker would face a real risk of being subjected to inhuman or degrading treatment within the meaning of that provision.'.

> It is also important to note that to conclude otherwise would mean that Member States are required, on the basis of the Visa Code, de facto to allow third-country nationals to submit applications for international protection to the representations of Member States that are within the territory of a third country. Indeed, whereas the Visa Code is not intended to harmonise the laws of Member States on international protection, it should be noted that the measures adopted by the European Union on the basis of Article 78 TFEU that govern the procedures for applications for international protection do not impose such an obligation and, on the contrary, exclude from their scope applications made to the representations of Member States. Accordingly, it is apparent from Article 3(1) and (2) of Directive 2013/32 that that directive applies to applications for international protection made in the territory, including at the border, in the territorial waters or in the transit zones of the Member States, but not to requests for diplomatic or territorial asylum submitted to the representations of Member States. Similarly, it follows from Articles 1 and 3 of Regulation No 604/2013 that that regulation only imposes an obligation on Member States to examine any application for international protection made on the territory of a Member State, including at the border or in transit zones, and that the procedures laid down in that regulation apply exclusively to such applications for international protection.

The Court does not rely solely on the texts but seems to link the impossibility of seeking asylum via a visa to an overall logic of European law. The Court goes beyond the very application of the Visa Code, which only regulates short stays, to indicate that no asylum application may be lodged outside the European territory, failing which it runs counter to the fundamental logic of the common European asylum system and, in particular, the Dublin Regulation. The Court could have limited its response to the applicability of the Visa Code.

4. A Right Understanding of the Visa Code?

The interpretation of the Visa Code in this case must be considered with respect to four points: the text, the criteria of intention, the forgotten possibility for a prolongation and the future.

4.1 The text

According to Article 25 of the EU Visa Code, a visa with limited territorial validity 'shall be issued exceptionally … when the Member State concerned considers it necessary on humanitarian grounds, for reasons of national interest or because of international obligations'. Since it was clear that Family X sought to remain on the Belgian territory in excess of 90 days, the Court held that the 'visa' could not be issued on the basis of the Visa Code. Four other arguments strengthened the ruling of the Court.

One of the conditions of Article 32 of the Visa Code provides that a visa must be denied 'if there are reasonable doubts as to … [the] intention to leave the territory of the Member States before the expiry of the visa applied for'. The Visa Code was enacted on the basis of Article 62(2)(b)(ii) of EU Treaty, which confers upon the Council the power to adopt 'rules on visas for *intended stays of no more than three months*'.[22] It would therefore go beyond the legal basis of the Visa Code to allow Member States to grant visas in excess of that three-month period.

To allow humanitarian visas to be granted to enable asylum claims would undermine Dublin Regulation. It would oblige States to open the doors of their embassies. The recast Asylum Procedures Directive governs 'applications … made in *the territory* … in the territorial waters or transit zones of Member States' but specifically excludes 'requests for … asylum submitted to *representations* of Member States'. In a similar vein, Regulation No 604/2013, in Articles 1 and 3, only makes mention of it applying to 'applications … made in the territory … in the territorial waters or transit zones of Member States'. In that case, the 'visa' application at hand made at the Belgian representation in Beirut fell outside the scope of EU law.

A *long-term stay* corresponds to Article 79(2)(a) TFEU which, under the umbrella of a 'common immigration policy', allows the EU Parliament and Council to set 'the conditions of entry and residence, and standards on the issue by Member States of long-term visas and residence permits'. Yet, at the material time, no such standards had been laid down. The net effect was that EU law did not cover the request of Family X, and as such, Belgium was required, as a matter of EU law, to deny it.

As the Court pointed out, there was a fine distinction. This requirement under EU law certainly did not mean that the Belgian State had to refuse the visa application. It simply meant that it could not be granted *as a mat-*

---

22 Emphasis added.

ter of EU law. The Belgian authorities would have been free, *as a matter of national law*, to grant the visa application if they so chose to. It seems, however, that this analysis is not convincing or, at least, was not the only option, for reasons of internal and external consistency of EU asylum law.

4.2 The Inconstancy of the Criteria of Intention

Firstly, the inconstancy of the criteria of intention must be pointed out. As underlined by the Advocate General, nothing in the Visa Code justifies the conclusion that the applicants' *intention* to apply for asylum once on Belgian territory could change either the nature or the subject of their application, or transform the application into an application for a stay longer than three months for at least four reasons.

Legally speaking, the criteria of intention is in itself a weak one. Largely interpreted, it could lead to a refusal of most of the tourist visas and it opens the doors for subjective analysis, even of hidden intents. To make this analysis at the stage of the admissibility, or of the considering the scope of application of a text, seems to be clearly testing the grounds.

Considering other decisions, the role played by these criteria in this case is at odds with the ruling of the tribunal in the EU-Turkey agreement case. There, the right criterion is formal and not linked to the intentions.[23] In paragraph 71, the Tribunal says that, 'independent of whether it constitutes a political statement (as maintained by the European Council, the Council and the Commission) or, on the contrary, a measure capable of producing binding legal effects (as the applicant submits), the EU-Turkey

---

23 As a reminder, the Court of First Instance, considered itself incompetent by virtue of the fact that the EU-Turkey agreement had paradoxically not been concluded by the European Council, but by the heads of state or government of its Member States. The press release, which made good reference to the 'EU' and the 'members of the European Council', is described by the Tribunal as having 'regrettably ambiguous terms'. The European Summit held in Brussels on 17 and 18 March 2016 was, in fact, a set of 'two separate events', a session of the European Council on the one hand, and an international summit with Turkey on the other. For 'reasons of cost, safety and efficiency' these meetings were held in the same building. The Court also considered that 'in practice' Member States had given the President of the Council 'a task of representation and coordination of the negotiations' while the President of the Commission was present during the negotiations in order to ensure 'the continuity of the political dialogue' with Turkey. Consequently, the EU-Turkey agreement had not been concluded by the Council and the Court of First Instance could not examine the substance of the application.

statement, as published via Press Release No 144/16, cannot be regarded as a measure adopted by the European Council, or, moreover, by any other institution, body, office or agency of the European Union, or as revealing the existence of such a measure that corresponds to the contested measure'.[24] Moreover, in the domestic procedures, it has not been contested that the applications in question were for short-term visas. The decision in first instance was confirmed in appeal by the ECJ.[25]

Short-term visas may be used to legally enter the territory and then, after that, to apply for a long-term stay permit: family reunification, work permit of residence. Legally speaking, it is neither impossible nor rare. Numerous legal bases exist, namely, in Belgian law, which allow so-called transfers of status. The Visa Code itself opens the door for this line of argument. A visa with limited territorial validity shall be issued exceptionally in the following cases: (a) when the Member State concerned considers it necessary on humanitarian grounds, for reasons of national interest or because of international obligations.

Even if it falls under the discretionary power of Member States, it does not preclude the possibility of respecting EU law. The ruling of ECJ in the Dublin *NS* case was very clear on EU law's control over the exercise of discretionary power. An examination of Article 3(2) of Regulation No 343/2003 shows that it grants Member States discretionary power, which forms an integral part of the Common European Asylum System provided for by the TFEU and developed by the European Union legislature. Paragraph 66 underlines that, as stated by the Commission, such discretionary power must be exercised in accordance with the other provisions of that Regulation.

In *MSS*, the European Court did not admit a contradiction between discretionary power and legal obligations to be respected. Article 3 § 2 of Dublin Regulation only allows the Member States the possibility of under-

24 EU Trib., Case T-192/16, EU:T:2017:128.

25 ECJ, Order in Joined Cases C-208/17 P and C-210/17 P [2018] *NF, NG and NM*, EU:C:2018:705. In three appeals against this order, the ECJ declared the appeals against these orders inadmissible in a laconic manner. In general, the Court criticises the applicants for a lack of consistency in their arguments. The latter merely summarise 'eight pleas in law without their arguments emerging clearly and precisely from the elements mentioned in a vague and confusing manner', and 'are limited to general statements' of disregard for Union law 'without indicating with the required precision either the elements criticised in the contested orders or the legal arguments which specifically support the application for annulment.' On this decision, read PA Van Malleghem, 'La Cour de justice refuse de revisiter la légalité de l'accord UE-Turquie' (2018) *Cahiers de l'EDEM*.

taking to examine an asylum application even if it is not obliged to do so under the criteria prescribed by the text. Hence, combined with Article 3 of the European Convention of Human Rights that prohibits torture and inhuman and degrading treatments and obligates States to take action to guarantee rights and not just to refrain from violating them, *Article 3 § 2 represents an obligation*,[26] for, in effect, a rule recognising a discretionary power of the States may be transformed into a guarantee of protection of human rights if this rule is interpreted through the prism of those latter rights that act as governing principles.

4.3 *The Forgotten Possibility for a Prolongation*

It is not only possible to convert a short-term stay permit into a long-term one but also to extend it beyond the period of validity for an authorised short-term stay.

Article 33 of the Visa Code stipulates that the period of validity and/or the duration of stay of an issued visa shall be extended where the competent authority of a Member State considers that a visa holder has provided proof of *force majeure* or humanitarian reasons preventing them from leaving the territory of the Member States before the expiry of the period of validity or the duration of stay authorised by the visa. Such an extension shall be granted free of charge.

---

26 '339. The Court notes that Article 3 § 2 of the Dublin Regulation provides that, by derogation from the general rule set forth in Article 3 § 1, each member State may examine an application for asylum lodged with it by a third-country national, even if such examination is not its responsibility under the criteria laid down in the Regulation. This is the so-called "sovereignty" clause. In such a case, the State concerned becomes the member State responsible for the purposes of the Regulation and takes on the obligations associated with that responsibility. 340. The Court concludes that, under the Dublin Regulation, the Belgian authorities could have refrained from transferring the applicant if they had considered that the receiving country, namely Greece, was not fulfilling its obligations under the Convention. Consequently, the Court considers that the impugned measure taken by the Belgian authorities did not strictly fall within Belgium's international legal obligations. Accordingly, the presumption of equivalent protection does not apply in this case.'.

5. Scope of Application of EU Asylum Law

The Court closes the door for further applications in the same legal framework, underlining that even a long-term visa application would not have fallen under the scope of application of EU asylum law.

The Court relies on the scope of application of the Dublin Regulation as well as the Procedures Directive. The Dublin Regulation mentions it as applying to 'applications ... made in the territory ... in the territorial waters or transit zones of Member States', whereas the Procedures Directive governs 'applications ... made in *the territory* ... in the territorial waters or transit zones of Member States' but specifically excludes 'requests for ... asylum submitted to *representations* of Member States'.[27] Even if this assumption is true, it hides an important part of EU asylum policy – that it does not limit itself to the territories of Member States.

Firstly, all the provisions on safe third countries are based on an assessment of events that occur outside of this territory. Secondly, the EU-Turkey agreement is a first step in the so-called new European asylum external policy. The EU could say until now that it is not EU law (the EU Tribunal ruled in this sense) but should this argument remain valid and is it in line of the reality in the future? Shall it be possible to argue that all those new agreements (like the Compacts) are not EU law?

Title V Article 78 TFEU, dedicated to the area of freedom, security and justice, contains a chapter 2 entitled 'Policies on Border-checks, Asylum and Immigration', according to which the EU shall adopt measures concerning partnership and cooperation with third countries for the purpose of managing inflows of people applying for asylum or subsidiary or temporary protection. It seems difficult to argue that EU asylum law is territorially limited to the geographical territory of EU countries, for the last developments illustrate a different reality.

In other cases, the ECJ did not hesitate to bring under the scope of EU law legal issues not directly linked to EU secondary law instruments, like nationality cases[28] or family reunification of family members of sedentary EU citizens.[29] Assuming a comprehensive approach of EU policies and legal framework only produces an erratic case law that is unable to generate guiding principles that are sufficiently consistent. To submit only one part of a policy and the legal instruments adopted to EU law and the Charter

---

27 § 49 of the procedures Directive.

28 ECJ, Case C-135/08 *Rottmann* [2010] EU:C:2010:104.

29 Again, just recently in ECJ, *K.A.*, EU:C:2018:308.

on the basis of formal distinctions is a bad solution, legally speaking, even if we understand that those distinctions are politically motivated.

6. Consequences on the Application of the EU Charter

Family X was not only claiming: 'Belgium, you *can* grant me a visa.' Their underlying argument was: 'Belgium you *must* grant me a visa because of your EU and international human rights obligations.' The obligations in question included the right to remain free from torture and inhumane or degrading treatment under Article 4 of the Charter and the right to claim asylum in accordance with the 1951 Refugee Convention under Article 18 of the Charter.

Was the Charter taken into consideration? The Charter applies only within the scope of EU law, even where Member States have a large margin of appreciation. For instance, concerning the Visa Code in *El Hasani*, the Court ruled in paragraph 36 that

Although it is true that in examining a visa application the national authorities have a broad discretion as regards the conditions for applying the grounds of refusal laid down by the Visa Code and the evaluation of the relevant facts, the fact remains that such discretion has no influence on the fact that the authorities directly apply a provision of EU law.

The Court continued, underlining that it is clear that the Charter is applicable where a Member State adopts a decision to refuse to issue a visa under Article 32(1) of the Visa Code.[30]

The above analysis seems relatively anodyne, for the more novel question is about extraterritoriality, as Family X was at risk of torture and degrading treatment *in Syria.* The Advocate General thought this was irrelevant. The Charter applies within the scope of EU law, regardless of any condition of territoriality. He noted that this conclusion was the necessary corollary to the *Åklagaren* principle that 'situations cannot exist which are covered in that way by EU law without those fundamental rights being applicable'.[31] This means that application of EU law also results in the application of fundamental rights, as both go hand in hand. The criterion is not based on geography but linked to the scope of EU law, which exceeds the territorial bounds of the EU.

---

30 ECJ, Case C-403/16 *El Hassani* [2017] EU:C:2017:960, §§ 36–37.
31 ECJ, Grand Chamber Case C-617/10 *Åklagaren v Fransson* [2013] EU:C:2013:105.

The Charter applies by virtue of EU law without any superadded condition of territoriality. In other words, it is the EU law that 'activates' the Charter, and not the connection to EU soil. To hold otherwise would also have the effect of removing the common visa policy from the purview of fundamental rights protection. The Advocate General went on to state that, unlike the ECHR, which requires an individual to be under the control or authority of the State, the EU Charter applies even when there is no such control or authority. In his view, therefore, it applies extraterritorially, but under *more lax* conditions than the ECHR.

7. *The scope of territorial jurisdiction of the European Convention of Human Rights*

Another argument invoked by the Belgian State was that the Charter, if applicable, had to be interpreted in the same sense as the ECHR. Under Article 52(3):

> In so far as this Charter contains rights which correspond to rights guaranteed by the ECHR, the meaning and scope of those rights shall be the same as those laid down by the said Convention. This provision shall not prevent Union law providing more extensive protection.

Does that 'scope' refer to the territorial scope of the ECHR? If so, the Charter rights are likely to apply, as the ECHR does, even abroad. Does that 'scope' also refer to the jurisdictional limit in Article 1 ECHR which seems to be absent from the Charter?

Those issues call for a clear way in the complex ECHR case law not on extraterritoriality, generally speaking, but on extraterritoriality in asylum and immigration cases. Among the various issues raised by the territorial application of ECHR in those fields, the one that is important here is the applicability to executive or adjudicative measures, which were specifically directed at persons residing abroad.[32]

---

32 Much in line with the passport cases brought before the Human Rights Committee, see namely Communication 125/1982 (Uruguay): '6.1. The Human Rights Committee does not accept the State party's contention that it is not competent do deal with the communication because the author does not fulfil the requirements of article I of the Optional Protocol. The question of the issue of a passport by Uruguay to a Uruguayan national, wherever he may be, is clearly a matter within the jurisdiction of the Uruguayan authorities and he is "subject to the jurisdiction" of Uruguay for that purpose.'.

In *Haydarie*,[33] which concerned the Dutch government's refusal to issue a provisional residence visa to a person living in Pakistan, the Court expressly discarded the argument that the Convention could not apply because the applicant was outside the jurisdiction of the State refusing to issue the visa. The Court considered that, as regards family life at issue in the present case – the existence of which is not in dispute – no distinction could be drawn between the two applicants living in the Netherlands and the three others currently residing in Pakistan. Under these circumstances, it did not find it necessary to answer the government's argument that the three applicants in Pakistan could not be regarded as finding themselves within the jurisdiction of the Netherlands within the meaning of Article 1 of the Convention.

The Court ruled in the same way as in family reunification cases where the applicant was still in their country of origin.[34] In all those family reunification cases, some family members were residents of a Member State. Does this conclusion that the protection is in force when the rights of people living in EU are at stake also apply when that is not the case? One has then to turn to the criteria of effective control, as in *Hirsi*, notwithstanding the fact that in *Hirsi* the applicants were on an Italian boat.

In the Chamber judgment in *Öcalan*,[35] the Court noted that the material difference with *Banković*[36] was that Mr. Öcalan was arrested and then had been physically forced to return to Turkey by Turkish officials; as a re-

33 ECtHR, *Haydarie and others v Netherlands* (2005) No 8876/04.

34 For instance, ECtHR, *Senigo Longue v France*, No 19113/09; *Tanda-Muzinga v France*, No 2260/10; *Ly v France*, No 23851/10; *Mugenzi v France*, No 52701/09.

35 ECtHR, *Ocalan*, No 46221/99.
In this case, the Turkish courts had issued seven arrest warrants for the applicant on the grounds that he had founded an armed band with a view to ending the territorial integrity of the Turkish State and for having instigated acts of terrorism. In February 1999, under controversial circumstances, he was taken on a plane to Nairobi airport in Kenya and interrogated by Turkish officials. He was transferred back to the Turkey. The European Court of Human Rights ruled that the facts fell within the jurisdiction of the Convention. The applicant had been arrested by members of the Turkish law enforcement officers inside an aircraft registered in Turkey, in the international area of Nairobi airport. As soon as he was handed over by Kenyan officials to their Turkish counterparts, the complainant was effectively placed under the authority of Turkey and therefore under the jurisdiction of that State, even though, in this case, Turkey had exercised its authority outside its territory. He had been physically forced by Turkish officials to return to Turkey and had been subject to their authority and guidance. control as soon as he is arrested and returned to Turkey.

36 ECtHR, *Banković*, No 52207/99.

sult, he was 'subject to their authority and control'. In its Grand Chamber judgment, the Court confirmed this proposition and found it 'common ground' that that arrest, followed by a physically enforced return, had brought Mr. Öcalan under the jurisdiction of Turkey[37]. In *Al-Saadoon and Mufdhi v the United Kingdom*,[38] the Court refers to the 'the total and exclusive *de facto*, and subsequently also *de jure*, control exercised over the premises where the individuals were detained'.[39]

In 2014, an interesting inadmissibility decision was made in *Abdul Whabak Khan*.[40] After having resided in the UK for years, he received an order to leave the territory, and finally left the UK for Pakistan. The Court's ruling was as follows:

The application was filed by six persons residing in Belgrade, Serbia. It was directed against 17 NATO Member States that were also parties to the European Convention of human rights. The applicants denounced NATO's bombing of the Serbian Radio and Television Headquarters in Belgrade. This act, committed as part of its air strike campaign during the conflict in Kosovo, had damaged the building and killed several people. As Serbia was not a Member State of the Council of Europe (until 2003), the case raised the question of the territorial application of the Convention.

The Court declared the application inadmissible. It conceded that international law does not exclude extraterritorial exercise of its jurisdiction by a State. However, this jurisdiction is generally defined and limited by the rights of territorial sovereignty of the other States concerned. Other criteria of jurisdiction are exceptional and require special justification, depending on the particular circumstances of each case. She added that the Convention is a multilateral treaty operating in an essentially regional context, and more particularly in the legal space of the Contracting States, of which it was clear that the Federal Republic of Yugoslavia was not part of. Therefore, not being convinced of the existence of any jurisdictional link between victims and Defendant States, the Court declared the application inadmissible.

37 ECtHR, GC, *Oçalan v. Turkey*, N° 6221/99, § 91: 'It is common ground that, directly after being handed over to the Turkish officials by the Kenyan officials, the applicant was effectively under Turkish authority and therefore within the "jurisdiction" of that State for the purposes of Article 1 of the Convention, even though in this instance Turkey exercised its authority outside its territory. It is true that the applicant was physically forced to return to Turkey by Turkish officials and was under their authority and control following his arrest and return to Turkey.'.

38 ECtHR, *Al-Saadoon and Mufdhi v the United Kingdom*, No 61498/08.

39 The main criteria are summarized by the key case *Al Skeini* ruled by the Grand Chamber on the 7 of July 2011.

40 ECtHR, dec., *Abdul Whabak Khan v. United Kingdom*, No. 11987/11.

> A State's jurisdictional competence under Article 1 is primarily territorial'. However, the Court recognised two principal exceptions to this principle, namely circumstances of 'State agent authority and control' and 'effective control over an area (see *Al-Skeini...*). In the present case, where the applicant had returned voluntarily to Pakistan, neither of the two principal exceptions to territorial jurisdiction applied. The Court noted that the applicant did not complain about the acts of British diplomatic and consular agents in Pakistan and remained free to go about his life in the country without any control by agents of the United Kingdom. His position was deemed to be different than those of the applicants in *Al-Saddoon and Mufdhi* (who were in British detention in Iraq and thus, until their handover to the Iraqi authorities, were under British authority and control) and the individuals in *Al-Skeini and others* (who had been killed in the course of security operations conduct by British soldiers in South East Iraq).[41]

The Court continued to distinguish between

> on the one hand, someone who was in the jurisdiction of a Contracting State but voluntarily left that jurisdiction and, on the other, someone who was never in the jurisdiction of that State. Nor is there any support in the Court's case law for the applicant's argument that the State's obligations under Article 3 require it to take this Article into account when making adverse decisions against individuals, even when those individuals are not within its jurisdiction.[42]

For those reasons, the Court ruled that

> there is support in the Court's case law for the proposition that the Contracting State's obligations under Article 8 may, in certain circumstances, require family members to be reunified with their relatives living in that Contracting State. However, that positive obligation rests, in large part, on the fact that one of the family members/applicants is already in the Contracting State and is being prevented from enjoying his or her family life with their relative because that relative has been denied entry to the Contracting State (see, for instance, *Abdulaziz, Cabales and Balkandali*, cited above). The transposition of that limited Article 8 obligation to Article 3 would, in effect, create an unlimited obligation on Contracting States to allow entry to an individual who

---

41 § 25.
42 § 26.

> might be at real risk of ill-treatment contrary to Article 3, regardless of where in the world that individual might find himself. The same is true for similar risks of detention and trial contrary to Articles 5 and 6 of the Convention.[43]

Considering *Al-Saadoon* and applying the criteria of the effective control, how is it possible to consider – even implicitly – that the Belgian State does not effectively exercise authority over its diplomatic offices? A difference could be deduced from the fact that, in the first case, the UK had explicitly decided to exercise its sovereign power in Iraq while the visa applicant was at the consulate at the time of making the application. Such a distinction would leave large parts of public actions on the side, out of the scope of judicial control. It is one thing to say that there is no general obligation to issue a visa, but it is yet another to exclude a decision on a procedure just to maintain its legality.

This decision takes us back to the current Belgian case law. After the ECJ ruling, some new decisions were made by the administrative court on the visa applications submitted by Syrian nationals. Most of the positive ones – that cancelled the administration's decision to reject the visa application – had been processed mostly on the basis of Article 8 ECHR rather than Article 3.[44] As in *Abdul Whabak Khan*, the positive side of Article 8 seems to offer a wider protection than Article 3 despite the absolute character of the protection offered by this provision.

8. *Access to Justice and the Criteria of the Availability of an Alternative*

The debate is not closed. In the short term, it is unfortunate that the last proposal to recast the Visa Code does not include the issue of humanitarian visas. On 11 December 2018, the European Parliament adopted in plenary a legislative initiative report on the introduction of a European humanitarian visa for the purpose of seeking international protection in the European Union.[45] One of the objectives of this measure is to reduce the number of deaths on migration routes. This report proposes the establishment of a humanitarian visa issued in Member States' embassies and consulates in third countries, which would provide persons wishing to apply for international protection the possibility of entering the European territory

---

43 § 27.

44 www.rvv-cce.be/sites/default/files/arr/A199384.AN.pdf.

45 www.europarl.europa.eu/doceo/document/A-8-2018-0328_EN.html?redirect.

through a legal and secure route. This humanitarian visa would give access to the EU territory, but only to the Member State issuing the visa and for the sole purpose of applying for international protection. The last proposal to recast the Visa Code did not follow the parliamentary request.

The following months and years will, of course, force the EU to choose an option for its asylum and immigration policy. *Firstly*, even if a regulation on humanitarian visas is not politically accepted, legal avenues must not be ignored. *Secondly*, even if the option seems to be more oriented to partnerships, resettlements, and subsequently to a collective approach, it is not conceivable to wrest a large part out of the control of the ECJ and the EU Charter in a field where human rights issues are so common yet tricky. *Thirdly*, how to also understand the message sent to the Member States that they are alone in resolving these important, fundamental issues?

A common guidance would have been valuable, because a *common* European asylum system is not a reality until the standards relating to its access are harmonised at the European level. By not meeting the first challenge, the European Union accepts that a significant proportion of immigration to the EU, that of the most vulnerable, is irregular. It then builds itself the spiral of the exit from a rule of law logic. By choosing to regulate immigration through instruments whose legal nature is ambiguous and unjustifiable through the usual channels of democratic control, the EU is creating a marginal policy, outsourced with respect to the institutions. Here, too, it escapes the logic of the rule of law.[46] Finally, by leaving States alone to face a fundamental challenge, EU courts are missing out on the role they can play in organising solidarity, both within and outside Europe.

The victims of the legal vacuum that this creates are firstly those without rights who flee and upon arrival have the greatest need for their rights to be restored. This decision is reminiscent of a recent decision of the European Court of Human Rights in *Naït-Liman* on the question of effective protection of human rights where the crucial issue of applicability was at stake.[47] It concerns the right of a refugee to file a civil claim at a Swiss court for damages relating to torture allegedly suffered in a third State, Tu-

---

46 JY Carlier and F Crépeau, 'Le droit européen des migrations: exemple d'un mouvement sans droit' (2017) *A.F.D.I.*; E Frasca, *Towards a privatisation of international protection? Private Sponsorship programmes in Europe and the Rule of Law*, Call for Papers from the ESIL Interest Group on Migration and Refugee Law: Migration and the Rule of Law.

47 On this case, see especially S Nkenkeu-Keck, 'L'arrêt *Naît-Liman c. Suisse* ou l'occasion manquée par la Cour européenne des droits de l'homme de renforcer l'effectivité du droit des victimes d'obtenir réparation de violation graves des droits

nisia. Specifically, the Grand Chamber examined whether – as a forum of necessity or as a matter of universal civil jurisdiction – the Swiss courts were required by Article 6(1) ECHR to examine the applicant's civil claim for compensation against Tunisia.

Like the Chamber, the Grand Chamber found that this was not the case, and considered that Member States were under no international law obligation to provide universal civil jurisdiction for torture. The Grand Chamber was clearly aware that its judgment could undermine access to redress mechanisms for torture victims: it doubly affirmed the 'broad international consensus recognising the existence of a right for victims of acts of torture to obtain appropriate and effective compensation',[48] commended States that had opened their legal systems to victims of torture abroad, and confirmed the principle of universal criminal jurisdiction.[49] In other words, while it considered that States are not under an obligation to provide for universal civil jurisdiction in torture cases, they are free to do so (like Belgium in *X & X*).

The forum of necessity is a private international law issue distinct from that pertaining to refugees. But both – victims of torture in a civil claim for compensation and those seeking to file an application for international protection – are faced with a search for a jurisdiction to bring them justice. Victims of torture are unable to introduce a case especially in the country of origin where the facts occurred, and those seeking international protection are obliged to escape their country of origin or residence to protect their basic human rights and have no other alternative than to file an application abroad. Such parallels must not just be assumed, but the dissenting opinion in *Naït-Liman* and the Advocate General's opinion in *X & X* underline similar issues about the effectiveness of human rights protection.

This lack of an alternative was emphasised by Advocate General Mengozzi in *X & X*.

> 175. Before concluding, allow me to draw your attention to how much the whole world, in particular here in Europe, was outraged and pro-

---

de l'homme' (2018) 116 *R.T.D.H.* 986; J Kapelanska-Pregowska, 'Extraterritorial jurisdiction of national courts and human rights enforcement: Quo valid Justitia' (2015) *International Community Law review* 425; C Ryngaert, 'From universal civil jurisdiction to forum of necessity: reflections on the judgment of the European Court of Human Rights in Nait-Liman' (2017) 100(3) *Rivista di diritto internazionale* 783; F Krenc, 'Chronique de la jurisprudence de la Cour européenne des droits de l'homme (1er janvier–30 juin 2018)' (2018) 6752 *Journal des tribunaux*.

48 §§ 97 and 218.

49 § 178.

> foundly moved to see, two years ago, the lifeless body of the young boy Alan, washed up on a beach, after his family had attempted, by means of smugglers and an overcrowded makeshift vessel full of Syrian refugees, to reach, via Turkey, the Greek island of Kos. Of the four family members, only his father survived the capsizing. It is commendable and salutary to be outraged. In the present case, the Court nevertheless has the opportunity to go further, as I invite it to, by enshrining the legal access route to international protection which stems from Article 25(1)(a) of the Visa Code. Make no mistake: it is not because emotion dictates this, but because EU law demands it.

This opinion could be read in parallel with two dissenting opinions in *Naït-Liman*. Judge Serguides concluded that 'the dismissal of the applicant's action without an examination of the merits by the Swiss courts impaired the very essence of the applicant's right of access to court' and that his consequent 'inability to seek redress' was 'equivalent to a denial of justice' (see paragraph 18 of that opinion). In other words, the fact that the applicant was precluded from bringing his claim before the Swiss courts amounted, in the circumstances of the present case, not only to a denial of procedural access to justice but also to a denial of effective subjective access to justice, and, in the final analysis, even to a denial of any substantive access to justice at all. Judge Dedov called positivism 'a dark side of international law'.

> We cannot find any morality and justice in international law which, on the one hand, allows tyrants and dictators to enjoy one of the best banking and medical care systems in the world and, on the other hand, refuses access to the courts for their victims. The majority chose to make a legal judgment, not a moral open-ended judgment, although the latter approach would be the most appropriate in the present case.

The development of human rights has led to the emergence of rights with a broad personal and territorial scope. Neither nationality nor administrative status determines the level of human rights guarantees. Although not universal, territorial jurisdiction exceeds the national territory or the territory of the organisation concerned. However, the protection of human rights continues to require institutional access to justice, whether through the possibility of applying to an authority with public authority or to a judge sanctioning non-compliance with the law. However, this access is not guaranteed. No one disputes that the applicants, both in *X & X* and *Naït Liman*, have no alternative to the application they made. The visa requested is intended to ensure access to a place where rights will be protected. The purpose of the proceedings in Switzerland is to obtain compensation for human rights violations. In both cases, the rights concerned belong to the hard core of absolute rights. International human rights jurisprudence has devoted considerable attention to due process and the effectiveness of remedies. Access to the judge before the procedure remains a less developed aspect, in particular through the criterion of the existence of an alternative to the procedural route used.

On this criteria of the availability of an alternative, an interesting parallel could be drawn with family reunification case law in Strasbourg. According the European Court of Human Rights, there is no right to family reunification. In the Grand chamber decision in *Jeunesse*, the judges recall in paragraph 107 that 'where immigration is concerned, Article 8 cannot be considered to impose on a State a general obligation to respect a married couple's choice of country for their matrimonial residence or to authorize family reunification on its territory.'[50]

But, in some cases, a balance between particular circumstances of the persons involved and the general interest could lead to consider that existence of a State's obligations to admit to its territory relatives of persons residing there and to determine the extent of this obligation. According to the Court, 'Factors to be taken into account in this context are the extent to which family life would effectively be ruptured, the extent of the ties in the Contracting State, whether there are insurmountable obstacles in the way of the family living in the country of origin of the alien concerned and whether there are factors of immigration control (for example, a history of breaches of immigration law) or considerations of public order weighing in favour of exclusion'. 'Insurmountable obstacles' are taken into consideration to examine if alternatives exist. When it is not the case, a positive obligation to grant a visa or a permit of stay could exist.

The Court tempered the requirement for such obstacles by noting that while there appeared to be 'no insurmountable obstacles for them to settle in Suriname.' It also reasoned that 'However, it is likely that the applicant and her family would experience a degree of hardship if they were forced to do so. When assessing the compliance of State authorities with their obligations under Article 8, it is necessary to take due account of the situation of all members of the family, as this provision guarantees protection to the whole family'.[51] Other decisions of the Court provide examples of such

---

50 ECtHR, GC, *Jeunesse v. Netherlands*, req. 12738/10, 03/10/2014.
51 Pt 117.

obstacles. They can be deduced from the applicant's refugee status, even if he or she has meanwhile become a citizen of the country of residence. In *Tuquabo-Tekle and others v. the Netherlands*, the Court rejected the State's argument that the mother had left her child in her country of origin 'of her own free will'. The Court recalls that she had left a civil war situation in Eritrea to seek asylum after her husband's death.[52] In the same spirit, in *Mubilanzila v. Belgium*, about a young girl in a detention centre, the Court underlined that 'family life was interrupted only because of the woman's flight from her country of origin out of serious fear of persecution within the meaning of the Geneva Convention of 28 July 1951 relating to the Status of Refugees'.[53] In all those rulings, the fact that there is no real or realistic possibility of a family life elsewhere than in the host country is relevant in the analysis of the case and in the balance carried out.

Moving away from the notion of a 'material' obstacle, the case law also uses the best interests of the child as a criterion for considering that there may be a right to family reunification. 'When children are involved, their best interests must be taken into account.... On this particular point, the Court recalls that there is a broad consensus, particularly in international law, that the best interests of children should be a primary consideration in all decisions affecting them.... This interest alone is certainly not decisive, but it must certainly be given significant weight. In order to ensure that the best interests of children who are directly concerned are effectively protected and given sufficient weight, national decision-making bodies must in principle examine and assess the factors relating to the convenience, feasibility and proportionality of a possible removal of their father or mother who is a third-country national'.[54] This more flexible approach, which combines taking into account the presence of children integrated into the social network of the country of residence and the difficulty of family life in a third country, rather than its impossibility, was already present in some cases. The aim was to find the 'most appropriate' way to allow family life. In the case *Şen v. the Netherlands*, the applicants, legally residing in the Netherlands, wished to be joined by their daughter who had remained in

52 ECtHR, *Tuquabo-Tekle and others v. Netherlands*, 1st December 2005, req. N° 60665/00, pt 47.
See also, in the case of recognized refugees, ECtHR, Mugenzi v. France, 10 July 2014, req. N° 52701/09 and Tanda-Muzinga v. France, 10 July 2014, req. N° 2260/10.

53 ECtHR, *Mubilanzila v. Belgium*, req. 12 October 2006, N° 3178/03, pt 75.

54 ECtHR, GC, *Jeunesse v. Netherlands*, pt 109. In the same sense, Nunez v. Norway, 28 June 2011, req. N° 55597/09, pt 84; Mugenzi v. France, 2014, pt 45.

Turkey for three years. The Court 'takes into account the age of the children concerned, their situation in their country of origin and their degree of dependence on parents'.[55] It concludes that there is a major obstacle to the return of Family Şen to Turkey. However, it seems that this judgment is more flexible than the usual case law of the time, since the Court balances the interests involved without requiring proof of an impossibility of reunification abroad. The arrival of the child in the Netherlands 'was the most appropriate way to develop a family life with her, especially since, given her young age, there was a particular requirement to promote her integration into the family unit of her parents, who were able and willing to take care of her'.[56]

This openness to a logic based on the existence, or not, of an alternative to migration is all the more paradoxical since it occurs here in reference to rights that are not absolute, in particular, not absolute rights such as the prohibition of torture and inhuman and degrading treatment. If the explanation is linked to the presence of family members on the territory of a Council of Europe country, then this criterion should be clarified since the Court does not use such a criterion in other cases where Article 3 is imple-

55 ECtHR, *Şen v. Netherlands*, 21 December 2001, req. N° 31465/96, pt 37. Contra, *Dec. I.A.A. and Others v. United Kingdom* (2016). With regard to the United Kingdom authorities' refusal to allow five children to enter the United Kingdom to be reunited with their mothers, the Court declares inadmissible the complaint based on the violation of Article 8. The mother had joined her second husband in the United Kingdom in 2004, leaving the children behind with her sister in Somalia. The children then moved to Ethiopia. As for the best interests of the child, the Court points out that 'The domestic courts accepted that it would be in the applicants' best interests to be allowed to join their mother in the United Kingdom. However, while the Court has held that the best interests of the child is a "paramount" consideration, it cannot be a "trump card" which requires the admission of all children who would be better off living in a Contracting State [...]. The present applicants' current situation is certainly "unenviable", as the domestic courts found. However, they are no longer young children (they are currently twenty-one, twenty, nineteen, fourteen and thirteen years old) and the Court has previously rejected cases involving failed applications for family reunification and complaints under Article 8 where the children concerned have in the meantime reached an age where they were presumably not as much in need of care as young children and are increasingly able to defend for themselves [...]. All of the applicants have grown up in the cultural or linguistic environment of their country of origin, and for the last nine years they have lived together as a family unit in Ethiopia with the older children caring for their younger siblings. None of the applicants has ever been to the United Kingdom, and they have not lived together with their mother for more than eleven years' (pt 46).

56 ECtHR, *Şen v. Netherlands*, pt 40.

mented in the context of extraterritorial jurisdiction, such as the use of force in Iraq.

While it is certain that claiming respect for fundamental rights in a situation with foreign elements, such as exile or migration, is, in fact, more difficult, these material obstacles must not be exacerbated by legal barriers. In his article on the philosopher Hannah Arendt entitled 'The dynamics of the egalitarian principle in the face of anti-Semitism and other racisms', François Rigaux expressed this fundamental requirement of formal equality.

> Undoubtedly, the egalitarian principle already suffers from deep cultural and economic inequalities, which trace an excessive separation between peoples and between individuals. But it is not the role of the law to reinforce these inequalities by covering them with a formal justification and trying to make them perpetual. On the contrary, the right has a dynamic function, its truth is in the future, not in the past, and the insufficient resources it offers must contribute to dismantling a network of injustices which, although traditional, are no less anachronistic.[57]

Belonging to a State dear to her cannot, as Hannah Arendt puts it, condition the 'right to have rights'. According to her, it is the difference between the rights belonging to a person and the right to claim those rights as belonging to them, which only citizenship guarantees. It shows how important it is, given the loss of authority of the *laws of nature* and religion, to belong to the nation as the basic place that also represents the source of rights that can be claimed. The stateless find themselves without rights within the organised and civilised humanity of nations. Hannah Arendt uses the image of the vicious circle as the process leading to extermination camps, with exclusion gradually taking root and gaining ground.

57 Free translation of: 'Sans doute le principe égalitaire souffre-t-il déjà des profondes inégalités, culturelles, économiques, qui tracent entre les peuples et entre les individus une séparation excessive. Mais ce n'est pas le rôle du droit de renforcer ces inégalités en les couvrant d'une justification formelle et en s'efforçant de les rendre perpétuelles. Au contraire, le droit a une fonction dynamique, sa vérité est dans le futur, non dans le passé, et les ressources insuffisantes qu'il offre doivent contribuer à démanteler un réseau d'injustices qui, pour être traditionnelles, n'en sont pas moins anachroniques', F Rigaux, 'La dynamique du principe égalitaire face à l'antisémitisme et autres racismes', *in* MC Caloz-Tschopp (ed), *Hannah Arendt, les sans-États et le 'droit d'avoir des droits'*, vol 1, Geneva Group 'Violence et droit d'asile en Europe' (Université ouvrière de Genève, L'Harmattan, 1998) 93.

> The civil wars that opened and marked the twenty years of an uncertain peace were not only more cruel and bloody than the previous ones; they led to the immigration of groups that, less happy than their predecessors of the religious wars, were not welcomed anywhere and could not be assimilated anywhere. Once they left their homeland, they found themselves without a homeland; once they abandoned their state, they became stateless; once they were deprived of the rights that their humanity conferred on them, they found themselves without rights, the dregs of the earth.

Hannah Arendt stressed the link between national sovereignty and human rights. Once people are no longer protected by a sovereign national State, they no longer have any guarantee of respect for human rights. Hannah Arendt criticises the human rights ideology for failing to recognise that political affiliation (citizenship, possession of a passport) as being fundamental, rather than the defence of abstract rights that remain fictional in the court of law.

Writing at a time when she was personally confronted with the condition of exile and statelessness, Hannah Arendt was also describing a time before the adoption of international texts protecting fundamental rights on a non-discriminatory basis and the establishment of safeguard mechanisms that could be used by any person regardless of nationality or domicile. These texts exist today but, even if the progress made has been enormous, it is not yet sufficient to cover all the gaps where access to justice remains tenuous. The challenge of the human rights and immigration case law is to prohibit a denial of the 'right to have rights'. Any analysis must be concerned with generating alternatives rather than ascribing the inevitability of a negative legal ruling to the dictates of the legal texts.

Hunting for legal loopholes is a reality in international law. It is at the heart of the 'extradite or punish' clauses, the rules declaring the most serious crimes imprescriptible and the creation of international tribunals to try some of them. The limits to these mechanisms are numerous – from the failure of many States to accede to them to the practical obstacles imposed by cumbersome procedures. These questions relate to the search for justice in a transnational situation.

The *Naït-Liman* decision illustrates the limits of the extension of so-called universal criminal jurisdiction to civil litigation concerning compensation. In criminal law, universal jurisdiction is exercised by a State that prosecutes the perpetrators of certain crimes, regardless of where the crime was committed, and regardless of the nationality of the perpetrators or victims. This is a derogation from the principle of territoriality, which is the basis for the exercise of jurisdiction in criminal matters. According to this norm, a person is prosecuted and tried by the authorities of the State on whose territory the offence was committed in accordance with the law in force in that State. This jurisdiction is combined with other traditional criteria of extraterritorial, but nevertheless classic, jurisdiction in criminal law: active personality, a criterion linked to the nationality of the perpetrator, and passive personality, which allows the State of which the victim is a national the jurisdiction over the matter. Universal jurisdiction refers to systems where the connecting link with the country of the forum is reduced or sometimes abolished.[58]

On the one hand, the problem of immunity was not dealt with in this case as the central issue was territorial jurisdiction. On the other hand, even if the Court considers that the right of victims of torture to obtain compensation, recognised under Swiss law, is a civil right protected by Article 6, it points out that the right of access to a court is not absolute. This right may be subject to limits in relation to which the State has discretion. The State's objective of ensuring the proper administration of justice and the effectiveness of domestic judicial decisions is considered legitimate and the Court understands the need to avoid diplomatic difficulties. As for proportionality, the Court points out that States that recognise universal jurisdiction in civil matters operating autonomously for acts of torture are currently the exception, so that an international custom cannot be identified. As for treaty law, while Article 14 of the Convention against Torture generally enshrines the right of victims of torture to obtain reparation, it is silent on how to effectively implement this right or the geographical scope of the States parties' obligation to do so.

As in international criminal law, in asylum law, the key issue is also the geographic scope of the obligations of the States, but more so even access to a territory where justice could be accessed. Hence, the crucial issue of access to justice as a preamble to a fair procedure is not a new challenge. It was discussed in a plenary hearing of the European Court of Human Rights almost half a century ago in *Golder*.[59] The origin of the legal dispute

---

58 D Vandermeersch, 'La compétence universelle en droit belge', in *Poursuites pénales et extraterritorialité = Strafprocesrech en extraterritorialiteit*, Dossier de la Rev. dr. pén., n°8, 2002, p. 41.
On international jurisdiction, see namely EU Parl., Policy Department for External Relations, F Jeßberger, J Krebs and C Ryngaert, Universal jurisdiction and international crimes: Constraints and best practices, EP/EXPO/B/COMMITTEE/FWC/2013-08/Lot8/21 EN September 2018 -PE 603.878.

59 ECtHR, Golder v United Kingdom, 21 February 1975, Appl. No o. 4451/70.

was the refusal of permission to consult a solicitor with a view to bringing a civil action for libel against a prison officer. The consequence was an exclusion of all matters of access to the courts. The applicant pleaded in Strasbourg that this decision violated Article 6 of the European Convention of Human Rights. The Court ruled:

> It would be inconceivable, in the opinion of the Court, that Article 6 para. 1 should describe in detail the procedural guarantees afforded to parties in a pending lawsuit and should not first protect that which alone makes it in fact possible to benefit from such guarantees, that is, access to a court. The fair, public and expeditious characteristics of judicial proceedings are of no value at all if there are no judicial proceedings.[60]

The British Government had submitted that expressions such as 'fair and public hearing', 'within a reasonable time', 'judgment', 'trial', and the like, clearly presupposed proceedings pending before a court. 'It does not, however, necessarily follow that a right to the very institution of such proceedings is thereby excluded'.[61] Even practically a criminal dispute or a civil procedure could begin prior to the referral procedure of the Trial Court. Returning to the fundamental principles, the Court underlined that the right to submit a claim to a court and the prohibition of denial of justice are some of the universally 'recognised' fundamental principles of law. The decision also highlighted the risk of a narrow interpretation of Article 6.

> Were Article 6 para 1 to be understood as concerning exclusively the conduct of an action which had already been initiated before a court, a Contracting State could, without acting in breach of that text, do away with its courts, or take away their jurisdiction to determine certain classes of civil actions and entrust it to organs dependent on the Government. Such assumptions, indissociable from a danger of arbitrary power, would have serious consequences which are repugnant to the aforementioned principles and which the Court cannot overlook.[62]

The message is clear, and entirely dedicated to a useful effect of the protection regime. The Court used a well-known phrasing: 'The Convention is

60 ECtHR, Golder, pt 35.
61 ECtHR, Golder, pt 32.
62 ECtHR, Golder, pt 34.

intended to guarantee not rights that are theoretical or illusory but rights that are practical and effective'.[63]

In the torts case of *Naït Liman*, the case law should accept going a step further than in *Golder*, even ruling in the same spirit. In this leading case, the Court of Strasbourg had to extend the material scope of a right but not to discuss its territorial scope. The right of access to justice in *Nait Liman* or in asylum is located upstream of access to the judicial institution itself, since it concerns the issue of whether the applicant is able to access a State which acknowledges an obligation towards him or her. In *Golder*, the Court emphasised that it was not enough for the proceedings before the judge to be fair. In asylum matters, it was not enough that a refugee right exists or that the principle of non-refoulement is guaranteed, it is necessary to have access to the debtor of these rights. A State that guarantees them must have obligations towards the asylum seeker. However, to do so, it is necessary, as the case law considers it, to have entered a geographical area where the State is bound by this obligation. This precondition is particularly paradoxical for the asylum seeker who is, by definition, in an extraterritorial situation that characterises flight. When called upon to rule, will the Strasbourg Court, as in *Golder*, opt for a teleological interpretation, giving useful effect to a right guaranteed by the Convention – here Article 6, here Article 3? The question is not as simple. The elasticity of the substantive scope of rights seems more natural than that of their territorial scope, even though in the end, in the light of the criterion of useful effect, the issues are similar.

9. *Bridging the Gaps in Access to Justice: the Global Compact for Refugees*

To avoid these gaps, one of the solutions lies in better cooperation. However, binding solutions must be adopted where there is a strong reluctance to do so.

A new instrument in asylum governance is the Global Compact for Refugees.[64] The Compact is in line with the process initiated in New York. The New York Declaration for Refugee and Migrants,[65] adopted by the

63 ECtHR, Golder, pt 18; see also *Airey c. Ireland*, 9 October 1979, Appl. N° 289/73, pt 24.

64 www.unhcr.org/gcr/GCR_English.pdf.

65 New York Declaration for Refugee and Migrants and Global Compact for Refugees, UN GAOR, Seventy-one Session, Agenda Items 13 and 117, UN Doc A/RES/71/1 (3 October 2016) ('New York Declaration').

United Nations at the General Assembly in September 2015, expressed the need to broaden the number and range of legal channels available for refugees admitted or resettled in third countries.[66] The need for more global solidarity was presented as a key issue for the future. The aim was to 'provide resettlement places and other legal pathways for admission on a scale that would enable the annual resettlement needs identified by the Office of the United Nations High Commissioner for Refugees to be met'.[67]

The Global Compact for Refugees consolidates those commitments. It was drafted by the UN High Commissioner for Refugees (UNHCR) in consultation with governments and other actors and adopted by the UN General Assembly in December 2018.

> The objectives of the global compact as a whole are to: (i) ease pressures on host countries; (ii) enhance refugee self-reliance; (iii) expand access to third country solutions; and (iv) support conditions in countries of origin for return in safety and dignity. The global compact will seek to achieve these four interlinked and interdependent objectives through the mobilization of political will, a broadened base of support, and arrangements that facilitate more equitable, sustained and predictable contributions among States and other relevant stakeholders.[68]

Just this sentence indicates that no binding mechanisms have emerged. This Compact evokes a wide range of reactions. They depend on the point of departure. The highly integrated system that the Compact offers does not represent an adequate response for meeting the diverse challenges at hand faced by migrants and host countries. At the same time, effective solutions are expected within the framework of the obligation of result as opposed to the obligation of means or conduct, which requires reasonable action towards the achievement of the desired result. It is important to distinguish between different categories of host countries so that the mechanisms put in place and the tools allocated directly respond to the positions

66 Point 77.

67 Point 78. 'Humanitarian admission programs, temporary evacuation programs such as evacuation for medical reasons, flexible arrangements to assist family reunification, private sponsorship for individual refugees and opportunities for labor mobility for refugees, including through private sector partnerships, and for education, such as scholarships and student visas figure among the opportunities to expand refugee admission.' (Point 79.).

68 Point 7.

they take with respect to migration and how that benefits refugees and asylum seekers.

The Compact offers African countries tools to build long-term solutions with refugees that are already on their territory. Fatima Khan and Cecile Sackeyfio[69] note that 'the Refugee Compact is also criticised for not changing the spatial allocation of refugees'. But

> while that may be the case, for the many women and children languishing in camps, the Compact can make a difference to 'the sheer waste of human potential' that is currently the *status quo*. As it stands, only a minority of refugees within African States can seek refuge elsewhere. Many are located within the African continent, often fleeing to neighbouring countries. Because of this, it remains important to nuance the responsibility-sharing dialogue. International cooperation to meet refugees *where they are* will do much not only to help host countries prosper, but to equalise opportunities for refugees within African nations'.

They advocate that

> in conclusion, it remains crucial to focus on the ways in which the Refugee Compact can benefit refugees, host communities, and host countries in Africa: that is, by addressing issues affecting resource-strained host countries and countries of origin that face large numbers of fleeing and repatriating people, but lack the mechanisms to cope. The Refugee Compact's human rights and humanitarian perspective has shifted the framework within which the refugee question is situated, to one which produces robust and tangible solutions: for refugee self-reliance and integration into urban spaces; for decreased usage of and need for refugee camps; for assessments of the reasons people seek refuge; and for shared and equitable international responsibility.

For Western countries facing the significant issue of access to their territory, the solutions proposed are weak. In 'The Global Cop-Out on Refugees', James Hathaway clarifies that

> the first and most critical priority—ironically not even addressed in the Global Compact—is access to protection. While we ought to promote assisted entry wherever that is feasible, the non-negotiable base-

---

69 F Khan and C Sackeyfio, 'What Promise Does the Global Compact on Refugees Hold for African Refugees?' (2019) *International Journal of Refugee Law*, eez002, https://doi.org/10.1093/ijrl/eez002.

> line commitment must be that refugees be allowed to access the international protection system in whatever country they can reach. No more barriers to entry, no more politics of *non-entrée*.'

The Compact does not meet this crucial challenge of the Global North (and other silent regions) to take their part, organise lawful access and real solidarity. It 'doesn't dependably get refugees to a place of protection; doesn't ensure dignified and empowering protection for the duration of risk; doesn't require meaningful burden and responsibility sharing; and doesn't guarantee solutions either for refugees or for their host communities'. He concludes,

> I think we need to call out this 'Compact' for what it really is—a 'cop-out'. We should be clear that we do not need a Compact 'on' refugees, in which refugees are simply the object, not the subject, of the agreement. It is high time for a reform that puts refugees—all refugees, wherever located—first, and which recognises that keeping a multilateral commitment to refugee rights alive requires not caution, but rather courage.

Cooperation mechanisms are essential but not sufficient. They allow exchanges of points of view and thus the adoption, or at least the hearing, of a different viewpoint. They are the best guarantee of measures and rules that target a problem as a whole, without legal gaps, and give impetus for further cooperation. But as a place for discussion, they can be sterile and dictated by political agendas. Without a binding instrument, especially considering that States are reluctant to assume obligations, blind spots remain. Asylum seekers seeking legal access to places of protection and justice are located firstly within the domain of the State, and especially asylum seekers who are victims of torture need the State for legal access to justice and protection. Even more than any other, borders must be places of law and not of lawlessness. Multiple risks, both actual and of denial of justice, converge there. This reality covers both the geographical borders of States and the borders of legal systems. If we fail to fill each gap, the weakest among us would be excluded from any protection.

In 'No Country, No Cry', Olivera Jokic[70] offers a timely reflection on gendered violence in migration contexts, which resonates paradoxically after decades of affirming and seeking some form of universal human rights

70 O Jokic, No country, no cry: Literature of women's displacement and the reading of pity, *Journal of Postcolonial Writing*, Volume 54, 2018 - Issue 6: Special issue: Refugee Literature, Pages 781-794.

protection. Especially for migrants and exiles, these rights stop at the border gates. Too often the judicial response is haunted by the fear of a resulting influx of claims for protection and compensation proceedings. However understandable that may be, the reflection should rather focus on how guaranteed rights risk being compromised if *places of effective protection* do not exist. It is one thing to ask about the risk of spill over from denunciations of violations, it is yet another to consider the actual risk to the substance of the rights if there is no hospitable port in which to moor.

Part 2.
Humanitarian Admission Under Domestic Law. Between Formalised Procedures and Informal Practices

Chapter 4: Humanitarian Admission to Italy through Humanitarian Visas and Corridors

Katia Bianchini[1]

Contents

---

1 Research Fellow in the Department of Law & Anthropology of the Max Planck Institute for Social Anthropology.

1 Introduction

This chapter offers insights on how humanitarian visas provide a complementary legal pathway to Europe by focusing on the Italian case. The key research question is to identify the legislation and practices on humanitarian visas in Italy. The chapter devotes particular attention to the implementation of the 'humanitarian corridors' (HCs), a programme set up by various Faith Based Organisations (FBOs) in collaboration with the Italian government in order to ensure safe arrivals of asylum seekers and vulnerable persons from countries of first refuge outside Europe. The HCs have been the only instance where Italy has used humanitarian visas on a relevant scale.

In section 2, the chapter explains what the HCs are, their legal basis, the essential elements, the selection criteria and processes, and how they are organised and implemented. It argues that the use of humanitarian visas through the model of the HCs can be replicated, but a number of risks also need to be addressed, including the problem of excessive reliance on the goodwill of the government in power for their realisation, uncertainty in the selection process of the beneficiaries, lack of due process guarantees, and burden shifting of essentially State functions to civil society. Accordingly, although the HCs represent a good practice, they cannot be an alternative to the current systems of reception or resettlement. In section 3, the chapter briefly sketches out few other situations where humanitarian visas have been used to ensure safe entry to refugees and critically notes that such instances have been limited to situations of emergencies. Section 4 summarises the findings and concludes that, to have a significant impact and comply with the international obligations, humanitarian visas shall be developed through legislation and through a harmonised approach at the European level. Section 5 explores whether and how a common EU framework on humanitarian visas is desirable, explores arguments in favour and against it, and makes policy recommendations.

It should be noted that, because the use of humanitarian visas in Italy is very recent, there is little literature available on the subject and some pieces of information are also conflicting. Therefore, I have integrated the texts with data from thirteen semi-structured interviews of experts and stakeholders in order to gain insights into how humanitarian visas are issued and how the humanitarian corridors programme works in practice.

The names of a minority of interviewees who requested that they not be disclosed are anonymised. The interviews were carried out in Italian, my mother tongue, and by telephone or Skype. I identified the interviewees through previous published research, publicly available information on the organisations' websites, as well as their own contacts and networks. In preparing for the interviews, I prioritised flexibility. Although I had written down a list of questions I wanted to ask, I allowed the respondents to expand, digress, or even talk about a particular topic and their own concerns,[2] so that many questions I ended up asking arose in the course of the conversation. I took notes during the interviews, and then asked the respondents to check their accuracy. I double-checked the data of the interviews with the information gathered through primary text sources and connected them to the literature and wider academic debates.

2 *Humanitarian corridors for beneficiaries of protection*

The HCs were born as a two-year-pilot project at the end of 2015 in response to the dangerous journeys and arrivals of refugees and migrants by sea. Indeed, the Central Mediterranean route, which connects North Africa (especially Libya and Egypt) to Italy is considered the deadliest migration route in the world. It is estimated that more than 15,200 people died between 2014 and February 2019.[3]

2 C Robson, *Real World Research*, 3rd edn (Förlag, John Wiley Sons, 2011) 280.

3 IOM, 'The Central Mediterranean Route: Migrant Fatalities. January 2014 – July 2017' (31 July 2017) 1 missingmigrants.iom.int/central-mediterranean-route-migrant-fatalities-january-2014-july-2017; IOM, 'Deaths by Route – Central Mediterranean Route' (February 2019) https://missingmigrants.iom.int/region/mediterranean?migrant_route%5B%5D=1376.

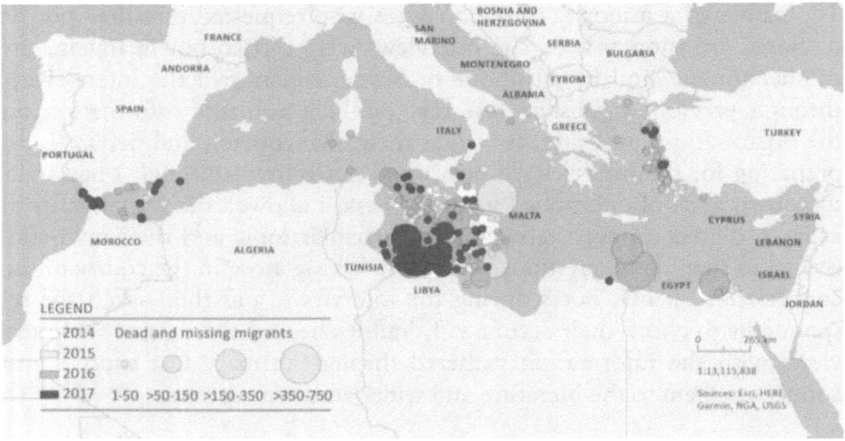

Source: IOM, 'The Central Mediterranean route: Migrant Fatalities. January 2014 – July 2017' (31 July 2017) 1 missingmigrants.iom.int/central-mediterranean-route-migrant-fatalities-january-2014-july-2017.

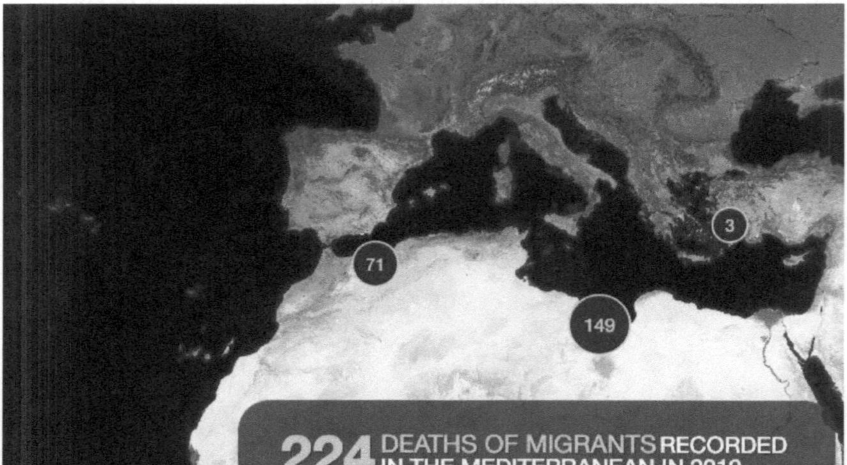

Source: IOM, 'Deaths by Route' (28 February 2019) https://missingmigrants.iom.int/region/mediterranean?.

In particular, the impetus for the realisation of the HCs came following the death of at least 800 migrants of multiple nationalities (including Syrian, Eritrean and Somali), which occurred while they were attempting to cross the Mediterranean on a shipwreck on 19 April 2015.[4] This tragedy brought the FBOs and other civil society actors together to study, propose and advocate for a safe and legal pathway for refugees to Italy. The outcome, after long negotiations with the Italian government, was the creation of the HCs. In brief, the HCs' aim is to allow the most vulnerable migrants and refugees to gain access to humanitarian visas, safe passage to Italy, lodge an asylum application upon arrival and encourage integration.[5] The participating associations, which are all FBOs, act as sponsors and cover most of the cost of the programme, including the reception and integration services.[6]

The next sub-sections explain in detail how the HCs work, placing particular emphasis on their legal basis, procedures, criteria for selection of the beneficiaries, and reception in Italy, with a view to assess their replicability as well as their shortcomings.

---

4 A Bonomolo and S Kirchgaessner, 'UN Says 800 migrants Dead in Boat Disaster as Italy Launches Rescue of Two More Vessels' *The Guardian* (Rome, 20 April 2015) www.theguardian.com/world/2015/apr/20/italy-pm-matteo-renzi-migrant-shipwreck-crisis-srebrenica-massacre; Interview with P Naso, Professor of History and Religion, Faculty of Literature, Sapienza University, and Coordinator, Mediterranean Hope Project (Rome, Italy, 26 April 2018).

5 Ministero degli Affari Esteri e della Cooperazione Internazionale, Minsitero dell' Interno e Comunita' di Sant'Egidio, Federazione delle Chiese Evangeliche e Tavola Valdese, 'Protocollo Tecnico per la Realizzazzione del Progetto "Apertura di Corridori Umanitari"' (15 dicembre 2015) ('Protocollo 15 dicembre 2015') 3-4; Ministero delgli Affari Esteri e della Cooperazione Internazionale, Ministero dell' Interno e Conferenza Episcopale Itlaiana e Comunita' di Sant'Egidio, 'Protocollo Tecnico per la Realizzazzione del Progetto "Apertura di Corridori Umanitari"' (12 gennaio 2017) ('Protocollo 12 gennaio 2017') 4-5; Ministero delgli Affari Esteri e della Cooperazione Internazionale, Minsitero dell' Interno e Comunita' di Sant'Egidio, Federazione delle Chiese Evangeliche e Tavola Valdese, 'Protocollo Tecnico per la Realizzazzione del Progetto "Apertura di Corridori Umanitari"' (7 novembre 2017) ('Protocollo 7 novembre 2017') 2-3; Ministero delgli Affari Esteri e della Cooperazione Internazionale, Minsitero dell' Interno e Conferenza Episcopale Itlaiana e Comunita' di Sant'Egidio, 'Protocollo Tecnico per la Realizzazzione del Progetto "Apertura di Corridori Umanitari"' (3 maggio 2019) ('Protocollo 3 maggio 2019') 2-3; M Collyer, M Mancinelli, F Petito, 'Humanitarian Corridors: Safe and Legal Pathways to Europe' (Policy Briefing, University of Sussex, Autumn 2017) 1.

6 P Morozzo della Rocca, 'I Due Protocolli d'Intesa sui "Corridori Umanitari" tra Alcuni Enti di Ispirazione Religiosa ed il Governo ed il loro Possibile Impatto sulle Politiche di Asilo e Immigrazione' (2017) 1 *Diritto, Immigrazione e Cittadinanza* 1, 9.

2.1 Legal basis of the humanitarian corridors

There is no provision in Italian legislation regarding the issuance of humanitarian visas. However the HCs became possible because they could be set up without adopting new legislation and within the existing legal and operational framework by relying on *Article 25 of Regulation n. 810/2009 of 13 July 2009* (Visa Code).[7] This Article provides Member States the possibility of issuing, in exceptional cases, visas with limited territorial validity for humanitarian reasons, national interest or on the grounds of international obligations. What is meant by 'humanitarian reasons' has not been clearly defined, but State practice shows that these kinds of visas have been issued for health reasons or protection needs.[8]

Article 25 must be read together with Article 1, which sets out the scope of the Code and states that the intended stay must not be longer than three months. There is no separate procedure in the Visa Code for lodging and considering an application for a humanitarian visa.

Despite the recent case of *X and X v Belgium*,[9] it is believed that Article 25 of the Visa Code can still be used as the legal basis for setting up humanitarian corridors in the future.[10] In that case, the issue at stake was whether Belgium had an obligation to issue a humanitarian visa to allow the applicants to travel to Belgium and apply for asylum there. However, the Court declined to reply and held that this was a matter of national law. In the case of the HCs, however, the parties involved do not intend to create any subjective right to a humanitarian visa.

7 Regulation (EC) 810/2009 establishing a community Code on Visas (Visa Code) [2009] OJ L 243/1, art 25; Protocollo 15 dicembre 2015 (n 5) 3 para 11(c); Protocollo 12 gennaio 2017 (n 5) art 4(c); Protocollo 7 novembre 2017 (n 5) 3 para 11(c); S Trotta, 'Safe and Legal Passages to Europe: A Case-Study of Faith-Based Humanitarian Corridors to Italy' (2017) UCL Migration Research Unit, Working Papers 2017/5, 27; Mediterranean Hope, 'Migrant Humanitarian Corridors Greenlighted in Italy' (1 January 2016) www.mediterraneanhope.com/2016/01/01/migrant-humanitarian-corridors-greenlighted-in-italy/; Sant'Egidio, 'Dossier: What are the Humanitarian Corridors' (29 February 2016) archive.santegidio.org/pageID/11676/langID/en/Humanitarian-Corridors-for-refugees.html.

8 U I Jensen, 'Humanitarian Visas: Option or Obligation?' (PE 509.986, European Parliament 2014) 41-48.

9 Opinion in C-638/16 *PPU X and X v Belgium* [2017] 4 WLR 89.

10 Interview with C Hein, Board Member and Founder, Italian Refugee Council, and Adjunct Professor, Department of Political Science, Luiss University (Rome, Italy, 26 April 2018).

In terms of the legal instrument chosen to carry out the programme, the parties agreed that it would be a '*protocollo*' (or, as labelled in the international context, 'Memorandum of Understanding' – MoU). An MoU is an administrative document which sets forth the aims, procedures, tools, responsibilities of the parties, as well as the validity and timeline of the project. MoUs are based on the collaboration between parties that intend to reach a common goal and normally do not have a legally binding force. They are more similar to a 'gentlemen's agreement' than a contract.[11] The MoUs of the HCs leave wide discretion to the administration and are written in carefully drafted general terms which allow the government to remain in as much control as possible. The MoUs create political and institutional responsibilities, but are not driven by the aim of creating enforceable subjective rights and making the visa process legally binding.

In regards to the use of *private sponsorship* on the part of the FBOs, the MoUs refer to the European Agenda on Migration, which hopes that the Member States use all legal channels to help people in need of protection, including assistance from private individuals and non-governmental organisations, humanitarian visas and family reunion.[12] Moreover, the MoU of 7 November 2017 mentions a European Commission's Communication of 27 April 2017, which recommends private sponsorships among other initiatives that States should support in order to increase the numbers of lawful entries into the country.[13]

2.2 *The MoUs for the humanitarian corridors: signatories, selection of countries and number of humanitarian visas*

The pilot project was set up by religious organisations and the Italian government with the first MoU in 2015 and was further expanded with two further MoUs in 2017 and one in 2019. In particular, the first MoU was signed on 15 December 2015 between the Federation of Protestant

11 S Calassi, 'L' Attivita' Amministrativa Negoziata nell' Analisi di Alcune Fattispecie nella Legislazione della Provincia Autonoma di Trento' (Master dissertation, Trentino School of Management 2011) 20.

12 Commission, 'A European Agenda on Migration' (Communication) COM (2015) 240 final. See: Protocollo 15 dicembre 2015 (n 5), 2 para 3; Protocollo 12 gennaio 2017 (n 5) 2 para 2; Protocollo 7 novembre 2017 (n 5) 2 para 3; Protocollo 3 maggio 2019 (n 5) para 7.2.

13 Commission, 'Delivery of the European Agenda on Migration' (Communication) COM (2017) 558 final; Protocollo 9 novembre 2017 (n 5) 2 para 4.

Churches (FCEI),[14] the Waldensian Church,[15] the Catholic Community of *Sant'Egidio*[16] and the Ministries of Interior and of Foreign Affairs. The second MoU was signed on 12 January 2017 between the Community of *Sant'Egidio*, the *Conferenza Episcopale Italiana* (Italian Episcopal Conference – CEI)[17] and the Ministries of Interior and of Foreign Affairs.[18] The third MoU had the same signatories as the first one, and was signed on 7 November 2017. The most recent MoU extended the MoU signed on 12 January 2017 and was signed on 3 May 2019 by Sant' Egidio, CEI and the Ministries of Interior and of Foreign Affairs.[19] The four MoUs, are very similar, apart from the descriptive part of the legal justifications in those dated 7 November 2017 and 3 May 2019, mainly due to references to latest declarations of the European Commission. Their aims, procedures, and implementation are the same.

On the basis of the first MoU, in the first six months, the Italian government agreed to issue a maximum of 150 humanitarian visas for persons in Morocco and 250 in Lebanon. At the end of the first six-month-period of its signing, it was agreed that, upon successful completion of the first phase, the project would be extended to Ethiopia, with the aim of involving, in particular, potential beneficiaries of protection from Eritrea, Soma-

---

14 FCEI was founded in 1967 and is comprised of various protestant Churches, including the Italian Evangelic Lutheran Church, Waldensian Church, Methodist Church, Salvation Army International, Christian Evangelical Baptist Union, Apostolic Church and St. Andrew's Church of Scotland in Rome. FCEI, 'Le Chiese Membro della FCEI' www.fcei.it/membri/.

15 The Waldensian Church is one of the Evangelic Churches. Chiesa Evangelica Valdese, 'Ci Presentiamo' www.chiesavaldese.org/aria_cms.php?page=16.

16 Sant'Egidio is a Catholic community founded in 1968. Over time, it has become a network of communities in more than 70 countries. Its activities focus on prayer, help for the poor, work for peace, and communicating the gospel. Sant'Egidio, 'The Community' www.santegidio.org/pageID/30008/langID/en/THE-COMMUNITY.html.

17 The CEI is the permanent assembly of Italian Bishops. It is a body which has particular importance regarding the relationship between the Italian State and the Catholic Church. Chiesa Cattolica Italiana www.chiesacattolica.it/la-conferenza-episcopale-italiana/.

18 Ministero delgli Affari Esteri e della Cooperazione Internazionale, Minisqtero dell' Interno e Comunita' di Sant'Egidio, Federazione delle Chiese Evangeliche e Tavola Valdese, 'Protocollo di Intesa per la Realizzazzione del Progetto "Apertura di Corridori Umanitari"' ('Protocollo 2017').

19 A Sofia, 'Intesa sui Corridori Umanitari al Viminale ma Salvini non c'e'.' *Il Fatto Quotidiano* (4 May 2019) www.ilfattoquotidiano.it/2019/05/04/intesa-sui-corridoi-umanitari-al-viminale-ma-salvini-non-ce-cei-attacca-caritas-al-lavoro-per-migranti-e-italiani/5153585/.

lia and South Sudan. Morocco and Lebanon were chosen on the grounds of being key 'transit countries' for high numbers of refugees and because of the presence of several organisations and Churches already involved in the matter.[20] Specifically, in Lebanon, the beneficiaries are mostly people fleeing from regional conflicts, and especially families and vulnerable persons[21] from Syria. In regards to Morocco, the beneficiaries of the project were meant to be both Syrians with preference for those recognized *prima facie* refugees by the UNHCR, and people in conditions of particular vulnerability coming from Sub-Saharan Africa. In total, the Italian government agreed to issue a maximum of 1,000 humanitarian visas between 2016 and 2017.[22] However, in Morocco, the project was not implemented, as the Moroccan authorities feared a pull-factor.[23] In Ethiopia, due to operational matters, it was not possible to issue visas under the first MoU, but only with the MoU of 12 January 2017. Under this agreement, a maximum of 500 humanitarian visas could be granted between 2018 and 2019.[24]

With the MoU dated 7 November 2017, the project has been further expanded in Morocco and Lebanon, with the aim of issuing a maximum of 1,000 humanitarian visas between 2018 and 2019.[25]

Finally, the MoU of 2019 saw the establishment of the humanitarian corridors in Ethiopia, Jordan, and Niger, where 600 humanitarian visas are to be issued between July 2019 and 2021.[26] Although the text of the MoU does not specify it, the inclusion of Niger was due to the need of providing

20 The choice of Lebanon was also based on the consideration of the many hosted Syrian refugees. Lebanon has a population of about 4 million people and hosts about 1.2 million refugees. Besides the Syrian refugees, the country hosts half a million Palestinians in camps. As a consequence, the country is overwhelmed by refugees. 'Beyond Good Intentions: Creating Safe Passage to Italy' (2016) 1 *Security Community* 30-31.

21 Section 2.3 of this chapter will further discuss the criteria of selection and how 'vulnerability' is understood.

22 Protocollo 15 dicembre 2015 (n 5) art 5.

23 Interview with D Pompei, Coordinator, Humanitarian Corridors for the Community of Sant'Egidio (Rome, Italy, 3 May 2018); Interview with O Forti, National Coordinator, Humanitarian Corridors for Caritas (Rome, Italy, 7 February 2019).

24 Protocollo 12 gennaio 2017 (n 5) art 5.

25 Protocollo 7 november 2017 (n 5) art 5.

26 The Protocol states that, with the agreement of the government, the period can be extended for another year if necessary. It also states that, with the agreement of the government, the programme can include persons who transit through other countries. Protocollo 3 maggio 2019 (n 5) art 5. Farnesina, 'Protocollo Tecnico per l' Apertura dei Corridori Umanitari' (6 May 2019) www.esteri.it/mae/it/

durable solutions to refugees the UNHCR evacuates from immigration detention centres in Libya.[27]

The total number of visas issued as of the end of January 2019 stood at 1,403 for people in Lebanon, and 500 for Ethiopia under the MoU of 12 January 2017.[28] It is reported that, an addendum to the MoU of 12 January 2017 modified it to include Iraqi Christians who had fled to Turkey as well Syrians with serious medical needs in Jordan who needed to be evacuated.[29]

2.3 *The process of identification and selection of beneficiaries for the humanitarian corridors*

The MoUs provide only general guidance on the essential steps in the process of examining beneficiaries' identification and issuing the humanitarian visas. The FBOs involved are in charge of preparing the list of potential beneficiaries and following the process from the beginning to the very end. The selection of the beneficiaries is made through actors on the field and takes a few months. For example, in Lebanon, the FBOs rely on two associations: Mediterranean Hope (a project of the Federation of Evangelical Churches – FCEI – and the Waldensian Church)[30] and *Operazione Colomba* (a project of the Community Papa Giovanni XIII). *Operazione Colomba* was chosen because their volunteers live in the refugee camp of Tel Abbas, they know the situation on the ground, and can help to build the beneficiaries'

sala_stampa/archivionotizie/comunicati/protocollo-tecnico-per-l-apertura-di-corridoi-umanitari.html.

27 Sir Agenzia d' Informazione, 'Corridori Umanitari: Forti (Caritas), "Al Via Secondo Protocollo anche dal Niger, Primi Arrivi tra Luglio e Ottobre, 47 Diocesi Coinvolte"' (3 May 2019) www.agensir.it/quotidiano/2019/5/3/corridoi-umanitari-forti-caritas-al-via-secondo-protocollo-anche-dal-niger-primi-arrivi-tra-luglio-e-ottobre-47-diocesi-coinvolte/.

28 Interview with S Scotta, Operator, Mediterranean Hope in Lebanon (Beirut, Lebanon, 28 January 2019).

29 Interview with Forti (n 23). Twenty persons were evacuated in Turkey and Jordan. Interview with C Pani, Head of Humanitarian Corridors in Ethiopia, Comunita' di Saint' Egidio (Rome, Italy, 15 February 2019).

30 Mediterranean Hope, 'Chi Siamo. Corridori Umanitari' www.mediterraneanhope.com/corridoi-umanitari/.

trust with the sponsoring FBOs.[31] Referrals from the UNHCR, *Medici Senza Frontiere* (Doctors Without Borders) and other organisations are also considered by the FBOs. In Ethiopia, the community of *Sant'Egidio* is directly on the field and makes the selection with the operational help of the CEI through Caritas and *Migrantes.*[32] The UNHCR, local churches, NGOs, as well as relatives or friends of beneficiaries in Italy may also refer individuals.[33] However, the beneficiaries themselves cannot make an application to be included in the programme.

The potential beneficiaries are carefully selected and undergo interviews[34] that allow an assessment of their needs, vulnerabilities, the urgency of the situation, and whether they can integrate and intend to stay in Italy upon arrival, as further explained in the next sub-section.

The list of beneficiaries is presented to the Italian embassy and the national authorities of the host country to carry out security checks and exclude pending legal cases. The list of potential beneficiaries is then screened by the Italian Ministry of Interior to prevent threats to the national security and public order. Whereas no particular problems have been encountered for the project in Ethiopia, it is reported that several cases were denied in Lebanon.[35] As there is no obligation on the part of the Italian authorities to give any explanation in case of refusal, the exact reasons for such decisions are unknown. According to the interviewees, it is likely that some cases were rejected because they could create diplomatic problems with countries of first asylum (for example, in situations of persons with multiple nationalities) or concerned people coming from areas where terrorist groups are active.[36] Others were denied because beneficiaries were

---

31 Interview with Coordinator, Community of Sant'Egidio (Rome, Italy, 19 April 2018); Operazione Colomba, 'Dove Siamo. Libano-Sirya. Progetto' www.operazionecolomba.it/dove-siamo/libano-siria/libanosiria-progetto.html.

32 Interview with Naso (n 4); Interview with Pompei (n 23); A Gagliardi, 'Corridori Umanitari, a Fiumicino 30 Profughi Siriani dal Libano' *Il Sole 24 Ore* (30 January 2018) www.ilsole24ore.com/art/notizie/2018-01-29/corridoi-umanitari-fiumicino-30-profughi-siriani-libano-160005.shtml?uuid=AEyDzpqD.

33 Interview with Pani (n 29).

34 The interviews are conducted by the FBOs or by local actors on behalf of the FBOs in refugee camps or temporary private accommodations. The interviews are then vetted by the FBOs' offices in Rome. Interview with B Chioccioli, Project and Communication Officer, Mediterranean Hope (Rome, Italy, 12 May 2018).

35 Interview with Scotta (n 28); Interview with G de Monte, Journalist, Communication Office, Mediterranean Hope (Rome, Italy, 12 February 2019).

36 Interview with Chioccioli (n 34). Refugees in Ethiopia are usually poorer than those in Lebanon, are seldom involved in politics, and attract fewer security concerns than refugees from the Middle East. Interview with Pani (n 29).

suspected of potentially engaging in secondary movements due to family links in other EU countries.[37]

For cases from Lebanon, the Italian Ministry of Interior may ask the UNHCR whether the information is consistent with the filed information and, if not, the case may not proceed.[38] For cases from Ethiopia, Turkey and Jordan, the UNHCR has been more involved since the beginning of the procedure and this situation does not occur.[39]

In case of approval, the list is forwarded to the Ministry of Foreign Affairs who will communicate to the consular authorities about the issuance of a visa with limited territorial validity in order to arrive in Italy.[40] In case of refusal, there is no right of appeal.

Before departure, the beneficiaries are required to take part in awareness sessions on the cultural, linguistic and social aspects of European culture and society. Once the beneficiaries receive their humanitarian visas and travel documents, the sponsoring associations will deal with their transfer to the Italian territory and pay the costs. [41]

2.4 Criteria to identify the beneficiaries

Central to the aim of the HCs is the provision of a safe and alternative means to dangerous migration routes to Europe and seek protection. Such an alternative is, however, available only to those who are identified as 'priority groups'. As any other humanitarian or resettlement programme, the HCs face the reality of choosing the beneficiaries from a large pool of refugees in need and justifying such choices.[42] Thus, according to the

---

37 Interview with Scotta (n 28).

38 ibid.

39 Interview with Forti (n 23). In Ethiopia, the government requires refugees to be registered with the UNHCR. Interview with Pani (n 29).

40 Collyer (n 5) 3. In Lebanon, the Italian consular authorities are in charge of issuing travel documents in case of lack of a passport, whereas in Ethiopia the Ethiopian government is responsible for that. To issue a travel document, the Ethiopian government requires the refugee to be registered with the UNHCR and reside in the place of registration. Interview with Pani (n 29).

41 Collyer (n 5) 3.

42 D Fassin, 'Inequalities of Lives, Hierarchies of Humanity: Moral Commitments and Ethical Dilemmas of Humanitarism' in I Feldman and M Ticktin (eds), *In the Name of Humanity: the Government of Threat and Care* (Durham, Duke University Press, 2010) 239-40; H C Markay, 'The Corridors Through the Keyhole: An Analysis of the Humanitarian Corridors Programme from Lebanon and Ethiopia to

MoUs, the beneficiaries are selected with reference to the following criteria:

a) Persons whom the UNHCR considers *prima facie* deserving refugee status;[43]
b) Persons who, although not falling under the former point, show a proved vulnerability situation due to their personal characteristics, age and health (for instance, women with children, victims of trafficking, elderly, persons with disability or affected by serious illnesses);[44]
c) Either one of the two criteria, as long its grounds and seriousness is proved, can justify the admission of a person to the project.

In complementary form and not in place of the previous criteria, the following factors will be considered:

d) Persons who can benefit from support in Italy from individuals, Churches or associations that have volunteered to provide hospitality and support for a substantial period in the initial phase;
e) Persons who already have a family or stable social network in Italy and have declared their intention to live and integrate in the country for that reason.[45]

2.4.1 'Vulnerability'

Even though the MoUs do not establish a clear definition of 'vulnerability', the concept seems to refer to situations where individuals with special

---

Italy' (Master dissertation, University of Oxford 2018) 21-22; Interview with researcher, Oxford University (Oxford, UK, 18 April 2018).

43 'A prima facie approach means the recognition by a State or UNHCR of refugee status on the basis of readily apparent, objective circumstances in the country of origin or, in the case of stateless asylum-seekers, their country of former habitual residence. A prima facie approach acknowledges that those fleeing these circumstances are at risk of harm that brings them within the applicable refugee definition.' UNHCR, 'Guidelines on International Protection No. 11: Prima Facie Recognition of Refugee Status' (2015) para 1. 'Although a prima facie approach may be applied within individual refugee status determination procedures it is more often used in group situations, for example where individual status determination is impractical, impossible or unnecessary in large-scale situations.' ibid para 2.

44 Protocollo 15 dicembre 2015 (n 5) 5 para 13(b), art 3.

45 Protocollo 15 dicembre 2015 (n 5) art 3; Protocollo 12 gennaio 2017 (n 5) art 3; Protocollo 7 novembre 2017 (n 5) art 3; Protocollo 3 maggio 2019 (n 5) art 3.

needs are particularly exposed to harm and lack the capacity to cope with the situation.[46] The term 'vulnerability' frequently appears in resettlement contexts and in the UNHCR Guidelines as a criterion for refugees to access protection, durable solutions or other protected entry procedures, and is subject to different understandings.[47] For instance, in the UNCHR resettlement programmes, the following categories of refugees are seen to have special needs: women and girls at risk; children and adolescents under physical threat, either unaccompanied or seeking to maintain family unit; persons with medical needs and victims of torture; and the elderly and the disabled.[48]

One main difference between the MoUs on one hand and the resettlement and reception programmes on the other is that the former expands the personal scope to qualify, as a person does not need to be registered with the UNHCR as a refugee or meet the 'refugee' definition.[49] This was indeed a key point negotiated by the FBOs with the Italian government: in Lebanon, the UNHCR had to suspend the registration of refugees as per instruction of the Lebanese Government as a result of which many Syrians would have been excluded from the programme.[50] However, the FBOs could not include unaccompanied minors under the category of 'vulnera-

---

46 Markay (n 42); for a discussion on vulnerability, see generally T Afifi and J Jäger, *Environment, Forced Migration and Social Vulnerability* (London, Springer, 2010).

47 UNHCR and International Detention Coalition, *Vulnerability Screening Tool. Identifying and Addressing Vulnerability: a Tool for Asylum and Migration Systems* (2016); UNHCR, 'UNHCR Resettlement Handbook. Division of International Protection' (revised edn, 2011) 182-84; Trotta (n 7) 10.

48 UNHCR (n 47) 243-99. In turn, the Reception Directive provides that 'Member States shall take into account the specific situation of vulnerable persons such as minors, unaccompanied minors, disabled people, elderly people, pregnant women, single parents with minor children, victims of human trafficking, persons with serious illnesses, persons with mental disorders and persons who have been subjected to torture, rape or other serious forms of psychological, physical or sexual violence, such as victims of female genital mutilation, in the national law implementing this Directive.' Directive (EU) 2013/33 laying down standards for the reception of applicants for international protection [2013] OJ L180, art 21; see also UNHCR and International Detention Coalition (n 47); UNHCR (n 47) 182-84; Interview with Pompei (n 23).

49 della Rocca (n 6) 13-14.

50 Trotta (n 7) 21; UNHCR, 'Syria Regional Refugee Response' (as of 16 September 2019) https://data2.unhcr.org/en/situations/syria; UNHCR, 'Lebanon. Overview 2015' http://reporting.unhcr.org/node/2520?y=2015#year.

ble people' due to the legal issues connected with them, in particular the need to appoint legal guardians.[51]

Clearly, the MoUs give the FBOs a wide margin of appreciation in the selection of the beneficiaries. The interviewees themselves confirmed this, as they all stressed that the goal of the HCs is to protect those considered 'the weakest'. But they also pointed to other specific deserving categories that could be included.[52] For instance, they focused on medical needs, on families (as opposed to individuals), on those who identified as gays and lesbians, but also on people who did not qualify for inclusion in family-reunion, resettlement or other programmes and would likely remain in refugee camps with no prospects of integration.[53] When asked about how they would select the beneficiaries, one of the operators explained that they were not concerned with applying legal standards but on finding practical solutions on the grounds of what they believe was fair and could make the programme work rather than following precise rules.[54] He added that the selection was difficult and sometimes overwhelming. Another operator explained that even among them, there may be different views on whom to include in the programme, and in case of disagreement, the decision was taken by their head office in Rome.[55] One study confirmed that different actors interpret 'vulnerability' in different ways according to their own understandings and aims: some actors may consider situations of 'extreme poverty'; others may include whole families who would otherwise remain stranded in refugee camps. It has also been reported that some beneficiaries were selected upon the request of the Italian government as they cooperated to an operation to rescue Italian hostages in Syria.[56]

In light of the above, it emerges that FBOs have developed an operational definition of 'vulnerability', which includes intersecting factors and components, thus allowing an assessment based on a more nuanced understanding of the beneficiaries' experiences and eligibility for the programme according to the specificity of the situations they face. However, these criteria have the effect of dividing 'refugees into sub-categories of deservedness', and in practice it may involve 'political and humanitarian' considerations

---

51 Interview with Naso (n 4).

52 Markay (n 42) 27.

53 Interview with Scotta (n 28); Interview with Coordinator (n 31); Trotta (n 7) 21.

54 Interview with A. Capannini, Volunteer, Operazione Colomba (Rome, Italy, 24 May 2018).

55 Interview with Scotta (n 28).

56 Trotta (n 7) 29.

rather than objective standards.[57] Moreover, the preference for family, women and children may reinforce the stereotype of lone male migrants as a threat.[58] And, finally, while limited groups of particularly vulnerable persons might be included in the programme, the majority of refugees are excluded,[59] raising moral dilemmas and issues concerning the fundamental principles of fairness and legal certainty.[60] Problems relating to the practice of identifying 'priority groups' is not unique to the context of the HCs. Indeed, they are inherent to humanitarian and resettlement projects in general, including those run by the UNHCR in collaboration with governments.[61] In a way, they are linked to the organisation and features of these programmes, especially their reliance on access to 'soft-law' instruments[62] and considerations such as States' discretionary will, wide appreciation of the selection criteria of the actors in charge of implementation, and the powerlessness of the refugees.[63]

Finally, one concern that has been pointed out is that, although the beneficiaries are selected independent of their religious affiliations, the process is carried out through the FBOs' networks and partners on site who may favour those they come into contact with more easily. However fieldwork research would be needed to support such a concern.[64] On this point, the experts that I interviewed for this study have all stressed that the selection of the beneficiaries is completely independent of their religious affiliation and the only aim of the project is to help people in need. This is confirmed by the fact that the majority of the beneficiaries are Muslims.[65]

The next section will further explore how 'vulnerability' in the context of the HCs is being balanced against other considerations.

---

57 S Fine, 'Faiths and the Politics of Resettlement' (2014) 48 *FMR* 53-54.

58 Trotta (n 7) 32.

59 ibid 11-12; E Fiddian, 'Relocating: the Asylum Experience in Cairo' (2006) 8 *Interventions* 295, 305-11.

60 J-Y Carlier, 'Des Droits de l'Homme Vulnérable à la Vulnérabilité des Droits de l'Homme, la Fragilité des Équilibres' (2017) 79 *Revue interdisciplinaire d'études juridiques* 175-204.

61 G Verdirame and B Harrell-Bond, *Rights in Exile. Janus-Faced Humanitarism* (Oxford, Bergham Books, 2005) 283, 285.

62 K B Sandvik, 'Blurring Boundaries: Refugee Resettlement in Kampala - Between the Formal, the Informal, and the Illegal' (2011) 34 *PoLAR* 11.

63 Verdirame (n 61) 286.

64 Trotta (n 7) 23.

65 Collyer (n 5) 3.

2.4.2 *Integration in Italy and avoidance of secondary movements*

The concepts of vulnerability and *prima facie* recognition of refugee status in the MoUs are qualified in light of pragmatic considerations. Specifically, the MoUs state that, in complementary form and not in substitution of the aforementioned criteria, it shall be taken into account whether the beneficiaries intend to live and integrate in Italy.[66] In practice, vulnerability and *prima facie* refugee status are bundled together with the challenges that the beneficiaries will face once uprooted and whether they will be able to grow and become self-sufficient in the new context.[67] In this regard, one interviewee explained that between a family composed of a mother and five young children and a family with more children, but with two approaching adulthood and capable of working, they would choose the latter, as they are more likely to become independent in a shorter period of time.[68] Some stakeholders stated that they are concerned about whether the relocation may have negative effects on the beneficiaries' well-being. They illustrated this very well with the case of elderly people: if they had already fled from Syria and have been living in refugee camps for some years, they will likely never integrate or manage to become independent in Italy. Their health may even deteriorate with a new settlement, and therefore they would not be chosen unless part of a family.[69]

In addition to the integration criterion, the MoUs require an assessment of whether the beneficiaries have any family or personal ties with Italy and whether they intend to settle down in the country, in order to limit or avoid secondary movements.[70] Stakeholders explained that they are becoming increasingly careful about this, as about 20 per cent of the beneficiaries from Lebanon left Italy after their arrival, and this may create problems with the government, as the programme relies on compliance with

66 Protocollo 15 dicembre 2015 (n 5) art 3; Protocollo 12 gennaio 2017 (n 5) art 3; Protocollo 7 novembre 2017 (n 5) art 3; Protocollo 3 maggio 2019 (n 5) art 3.

67 Interview with Pani (n 29).

68 ibid.

69 Interview with M Bonafede, Representative, Waldensian Church at the Italian Federation of Evangelic Churches, and Promoter, Humanitarian Corridors (Turin, Italy, 13 May 2018); Interview with Chioccioli (n 34); A Ager, 'Health and Forced Migration' in E Fiddian-Qasmiyeh and others (eds), *The Oxford Handbook of Refugee and Forced Migration Studies* (Oxford, Oxford University Press, 2014) 439.

70 Protocollo 15 dicembre 2015 (n 5) para 11(d), art 3; Protocollo 12 gennaio 2017 (n 5) art 4(d); Protocollo 7 novembre 2017 (n 5) art 3; Protocollo 3 maggio 2019 (n 5) art 3.

the rules.[71] Therefore, FBO's *operatori* (literally operators, but essentially volunteers and employees) try to understand whether the beneficiaries' migration project is actually to remain in Italy. The *operatori* now tend not to select individuals with family members in other European countries.[72] In this regard, Caritas is strengthening the beneficiaries' preparation before departure by informing them of the difficulties which they may face in Italy.[73] These efforts address the Italian government's desire of being in control of its borders as well as of not permitting the beneficiaries to bypass EU immigration law upon arrival.[74] Thus, it is clear that the negotiated objectives of the programme with the government – helping the most vulnerable, maintaining the reputation of having a humane migration policy, and protecting the EU borders – create constraints and grey areas during the selection process.[75]

2.5 Reception of beneficiaries: legal status and support provided after arrival

Once they arrive in Italy, the beneficiaries go on to lodge the asylum application at the airport. The FBOs support them with legal assistance and transfer them to different cities across the country.

Upon receipt of the asylum claim, the Ministry of the Interior shall forward the relevant files to the Territorial Commission in charge of the asylum decision.[76] For these applicants, the asylum procedure takes a much shorter time than usual – only six months compared to an average of two years.[77] In part, this is due to the fact that security checks are carried out beforehand but also owing to the FBOs' ability to speed up the processing of the applications thanks to connections with the Ministry of the Interior in Rome.[78] At the end of November 2018, the number of applicants from Lebanon who obtained the refugee status amounted to 751. Three received subsidiary protection (five years' leave to remain) and six a permit to stay

71 This figure applies only to the beneficiaries who arrived from Lebanon. Interview with Bonafede (n 69); Interview with de Monte (n 35). There is no available data of the beneficiaries who arrived from Ethiopia.
72 Interview with Bonafede (n 69).
73 Interview with Forti (n 23).
74 Markay (n 42) 32-33.
75 ibid 33.
76 Protocollo 15 dicembre 2015 (n 5) art 4; Protocollo 12 gennaio 2017 (n 5) art 4; Protocollo 17 novembre 2017 (n 5) art 4.
77 Collyer (n 5) 3.
78 Trotta (n 7) 23.

on humanitarian grounds (between six months and two years' leave to remain).[79] The other applicants are still awaiting a decision on their cases.[80] Over 95 per cent of the applicants from Ethiopia, Jordan and Turkey whose cases were finalised have received refugee status and the others subsidiary protection but the exact numbers have not yet been made public.[81]

The form of support provided by the FBOs has been formalised with the Italian government and creates a parallel structure of reception outside that of the State.[82] Refugees, as well as beneficiaries of other forms of international protection, are immediately immersed into local communities instead of being placed in reception centres. Besides providing accommodation and support, the FBOs assist the refugees and beneficiaries of international protection with reaching their integration goals through language acquisition and work training, as well as with obtaining social benefits once the primary reception phase has been completed, in order to stabilise their position in Italy and prevent secondary movements.[83] The Italian government provides healthcare, schooling, integration services and, if the beneficiaries cannot integrate in the labour market, the support of welfare benefits.[84] The recent Decree Law 840/2018 (*Salvini Decree*) requiring a certificate of residence[85] in Italy to access health care has been detrimental to asylum seekers, who are normally unable to obtain such a certificate, and this has complicated the reception system for the beneficiaries of the HCs.

---

79 Both permits are renewable.

80 Interview with de Monte (n 35). It should be noted that the recent Legislative Decree 113/2018 has abolished the general humanitarian permission which allowed lawful residence in case a person did not qualify for refugee status but serious reasons based on humanitarian considerations or international obligations justified it. Humanitarian permission has now been limited to medical cases, or cases related to natural disasters or particular acts of civil engagement. DL 113/2018; C Padula, 'Quale Sorte per il Permesso di Soggiorno Umanitario Dopo il DL 113/2018?' (Associazione per gli Studi Giuridici sull'Immigrazione, 21 November 2018) www.asgi.it/asilo-e-protezione-internazionale/permesso-umanitario-dopo-decreto-11-2018/.

81 Interview with Forti (n 23); Interview with Pani (n 29).

82 Trotta (n 7) 26.

83 Protocollo 15 dicembre 2015 (n 5) art 3(11); Protocollo 12 gennaio 2017 (n 5) art 4(d); Protocollo 7 novembre 2017 (n 4) 4-5 para 10(d); Interview with Coordinator (n 31).

84 Interview with Pompei (n 23).

85 Only persons who have a regular residence permit can register in the lists of residents of the local town-hall. See eg Comune di Milano, 'Iscrizione Anagrafica per Cittadini Stranieri Extra UE' www.comune.milano.it/servizi/iscrizione-anagrafica-per-cittadini-extra-ue.

However, in some cases, the FBOs have been able to circumvent this new provision by negotiating with the local health services (*Associazione Santitaria Locale - ASL*) to accept the de facto residence of the applicants.[86]

The FBOs provide different kinds of services. For instance, the Waldensian Church and the FCEI tend to provide reception in small centres and hire external personnel, whereas the community of *Sant'Egidio* and Caritas are more based on mobilising resources within the religious community.[87] These differences make it difficult to evaluate the reception standards of the alternative systems although it is reported that there is a structure that coordinates the dispersal and allocation of the beneficiaries, taking into consideration their characteristics and needs.[88] Overall, this quality of reception seems to understand integration not only as a goal, but as a two-way process, in the sense that is dependent 'as much on the attitudes and actions of host country governments, institutions, service providers, communities and individuals as it is on the stance of migrants themselves, and needs to be sustainable.'[89] Moreover, according to some research, programmes based on private sponsorships like this are more successful in achieving long-term integration than government-sponsored programmes. This is due to the fact that the bond between the sponsor and the refugee is more personal and stronger, facilitating social cohesion.[90] It has also been noted that in Italy, public institutions have set up minimal interventions to facilitate integration into society and as a result refugee treatment has resembled that of economic migrants: social networks are crucial for finding employment and civil society organisations are the reference point for many needs.[91]

---

86 Interview with Pani (n 29).

87 Trotta (n 7) 26.

88 della Rocca (n 6) 13, 29.

89 G Craig, 'Migration and Integration. A Local and Experimental Perspective' (2015) University of Birmingham, IRiS Working Paper Series 7/2015, 64. The Italian authorities' integration approach is explained in the next paragraphs of this section.

90 della Rocca (n 6) 26-30; E Y Krivenko, 'Hospitality and Sovereignty: What Can We Learn From the Canadian Private Sponsorship Program?' (2012) 24 *IJRL* (2012) 579, 595-96; M Lanphier, 'Sponsorship: Organizational, Sponsor, and Refugee Perspectives' (2003) 4 *Journal of International Migration and Integration* 237, 245–46.

91 M Abrosini, 'Better than Our Fears? Refugees in Italy: Between Rhetorics of Exclusion and Local Projects of Inclusion' in S Kneebone, D Stevens, L Baldassar (eds), *Refugee Protection and the Role of Law* (London, Routledge, 2014) 235, 241.

Initially, FBOs provided support for about one year, but recently they extended it to about two years, as practice had shown that it was difficult for the refugees to become self-reliant in a shorter timeframe.[92] If the beneficiaries' independence has not been achieved within this period, support can be extended until necessary. Thus the beneficiaries might be provided with accommodation and support for a longer period than other asylum seekers, who instead can rely on it only until the final decision of their international protection application – or a maximum of six months 'grace period' after its adoption.[93] Furthermore, FBOs have an approach to reception services which is usually heavily reliant on volunteers and parishes and of better quality than those provided by the State.[94] In this regard, State-run emergency reception services (*Centri di Accoglienza Straordinaria - CAS*) that had to be provided for limited periods of time while asylum seekers waited to be moved to more long-term accommodation facilities (*Sistema di Protezione per Richiedenti Asilo e Rifugiati - SPRAR*) were often used to accommodate people for longer periods of time. Due to the high number of migrants arriving by sea and the decrease of secondary movements from Italy, CAS, once meant for situations of emergency, is now hosting about 80 per cent of asylum seekers, and this has become the norm.[95] With Decree Law 840/2018, SPRAR can accommodate only recognised refugees and unaccompanied-minor asylum seekers, whereas all other asylum seekers are hosted in centres of first reception (i.e., CAS, *Centri governativi di prima accoglienza* (CARA)). This measure has been heavily criticised as CAS and CARA lack effective integration programmes.[96] Moreover, CAS and CARA reception services are in general of lower quality than those provided by SPRAR. However, even within SPRAR there are many quality variations regarding the services provided, mostly because when SPRAR are privately managed, profit considerations may compete with their original aim.[97] Additionally, city councils' hostility and refusal

---

92 Interview with Coordinator (n 31).

93 P Gois and G Falchi, 'The Third Way. Humanitarian Corridors in Peacetime as a (Local) Civil Society Response to a EU's Common Failure' (2017) 25 *Revista Interdisciplinar da Mobilidade Humana* 59, 69; della Rocca (n 6) 13, 27.

94 Gois (n 93) 70.

95 Interview with social worker (Genoa, Italy, 24 April 2018).

96 E Lorusso, 'Decreto Sicurezza, Si dal Senato. Ecco Cosa Prevede' *Panorama* (7 November 2018) www.panorama.it/news/politica/decreto-sicurezza-legge-senato-contenuti-cosa-cambia-immigrazione/; A Camilli, 'Tutte le Obiezioni al Decreto Salvini' *Internazionale* (27 September 2018) www.internazionale.it/bloc-notes/annalisa-camilli/2018/09/27/obiezioni-decreto-salvini-immigrazione-sicurezza.

97 della Rocca (n 6) 27-28.

to be involved with SPRAR's management due to fears of unpopularity among the electorate, has shifted the responsibility for dealing with reception services to the Ministry of the Interior, which, however, cannot provide the same social connections and integration options that local bodies otherwise would.[98] In light of this complex situation, arguments have been raised about the HCs creating a 'privileged channel of protection' and discriminating between asylum seekers. However, Susanna Trotta argues that the privileged aspects of the reception services have been used as an opportunity for lobbying for the improvement of the general support system.[99]

2.6 *Perspectives for enhancement and replication of the humanitarian corridors in other countries*

Both the Italian government and the religious groups involved in the HCs underline the 'replicability' of the project, as exemplified by the adoption of similar initiatives in France, Belgium, Andorra and San Marino.[100] In this respect, 'replicability' means that the HCs could be based on different legal frameworks and forms and adopt a flexible approach. It could also mean that the initiative be started and supported by non-faith-based groups.[101] The actors in each country could decide how to best manage collaborations and available resources. However, one of the main aims of the HCs is to actively address the ongoing refugee influx and manage protected entries from the bottom-up.[102] Similarly, community-led assistance provides not only material reception, but also an effective system of integration into society through volunteers and networks. In Italy, the FBOs played a crucial role in establishing and implementing the HCs.[103] In the previous decades, these FBOs gained specific experience and competence on refugees and resettlement matters since they have been involved in reception and integration services for refugees in Italy as well as in humani-

98 ibid 28.

99 Trotta (n 7) 24. Paolo Morozzo della Rocca also underlines the FBOs' goal to realise a best practice model of reception based on cooperation and support of other institutions and local communities. della Rocca (n 6) 29-30.

100 Collyer (n 5) 4; Trotta (n 7) 27; Ministro degli Affari Esteri e della Cooperazione Internazionale, 'Humanitarian Corridors' www.esteri.it/mae/en/politica_estera/temi_globali/diritti_umani/i-corridoi-umanitari.html.

101 Trotta (n 7) 34.

102 Collyer (n 5) 4.

103 Historically, FBOs have been playing an important role as far as the shaping of Italian immigration policies and legislation. Trotta (n 7) 27-28.

tarian initiatives in transiting countries. Their reputation and professionalism persuaded the Italian government to support the HCs. Additionally, these FBOs committed to use their networks of contacts with other international and national actors, as well as to fund the project: the Waldensian Church and the Community of *Sant'Egidio* rely on donations of two schemes that allow taxpayers to give them a small percentage of their income tax; other FBOs receive donations from private citizens, local authorities, transnational networks and fundraising events.[104]

Jessica Eby and others have stressed that in the United States, NGOs and FBOs are in charge of delivering a wide range of services concerning the resettlement programme and it would be impossible without their work and support.[105] Confirming this and other previous studies, the FBOs in Italy have been and continue to be key actors who are not just implementing partners, but advocates for the protection of refugees.[106] In the HCs context, they have engaged in lobbying activities to support the project at the national, European and international levels, in communicating the project to the public, and in trying to change the perspectives on refugees in Italy. For instance, they stress the refugees' personal experiences to show that they are not a threat. The result has been that even mainstream media has presented the HCs as an example of solidarity, which, at the same time, addresses citizens' concerns regarding safety and security. Moreover, such messages have been reinforced by the support of Pope Francis, the former Italian Prime Minister Paolo Gentiloni, and the UNHCR.[107] There have been very few isolated criticisms, voiced most recently in the 2018 electoral campaign.[108]

The aim of civil society has been described as not being 'revolutionary' but as providing a model that could incentivise State actors to adopt similar initiatives.[109] Some stakeholders hope that the HCs will contribute not only to developing the use of humanitarian visas on a larger scale, but also to expanding private sponsorship as an ordinary legal channel beyond situations of vulnerability.[110] Others, such as the Federation of Evangelic Churches, are lobbying to introduce humanitarian corridors at the Euro-

---

104 Interview with Coordinator (n 31); Trotta (n 7) 24.
105 ibid 6; J Eby and others, 'The Faith Community's Role in Refugee Resettlement in the United States' (2011) 24 *JRS* 586-87.
106 Trotta (n 7); Eby (n 105) 586-87.
107 Collyer (n 5) 2.
108 Interview with Pompei (n 23).
109 Markay (n 42) 53-54.
110 Interview with Pompei (n 23).

pean level through European Union legislation, European funds, agreements between different States, the European Union, NGOs and FBOs.[111] In this regard, in December 2018, the Committee on Civil Liberties, Justice and Home Affairs (LIBE Committee) of the European Parliament, agreed to request the Commission to adopt legislation establishing a European Humanitarian Visa by 31 March 2019.[112] However the Commission rejected the proposal acknowledging that it is not politically feasible, and stating that the new common resettlement framework already addresses the issues at stake.[113] In the absence of a common EU framework and national legislation, one constraint to replicating and expanding the HCs is that Article 25 of the Visa Code states that humanitarian visas are to be used only in 'exceptional' cases and when the Member State 'considers it necessary' rather than to comply with enforceable obligations.

Furthermore, as they rely on the solidarity and goodwill of local communities, HCs cannot be an alternative to resettlement or other protected entry procedures – especially owing to the high costs and the limited num-

---

111 Interview with Naso (n 4); Mediterranean Hope, 'Humanitarian Corridors Presented at the European Parliament' (Rome, 7 December 2017) www.mediterraneanhope.com/ 2017/12/07/humanitarian-corridors-presented-at-the-european-parliament/.

112 European Parliament, 'Humanitarian Visas to Avoid Deaths and Improve Management of Refugee Flows' (11 December 2018) www.europarl.europa.eu/news/en/press-room/20181205IPR20933/humanitarian-visas-to-avoid-deaths-and-improve-management-of-refugee-flows; European Parliament, 'Humanitarian Visas Would Reduce Refugees' Death Toll' (3 December 2018) www.europarl.europa.eu/news/en/press-room/20181203IPR20713/ humanitarian-visas-would-reduce-refugees-death-toll; Interview with Hein (n 9).

113 European Parliament, Legislative Train, 'Proposal for a Regulation on Establishing a European Humanitarian Visa' (June 2019) 2.
The New Resettlement Framework will replace the current ad-hoc schemes and set two-year plans for resettling refugees. The new legislation will provide a common set of procedures for the selection and treatment of resettlement candidates and also ensure financial support from the EU budget. K Bamberg, 'The EU Resettlement Framework: from a Humanitarian Pathway to a Migration Management Tool' (Discussion Paper, European Migration and Diversity Programme, European Policy Centre 2018); European Parliament (n 112) However, the Resettlement Framework only includes persons who have already been recognised as refugees, and who also fulfil other vulnerability or geographical criteria. In addition, Member States will continue to decide to whom, and how many people, they will grant protection. In any case, the Commission also stated that it would include in its assessment of the application of the Union Resettlement Framework whether additional measures for admission to the territory of the Member States are needed. European Parliament (n 113) 2-3.

ber of beneficiaries they can support.[114] Consequently, at present, the HCs cannot be seen as an alternative to the current public system of reception or resettlement or as a substitute to other entry protected procedures because they lack the resources to deal with their dimension.[115] They can nevertheless be considered a complementary pathway.[116] One test showing whether the HCs have been really successful or not will depend on their expansion beyond civil society and becoming a structural model with the collaboration of the government and international institutions.[117]

2.7 *Shortcomings*

For the HCs to become a structural model, a number of matters need to be addressed. First of all, in section 2.4.1 of this chapter, it was discussed that the FBOs involved have come to develop a preference for deciding cases on the grounds of practical considerations,[118] which emphasise the special circumstances and problems of each potential beneficiary, recognising the differences, and not attempting to fit them into a system of general rules.[119] The flexible criteria to select the beneficiaries allow wide discretion over the choice of whom to include in the programme, and this helps to find creative solutions in the difficult and complex settings where they take place. On the other hand, the data confirm previous works in the field of administrative justice, arguing that, in this kind of decision-making, perceptions of justice, deservedness, and goals are based more on political and humanitarian considerations than on legal standards. In other words, the decisions are not taken in a vacuum; they are value-driven rather than founded on a legal framework. FBOs operate according to their own values which somehow are never completely neutral, as advocating for justice or peace work is never neutral.[120] So the risk is of emphasising suffering over rights and of substituting charity for the law.[121] Similarly, due process

---

114 della Rocca (n 6) 29.

115 Jensen (n 8) 8; della Rocca (n 6) 29.

116 della Rocca (n 6) 29.

117 Markay (n 42) 50.

118 M Hertogh, 'Through the Eyes of Bureaucrats: How Front Line Officials Understand Administrative Justice' in M Adler, *Administrative Justice in Context* (Oxford, Hart Publishing, 2010) 203-04.

119 ibid 203, 212.

120 E Ferris, 'Faith and Humanitarianism: It's Complicated' (2005) 24 *JRS* 606, 618.

121 Markay (n 42) 52; D Fassin, 'The Precarious Truth of Asylum' (2013) 25 *Public Culture* 39, 49.

guarantees, including access to information, right to a motivated decision, and an effective remedy, are not provided for. Accordingly, the fundamental principles of legality (requiring that every administrative decision that affects rights and freedoms is based on a statutory basis) and equality (requiring equal treatment of all persons in equal circumstances) are set aside in favour of more practical and informal solutions.[122] Therefore, there is the need to better define and address the selection criteria in a binding legal framework. Whereas the parties involved could set up the programme using the legal instrument of MoUs, it would be desirable that international protection initiatives be regulated by an act of Parliament and undergo the usual Constitutional guarantees for the passage of legislation. It is acknowledged that it is questionable as to whether the Italian government had the political force to obtain parliamentary support for such a project and, for some refugee advocates and FBOs, the present approach far outweighs the downfalls. In other words, if civil society had not engaged in this project, the beneficiaries might still be facing security problems in Lebanon or Ethiopia.[123] Overall this political choice is in line with the fragmented and ad hoc responses that Italy has given to the immigration phenomenon in the last twenty years, instead of adopting a clear and comprehensive plan to govern and manage it.

Second, this matter is strictly connected to that of accountability and professionalism of the actors involved. Most work of the FBOs is not recorded or quantified and, consequently, it is difficult to make an assessment of their assistance and decisions.[124] Nevertheless, it has also been discussed that several FBOs adopt a professional framework and approach, for instance, by hiring professionals, adopting high professional standards, and avoiding any activity that can be considered of missionary nature.[125] Moreover, under pressure from governments and other NGOs, they may have to comply with codes of conduct which prohibit discriminating on the basis of religion.[126] It has been pointed out that further research could look into different understandings of professionalisms as well as of humanitarian work that takes faith into account and how, at the same time, they satisfy the 'fundamental principles of impartiality, independence and neu-

---

122 Hertogh (n 118) 203, 211.

123 Markay (n 42) 51-52.

124 Ferris (n 120) 610; A Ager, 'Faith and the Secular: Tensions in Realising Humanitarian Principles' (2014) 48 *FMR* 16-18; Trotta (n 7) 9.

125 Ferris (n 120) 610; Trotta (n 7) 9.

126 Ferris (n 120) 615.

trality'.[127] This would require considering 'the role of faith in the personal experiences of both aid workers and beneficiaries alike'.[128] It may also involve investigating the motivations of FBOs and the type of work that they do and fund, as well as whether and to what extent religious activities, such as prayer and worship, are integrated into humanitarian work.[129]

Finally, another debate concerns the FBOs' role in resettlement and migration programmes. Whereas their involvement has changed governments' protection policies as far as the diversification and numbers of beneficiaries,[130] as confirmed in the case of the HCs in Italy, where civil society has contributed to stimulate debate and State action, it has been argued that the diversification of actors in this area has shown the risks when the responsibility for disadvantaged groups is ceded to civil society and the burden is shifted from State to private actors.[131] This is an important issue to address because far-reaching solutions require concerted action among humanitarian, political, security and development actors rather than responses of individual organisations.[132] If civil society is left to do everything, it will 'fall short of its own objectives in something'.[133] Moreover, the adoption of safe and legal pathways should be seen as an obligation arising from international law rather than an exception to national immigration policies.[134]

3 Other uses of humanitarian visas and instances of ad-hoc entry measures

Interviewees have confirmed that humanitarian visas issued on the basis of Article 25 of the Visa Code have been used in some isolated cases apart from humanitarian corridors. There are no statistics that inform on how

127 Trotta (n 7) 9; Ager (n 124) 16-18.

128 Trotta (n 7) 9.

129 Ferris (n 120) 614-15.

130 Trotta (n 7) 7; Krivenko (n 90) 579; B Treviranus and M Casasola, 'Canada's Private Sponsorship of Refugees Program: a Practitioners Perspective of its Past and Future' (2003) 4 *JIMI/RIMI* 177.

131 Trotta (n 7) 6; M Gottwald,'Burden Sharing and Refugee Protection' in Fiddian-Qasmiyeh and others (n 69) 525, 533, 535; G Loescher, 'UNHCR and Forced Migration' in Fiddian-Qasmiyeh and others (n 69) 214, 217. The stakeholders that I interviewed all agreed on this point and stated that their responsibility shall be shared with the State's.

132 Gottwald (n 131) 534.

133 Markay (n 42) 49.

134 ibid 55.

many times humanitarian visas have been issued. The data suggest that humanitarian visas were issued in exceptional cases to ensure protection to persons who were in urgent need. For instance, in the past years, the *Consiglio Italiano dei Rifugiati* (CIR) [Italian Refugee Council] was able to negotiate about 20 visas with the government for asylum seekers who had family ties in Italy. It is believed that an individual approaching an Italian embassy alone, without support from NGOs in Italy would be unable to obtain such a visa.[135] On the other hand, even if the Law Clinic at the University of Brescia, supported by the Red Cross, applied for a humanitarian visa on behalf of a client under Article 25 of the Visa Code, it was unsuccessful. Students working in the Law Clinic had contacted the Italian Ministry of the Interior to ask clarification on the criteria to obtain a humanitarian visa and they were informed that applicants needed to prove there were grounds for persecution. Although the applicant was a widow with three children, whose husband and other two children were killed by terrorists, and she had a brother in Italy willing to sponsor her, the Ministry of the Interior refused the case on the grounds that the applicant could not demonstrate that she faced persecution in her country. One reported difficulty in this case was to provide evidence of persecution while still living in Pakistan, as both the Pakistani authorities and the local UNHCR were reluctant to assist.[136]

---

135 Interview with Hein (n 10). See also the recent decision of the Tribunale Ordinario di Roma dated of 21 February 2019. In this case, the Civil Court in Rome dealt with the humanitarian visa application on behalf of a Nigerian unaccompanied child to join his mother and brother in Italy. The child had been detained in immigration centres in Libya and needed urgent medical treatment. The International Organization for Migration (IOM) assisted the child to contact his mother and set up a detailed medical plan with a hospital in Italy. However, IOM was unable to receive a visa for the child. The Civil Court recognised that the application could be submitted under Article 25 of the Visa Code Court and ordered the Ministry of Foreign Affairs to issue a humanitarian visa and a travel permit to the child. The Court considered factors such as the child's health, the availability of medical treatment in Nigeria or Libya, and the right to family life under Article 8 of the ECHR as well as the Italian Constitution. Tribunale Ordinario di Roma, Ordinanza 21.02.2019 www.asgi.it/wp-content/uploads/2019/05/Tribunale-di-Roma-visto-umanitario-per-msna-in-Libia.pdf.

136 Telephone conversation with C di Stasio, Lecturer, Faculty of Law, University of Brescia (Brescia, Italy, 26 April 2018); C di Stasio, 'The "Immigration and Asylum Clinic" of the University of Brescia Facing the Problem of Immigration in Europe: New Challenges to the Effectiveness of Migrants' Rights' (2017) 4 *German Journal of Legal Education* 192, 214-17.

In this context, it should be mentioned that recently Italy carried out a few evacuations of migrants detained in immigration centres in Libya. These evacuations have been labelled HCs, although they were not based on a MoU or any other public document. Furthermore, the beneficiaries were selected by the UNHCR and the reception provided by the State. The Italian government organised and financially supported the transfer to Italy through the Italian Air Force. The Catholic Church, through Caritas, as well as the Italian government were involved with the evacuation logistics and the reception of the beneficiaries.[137] The beneficiaries were migrants from Eritrea, Ethiopia, Somalia, Cameroon and Yemen, and included single mothers, unaccompanied minors, and disabled people. Once in Italy, the beneficiaries received medical care, were dispersed through reception facilities in the country and allowed to apply for asylum.[138] These evacuations were carried out in response to the UNHCR's appeal made in December 2017 calling governments for resettlement places for vulnerable migrants stranded in Libya, as many asylum seekers, refugees and stateless persons there face serious violations of human rights, including indefinite and arbitrary detention.[139] Following the agreement, which the Italian government had entered into with Libya in July 2017 to prevent boats

137 'Corridori Umanitari: Caritas, altre 150 Persone Arrivate in Sicurezza dalla Libia' *Servizio di Informazione Religiosa* (15 February 2018) www.agensir.it/quotidiano/2018/2/15/corridoi-umanitari-caritas-altre-150-persone-arrivate-in-sicurezza-dalla-libia/; 'Come Funziona il "Corridorio Umanitario" dalla Libia' *Il Post* (3 January 2018) www.ilpost.it/2018/01/03/libia-migranti-corridoio-umanitario/.

138 'Come Funziona il "Corridorio Umanitario" dalla Libia' *Il Post* (3 January 2018) www.ilpost.it/ 2018/01/03/libia-migranti-corridoio-umanitario/.

139 Between November 2017 and 7 December 2018, UNHCR concluded 24 evacuations in Libya of over 2,600 refugees. The refugees were transferred to Italy (312), Niger (2.202), and Romania (94). UNHCR, 'Con Quasi 2.500 Persone Evacuate dalla Libia, l' UNHCR Chiede Piu' Posti per il Reinsediamento e la Fine della Detenzione' (23 November 2019) www.unhcr.it/news/comunicati-stampa/quasi-2-500-persone-evacuate-dalla-libia-lunhcr-chiede-piu-posti-reinsediamento-la-fine-della-detenzione.html; 'Evacuazione del Primo Gruppo di Rifugiati dalla Nuova Struttura in Libia' (7 December 2018) www.unhcr.it/news/comunicati-stampa/ evacuazione-del-primo-gruppo-rifugiati-dalla-nuova-struttura-libia.html; V Piccolillo, 'Salvini Accogli 51 Migranti dal Niger: "Porte Spalancate a Chi Scappa dalla Guerra, Chiuse a Chi la Porta da Noi"' *Corriere della Sera* (14 November 2018) roma.corriere.it/notizie/cronaca/18_novembre_14/roma-salvini-accoglie-51-migranti-niger-arrivati-corridoi-umanitari-448ad8e8-e801-11e8-b8c4-2c4605eeaada.shtml; A Ziniti, 'Migranti, 51 in Italia con Corridoio Umanitario dal Niger' *La Repubblica* (14 November 2018) www.repubblica.it/cronaca/2018/11/14/news/ migranti_51_in_arrivo_in_italia_con_corridoio_umanitario_da_niger-211626594/.

from leaving the Libyan coast and trafficking people into Italy, as well as deportation agreements between several EU governments and Sudan, the problem of migrants' human rights violations in transit even intensified.[140]

In the past, besides these instances, Italy adopted ad hoc mechanisms based on political decisions to allow asylum seekers and refugees to enter the country. For instance, three 'informal' resettlement operations from Libya took place between 2007 and 2010. On this occasion, 150 Eritrean refugees selected by UNHCR were transferred to Italy, where they applied for asylum. The Italian Embassy issued a Visa with Limited Territorial Validity for tourism/courtesy reasons to allow the beneficiaries to travel and be admitted into the territory.[141]

Another evacuation operation involved 160 Palestinian refugees living in the Al Tanf camp at the Syrian-Iraqi border. At the end of 2009, upon UNHCR's referral, these refugees were transferred to Italy, where they sought asylum. Similar to the previous case, the Italian Embassy issued a Visa with Limited Territorial Validity for tourism/courtesy reasons. [142]

In March 2011, two humanitarian evacuations from Libya took place in order to ensure safety to 108 persons originating from Eritrea and Ethiopia who were transferred from Tripoli to Italy. Following the plea by the Bishop of Tripoli, Habeshia Association and Italian Refugee Council, the Ministry of the Interior and the Ministry of Foreign Affairs agreed to urgently evacuate these persons through the Italian Air Force. Unlike the previous 'informal' resettlement operations, these evacuations took place without UNHCR's involvement. Moreover, due to time constraints, no visa was issued to these individuals who applied for asylum upon arrival.[143]

---

140 M Perrone, 'Migranti, il Patto con la Libia Frena gli Arrivi: da Luglio – 68 %' *Il Sole 24 Ore* (27 August 2017) www.ilsole24ore.com/art/notizie/2017-08-26/migranti-patto-la-libia-frena-arrivi-221553.shtml?uuid=AE QsV7HC&refresh_ce=1; The Editorial Board, 'Italy's Dodgy Deal on Migrants' *New York Times* (25 September 2017) www.nytimes.com/2017/09/25/opinion/migrants-italy-europe.html; D Walsh and J Horowitz, 'Italy, Going it Alone, Stalls the Flow of Migrants. But at What Cost?' *New York Times* (17 September 2017) www.nytimes.com/2017/09/17/world/europe/italy-libya-migrant-crisis.html; P Kingsley, 'Migration to Europe is Down Sharply. So is it Still a "Crisis"?' *New York Times* (27 June 2018) www.nytimes.com/ interactive/2018/06/27/world/europe/europe-migrant-crisis-change.html?module=inline.

141 Consiglio Italiano per i Rifugiati, 'Ponti non Muri. Garantire l'Accesso alla Protezione nell'Unione Europea' (2015) 69; Jensen (n 8) 44.

142 ibid.

143 C Hein and M de Donato, 'Exploring Avenues for Protected Entry in Europe' (ONLUS 2012) 45.

In May 1990, at the beginning of the Yugoslav war, hundreds of Albanians occupied some Embassies in Tirana. At that time, Italy, France and Germany granted refugee status automatically to those who occupied their Embassies. On July 13th 1990, 3,800 Albanians were transferred to Italy. 804 out of them remained in Italy and were given refugee status without going through the ordinary asylum procedure.[144]

In light of this scenario, it can be concluded that, in exceptional situations of emergencies, when asylum seekers and vulnerable people had to travel to Italy, a number of practical and ad hoc mechanisms were adopted, including temporary protection, tourist visas, and humanitarian evacuations. However, such cases are based on political decisions and do not represent reliable and transparent pathways. Moreover, this discretion over procedures and criteria to obtain humanitarian visas create fluctuating policies and uncertainty over the implementation of Article 25 of the Visa Code at the broader European level.[145] Considering the above, the next section discusses the need for a harmonised European approach in this area.

4 *Value of a common EU framework on protection entries*

4.1. The debate on the need of EU legislation on protected entries

In the context of protected entries in Europe, there seems to be agreement on the need to expand admission programmes, but whether and how a common EU binding framework should be adopted is contested. Research demonstrates that, similar to Italy, other EU States have issued humanitarian visas for specific groups of refugees as acts of goodwill rather than legal obligations.[146] Alternative safe and legal pathways to protection in Europe,

144 ibid 44.

145 P Hanke, M Wieruszewski and M Panizzon, 'The "Spirit of the Schengen Rules", the Humanitarian Visa, and Contested Asylum Governance in Europe – The Swiss Case' (2019) 48 *Journal of Ethnic and Migration Studies* 1361, 1368.

146 W van Ballegooij and C Navarra, 'Humanitarian Visas. European Added Value Assessment Accompanying the European Parliament's Legislative Own-Initiative report (Rapporteur: Juan Fernando López Aguilar)' (European Parliamentary Research Service, July 2018) 42; A Sánchez Legido, 'El Arriesgado Acceso a la Protección Internacional en la Europa Fortaleza: la Batalla por el Visado Humanitario Europeo' (2017) 57 *Revista de Derecho Comunitario Europeo* 433, 451.

such as resettlement,[147] have also been forged on the basis of a voluntary approach due to a variety of factors, including lack of reception services, lack of embassies' staff to deal with applicants, and above all lack of political will.[148] Aims and objectives of safe and legal channels are often imprecisely specified, and there are no sufficient standards to hold governments accountable for their implementation. Given the wide discretion of national authorities in this area, States' practices strongly reflect their own national interests.[149]

On the one hand, the proponents of a common European framework on protected entries argue that, first of all, they are necessary to improve protection. Due to the shortage of legal routes of entry to the EU territory, potential asylum seekers and other migrants resort to irregular and dangerous journeys with the help of smugglers and traffickers. This has consequences not only for migrants but for States as well. Harmonised protected entries could be an effective means to ensure safe arrivals, prevent unauthorised migrants, enhance security and identity checks and fight against organised crime.

Second, to build a credible asylum policy in Europe, the EU must identify concrete instruments to adequately balance the tension between the international obligations to admit protection-seekers and Member States' sovereign power to control access to their territory.[150] The EU adopted the 'asylum acquis' to avoid fragmentation in refugee policies and practices across the common area,[151] but to ensure uniform understanding of the rights at stake, predictability and legal certainty, a coordinated action regarding protected entries is required.[152]

Third, a unitary framework could balance the uneven distribution of the refugee burden, which is unfair to countries of first refuge and tran-

---

147 A Radjenovic, 'Resettlement of Refugees: EU Framework' (Briefing EU Legislation in Progress, European Parliamentary Research Service 2017) 5.

148 ibid.

149 Hanke (n 145) 1366; van Ballegooij (n 146) 42.

150 S Velluti, *Reforming the Common European Asylum System – Legislative Developments and Judicial Activism of the European Courts* (London, Springer, 2014) 106.

151 T P Spijkerboer, 'Full Circle? The Personal Scope of International Protection in the Geneva Convention and the Draft Directive on Qualification'; G Noll, 'International Protection Obligations and the Definition of Subsidiary Protection in the EU Qualification Directive'; and F Julien-Laferrière, 'Le Statut des Personnes Protégées' in D U de Sousa and P De Bruycker (eds), *The Emergence of a European Asylum Policy* (Brussels, Bruylant, 2004) 167, 183, 195.

152 van Ballegooij (n 146) 60.

sit.[153] This could also improve the meaning of the principle of solidarity and fair responsibility sharing set out in Article 80 of the Treaty on the Functioning of the European Union (TFEU)[154] for the future of the Common European Asylum System (CEAS). For instance, Italy has been demanding concrete solidarity from other EU Member States in dealing with sea arrivals.[155] Additionally, the Schengen system has been under pressure, especially since the 'refugee crises', as it depends on the ability to coordinate the management of external borders and prevent inflows of irregular migrants and secondary movements.[156]

On the other hand, States raise various concerns regarding a common EU framework on protected entries, including whether they would be compatible with international human rights and EU law; where processing centres would be located and how to avoid that they could be overburdened; how protection seekers would have access to embassies or processing centres;[157] the risk for host States of becoming a magnet for even more asylum seekers; decrease of control over migration;[158] feasibility of return to the country of origin for those who receive a denial of their international protection application.[159]

In response, I argue that the EU could adopt a potential wide range of measures to address these issues, such as humanitarian visas, sponsorship

153 Velluti (n 150) 106.

154 'The policies of the Union set out in this Chapter and their implementation shall be governed by the principle of solidarity and fair sharing of responsibility, including its financial implications, between the Member States. Whenever necessary, the Union acts adopted pursuant to this Chapter shall contain appropriate measures to give effect to this principle.' Treaty on the Functioning of the European Union [2016] OJ C202/78, art 80.

155 Abrosini (n 90) 235, 240; Il Fatto Quotidiano, 'Migranti, Commissione EU Risponde alla Richiesta di Aiuto di Moavero: "Ridistribuzione? Chieda a Stati Membri"' (26 April 2019) www.ilfattoquotidiano.it/2019/04/26/migranti-commissione-ue-risponde-alla-richiesta-di-aiuto-di-moavero-redistribuzione-chieda-a-stati-membri/5135777/; 'Migrant Crisis: Italy to Accept Arrivals Until Deal Reached' *BBC* (23 July 2018) www.bbc.com/news/world-europe-44933122.

156 M Savino, 'Refashioning Resettlement: from Border Externalization to Legal Pathways for Asylum' in S Carrera and others (eds), *EU External Migration Policies in an Era of Global Mobilities: Intersecting Policy Universes* (Leiden, Brill Nijhoff, 2019) 81-104.

157 J McAdam, 'Extraterritorial Processing in Europe' (Policy Brief 1, The Andrew and Renata Centre for International Refugee Law, University of New South Wales 2015) 6.

158 A Betts, 'Resettlement: Where's the Evidence, What's the Strategy?' (2017) 54 *FMR* 73-74.

159 M de Donato Cordeil and C Hein, 'Ponti Non Muri (CIR 2015) 92.

programmes, resettlement, family reunification, education or labour opportunities.[160] The legal framework should be carefully designed in order to guarantee fundamental rights, objective selection criteria and screening of applicants. Cooperation and equitable responsibility regarding administrative capacity and financial resources should be a central component,[161] and strong incentives and commitment to take host countries' interests under consideration would be crucial.[162] Also, the adoption of a clear set of rules will increase better predictability of arrivals, and 'preparation and coordination of post-arrival arrangements' such as reception services.[163] At present, it is not foreseeable when and how 'spontaneous arrivals' may occur, nor evaluate their circumstances, and asylum seekers are registered only after arrival and if they have contacts with the authorities. [164] While a discussion of all the available options regarding the introduction of protected entries is beyond the scope of this chapter,[165] as its focus is on humanitarian visas, it is acknowledged that humanitarian visas should be complementary to other protected entry procedures and the CEAS, and they are not a substitute for them.[166] Humanitarian visas could be used as a response to specific refugee situations, alongside strategies within countries of first asylum and within the countries of origin.[167]

In light of this, the next section aims at identifying a number of recommendations to set up common legislation for humanitarian visas. These recommendations draw from the Italian experience and aim at addressing the main legal shortcomings that have been observed (i.e., the absence of a legal instrument setting out clear criteria to identify beneficiaries and due process guarantees; no subjective right to a humanitarian visa).

---

160 UNHCR, 'Complementary Pathways for Admission of Refugees to Third Countries. Key Considerations' (2019) 5.

161 McAdam (n 157) 11; de Donato (n 159) 86.

162 McAdam (n 157) 10.

163 van Ballegooij (n 146) 62.

164 ibid.

165 K Pollet, 'A Common European Asylum System under Construction: Remaining Gaps, Challenges and Next Steps' in V Chetail, P De Bruycker and F Maiani, *Reforming the Common European Asylum System* (Boston, Brill Nijhoff, 2016) 74, 90.

166 J van Selm, 'Expanding Solutions for Refugees: Complementary Pathways of Admission to Europe' (European Resettlement Network 2018).

167 Betts (n 158) 73-75.

4.2. *Recommendations for the adoption of common legislation on humanitarian visas*

A new EU instrument that provides for humanitarian visas should be adopted to allow protection seekers to reach a Member State's territory in order to lodge an application for international protection. In line with the draft report of the European Parliament to the Commission, the humanitarian visa shall have limited validity and the Member State issuing it should be responsible to deal with the request for protection.[168] Member States shall be under an obligation to issue the humanitarian visa to persons seeking international protection when that is the only way to comply with international law, including the Refugee Convention, the European Convention on Human Rights, as well as the duties under Article 4 (prohibition of torture and inhuman or degrading treatment) and Article 19(2) (protection in the event of removal, expulsion and extradition) of the EU Charter of Fundamental Rights (CFR).[169] This argument is also supported by the ECtHR decision in the case of *Hirsi Jamaa and Others v Italy*, indicating that once a person is within a Member State's jurisdiction, which is unquestionably the situation when they present themselves to an embassy, 'that Member State must enable access to a procedure to verify whether the principle of *non-refoulement* would be violated upon return'.[170] The criteria should be assessed on a *prima facie* basis and a visa shall be issued when an 'arguable claim' of exposure to a real risk of serious harm or a well-founded fear of persecution has been established.[171] This would best reflect the

168 European Parliament, European Parliament Resolution of 11 December 2018 with Recommendations to the Commission on Humanitarian Visas (2018/2271(INL)) (11 December 2018) (P8_TA(2018)0494).

169 The Charter of Fundamental Rights of the European Union which must be complied with by Member States when implementing EU law. Charter of Fundamental Rights of the European Union [2012] OJ C326/02 (Charter EU); European Commission, 'Incorporating Fundamental Rights into EU Legislative Process. Strategy and proposals for embedding fundamental rights in EU law' ec.europa.eu/info/aid-development-cooperation-fundamental-rights/your-rights-eu/eu-charter-fundamental-rights/application-charter/incorporating-fundamental-rights-eu-legislative-process_en.

170 Pollet (n 165) 74, 91. See *Hirsi Jamaa and Others v Italy* App no 27765/09 (ECtHR, 23 February 2012) para 133.

171 Note that the concept of 'arguable claim' is not the same as 'admissible application'; it denotes a much lower threshold. See eg, *TI v UK* which the ECtHR considered 'arguable', but subsequently dismissed as 'inadmissible' after a thorough examination of the case. *TI v UK* App no 43844/98 (ECtHR, 7 March 2000).

declarative nature of refugee status,[172] and avoid the difficulties associated with selecting a pool of 'vulnerable' applicants, as well with offshore processing schemes, such as those pertaining to fair processing guarantees, remedies with suspensive effect, and effective judicial protection abroad. At the same time, it will allow the authorities to remain in control of the procedure.[173]

4.2.1 Subjective right

Therefore, a subjective right to apply for a humanitarian visa should be recognised as long as the qualifying criteria are met and the entry procedures are followed.[174] This is in line with the Recast Qualification Directive, which imposes an obligation on Member States under Articles 13 and 18 to grant the relevant protection status to the individual meeting the qualification criteria set out in the Directive.[175] Also, the Recast Qualification Directive does not include any geographical scope to its application.

Regarding the instrument to adopt, it shall be legally binding, as the objective pursued must be line in with *non-refoulement* obligations and fundamental rights. A non-binding recommendation will not be enough to guarantee compliance. To minimise deviation from common obligations under EU law, the best choice between a Directive or a Regulation is the latter. This is also the instrument chosen for the visa acquis, the Schengen Borders Code (SBC), and the new phase of the CEAS. A regulation would preserve the integrity and ensure the effective functioning of the rules as they would be directly applicable in all Member States.[176] Whereas in the

172 The Qualification Directive acknowledges in recital 21 that '[t]he recognition of refugee status is a declaratory act'. European Parliament and Council Directive 2011/95/EU of 13 December 2011 on standards for the qualification of third-country nationals or stateless persons as beneficiaries of international protection, for a uniform status for refugees or for persons eligible for subsidiary protection, and for the content of the protection granted (recast) [2011] OJ L 337/9, recital 21.

173 van Ballegooij (n 146) 72.

174 de Donato (n 159) 118.

175 European Parliament and Council Directive 2011/95/EU (n 172) arts 13, 18.

176 It has been proven that when Member States are left with 'the choice of form and methods' of implementation, different criteria and procedures as well as standards of application arise. van Ballegooij (n 145) 82. The Common Asylum System has already revealed differences between Member States in the ways rules are interpreted and applied, creating divergences in recognition rates and types

past it was argued that a common legal framework on humanitarian visas could be included in the Visa Code, this would not be appropriate as its scope is to cover short-stay visas only.[177] In addition, the SBC, which sets rules on the monitoring of persons crossing the EU's external borders, does not address the situation of asylum seekers, notwithstanding the references to *non-refoulement* and obligations concerning access to international protection in its Articles 3 and 4.[178] This view was confirmed by the CJEU in *X and X v. Belgium* where it found that the Code does not create a subjective right to a humanitarian visa.[179]

4.2.2 *Procedural guarantees*

Procedural guarantees could be derived from the CFR as well as the principles of European Union law, including the right to good administration

of protection granted, which is why the review of the 'asylum package' represents a more integrated approach, and supports the transformation of Directives into Regulations. European Asylum Support Office, *Annual Report on the Situation of Asylum in the European Union 2016* (2017) 26, 48; European Asylum Support Office, *Annual Report on the Situation of Asylum in the European Union 2017* (2018) 166; European Commission, 'Completing the Reform of the Common European Asylum System: Towards an Efficient, Fair and Humane Asylum Policy' (13 July 2016) europa.eu/rapid/press-release_IP-16-2433_en.htm.

177 van Ballegooij (n 146) 69.

178 Hanke (n 145) 1370; U I Jensen, 'Humanitarian Visas: Option or Obligation?' (PE 509.986, European Parliament 2014); V Moreno-Lax and C Costello, 'The Extraterritorial Application of the Charter: From Territoriality to Facticity, the Effectiveness Model' in S Peers and others, *The EU Charter of Fundamental Rights. A Commentary* (Oxford, Hart Publishing, 2014) 1657–83.

179 See text between footnotes 7 and 10 in this chapter. Hanke (n 145) 1371; V Moreno-Lax, 'Asylum Visas as an Obligation under EU Law: Case PPU C-638/16 X, X v État Belge (Part I)' (16 February 2017) *EU Immigration and Asylum Law and Policy* eumigrationlawblog.eu/asylum-visas-as-an-obligation-under-eu-law-case-ppu-c-63816-x-x-v-etat-belge/; V Moreno-Lax 'Asylum Visas as an Obligation under EU Law: Case PPU C-638/16 X, X v État belge (Part II)' (21 February 2019) *EU Immigration and Asylum Law and Policy* eumigrationlawblog.eu/asylum-visas-as-an-obligation-under-eu-law-case-ppu-c-63816-x-x-v-etat-belge-part-ii/.

and effective remedy in line with Articles 41[180] and 47[181] of the CFR.[182] A minimum set of procedural guarantees should therefore be provided, such as access to information, interpreters, right to a hearing, a motivated decision and an effective remedy.[183] Decisions should be made by competent personnel, with adequate knowledge and specialised training.

In case of negative decisions, the right to an effective remedy, which includes the right to a hearing before an independent and impartial tribunal, in accordance with Article 47 of the CFR, must be available.[184] In situations of emergencies involving the risk of irreversible harm, an automatic suspensive effect should be set up.[185] This option may translate in the issuance of a permit for immediate evacuation when imminent danger is faced.[186]

---

180 '1. Every person has the right to have his or her affairs handled impartially, fairly and within a reasonable time by the institutions and bodies of the Union. 2. This right includes: the right of every person to be heard, before any individual measure which would affect him or her adversely is taken; the right of every person to have access to his or her file, while respecting the legitimate interests of confidentiality and of professional and business secrecy; the obligation of the administration to give reasons for its decisions. 3. Every person has the right to have the Community make good any damage caused by its institutions or by its servants in the performance of their duties, in accordance with the general principles common to the laws of the Member States. 4. Every person may write to the institutions of the Union in one of the languages of the Treaties and must have an answer in the same language.' Charter EU (n 169) art 41.

181 'Everyone whose rights and freedoms guaranteed by the law of the Union are violated has the right to an effective remedy before a tribunal in compliance with the conditions laid down in this Article. Everyone is entitled to a fair and public hearing within a reasonable time by an independent and impartial tribunal previously established by law. Everyone shall have the possibility of being advised, defended and represented. Legal aid shall be made available to those who lack sufficient resources in so far as such aid is necessary to ensure effective access to justice'. Charter EU (n 169) art 47.

182 However, the Recast Reception Conditions Directive and the Recast Asylum Procedures Directive would not apply due to their geographical limitation. K Pollet (n 165) 74, 91, 93.

183 ibid 74, 91.

184 V Moreno-Lax, *Accessing Asylum in Europe* (Oxford, Oxford University Press, 2017) 395-459.

185 See, among many others, *Sultani v France*: 'un recours dépourvu d'effet suspensif automatique ne satisfaisait pas aux conditions d'effectivité de l'article 13 de la Convention'. [an appeal deprived of automatic suspensive effect does not satisfy the effectiveness requirements of article 13 of the Convention.]. *Sultani v France* App no 45223/05 (ECtHR, 20 September 2007) para 50.

186 van Ballegooij (n 146) 73.

To address States' concerns on detrimental effects that the adoption of these arrangements may entail, especially fears of a pull factor, the issuance of humanitarian visas could be progressive and be first introduced in countries where the presence of persons from top refugee-producing States is most demanding and there is either a presumption of lack of safety/need for protection from *refoulement*[187] or the need to relieve the hosting countries from high influxes of refugees. A strategy of controlled roll-out in progressive phases in selected countries would be required.[188] Also, discussions and agreements with third countries on the consequences for them regarding hosting additional international protection seekers at least temporarily should be carried out.[189]

Whether this proposal would be a viable option for significant numbers of refugees has not been tested yet, but it certainly has potential and should be further explored.

5 Conclusion

The focus of this chapter has been on the HCs, as they had more impact than other instances when humanitarian visas have been used. The HCs were born as a pilot project at the end of 2015. The three most important features of the HCs highlighted here are: (1) the aim of creating a legal pathway to admission for people who need international protection, taking into consideration State's concerns such as security issues; (2) the focus on a wide understanding of vulnerability of the beneficiaries, encompassing those who would qualify for asylum, assessed together with integration potential and avoidance of secondary movements; (3) the FBOs' role, sponsorship, and involvement from the selection process to the reception and community-based integration activities. Moreover, the HCs have given an opportunity for lobbying towards a wider use of humanitarian visas and private sponsorship projects. It was pointed out that in Italy, the HCs were possible due to the influence that the catholic groups have often played in immigration policy and legislation, both through direct lobbying of political parties and call-up of the public.

Whereas a drawback of the HCs and the use of humanitarian visas in general in Italy is that they are based on non-binding instruments and the

187 van Ballegooij (n 146) 74.
188 ibid 75.
189 Pollet (n 165) 74, 93.

sovereign discretion of the State, the recourse to soft law and discretionary mechanisms was a necessary evil given the lack of international legal obligations. In order to have a significant impact in the context of the issues that they try to address, the HCs would require to be extended, expanded and developed at the European level.[190] For an effective programme, responsibility for protection should be shared between civil society and the State, and regulated by law. At the European level, a harmonised policy approach to alternative pathways would be needed for those who seek protection and are still in transit countries. In particular, a uniform understanding of rights and qualification criteria for the issuance of humanitarian visas would be required in order to adopt a coordinated action in compliance with EU values and principles. Without it, 'legal certainty, foreseeability, and the similar application and implementation of the relevant rules cannot be guaranteed.'[191] Member States and asylum seekers' trust in the system 'depends on the existence of a level playing field, which Member States acting alone cannot provide'.[192] While it is recognised that this proposal may clash with reality, it has a number of merits, which, among others, would address the protection gaps present in CEAS, increase control over the visa application process, and allow for better screening of beneficiaries and predictability of arrivals.

190 M Collyer (n 5) 4.
191 van Ballegooij (n 146) 60.
192 ibid.

Appendix

Interviewee	Affiliation	Date of interview and location of interviewee
M Bonafede	Representative, Waldensian Church at the Italian Federation of Evangelic Churches; Promoter, Humanitarian Corridors	Turin, Italy, 13 May 2018
A Capannini	Volunteer, Operazione Colomba	Rome, Italy, 24 May 2018
B Chioccioli	Project and Communication Officer, Mediterranean Hope	Rome, Italy, 12 May 2018
Coordinator	Community of Sant'Egidio	Rome, Italy, 19 April 2018
O Forti	National Coordinator, Humanitarian Corridors for Caritas	Rome, Italy, 7 February 2019
C Hein	Board Member and Founder, Italian Refugee Council; Adjunct Professor, Department of Political Science, Luiss University	Rome, Italy, 26 April 2018
G de Monte	Journalist, Communication Office, Mediterranean Hope	Rome, Italy, 12 February 2019
P Naso	Professor of History and Religion, Faculty of Literature, Sapienza University; Coordinator, Mediterranean Hope	Rome, Italy, 26 April 2018
C Pani	Head of Humanitarian Corridors in Ethiopia, Community of Sant'Egidio	Rome, Italy, 15 February 2019
D Pompei	Coordinator, Humanitarian Corridors, Community of Sant'Egidio	Rome, Italy, 3 May 2018
Researcher	Oxford University	Oxford, UK, 18 April 2018
S Scotta	Operator, Mediterranean Hope in Lebanon	Beirut, Lebanon, 24 May 2018 and 28 January 2019
C di Stasio	Lecturer, Faculty of Law, University of Brescia	Brescia, Italy, 26 April 2018
Social worker	Social services	Genoa, Italy, 24 April 2018

Chapter 5:
Humanitarian Admission to Germany – Access vs. Rights ?

Pauline Endres de Oliveira[1]

Contents

---

1 Lawyer at the bar of Berlin and PhD Fellow at the Justus-Liebig-University Gießen, with a focus on legal access to protection in the EU. The author worked as consultant for UNHCR Germany during the implementation of the Humanitarian Admission Schemes for Syrians from 2014 to 2016 and is member of Amnesty International's expert commission on asylum. Special thanks to Rebecca Einhoff, UNHCR Germany, and Nikolas Feith Tan, Danish Institute for Human Rights, for their valuable comments and insights.

6.1 *Introduction*

Legal access to protection is one of the most contested issues in refugee law.[2] In the absence of an explicit entry right for refugees, humanitarian admission seems to be promising for individuals and States by offering a method of safe as well as regulated arrival in receiving countries.[3] After the CJEU indicated that it is within the Member States' jurisdiction to issue a 'humanitarian visa' to access an asylum procedure in the EU,[4] the German Constitutional Court emphasised the fact that there is no such option in national law.[5] As regards Germany, the term 'humanitarian visa', therefore, refers to existing visa schemes with humanitarian scope, ranging from

2 See further P Endres de Oliveira, 'Legaler Zugang zu internationalem Schutz – Zur Gretchenfrage im Flüchtlingsrecht' (2016) *Kritische Justiz* 49(2) 167.

3 See, for instance, F McKay, S L Thomas and S Kneebone, 'It would be ok if they came through the proper channels': Community Perceptions and Attitudes Towards Asylum Seekers' *Australia Journal of Refugee Studies* (2015) 25(1) 113; see also J v Selm, 'The Strategic Use of Resettlement: Changing the Face of Protection?' (2004) Refuge 22, 43: 'if a country resettles refugees, as opposed to seeing them arrive spontaneously, the authorities know who they are, the people enter legally, and the process can be managed.'.

4 See Case C-638/16 *X. and X. vs. Belgium*, ECLI:EU:C:2017:173; for a critical discussion see P Endres de Oliveira, 'Humanitäre Visa für Flüchtlinge, Teil 1: Nicht mit der EU' and C Ziebritzki, 'Humanitäre Visa für Flüchtlinge, Teil 2: Wirklich keine Angelegenheit der EU?' (2017) *Verfassungsblog* 09 March 2017.

5 See BVerfG 2 BvR 1758/17, Judgement of 11 October 2017, para. 16.

individual admission to large scale ad hoc schemes and permanent resettlement. One thing all of these 'protected entry procedures'[6] have in common is that a residence permit on humanitarian grounds is granted immediately upon arrival, without an asylum procedure.[7] Humanitarian admission has a long tradition in Germany, going back to 1956, when approximately 13,000 refugees from Hungary were admitted (to Western Germany).[8] Since 2013, humanitarian admission programmes have focused on the conflict in Syria, enabling the legal entry of over 44,000 individuals from Syria and its neighbouring countries. Beneficiaries are mostly individuals with special needs as well as personal links to Germany.

This chapter analyses different methods of humanitarian access to Germany by outlining existing legal grounds and respective procedures. Thereby, it compares the status of beneficiaries to the status granted in national asylum procedures. A particular focus lies on protection seekers from Syria as the largest group of asylum seekers as well as the main beneficiaries of humanitarian admission. The analysis shows that their status, and therewith the quality of protection, does not merely depend on the individual circumstances of the case, but on external factors such as how and when individuals arrived in Germany.

---

6 See further on this notion Noll, Gregor / Fagerlund, Jessica / Liebaut, Fabrice, 'Study on the Feasibility of Processing Asylum Claims Outside the EU against the Background of the Common European Asylum System and the Goal of a Common Asylum Procedure' EU Commission / Danish Centre for Human Rights (Brussels 2002), 21.

7 The term therewith also differs from the notion of 'humanitarian visa' as used by the European Parliament in its resolution of 11 December 2018 with recommendations to the Commission on Humanitarian Visas (2018/2271(INL)), available at http://www.europarl.europa.eu/sides/getDoc.do?pubRef=-//EP//TEXT+TA+P8-TA-2018-0494+0+DOC+XML+V0//EN&language=EN, [last accessed 15 July 2019].

8 See B Huber/J Eichenhofer/P Endres de Oliveira, Aufenthaltsrecht (C.H. Beck, 2017) 107 ff., with reference to the provisions of the former 'Kontingentflüchtlingsgesetz' (HumHAG) that also served as the basis for the admission of around 35,000 Vietnamese 'boat people' between 1970 and 1980, and around 350,000 refugees from Bosnia during the 1990s; for a detailed overview of all cases of humanitarian admission to Germany, see Grote, Janne, 'Humanitarian Admission Programmes in Germany for Beneficiaries of Protection from Syria' (2017) Federal Office for Migration and Refugees, German National Contact Point oft he European Migration Network, 15.

6.2 Admission in exceptional individual cases

When considering legal access options for individuals in need of protection, Section 22 of the German Residence Act[9] is of particular interest. In contrast to admission schemes targeting specific situations and group admission based on quotas (regulated in Section 23 Residence Act, see below at 6.3 ff.), Section 22 Residence Act allows for an *individual* 'admission from abroad'. It is therewith possible to approach a German representation with an individual request for a visa on the basis of this provision, which reads as follows:

> A foreigner may be granted a temporary residence permit for the purpose of admission from abroad in accordance with international law or on urgent humanitarian grounds. A temporary residence permit must be granted if the Federal Ministry of the Interior or the body designated by it has declared, so as to uphold the political interests of the Federal Republic of Germany, that the foreigner is to be admitted. [...]

An admission 'in accordance with international law' (sentence 1 Alt. 1) is meant to cover cases of international commitments, as, for instance, on the basis of bi- or multilateral agreements, or respect for the interests of other States and international organisations. The requirement of 'urgent humanitarian grounds' (sentence 1 Alt. 2) can apply to particularly exceptional situations of humanitarian needs, such as cases of severe illness and extreme emergency situations, that differ from the general situation in the country of origin. Thus, the need to flee from an internal conflict, as, for instance, the conflict in Syria, is not considered 'urgent humanitarian grounds'. The provision has therefore been of little use to individuals trying to flee Syria and seek protection through humanitarian admission in Germany. Additionally, there is the unwritten requirement to demonstrate *links to Germany*.[10] Although family reunification is generally not covered by this provision, a recent example of its application is the granting of visas to family members of unaccompanied minors with subsidiary protection status in particularly exceptional cases, after family reunification rights of beneficiaries of subsidiary protection had been restricted in 2016 (see below at

9 Residence Act of 25 Feb. 2008 (*Aufenthaltsgesetz*), available at: www.gesetze-im-internet.de/englisch_aufenthg/ [last accessed 15 July 2019].

10 See Huber/Eichenhofer/Endres de Oliveira (n 8) 116, with further references.

6.7.2).[11] Relevant examples of admissions following a declaration of the Federal Ministry of the Interior to 'uphold the political interests' of Germany (sentence 2) are admissions of local Afghan staffmembers of the German Mission in Afghanistan (part of NATO's ISAF mission) and their family members. This has been an option since 2013 for individual applicants independent of a quota on the basis of a so-called 'risk notifications'.[12] Another recent example is the admission of members of the civil defence unit 'White Helmets'[13] and their families from Syria.[14]

The examples show that while Section 22 allows for an individual admission from abroad, beneficiaries are mostly individuals belonging to certain groups. All in all, Section 22 is of little practical relevance.[15] As in all of the access options described hereafter, the decision to grant access to Germany via humanitarian visa is a discretionary act, an expression of national sovereignty.[16] Only errors in assessment or a failure to exercise discretion are subject to judicial scrutiny. Due to its highly exceptional character and a range of unwritten requirements, Section 22 is rarely applied. In comparison to the (group) admission schemes discussed hereafter, admission numbers in that catgory are therefore very low.

6.3 Quota-based admission at federal level: Ad hoc schemes for individuals fleeing Syria

In light of the highly exceptional character of Section 22, the focus of humanitarian admission in Germany lies on quota-based governmental pro-

---

11 See H Cremer, 'Kein Recht auf Familie für subsidiär Schutzberechtigte? Zur Anwendung von § 22 Satz 1 AufenthG nach den Vorgaben der UN-Kinderrechtskonvention', *Asylmagazin* 3/2018, 65; see also Anna Schmitt und Sebastian Muy, '"Aufnahme aus dem Ausland" beim Familiennachzug – Anwendung des § 22 Satz 1 AufenthG beim Familiennachzug zu subsidiär Schutzberechtigten', *Asylmagazin* 6/2017, 217.

12 See Grote (n 8) 17 f., 21 and 24, with details on the selection process and actors involved; see also Deutscher Bundestag, Wissenschaftliche Dienste 'Humanitärer Schutz für afghanische Ortskräfte' - WD 3 – 3000 – 170/16.

13 See https://whitehelmets.org/en/ [last accessed 15 July 2019].

14 See https://resettlement.de/aufnahme-von-weisshelmen-in-deutschland/ [last accessed 15 April 2019].

15 See Huber/Eichenhofer/Endres de Oliveira (n 8) 115; see also P Endres de Oliveira, 'Schutz syrischer Flüchtlinge in Deutschland – Welche Möglichkeiten für einen sicheren Aufenthalt gibt es?' *Asylmagazin* 9/2014, 284, 289.

16 See BVerwG 1 C 21.10, Judgement of 15.11.2011, para.10.

grammes, targeting specific situations and groups of people. In contrast to Section 22, there is no general option of applying for an individual admission. Admissions follow specific 'admission orders' (*Aufnahmeanordnungen*) from the Federal Ministry of the Interior, issued in accordance with the supreme *Land* authorities.[17] The 'admission orders' determine the details of the procedure as well as admission criteria regarding potential beneficiaries. In the following, the focus lies on Section 23 subsection 2 Residence Act, which foresees admission at federal level 'when special political interests' apply and reads as follows:

> In order to safeguard special political interests of the Federal Republic of Germany, the Federal Ministry of the Interior may, in consultation with the supreme Land authorities, order foreigners from specific states or certain categories of foreigners defined by other means to be granted approval for admission by the Federal Office for Migration and Refugees. [...] The foreigners concerned shall be issued a temporary residence permit or permanent settlement permit, in accordance with the approval for admission. [...]

This provision has been the legal basis for various admission schemes at federal level, such as the admission of 2,500 Iraqi nationals from Jordan and Syria in 2009 and 2010, as well as the admission of Jewish immigrants from the former Soviet Union, which is still ongoing.[18] In recent times, the focus has lain on the admission of individuals who fled the conflict in Syria ('HAP Syria' 1 – 3 and 'HAP Turkey').

6.3.1 HAP Syria 1 – 3: Procedure and beneficiaries

The first *Humanitarian Admission Programme for Beneficiaries of Protection from Syria, its Neighbouring Countries, Egypt and Libya* (HAP Syria 1) was launched in May 2013, following urgent calls from civil society, UNHCR

---

17 For a listing of respective admission orders as well as information on arrivals from 2015 to 2019 through legal access schemes in Germany (including information on numbers, first country of refuge, nationality and residence permit), see https://resettlement.de/en/current-admissions/ [last accessed 15 July 2019].

18 Jewish immigrants receive a permanent residence permit immediately upon arrival on the basis of Section 23 subsection 2 sentence 3 Residence Act, see further Huber/Eichenhofer/Endres de Oliveira (n 8) 122 f.

and the German Parliament.[19] The federal minister of the interior agreed with the interior ministers and senators of the federal *Länder* on the admission of 5,000 particularly vulnerable individuals for the duration of the conflict. Two additional admission programmes followed with quotas of 5,000 places in December 2013 (HAP Syria 2) and 10,000 in July 2014 (HAP Syria 3). Admissions mainly took place from Syria, Lebanon, Egypt and Libya.[20] Together with the Goethe Institute, the International Organization for Migration (IOM) assisted in providing travel and pre-departure information, including cultural orientation. During the respective visa procedures, embassies cooperated with the local immigration offices, which were responsible for issuing residence permits upon arrival.[21] All of these federal programmes have ended.

The Federal Office for Migration and Refugees selected the beneficiaries on the basis of respective case referrals. Individuals qualifying for HAP Syria 1 were initially identified by UNHCR and Caritas Lebanon as well as German missions in the region on the basis of the admission criteria as set out for each programme. The requirements were specified in the respective 'admission orders' and adjusted over time. HAP Syria 2 and 3 also allowed for the federal *Länder* to propose individuals for an admission. Beneficiaries of the three HAP Syria were mainly Syrian nationals, however, HAP Syria 2 and 3 also included stateless Palestinians and Kurds from Syria on an individual basis. The selection was not merely based on humanitarian criteria (such as medical needs, women-at-risk, or other forms of vulnerability). The schemes particularly targeted individuals demonstrating 'links to Germany', or the 'the ability to make a contribution to the reconstruction of Syria' at the end of the conflict.[22] Individuals with a criminal record or under the suspicion of membership of a terrorist or criminal organisation, or believed to have engaged in any kind of activities considered as a danger for international peace and security, were excluded from admission.

---

19 Sachverständigenrat deutscher Stiftungen für Integration und Migration (SVR), 'Sicherer Zugang – Die humanitären Aufnahmeprogramme für syrische Flüchtlinge in Deutschland' (2015), 14.

20 Admission orders are available at https://resettlement.de/humanitaere-aufnahme-programme/ [last accessed 15 July 2019].

21 See SVR (n 19) 16 for detailed information on the selection process.

22 See further Grote (n 8) 25, pointing out that the first priority of HAP 1 was to oversee the humanitarian situation of the individual applicant, the first priorities of HAP 2 and 3 were links to Germany.

6.3.2 Admissions on the basis of the EU-Turkey-Statement: HAP Turkey

In addition to the three HAP Syria, Germany reassigned 13,694 places originally foreseen to comply with the EU relocation programme[23] to the admission of Syrians from Turkey ('HAP Turkey'), following the EU-Turkey-Statement[24] of March 2016.[25] These admissions are based on 'admission orders' of the German Federal Ministry of the Interior in accordance with the supreme *Land* authorities of the federal *Länder*, foreseeing admission of up to 500 individuals per month until 31 December 2019.[26] Beneficiaries are selected by the German Federal Office for Migration and Refugees on the basis of proposals made by UNHCR in cooperation with the Turkish asylum authority (Directorate General of Migration Management, DGMM). There has been criticism regarding a lack of transparency of the selection criteria applied by the DGMM, which has the right of proposal.[27] While beneficiaries were initially granted a residence permit on the basis of Section 23 subsection 4 Residence Act (resettlement, see below at 6.5), admissions are now based on Section 23 subsection 2 Residence Act. As further discussed below (at 6.7), this distinction is not irrelevant, since the scope of rights granted upon arrival varies substantially depending on the legal basis of the admission.

---

23 For information on Member States' Support to the Emergency Relocation Mechanism as of 30 October 2018 see https://ec.europa.eu/home-affairs/sites/homeaffairs/files/what-we-do/policies/european-agenda-migration/press-material/docs/state_of_play_-_relocation_en.pdf [last accessed 15 July 2019].

24 EU-Turkey Statement, Press Release, 18 March 2016, available at: www.consilium.europa.eu/en/press/press-releases/2016/03/18-eu-turkey-statement/ [last accessed 15 July 2019].

25 See further on resettlement under the EU Turkey Statement, C Ziebritzky in this volume.

26 The latest 'admission order' of 21 December 2018 is available at https://www.bmi.bund.de/SharedDocs/downloads/DE/veroeffentlichungen/themen/migration/humanitaere-aufnahmeprogramme/aufnahmeanordnung-8.pdf?__blob=publicationFile&v=1 [last accessed 15 July 2019]; for information on latest arrivals see https://resettlement.de/en/current-admissions/ [last accessed 15 July 2019].

27 See E Lutter/V Zehnder/E Knezevic, 'Resettlement und humanitäre Aufnahmeprogramme – Rahmenbedingungen und Herausforderungen der aktuellen Aufnahmeverfahren in der Praxis, *Asylmagazin* 1-2/2018, 29, 33.

6.4 Humanitarian admission schemes at Länder level

Besides humanitarian admission at federal level, there is the possibility of an admission at *Länder* level according to Section 23 subsection 1 Residence Act, providing that:

> The supreme *Land* authority may order a temporary residence permit to be granted to foreigners from specific states or to certain groups of foreigners defined by other means, in accordance with international law, on humanitarian grounds or in order to uphold the political interests of the Federal Republic of Germany. The order may be issued subject to the proviso that a declaration of commitment be submitted in accordance with Section 68. In order to ensure a nationwide uniform approach, the order shall require the approval of the Federal Ministry of the Interior.

Again, there is no institutionalised admission procedure. Details regarding an admission on the basis of this provision are outlined in the respective 'admission orders'. Prominent examples of admissions based on this provision are the private sponsorship schemes for relatives of Syrian nationals implemented from 2013 onwards.

6.4.1 Private sponsorship programmes for relatives of Syrian nationals in Germany

Instead of extending existing options of family reunification or applying Section 22 Residence Act more broadly for relatives of Syrian nationals already living in Germany,[28] the temporary ad hoc schemes at federal level have been complemented by temporary admission schemes at *Länder* level since 2013 (in all federal *Länder* except Bavaria). These *Länder* schemes were particularly designed for Syrians with first or second degree relatives in Germany. They qualify as 'private sponsorship programmes',[29] since the main requirement is a 'declaration of commitment' (*Verpflichtungserklä-*

---

28 See further on Syrian immigrant population in Germany, N J Ragab/L Rahmeier/M Siegel, 'Mapping the Syrian Diaspora in Germany – Contributions to Peace, Reconstruction and Potentials for Collaboration with German Development Cooperation' (2017), Maastricht Graduate School of Governance, 15.

29 See further on private sponsorship, European Commission, *Study on the feasibility and added value of sponsorship schemes as a possible pathway to safe channels for admission to the EU, including resettlement* (2018).

rung) from a private sponsor in Germany undertaking to cover the accommodation and living expenses of the applicant. So far, the schemes have offered legal entry to over 24,000 individuals and are partly still ongoing.[30] Beneficiaries live in Germany with a residence permit based on Section 23 subsection 1 Residence Act. Although the target group can be the same (eg individuals fleeing the conflict in Syria), a residence permit based on Section 23 subsection 1 entails several restrictions compared to the residence permit granted to individuals admitted through the federal admission programmes or resettlement – and even more so in comparison to a residence permit granted to Convention refugees[31] on the basis of a national asylum procedure (see further below at 6.7). The quality of protection is not the only controversy raised by these private sponsorship schemes.

6.4.2 Controversies raised by private sponsorship: Duration of financial commitments

On the one hand, private sponsorship schemes can empower civil society by offering an option to actively engage in the safe entry of protection seekers. The personal contact between beneficiaries and sponsors has also proven to enhance the general social acceptance of humanitarian admission and facilitate integration.[32] On the other hand, the requirement of providing financial guarantees partly shifts the humanitarian responsibility of the State to civil society, and risks overstraining the financial capacities of the respective sponsors.[33] A particular example in this regard were the high financial burdens related to medical costs. Here, the *Länder* eventual-

30 There are ongoing programmes in Berlin, Brandenburg, Hamburg, Schleswig-Holstein and Thuringia; for an overview see https://resettlement.de/current-admissions/ [last accessed 15 July 2019].

31 See Article 1A of the Refugee Convention (UN General Assembly, *Convention Relating to the Status of Refugees*, 28 July 1951, United Nations, Treaty Series, vol. 189, 137, available at: https://www.refworld.org/docid/3be01b964.html [last accessed 15 July 2019].

32 See SVR (n 19) 23.

33 See for instance, C Schwarz, 'German Refugee Policy in the Wake of the Syrian Refugee Crisis', in: E Aksaz and J-F Pérouse (ed.), *"Guests and Aliens": Re-Configuring New Mobilities in the Eastern Mediterranean After 2011 – with a special focus on Syrian refugees* (2016) 1, 4; see also more generally S Labman, 'Private Sponsorship: Complementary or Conflicting Interests?', *Refuge* (2016) 32(2) 67; P T Lenard, 'Resettling Refugees: Is Private Sponsorship a Just Way Forward?' *Journal of Global Ethics* (2016) 12(3) 300; G Richie, 'Civil Society, the State, and Private

ly resumed responsibility for covering the health insurances of beneficiaries. However, a remaining issue is the duration of the declaration of commitment.[34] Until 2016, the declarations of commitment were of unlimited validity in most of the *Länder* schemes, putting the sponsors under great duress. Since the financial guarantees were granted within a visa procedure for a specific residence permit (on the basis of Section 23 subsection 1 Residence Act), several beneficiaries of the *Länder* schemes applied for asylum upon arrival, hoping that a potential change to Convention refugee status (on the basis of Section 25 subsection 2 Alt. 1 Residence Act) would release their relatives from the declaration of commitment. The following increase in asylum applications and judicial appeals put administrative and judicial bodies under pressure, taking away the advantages such an admission scheme offers by not depending on an asylum procedure.[35] A legislative change introduced with the Integration Act (*Integrationsgesetz*) on 7 July 2016 put an end to debates regarding all future admissions: Section 68 subsection 1 sentence 4 Residence Act now provides for a five year duration of the declaration of commitment, independent of the (humanitarian) status of the beneficiary.[36] This was followed by a decision of the Federal Administrative Court of January 2017 regarding a prior case in which the court stated that a change of (humanitarian) status would not release the sponsors from their obligation to provide financial support for the respective applicants.[37] Although there is now a limitation of guarantees, a commitment to cover all costs over five years can still be a heavy burden. This consideration seems to have influenced the design of the current pilot programme 'NesT'. Before drawing attention to this new method of admission, the next section will discuss the German resettlement programme to complete the picture of established humanitarian access methods.

Sponsorship: The Political Economy of Refugee Resettlement' *International Journal of Lifelong Education* (2018) 37(1) 1.

34 To ease the financial burden of sponsors, the civil society organisation 'Flüchtlingspaten Syrien' (*Syrian Refugee Sponsors*) started to collect contributions and coordinate sponsorships, for more information see https://fluechtlingspaten-syrien.de.

35 See further Endres de Oliveira (n 15) 178.

36 See also Section 68a of the Residence Act, stipulating that financial commitments declared before the 6 August 2016 (entry into force of the Integration Act) expire after three years.

37 BVerwG 1 C10.16, 26 January 2017; for a critical discussion see M Riebau/C Hörich, 'Der Streit um die Verpflichtungserklärung geht weiter' *Asylmagazin* 7-8/2017, 272.

6.5 The German resettlement programme

Humanitarian admission based on fixed quotas is often generally referred to as 'resettlement'. This can be misleading as there are substantial differences between the *ad hoc* admission schemes described thus far and a permanent resettlement programme. Differences exist with regard to scope, procedure, admission quota and rights granted to beneficiaries upon arrival. Defined by UNHCR as one of the three 'durable solutions' (alongside voluntary repatriation and integration), 'Resettlement involves the selection and transfer of refugees from a State in which they have sought protection to a third State which has agreed to admit them – as refugees – with permanent residence status'.[38] In contrast to the long history of *ad hoc* humanitarian admission, a permanent resettlement programme in cooperation with UNHCR with a focus on protracted refugee situations has only recently been established in Germany. One of the driving forces behind the implementation was the *Save-me* campaign, launched in 2008 by various actors from civil society.[39] A decision by the Conference of Interior State Ministers in December 2011 opened the way for a pilot resettlement programme from 2012 to 2014 with an initial quota of 300 individual admissions per year. A permanent institutionalised scheme has been in place since 2014.[40] In 2015, Germany raised its permanent quota to 500 individuals per year and implemented a separate legal basis for resettlement in Section 23 subsection 4 Residence Act.[41] It provides that

> In consultation with the supreme *Land* authorities, the Federal Ministry of the Interior may, within the context of resettling persons seeking protection, order that the Federal Office for Migration and Refugees grant approval for admission to certain persons seeking pro-

---

38 See UN High Commissioner for Refugees (UNHCR), *Resettlement Handbook* (2011) 3, available at https://www.unhcr.org/protection/resettlement/4a2ccf4c6/unhcr-resettlement-handbook-country-chapters.html [last accessed 15 July 2019]; see also UNHCR, *Protracted Refugee Situations*, Doc. EC/54/SC/CRP.14, 10 June 2004, 1.

39 For more information see https://www.proasyl.de/material/save-me-fluechtlinge-aufnehmen/ [last accessed 15 July 2019].

40 See Grote (n 8) 13 ff.

41 This change was governed by the *Act to Redefine the Right to Stay and the Termination of Residence* (Gesetz zur Neubestimmung des Bleiberechts und der Aufenthaltsbeendigung). Before this statutory change, resettlement admissions were based on Section 23 subsection 2 Residence Act.

tection who have been selected for resettlement (resettlement refugees). [...]

6.5.1 Beneficiaries of resettlement

Germany has engaged in resettlement from Lebanon, Sudan, Egypt, Turkey, Tunisia, Syria and Indonesia. Recent admissions focussed on Jordan, Egypt, Ethiopia, Lebanon and Niger.[42] Similar to the ad hoc admission schemes discussed above, details regarding the procedure and admission criteria are not outlined directly in the Residence Act, but in a specific 'admission order'. Individuals admitted through resettlement generally fulfil at least one UNHCR criterion of particular vulnerability.[43] The proportion of women with special risk exposure, or individuals with particular physical or legal needs, such as elderly people or children, is therefore higher than in national asylum procedures.[44] Additionally, there are admission criteria without any humanitarian scope, such as particular links to Germany, as well as other factors indicating the 'integration potential' of the respective individual – for instance the educational level, professional background, language skills, religious affiliation and age.[45] A study analysing the relevance of such 'utilitarian considerations'[46] raises the question of 'whether the resettlement programme is based on an interest in the selection of "desired refugees" or whether the humanitarian concern for protection is foremost'.[47] On the basis of an evaluation of statistical data regarding the background of individuals admitted through resettlement to Germany from 2012 to 2014, the authors conclude that Germany consistently complied with the three key principles of resettlement as proclaimed by UNHCR (that is protection of individuals at risk, providing

42 An overview of recent admissions is available at https://resettlement.de/aktuelle-aufnahmen/[last accessed 15 July 2019].

43 Detailed information on the resettlement criteria of UNHCR is available at https://www.unhcr.org/protection/resettlement/558c015e9/resettlement-criteria.html [last accessed 15 July 2019].

44 See T Baraulina, M Bitterwolf (2018): Resettlement in Germany – What is the programme for particularly vulnerable refugees accomplishing? Issue 04/2018 of the Brief Analyses of the Migration Integration and Asylum Research Centre at the Federal Office for Migration and Refugees, Research Centre.

45 See Grote (n 8) 24.

46 This term is used in the feasibility study on protected entry procedures to describe admission criteria particularly promoting State interests, see Noll et. all (n 6) 5.

47 See Baraulina/Bitterwolf (n 44) 3.

durable solutions and international solidarity),[48] despite the additional national admission criteria.[49]

6.5.2 *Resettlement procedures*

There is no possibility for individuals to apply directly for resettlement to Germany. The identification and selection of beneficiaries follows the general steps of the UNHCR resettlement programme.[50] The Federal Office for Migration and Refugees conducts a preliminary assessment of cases preselected by UNHCR, focussing on plausibility, matching of national admission criteria and security considerations. This is followed by personal interviews with potential beneficiaries. After a positive decision from the Federal Office for Migration and Refugees, the German embassy in the region conducts the visa procedure, which mainly consists of identity and security checks. IOM assists with medical screenings, pre-departure-orientation and the organisation of charter flights to Germany.[51] Upon arrival in Germany, resettlement refugees are received by officials of the Federal Office for Migration and Refugees at the airport, where further security screenings take place before they are transferred to the initial reception centres in Friedland (Lower Saxony).[52] The local immigration office is responsible for granting a residence permit on the basis of Section 23 subsection 4 Residence Act.

In contrast to the traditional UNCHR definition of (permanent) status, Section 23 subsection 4 provides for a *temporary* 'resettlement refugee' status, which is similar, but not the same as the status granted to Convention refugees on the basis of a national asylum procedure (see further below at 6.7). All in all, resettlement is now well established in terms of admission criteria, procedure, and cooperation with UNHCR. It is therefore questionable whether mandatory requirements regarding the selection of indi-

48 See UNHCR *Resettlement Handbook* (n 38), 36 ff.
49 Baraulina/Bitterwolf (n 44) 10 f.
50 For further information on the UNHCR resettlement programme see https://www.unhcr.org/resettlement.html, [last accessed 15 July 2019].
51 See Huber/Eichenhofer/Endres de Oliveira (n 8) 124; see also Grote (n 8) 19.
52 Further information on the reception in Friedland is available at https://www.bamf.de/SharedDocs/Dossiers/DE/resettlement-dossier-2018.html?nn=1367526&notFirst=true&docId=10785132 [last accessed 15 July 2019].

viduals or target countries potentially introduced by a new Resettlement Regulation[53] at EU level would benefit the programme in Germany.

6.5.3 *Germany's commitment to the EU resettlement programme: A game of numbers*

In 2016 and 2017, Germany took part in the EU resettlement pilot programme, committing to an admission of a total of 1600 resettlement refugees within two years. This quota replaced (and raised) the annual quota of 500 admissions. A comparably impressive number of admissions was announced for 2018 and 2019: A total of 10,200 places was offered as part of Germany's commitment to the European resettlement framework.[54] For 2020, 5500 places were announced. This raise shows a growing commitment to humanitarian admission. However, the number also add to the confusion of resettlement with other humanitarian access options, because they actually divide themselves over different admission schemes.[55] As will be discussed below (at 6.7), this is not irrelevant in light of differences in status rights depending on the legal basis of the admission. The largest part of the announced 5500 admissions for 2020 covers admissions under 'HAP Turkey' on the basis of Section 23 subsection 2 Residence Act (see above at 6.3.2). Another 200 places are foreseen for an admission at *Länder* level in Schleswig-Holstein on the basis of Section 23 subsection 1 Residence Act. Actual resettlement on the basis of Section 23 subsection 4 is foreseen for in total of 1900 admissions. [56] Eventually, the upcoming 'NesT programme' will provide for admission of up to 400 individuals, who will also be granted 'resettlement refugee status' on the basis of Section 23 subsection 4 Residence. The next section will now draw attention to this new method of admission to Germany.

---

53 Proposal for a REGULATION OF THE EUROPEAN PARLIAMENT AND OF THE COUNCIL establishing a Union Resettlement Framework and amending Regulation (EU) No 516/2014 of the European Parliament and the Council, COM/2016/0468 final - 2016/0225 (COD).

54 https://resettlement.de/current-admissions/ and https://eur-lex.europa.eu/LexUriServ/LexUriServ.do?uri=OJ:L:2012:092:0001:0003:EN:PDF, [last accessed 6 January 2020].

55 For an overview see https://resettlement.de/resettlement-aufnahmen-in-2018-und-2019/[last accessed 15 July 2019].

56 See https://www.tagesschau.de/inland/fluechtlinge-umsiedlung-101.html [last accessed 6 January 2020].

6.6 *Combining resettlement with community sponsorship: The NesT-Programme*

The private sponsorship schemes at *Länder* level have shown that personal contact between individuals in need of protection and civil society can enhance the social acceptance of humanitarian admission.[57] Individual relations can also facilitate integration, allowing for more options of participation in social life. The pilot programme 'NesT'[58] combines these positive aspects of private sponsorship with elements of traditional resettlement, setting new standards for community sponsorship in Germany. It has been designed in cooperation with UNHCR, various members of civil society and the support of the Bertelsmann and Mercator Foundations. Beneficiaries are identified and pre-selected by UNHCR and granted a residence permit on the basis of Section 23 subsection 4 Residence Act upon arrival.

6.6.1 *The mentorship scheme as novelty to resettlement*

In contrast to traditional resettlement, the NesT programme foresees a mentoring scheme, including financial as well as non-material (integration) support from civil society. The Federal Office for Migration and Refugees is responsible for mentorship applications. If the application is approved, it proposes allocating a single person or family, previously selected from the UNHCR proposals, to interested mentors. If possible, the first contact between mentors and beneficiaries is to be established before arrival. The first personal encounter is then meant to take place in the presence of the staff members of Caritas in Friedland, where beneficiaries are to be offered orientation classes upon arrival.[59] While anyone can become a mentor – institutions, associations and individuals alike – individuals have to apply in a group of at least five, of whom two are to be the main contact persons. In contrast to the financial commitment required by the *Länder* schemes, 'mentors' are only asked to provide for the basic rent dur-

57 See SVR (n 19) 23.

58 See https://www.neustartimteam.de [last accessed 6 January 2020]. In late 2019, two individuals and three families have already entered Germany on the basis of NesT.

59 See the information provided by the Federal Ministry of the Interior at a conference in January 2019, available at https://www.akademie-rs.de/fileadmin/user_upload/download_archive/migration/20190126_wuertenberger_nest.pdf [last accessed 15 July 2019].

ing a period of *two years* (to be transferred in advance on a fiduciary account). Non-material support is required during a period of *one year* and consists of being the main contact person, offering support with finding a living space, a job, a place at a school or a vocational training, assistance with administrative issues, accompanying beneficiaries to official appointments, helping with translations etc. Further details regarding the mentorship are provided at a one-day information event free of charge, organised by the national contact point for civil society (*Zivilgesellschaftliche Kontaktstelle*, ZKS), an institution implemented for the sole purpose of assisting in the implementation of the programme. During the initial pilot phase of the programme, the ZKS consists of representatives of the German Caritas, the German Red Cross and the Evangelical Church of Westphalia. The latter finances the ZKS together with the Bertelsmann and Mercator Foundations.[60]

6.6.2 NesT – Weak resettlement or improved private-sponsorship?

Declaring admissions under the NesT programme as 'resettlement' has advantages and drawbacks with a view to offering legal access to protection: On the one side, the State relies on civil society to fulfil its commitments to resettlement. Here, an important aspect is the additionality of admissions: Replacing (parts of) the annual resettlement quota by such a private sponsorship scheme would certainly narrow and not enhance the possible scope of protection offered through humanitarian admission. On the other side, the financial commitment of 'mentors' part of the NesT programme is not as broad as the commitment of sponsors of the *Länder* schemes. From this perspective, the NesT programme can be seen as an improved form of private sponsorship. Moreover, beneficiaries of the NesT programme are granted the status of resettlement refugees – and therewith the strongest status to be achieved through humanitarian admission. This tackles the issue of how access and rights relate to each other, to be discussed in the following.

60 See information available at https://www.unhcr.org/dach/de/30736-neues-aufnahmeprogramm-nest-vorgestellt.html [last accessed 15 July 2019].

6.7 *Access vs. rights?*

This section discusses how the rights granted to individuals in need of protection vary depending on external factors such as the method and time of their arrival. Existing differences in status rights have led to harsh criticism of humanitarian admission, described as a 'neo-liberalization of refugee policies'[61] and 'containment of refugee flows'.[62] At first sight, there seems to be a trade-off between access and rights to the detriment of the protection seeker. Most affected are protection seekers from Syria, as they are not only the largest group of asylum seekers,[63] but also the main beneficiaries of humanitarian admission; they live in Germany with different resident permits and therewith different rights, depending on how and when they arrived. However, when comparing the rights accorded to beneficiaries of different humanitarian admission schemes and resettlement with the rights of individuals granted Convention refugee or subsidiary protection status on the basis of a national asylum procedure, the picture becomes more complex: With regard to crucial rights, such as permanent settlement and family reunification, resettlement refugees are in a stronger position than beneficiaries of subsidiary protection who arrived in Germany after 2016 – and therefore after the number of 'spontaneous asylum seekers' had increased significantly. The critizised trade-off between access and rights has since been replaced by a favourable treatement of individuals who accessed Germany legally, particularly through resettlement. To illustrate this changing correlation of access and rights, this section will at first discuss the quality of protection with respect to the method of arrival. A focus will thereby lie on the initial reception, the duration of the residence permit, options of permanent settlement as well as access to employment and language courses. Family reunification will be discussed separately in a second step, as it particularly exemplifies how not only the method but also the time of arrival affects the quality of protection.

---

61 Schwarz (n 33) 4.

62 See C Tometten, 'Resettlement, Humanitarian Admission, and Family Reunion: The Intricacies of Germany's Legal Entry Regimes for Syrian Refugees', Refugee Survey Quarterly, 2018, 37, 200 and 203.

63 Statistics of the German asylum authority BAMF are available at http://www.bamf.de/DE/Infothek/Statistiken/Asylzahlen/Asylgeschäftsstatistik/asylgeschaeftsstatistik-node.html [last accessed 15 April 2019].

6.7.1 *The quality of protection and the method of arrival*

Protection seekers who arrive in Germany 'spontaneously' have to undergo a national asylum procedure, which can lead to either a status based on the national right to asylum,[64] international protection (Convention refugee or subsidiary protection status[65]) or a status based on a national deportation ban.[66] The national right to asylum and Convention refugee status lead to the strongest humanitarian status in Germany.[67] An equally strong legal position cannot be achieved through ad hoc humanitarian admission nor resettlement. Individuals who enter Germany through any of the above discussed admission schemes, including resettlement, receive a temporary residence permit upon arrival, which varies depending on the legal basis of the admission and is generally less favourable than the residence permit granted to Convention refugees. However, the legal position of resettlement refugees comes very close to Convention refugee status.

6.7.1.1 *Reception and place of residence*

A particular feature of resettlement and *federal* humanitarian admission schemes is the initial accommodation at the special reception centre in Friedland. Beneficiaries are offered 14-day-orientation and language courses before they are allocated to different communities across Germany. This kind of special initial reception is not offered to asylum seekers, nor to beneficiaries of private sponsorship schemes at *Länder* level. Regarding the place of residence, the situation of individuals admitted through resettlement and *federal* humanitarian admission programmes is similar to asylum seekers who have been granted a protection status on the basis of a national asylum procedure: The allocation is determined by a specific distribu-

64 See Article 16a subsection 1 of the German Constitution. The issuance of the respective residence permit is based on Section 25 subsection 1 Residence Act.

65 The issuance of the respective residence permit is based on Section 25 subsection 2 alt. 1 (Convention refugee status) or subsection 2 alt. 2 (subsidiary protection) 2 Residence Act.

66 A residence permit issued due to a national deportation ban is based on Section 25 subsection 3 Residence Act.

67 Due to the exclusion clause (national safe-third-country concept) enshrined in Article 16a subsection 2, a status based on the national right to asylum is hardly ever granted.

tion key, the 'Königssteiner Schlüssel'.[68] Individuals who entered Germany through private sponsorship at *Länder* level or the new NesT programme on the basis of a declaration of commitment are allocated in the same administrative district as the respective sponsor or mentor.[69]

6.7.1.2 *Duration of stay and options of permanent settlement*

The duration of stay and options of permanent settlement differ widely. Here lies the first difference between resettlement refugees and beneficiaries of other humanitarian admission schemes. As with Convention refugees, resettlement refugees are granted a residence permit with an initial duration of three years. A permanent residence permit shall be granted after three or five years depending on how well integrated the respective person is, in particular concerning language skills and financial subsistence.[70] In contrast to resettlement, with its focus on a durable solution, humanitarian admission schemes are based on the assumption that beneficiaries only need 'temporary protection' for the duration of a specific conflict. Individuals who arrived in Germany through an *ad hoc* admission scheme at federal or *Länder* level are therefore in a less favourable position than resettlement refugees: While the duration of their residence permit varies from two to three years, depending on the respective 'admission order', a permanent residence permit can only be granted after five years at the earliest, with high thresholds regarding the necessary level of language skills and subsistence.[71] Resettlement refugees are also in a stronger pos-

---

68 See Section 12a Residence Act; for a critical discussion of this provision with respect to beneficiaries of international protection, see Huber/Eichenhofer/Endres de Oliveira (n 8) 162 ff.

69 As in all cases of a mandatory allocation of residence in Germany, the requirement may be lifted for urgent humanitarian reasons or as soon as the respective individual is no longer dependant on social benefits or the financial commitment of a sponsor.

70 See Section 26 subsection 3 Residence Act. While the threshold regarding the necessary level of German (C1 GER) and subsistence is still difficult to meet when applying for a permanent residence permit after three years, the conditions are easier to meet after five years: A lower level of German (A2 GER) and subsistence is needed.

71 See Section 26 subsection 4 Residence Act. Under Section 23 subsection 2 sentence 3 Residence Act, there is also the option of granting a permanent resident permit directly upon arrival, see further Huber/Eichenhofer/Endres de Oliveira (n 8) 122 f.

ition than beneficiaries of subsidiary protection, who are mostly granted a residence permit for the duration of one year, and do not benefit from the option of optaining a permanent resident permit under privileged conditions.[72]

6.7.1.3 Access to work, social benefits and language courses

The residence permits granted to beneficiaries of international protection as well as to individuals who enter Germany legally through federal admission or resettlement allow for both employment and freelance work. In contrast, individuals admitted through private sponsorship schemes at *Länder* level have to obtain a separate work permit to be able to take up employment, and are only allowed to take up freelance work in exceptional cases.[73] Although anyone in financial need can, in principle, claim social benefits in Germany, the financial commitment required for an admission through private sponsorship allows the State to take recourse against the respective sponsor. Another drawback of a residence permit following an admission on the basis of Section 23 subsection 1 Residence Act lies in the restricted access to language courses: While all beneficiaries of international protection as well as individuals admitted through the federal admission schemes and resettlement have the unconditional right to attend integration courses offered by the Federal Office for Migration and Refugees,[74] beneficiaries of private sponsorship at *Länder* level do not have this privilege. All in all, admission through private sponsorship at *Länder* level results in the weakest status that can be obtained through humanitarian admission.

6.7.1.4 The travel document as 'Achilles heel' of resettlement refugee status

Resettlement refugees are granted a status similar[75] to Convention refugees, and therefore the strongest form of protection through legal ad-

72 See Section 26 subsection 3 Residence Act.

73 See Section 4 subsection 2 Residence Act and 31 Employment Regulation, as well as Section 21 Residence Act.

74 See Section 44 subsection 1 Residence Act.

75 Since resettlement aims at offering a 'durable solution', it can be questioned why resettlement refugees are not granted Convention refugee status. For a critical assessment of this issue see Tometten (n 62) 187.

mission. The 'Achilles heel' is the travel document: A Convention travel document on the basis of Article 28 Refugee Convention is only issued to Convention refugees. Resettlement refugees – as well as beneficiaries of all other schemes and subsidiary protection – can only apply for a national travel document for aliens (*Reiseausweis für Ausländer*).[76] Such a travel document is issued on a discretionary basis in case the applicant can prove that he or she is unable to obtain a passport 'by reasonable means', a threshold often difficult to overcome. This situation is therefore pointed out as a major problem in practice.[77]

6.7.2 *The changing laws and policies regarding family reunification*

The following discussion considers both: family reunification as a right of beneficiaries of protection in Germany as well as family reunification as access method for relatives abroad. A particular focus lies on changing laws and policies restricting the right to family reunification of beneficiaries of subsidiary protection. The resulting difference to the legal position of resettlement refugees is particularly striking and illustrates how there is not only a correlation between the quality of protection and the access method, but also the time of arrival.

6.7.2.1 *Family reunification depends on the method of arrival*

Individuals admitted through ad hoc admission schemes at federal or *Länder* level have only very limited options of uniting with their family members in Germany.[78] The underlying assumption is that the immediate family should have entered together in the course of the admission. Although this argument could equally apply to resettlement procedures,[79] resettle-

76 See Sections 5 and 6 of the Ordinance on Residence.

77 See Lutter/Zehnder/Knezevic, (n 27) 34; see also Tometten (n 64) 195, 198 further discussing differences in options of naturalisation.

78 According to Section 29 subsection 3 Residence Act, family reunification with members of the nuclear family *may* only be granted 'for reasons of international law, on humanitarian grounds or in order to safeguard political interests of the Federal Republic of Germany'.

79 As stated by Baraulina/Bitterwolf (n 44) 8: 'The norm that families should be resettle together if possible plays a central role in the German resettlement programme. In the admission year 2012, for example, the proportion of people ad-

ment refugees in Germany enjoy the same privileges as Convention refugees: They have a right to family reunification with members of the nuclear family.[80] When exercising this right within three months upon the recognition of their status, Convention and resettlement refugees do not have to demonstrate sufficient financial means to provide for the living expenses of their family members,[81] nor do spouses abroad have to demonstrate German language skills.[82] Furthermore, the reunification of unaccompanied minors with their parents does not depend on the ability to secure the livelihood of the family nor to provide sufficient living space.[83] Here again, the legal position of resettlement refugees is not only stronger compared to beneficiaries of other legal access methods, but also compared to beneficiaries of subsidiary protection. As discussed in the following, the latter have very restricted options for reuniting with their family.[84]

6.7.2.2 *Family reunification depends on the time of arrival: The changing laws and policies regarding beneficiaries of subsidiary protection*

Resettlement refugees were not always in a stronger position than beneficiaries of subsidiary protection. Existing differences with regard to family reunification rights of beneficiaries of subsidiary protection are the result of statutory changes accompanied by changing recognition policies in national asylum procedures. These changes influenced options of family reunification and therewith again legal access. The developments can be traced as follows: In 2012, asylum applicants from Syria were mainly granted subsidiary protection in national asylum procedures.[85] At the time, the Federal Office for Migration and Refugees did not follow the UNHCR recommendations, which suggested that the majority of individuals fleeing Syria qualified for Convention refugee status due to the specific circum-

---

mitted with their close or extended family was 73 %. In 2014, 88 % of all those admitted came to Germany together with family members'.

80 The 'nuclear family' consists of the spouse and underage children, as well as the parents of unaccompanied minors.

81 See Section 29 subsection 2 sentence 2 Residence Act.

82 See Section 30 subsection 1 sentence 3 No. 1 Residence Act.

83 See Section 36 subsection 1 Residence Act.

84 See Section 36a Residence Act.

85 See Bundesamt für Migration und Flüchtlinge, Entscheiderbrief 3/2012, available at http://www.bamf.de/SharedDocs/Anlagen/DE/Publikationen/Entscheiderbrief/2012/entscheiderbrief-03-2012.pdf?__blob=publicationFile last accessed 15 March 2019].

stances of the conflict.[86] This distinction in status mattered significantly then: While Convention refugees could (and still can) apply for family reunification under privileged conditions, the requirement of (showing proof of) being able to provide for housing and livelihood rendered family reunification nearly impossible for individuals with subsidiary protection status at the time.[87] From the end of 2014 onwards, the administrative decision policy changed. Applicants from Syria were mostly granted Convention refugee status, reaching a recognition rate of over 97 percent in 2015.[88] This change in policy was certainly influenced by the high number of court decisions overruling former administrative decisions. But there was also an important legislative change, which has to be added to the picture: In August 2015, family reunification rights of individuals granted subsidiary protection were adjusted to match the legal situation of Convention refugees. This was in line with the overall objective at EU level in terms of achieving a 'uniform status' of international protection.[89] With regard to family reunification, it did therefore not matter anymore whether a person was granted refugee or subsidiary protection status. This could of course be a coincidence, if it were not for another legislative change to turn the picture upside down again. In March 2016, the provision on the right to family reunification of individuals with subsidiary protection status was suspended for two years. This followed the high increase of asylum applications in the year 2015. During the debates preceding this legislative step, it was argued that asylum seekers from Syria (the largest group of asylum applicants) would merely be affected by this suspension, as they were

86 See UN High Commissioner for Refugees (UNHCR), *Guidelines on International Protection No. 12: Claims for refugee status related to situations of armed conflict and violence under Article 1A(2) of the 1951 Convention and/or 1967 Protocol relating to the Status of Refugees and the regional refugee definitions*, 2 December 2016, HCR/GIP/16/12, available at: https://www.refworld.org/docid/583595ff4.html [last accessed 15 July 2019].

87 This situation led to a high number of appeals at the administrative courts, which eventually leaned towards refugee status, see further P Endres de Oliveira, 'Wer ist Flüchtling? Zum Hin und Her der Entscheidungspraxis zu Asylsuchenden aus Syrien', Verfassungsblog 22 December 2016, available at https://verfassungsblog.de/wer-ist-fluechtling-zum-hin-und-her-der-entscheidungspraxis-zu-asylsuchenden-aus-syrien/ [last accessed 15 July 2019]; for an overview on current judicial decisions regarding cases of Syrian applicants see https://www.asyl.net/laender/Syrien [last accessed 15 July 2019].

88 See the statistics of 2015, 35, available at https://www.bamf.de/SharedDocs/Anlagen/DE/Publikationen/Broschueren/bundesamt-in-zahlen-2015.pdf?__blob=publicationFile [last accessed 15 July 2019.

89 See Art. 1 Directive 2011/95/EU.

mostly granted Convention refugee status in asylum procedures. However, this did not hold true, since the decision policy simultaneously changed once more. From 2016 onwards, applicants from Syria were largely granted subsidiary protection status again. Up until today, the rights of beneficiaries of subsidiary protection remain very restricted. Instead of lifting the suspension after two years, a new provision was introduced in August 2018, regulating family reunification for beneficiaries of subsidiary protection on a discretionary basis. Section 36a Residence Act now states that family members *can* reunite on the basis of 'humanitarian grounds'.[90] Additionally, amissions are restricted to 1,000 cases per month.[91] All in all these developments reveal the changing dynamics between access and rights.

6.8 Conclusion

Humanitarian admission leads the way in terms of offering safe as well as regulated access to protection in Germany. Although there is no humanitarian visa to access the national asylum procedure, there are various visa schemes with humanitarian scope qualifying as 'protected entry procedures'. While there are only few cases of individual admission from abroad, the focus in Germany lies on *ad hoc* group admission schemes on the basis of fixed quotas. Since 2013, ad hoc admission schemes have increased at federal and *Länder* level, facilitating the legal entry of over 44,000 individuals fleeing the conflict in Syria. Thereby, admission at *Länder* level has relied on private sponsorship. Particular progress has been made with regard to a permanent resettlement scheme in cooperation with UNHCR, with admission quotas increasing every year. A novelty since 2019 is the pilot programme NesT, a hybrid between resettlement and private sponsorship. In contrast to resettlement, ad hoc admission programmes envision a higher number of admissions in a relatively short amount of time, even directly from the country of origin. They offer the flexibility of adjusting procedures, admission criteria and status rights up-

---

90 See further M Kalkmann, Das Familiennachzugsneuregelungsgesetz, *Asylmagazin* 7-8/2018, 232.

91 See further http://www.bamf.de/DE/Fluechtlingsschutz/FamilienasylFamiliennachzug/familienasyl-familiennachzug-node.html; comprehensive information on family reunification for beneficiaries of protection in Germany is available at https://familie.asyl.net/start/as well as at https://fap.diplo.de/webportal/desktop/index.html#start [both last accessed 15 July 2019].

on arrival. While humanitarian admission can be a win-win tool for individuals and States, the private sponsorship schemes implemented at *Länder* level have raised a number of controversies regarding the legal situation of sponsors and beneficiaries upon arrival. Lessons learned have influenced the design of the NesT programme, providing beneficiaries with the same rights as resettlement refugees.

All in all, the legal status of beneficiaries varies substantially depending on the method and time of arrival. The strongest form of protection can only be achieved through a national asylum procedure when Convention refugee status is granted. In the 'hirarchie of rights' resettlement refugee status comes next, offering an almost equally strong legal position. The situation of beneficiaries of an ad hoc admission scheme at federal level is comparable to the situation of beneficiaries of subsidiary protection following a national asylum procedure: In contrast to Convention and resettlement refugees, respective individuals face restrictions with regard to options for permanent settlement and especially family reunification. Eventually, the status of individuals entering Germany through private sponsorship at *Länder* level is the weakest. Beneficiaries face various restrictions, ranging from access to language courses, employment, social benefits, family reunification and options of permanent settlement.

As shown, the comparably weak status of beneficiaries of subsidiary protection is the result of changing recognition policies in national asylum procedures, accompanied by legislative changes restricting the right to family reunification and therewith to legal access. These changes followed the high increase of 'spontaneous arrivals' in Germany and have particularly affected the situation of protection seekers from Syria, as the largest group of asylum seekers and main beneficiaries of humanitarian admission. Their legal situation particularly illustrates the interplay between access and rights. Individuals with similar backgrounds, sometimes even from the same family, live with different residence permits and thus with different rights, depending on how and when they arrived in Germany. These differences not only impact on the individuals but can also burden administrative structures, as has been seen with the increase in asylum applications from beneficiaries of *Länder* schemes or the judicial appeals by Syrians only granted subsidiary protection in national asylum procedures. All in all, the quality of protection should be determined by individual protection needs and not the method or time of arrival.

Chapter 6: Humanitarian Admission to Belgium

Serge Bodart[1]

Contents

Introduction

There are no humanitarian admission procedures in Belgian law, which provides for neither the delivery of humanitarian visas nor any other kind of protected entry procedure. These are left to the discretion of the Minister in charge and his/her Secretary of State for Asylum and Migration. It is therefore quite challenging for myself as a judge at the Council for Aliens Law Litigation ('Council') to give a comprehensive overview of the national practice on humanitarian visas in Belgium. Those who receive such visas have no reason to litigate, and the Council does not review their files. Those whose application for such visa is rejected face major practical issues in bringing their case before the Courts, to the extent that the case law is scarce. Moreover, and as discussed hereafter, few reliable data are available on the practices of the authorities in the delivery of humanitarian visas.

This chapter will nonetheless attempt to present the state of affairs in this matter, which has raised (and is still raising) considerable controversies at the national level and ultimately led to the CJEU ruling in *X. and X.* It is divided into three parts. Section 2 clarifies the content of the relevant legislation, the Aliens Act of 15 December 1980, which is silent on the is-

1 Member of the Council of State, First President of the Council for Alien Law Litigation.

sue of humanitarian visas. Section 3 explores the relevant administrative practices and case law, which are in their infancy. Section 4 concludes the chapter by highlighting the many pending questions that neither the legislation nor the case law has managed to answer so far.

1 The Legislation

Entry into Belgian territory, the stay in the territory, and the establishment and the removal of foreigners from Belgian territory are ruled by a law of 15 December 1980.[2] For ease of readability, that law will hereafter be referred to as the 'Aliens Act'. The Aliens Act has been frequently amended since its introduction in 1980, but some of the principal stipulations remain unchanged, including the conditions under which a person is to be allowed to enter the territory.

The words 'humanitarian visa' do not appear in the text of the Aliens Act, which does not establish any criteria or procedures for obtaining such a visa. Therefore, these visas are subject to the general rule regarding the entry and the stay in the country.

The rules are rather simple:

1) nobody is allowed to enter the country if he/she is not in possession of the required documents;
2) one of the required documents is a visa, except when there is an exemption foreseen by international treaty or by law;
3) the visa is delivered outside the country, by a consular or diplomatic post;
4) the visa is in principle for a short stay (90 days);
5) for a longer stay, two possibilities exist:

- Some aliens benefit from a right to stay by virtue of the Aliens Act, such as EU citizens and family members of an alien who is legally staying within the territory. As explained in Section 3, this latter category is of great interest for the topic we are dealing with.
- Others must rely on the discretionary power of the 'Minister'[3] who may allow anyone to enter and stay on Belgian territory. In principle, such

2 Loi du 15 décembre 1980 sur l'accès au territoire, le séjour, l'établissement et l'éloignement des étrangers.

3 The Aliens Act refers to the 'Minister', but the responsibility may also be exerted by a secretary of state attached to a minister. This was, in fact, the case for years. Since December 2018, however, a Minister is fully responsible for this matter. This

authorisation must be requested from outside the Belgian territory.[4] The Aliens Act thus establishes the discretionary power of the Minister to grant a visa for whatever reason.

Besides the Aliens Act, Article 25(1)(a) of the EU Visa Code, which as a regulation is directly applicable, mentions the possibility for a Member State to deviate from certain rules of this code including, inter alia, when the Member State concerned considers it necessary on humanitarian grounds. Since the ruling in *X. and X.*,[5] we know that this provision may not be relied upon for long-term stays, as the Visa Code regulates short-term visas only. Since *X. and X.*, we also know that, as no measure has been adopted by the EU legislature with regard to the conditions governing the issue of long-term visas and residence permits, be it on humanitarian or on any other grounds, this matter falls solely within the scope of national law. Consequently, we could conclude that, legally speaking, the humanitarian visa referred to in Article 25(1)(a) of the Visa Code may only be granted for a short stay. However, this conclusion is not completely consistent with the practice.

2 *The Administrative Practices and Case Law*

A consequence of the vagueness of the Aliens Act is that it is very difficult to have a clear idea of the actual practices of the administrative authorities regarding humanitarian visas. As there is no provision that explicitly defines the category 'humanitarian visa', the available statistical data are scarce and need to be treated with caution; they are based merely on an empirical classification made by the consular and diplomatic posts.

According to MYRIA, the Federal Centre on Migration,[6] 1,182 humanitarian visas were issued in 2016, the large majority of which (905) were for

---

Minister is also in charge of social welfare and public health. The term 'Minister' must therefore be understood as the 'Minister in charge of asylum and migration or his Secretary of State'.

4 Under exceptional circumstances, aliens already staying irregularly in Belgium may request regularisation of their stay on humanitarian grounds. As this chapter is dealing with humanitarian visas, it does not detail that specific procedure.

5 Case C-638/16 PPU *X and X* [2017] EU:C:2017:173.

6 MYRIA, *La Migration en Chiffres* (Brussels, MYRIA, Myriatics 7, June 2017) <www.myria.be/files/Myriatics_FR_v 4.pdf> (accessed 25 November 2019).

short stays.[7] Quite surprisingly given the reasoning of the CJEU in *X. and X.*, most of the short-term humanitarian visas were granted as part of the resettlement of refugees and asylum seekers in the framework of international or domestic initiatives. This trend is not limited to 2016. Declercq claims that, in 2015, 77 per cent of the visas for a short stay granted on humanitarian grounds were issued in the context of resettlement of refugees and asylum seekers.[8] This practice may be viewed as being in contradiction to the *X. and X.* ruling and was, consequently, revoked in March 2017. Humanitarian visas are now mainly granted for long stays. According to Myria, 2,125 long-stay and only 236 short-stay humanaitarian visas were granted in 2017.[9] However, the previous administrative practice was perfectly coherent from an administrative and political point of view: a short-stay visa is granted to the aliens to let them legally enter the Belgian territory, where they can then apply for international protection. This application is subsequently dealt with by the competent authority in an accelerated procedure. I am afraid that we cannot understand the real significance of *X. and X.* if we do not analyse this judgment in relation to that well-established practice. This is further discussed hereafter.

Another major category of aliens who apply for humanitarian visas includes those who do not meet the legal requirements for family reunification, but invoke additional humanitarian circumstances on the basis of Article 8 ECHR. In such cases, the visas applied for, and sometimes granted, are generally long-term visas. But here again the available information is so limited that there is no clear understanding of how humanitarian visas are delivered for these reasons nor on the reasons which are considered valid

7 According to another source, the data are slightly different: 1,185 visas issued, 901 of which were for short stays (Ch. Repr. Sess. 2017-2018, QRVA 54 138, 04/12/2017).

8 A. Declercq, 'Het humanitair visum: balanceren tussen soevereine migratiecontrole en respect voor de mensenrechten' (2017) *T. Vreemd.* at 131. It has to be noted that the author bases her estimate on a comparison between the official data regarding the total number of humanitarian short-term visas granted and the available, not necessarily official, information on the relevant humanitarian operations. It must therefore be seen as a simple approximation that possibly underestimates the proportion of visas that are granted on the basis of a first selection made by the State in relation to those granted on the basis of the individual initiative of the applicant.

9 MYRIA, *La migration en chiffres et en droits 2018* (Brussels, MYRIA, 2018) at 38-40.

by the authorities.[10] The case law allows us to grasp the motives for rejecting these applications, but not those for accepting them.

To have a better understanding of how the administration and the Minister apply the discretionary power the law gives them, it is therefore necessary to have a look at the case law.

Any administrative decision regarding entry into the territory, the stay, the residence or the removal of foreigners may be contested by lodging an appeal with the Council for Alien Law Litigation (hereafter 'the Council'). Against the judgments of this administrative court, an appeal on the points of law may be lodged, if certain conditions are met, before the Council of State, Belgium's supreme administrative court.

The Council has the power to annul a decision taken by the Minister or his/her administration. The appeal does not automatically suspend the decision, but the judge can decide to suspend the execution of the decision challenged, sometimes in a procedure of extreme urgency, if there is a serious argument that could lead to annulment and if the immediate execution of the decision risks causing severe damage that could not be repaired by the annulment of the decision.

The Council frequently recalls that the law gives the Minister a wide margin of discretion and that the issuance of a residence permit is not a right but a favour. However, this wide margin of discretion does not release him/her from the obligation to reply to the arguments invoked by the applicant in support of the visa application. The decision to reject a visa application must clearly state why these arguments were not sufficient to justify the granting of the visa.

In the appeals lodged against a decision to refuse a so-called humanitarian visa, the issues at stake are frequently related to the violation of two Articles of the ECHR: Article 8 (Right to Respect for Private and Family Life) and Article 3 (Prohibition of Torture).

When a violation of Article 8 is alleged, the Council refers to the case law of the ECtHR and considers that even if the concerned person is not present within the territory of the Contracting State, 'the Contracting State's obligations under that provision may, in certain circumstances, require family members to be reunified with their relatives living in that Contracting State'.[11] To evaluate the extent of that positive obligation in

---

10 277 visas granted in 2016 and 777 applications during the same year, see MYRIA (n 6); In 2017, the data are quite different, 2.125 visas granted and 279 refusals but there is no available information about the distribution between asylum related applications and other grounds for granting the visa, see: MYRIA (n 9) at 39.

11 e.g. judgment of 22 December 2017, no 197238.

the concrete cases that are brought before him, the Council performs a case-by-case analysis in which great importance is given to the facts and reasons mentioned in the contested decisions.

For instance, the Council annulled a decision refusing a visa to a young Syrian man who had been tortured and suffered serious trauma. The applicant wanted to be reunited with his brother, who had been granted refugee status in Belgium. He provided medical evidence in support of his application, as well as various documents from the UNHCR and the tracing service of the Red Cross to establish his strong dependence on his brother.[12] The Council also considers that being recognized as a refugee in Belgium implies the impossibility of pursuing a family life in the country of origin. For that reason, the State must take that particular circumstance into account when deciding on a visa application introduced by the family members of a refugee, even when the conditions set out by the law for a family reunification visa are not fulfilled.[13] In other cases, the Council held that a *de facto* family life between a child and his or her stepmother has to be taken into account, especially when it is not disputed that the biological parents are dead or disappeared.[14] Generally speaking, when specific humanitarian circumstances are invoked, the administration cannot refuse the visa on the sole consideration that the claimant does not fall into the categories entitled to a right to family reunification as set out by the law.[15] On the other hand, the responsibility lies with the applicant to communicate the relevant information to the consular authority.[16]

The problematic is a bit different and more complicated when dealing with Article 3 ECHR. In the case of *Abdul Wahab Khan v. UK*, the Court excluded the transposition of the Article 8 ECHR positive obligation to Article 3 ECHR.[17] The Court considers that extending its reasoning under Article 8 ECHR to Article 3 ECHR 'would, in effect, create an unlimited

---

12 Judgment of 29 February 2016, no 163192.

13 Judgment of 14 June 2016, no 169761 Art 10, § 1, 5° to 7°, Aliens Act, gives a limitative list of the family members who may be taken into account for a family reunification, Art 10 § 2 further requires that certain income and housing criteria be met. Those conditions are slightly different for EU citizens (art 40 and 40bis) as well as for Belgian nationals who want to reunify with an alien family member (art 40ter).

14 Judgments of 28 April 2017, no 186197 and 186198.

15 Judgment of 31 October 2017, no 194545 (ascendant of an adult foreigner in Belgium).

16 Judgment of 28 July 2017, no 190162.

17 It has to be noted that the Court made this statement in response to the 'applicant's argument that the State's obligations under Article 3 required it to take that

obligation on Contracting States to allow entry to an individual who might be at real risk of ill-treatment contrary to Article 3, regardless of where in the world that individual might find himself'.[18] Some recent judgments of the Council follow the principle set out in *Abdul Wahab Khan* and conclude that no positive obligation for the State arises from Article 3 ECHR.[19]

These judgments were rendered in the ordinary annulment procedure. However, the Council must often deal with litigation on humanitarian visas in the so-called 'extreme urgency procedure'. The judgment is then adopted in a strict time frame and is provisional and limited to the question of whether the execution of the decision should be suspended or not, pending the examination of the appeal in the ordinary annulment procedure. A distinctive feature of this procedure is that the Council has to make an *ex nunc* and complete examination of the case, especially regarding the risk of a violation of a fundamental right to which no derogation is possible according to art. 15(2) ECHR. In an order adopted in 2013, the Council of State ruled that, given the absolute character of Article 3 ECHR, the Council made no error of law when ordering the suspension of a refusal to grant a short-term humanitarian visa because of an arguable claim that such refusal would have exposed the applicant to Article 3 ECHR violations.[20] The issue of the jurisdiction of the Belgian State in the meaning of Article 1 ECHR was not raised then.

Besides issues under Article 1 ECHR regarding the extraterritorial scope of Article 3 ECHR, the question of whether the extreme urgency procedure applies to visa applications arises. The relevant provision in the Aliens Act[21] only considers the return or the refoulement of a foreigner, but part of the case law recognizes that an extreme urgency may also occur in other situations and that in regard to the non-suspensive effect of the appeal, this procedure is the only way to offer an effective remedy. The problem is, of course, that the suspension of a decision to refuse a visa does not mean that

---

provision into account when making adverse decisions against individuals, *even when those individuals were not within its jurisdiction*' (emphasis added). In this case, the Court found no territorial jurisdiction in respect of an immigrant applicant who had voluntarily returned to his country of origin. See: *Abdul Wahab Khan v the UK* (App No 11987/11) ECHR (dec.) 28 January 2014 at para 26.

18 ibid. at para 27.

19 Judgment of 22 December 2017, no 197201; Judgment of 22 December 2017, no 197 238; Judgment of 23 April 2018, no 202817.

20 Order of 22 May 2013, no 9681 *Revue de droit des étrangers* 173 at 258.

21 Art. 39/82, § 4, al. 2, of the Aliens Act.

the applicant is granted a visa. The only effect is that the administration has to take a new decision, and even this is not uncontroversial.

Additional and major issues arise when the administration refuses to adopt a new decision or adopts a new decision that rests on reasons that are almost identical to the ones the Council had deemed insufficient. This practice gave rise to a judiciary saga at the end of 2016. In September 2016, the administration rejected the application of a Syrian Christian family living in Aleppo for a short-stay visa on humanitarian grounds. In short, the reasons for the refusal were that the applicants had no particular and close relationship with Belgium and that they, in fact, did not intend to come for a short stay, but to apply for asylum. A judgment of the Council decided on 7 October 2016[22] to suspend the execution of the decision due to a failure to address arguments regarding a possible violation of Article 3 ECHR. The judgment also ordered the administration to take a new decision. On 10 October, the administration adopted a similar decision that did not address the criticisms expressed in the ruling of the Council; the Council, therefore, again ordered the suspension of the decision.[23] On 17 October, a new yet still similar decision was adopted by the administration, prompting a new appeal before the Council and a new suspension order. The Council then decided to order the authority to deliver a pass or a visa for a short stay to the claimants.[24] To say it in non-legal language, that decision of the Council was a bit *rock'n roll* because it is generally agreed that the Council has no competence to issue a positive injunction to the Minister or his administration because such competence is not attributed to it by the Aliens Act.

The Secretary of State who was at the time in charge of asylum and migration built a political campaign around that case (and became very popular through it), letting it be known that he would not obey the order of the Council. He also lodged an appeal with the Council of State. The claimants then applied to different tribunals and courts to compel the Secretary of State to respect the decision of the Council. They won the case at different levels, but in vain: the Minister still refused to deliver the visa, claiming that he would wait until the judgment of the Council of State, although the appeal before this supreme administrative court does not suspend the decision of the Council.

22 Judgment of 7 October 2016, no 175973.
23 Judgment of 14 October 2016, no 176363.
24 Judgment of 20 October 2016, no 176577.

On 31 October, a new but similar case was brought before the Council. This time, mindful of the tumult caused by the previous case and hoping to avoid further discrepancies in the case law as some judges disagreed with the reasoning of their colleague,[25] the previous First President of the Council took the decision to refer the case to the general assembly of the Council. The general assembly considered it necessary to apply for two preliminary rulings, one from the Belgian Constitutional Court and other from the CJEU.

The question to the Constitutional Court concerned the competence of the Council to deal with extreme urgency requests against denials of visa applications. Briefly, the purpose behind the question was to know whether or not the Aliens Act must be interpreted in a way that restricts the procedure in extreme urgency for return decisions *lato sensu*, and whether such an interpretation is compatible with the principles of equality and non-discrimination and with the right to an effective remedy. As we will see, these questions remain unanswered.

The questions asked to the CJEU concerned the interpretation of Article 25(1)(a) of the Visa Code. What is meant by the words 'international obligations'? Does this provision impose a positive obligation when a decision risks interfering with the rights guaranteed by the ECHR, the Geneva Convention, and Articles 4 and 18 of the Charter? A subsidiary question addressed the possible impact of existing links with the Member State to which the visa application was made (one of the grounds for the refusal was the absence of a close relationship with Belgium).[26]

---

25 See, e.g., Judgment of 17 June 2016, no 170076; in that judgment the judge considered that the procedure in extreme urgency is, in principle, not applicable to challenges regarding the refusal to grant a visa.

26 These questions were laid out in *X and X* (n 5): (1) Do the "international obligations" referred to in Article 25(1)(a) of the Visa Code cover all the rights guaranteed by the Charter, including, in particular, those guaranteed by Articles 4 and 18, and do they also cover obligations which bind the Member States, in the light of the ECHR and Article 33 of the Geneva Convention? (2) (a) Depending on the answer given to the first question, must Article 25(1)(a) of the Visa Code be interpreted as meaning that, subject to its discretion with regard to the circumstances of the case, a Member State to which an application for a visa with limited territorial validity has been made is required to issue the visa applied for, where a risk of infringement of Article 4 and/or Article 18 of the Charter or another international obligation by which it is bound is established? (b) Does the existence of links between the applicant and the Member State to which the visa application was made (for example, family connections, host families, guarantors and sponsors) affect the answer to that question?'.

And as we know, the Court decided not to answer or, more precisely, not to answer frankly, as it found that the Visa Code was not applicable. According to the Court, it was 'apparent [...] that the applicants in the main proceedings submitted applications for visas [...] with a view to applying for asylum in Belgium immediately upon their arrival in that Member State and, thereafter, to being granted a residence permit with a period of validity not limited to 90 days'.[27] Such an application does not aim to obtain a short-term visa and consequently does not fall within the scope of the Code. The Court added that 'since [...] no measure has been adopted, to date, by the EU legislature on the basis of Article 79(2)(a) TFEU, with regard to the conditions governing the issue by Member States of long-term visas and residence permits to third-country nationals on humanitarian grounds, the applications at issue in the main proceedings fall solely within the scope of national law'.[28]

This could have been the only reason for the ruling. Yet the Court added two *obiter dicta* that are maybe more important than the main reason for its ruling. In what appears to be an *ad absurdum* argument, it tries to demonstrate that no other reasoning could have been compatible with the scope of EU asylum law. Firstly, according to the Court, 'to conclude otherwise [...] would be tantamount to allowing third-country nationals to lodge applications for visas on the basis of the Visa Code in order to obtain international protection in the Member State of their choice, which would undermine the general structure of the system established by Regulation No 604/2013 (the Dublin Regulation)'.[29] Secondly, it 'would mean that Member States are required, on the basis of the Visa Code, *de facto* to allow third-country nationals to submit applications for international protection to the representations of Member States that are within the territory of a third country [while] the measures adopted by the European Union [...] that govern the procedures for applications for international protection do not impose such an obligation and, on the contrary, exclude from their scope applications made to the representations of Member States'.[30]

---

27 Ibid. at para 42.

28 Ibid. at para 44.

29 Ibid. at para 48.

30 The Court then referred to Art 3(1) and (2) of the Directive 2013/32/EU of the European Parliament and of the Council of 26 June 2013 on common procedures for granting and withdrawing international protection [2013] OJ L180/60 and to the Regulation (EU) No 604/2013 of the European Parliament and of the Council of 26 June 2013 establishing the criteria and mechanisms for determining the

With this reasoning, the Court clearly tries to demonstrate that agreeing to the possibility of submitting an application for a short-term humanitarian visa based on the need for international protection would not be compatible with the common European asylum system. It could be understood as a way for the Court to indirectly signify to the Council that there are no 'positive obligations' under EU law to deliver a visa in the case of a risk of violation of Article 3 ECHR. The Court did not limit itself to stating that the question falls outside its area of competence; it also indicated that there is no right to seek asylum from abroad under EU law. The outcome of the *X. and X.* ruling then converges with the ECHR's reasoning in *Abdul Wahab Khan*, albeit in a less direct and gentler formulation.

One may doubt, however, that this will bring the controversies to an end. The European Parliament took steps towards establishing a European Humanitarian Visa that would give access to European territory – that is, the territory of the Member State issuing the visa exclusively – for the sole purpose of submitting an application for international protection.[31] Moreover, the other Belgian humanitarian visa case mentioned earlier has led to further litigation before the ECtHR (*M.N. and Others v. Belgium*).[32] Contrary to the application in *Abdul Wahab Khan*,[33] the application in *M.N.* was declared admissible. The Grand Chamber held a hearing on 24 April 2019. It remains to be seen whether the ECtHR will add a new chapter to the saga.

Conclusion: The Pending Questions

As the visa saga seems far from being over, this conclusion limits itself to highlighting some legal questions that remain unresolved.

First, and from the Belgian perspective, is the question of the right to an effective remedy against denials of visa applications. As discussed earlier in the chapter, a preliminary ruling was referred to the Constitutional Court

---

Member State responsible for examining an application for international protection lodged in one of the Member States by a third-country national or a stateless person [2013] OJ L180/31.

31 European Parliament resolution of 11 December 2018 with recommendations to the Commission on Humanitarian Visas, 2018/2271(INL). On that initiative and subsequent developments, see the contribution of Eugenia Relaño Pastor in this volume.

32 Application no 3599/18.

33 *Abdul Wahab Khan v. United Kingdom* (n 17) at para 26.

regarding the admissibility of an appeal made in extreme urgency against a refusal to issue a visa. However, after the ruling by the CJEU, the Council considered it unnecessary to wait for a complementary ruling by the Constitutionnal Court, and rejected the application.[34] Consequently, the Court struck the case off the list. The Council tried to put the same question in another case, but the Court determined that its reply was not necessary to decide on the case and left the question unanswered.[35] In a few cases this uncertainty may lead to discrepancies in the case law. Anyway, even if the Council considers it admissible to lodge an appeal in extreme urgency against a refusal to issue a visa, it does not necessarily imply that the remedy is effective. What happens when the Minister does not comply with the ruling of the Council? There is little chance that lawmakers would consider giving to the Council the competence of issuing a visa in such case.

A second pending question relates to the logic behind the *obiter dicta* of the CJEU in *X. and X.*: Does the Dublin regulation always prevent asylum seekers from submitting their applications for international protection to the Member State of their choice? It clearly does so in many cases, but not when the asylum seeker was granted a visa by a Member State, which is then responsible for dealing with the asylum application. In practice, such a visa is granted because the Member State was not aware of the applicant's intention to apply for international protection once he or she arrived on its territory. But is this really what the CJEU means – that Dublin III and, more generally the CEAS, encourage fraud and lies? And *quid* for the other people, i.e., those who do not travel with a visa? It is a fact that they have no choice but to risk their lives in the Mediterranean Sea, to pay exorbitant amounts to a mafia of smugglers, to cross the borders illegally. However, do we have to admit that this is the logic beyond the CEAS? I would say no, and I am sure that it is not what the Court had in mind. But why, then, would it be contrary to Dublin III and to the APD (directive on procedures) to allow some individuals to seek safety through a legal way? Would it, in particular, really 'undermine the general structure of the system established by Regulation No 604/2013'?[36] In any case, the Court does not exclude the possibility that Member States grant humanitarian visas according to national law, and we have seen that Belgium continued to grant such long-stay visas even after the ruling of the CJEU. The ruling is then maybe nothing more and nothing less than a reminder that, in a matter

34 Judgment of 30 March 2017, no 184 913.
35 Judgment of 18 October 2018, n° 141/2018.
36 *X and X* (n 5) at point 48.

where questions of sovereignty are pervasive, the scope of application of EU law has to be understood in a very strict, even restrictive, way.

Lastly, what is the meaning of the reference to the 'international obligations' in Article 25(1)(a) of the Visa Code? *X. and X.* made it clear that it cannot be used as a means to indirectly apply for long-term international protection status. But the question remains: to what kind of international obligation does it refer? Not to Article 8 ECHR, which *prima facie* also presupposes a long-term stay. To what then? I could not find any examples of such 'international obligations' that would warrant a short stay for humanitarian reasons in the Belgian case law or in administrative practice, except in the context of the resettlement of refugees.

Do we have to conclude from *X. and X.* that the delivery of short-term humanitarian visas to implement resettlement programs is necessarily contrary to the Visa Code? That seems to be how the Belgian authorities read it. But is this really the intended consequence of the ruling? The message is rather that this remains a matter of sovereignty. EU law does not prevent a Member State from applying Article 25(1)(a) to grant short-term humanitarian visas if it wishes to do so, but the State cannot be forced to grant such a visa to an individual submitting an application on his own.

The confrontation between this well-established State practice, which *in se* offers significant advantages from a humanitarian perspective, and the legal reasoning of the CJEU results from the fact that the Court, consciously or not, establishes the discretionary competence of the Member States to decide on humanitarian visa applications. There is nothing abnormal or shocking here. An issue may arise, however, when that discretionary competence is exercised in an arbitrary way. In this respect, it is worth noting that controversies have recently arisen in Belgium regarding the delivery of humanitarian visas to Syrian asylum seekers, as it appeared that the Secretary of State who was at the time in charge relied on a private individual – a member of the Assyrian community in Belgium – to help him select the Christian Syrians to whom he issued humanitarian visas. This informal intermediary is now charged with various criminal offences, including smuggling, as he would have requested payment from the asylum seekers. Such abuses are likely to occur when the limits of the discretionary competence are too vague and when no clear criteria or procedures are established. The international obligations of a State open a doorway that may allow the judge, as well as the administrative authority, to build a framework within which discretionary competence may be exercised without falling into arbitrariness. With *X. and X.*, an opportunity has been missed to give concrete form to that framework.

Part 3.
Claiming Humanitarian Admission. Survival Strategies and Litigation Attempts

Chapter 7: Unpacking Vulnerability: An Ethnographic Account of the Challenges of Implementing Resettlement Programmes in a Refugee Camp in Uganda

Sophie Nakueira[1]

Contents

---

1 Research Fellow in the Department of Law & Anthropology, Max Planck Institute for Social Anthropology.

Introduction

Legal scholarship on refugees often describes refugee strategies that fall outside the 'formal' state-approved channels in two opposing terms – legal and illegal. An anthropological approach enables us not only to understand how these strategies emerge but also to interpret them in ways that are meaningful for addressing the issues that such policies produce. To this end I conducted an ethnographic approach which entailed relying on empirical evidence to make my interpretations.

Proceeding with the definitional problem that is implicit in the eligibility for resettlement, I show how the UNHCR vulnerability categories have been complicit in creating or constructing personhood in Nakivale settlement in ways that reify these categories and specific narratives of suffering to the exclusion of others for resettlement purposes. I argue that although resettlement programmes are intended to take the most vulnerable refugee populations out of their countries of asylum and provide them with better protection in countries in the West, they act as a governance tool that controls refugee population outflow in practice. Therefore, viewed from the broader lens of migration control, I contend that UNHCR's vulnerability criteria, and the bureaucratic processes that determine the 'desired' candidate for resettlement, act as regulatory tools for migration control in a humanitarian context.[2] In discussing the multiple issues that are raised here, I draw on diverse disciplines to make sense of the resettlement scheme as a tool of governance. Before concluding, I discuss the challenges of implementing such a policy in a context where majority of the refugee population is vulnerable ab initio by showing the challenges of achieving the objectives of international humanitarian law and the implementation gaps of the resettlement policy in practice.

We are living in a time where policy debates on migration and asylum have diverted attention from 'humanitarian relief to security threats and cost'.[3] More countries are calling for border closures and there is a rise in nationalist and protectionist sentiments. The increasing externalisation of

2 K Bergtora Sandvik, 'Introduction: Refugee Resettlement as Humanitarian Governance. Power Dynamics' in A Garnier et. al. (eds), *Refugee Resettlement: Power, Politics and Humanitarian Governance* (New York, Berghahn Books, 2018) 65.

3 C Krishnadev, 'How Technology Could Revolutionalize Refugee Resettlement' (2019) *The Atlantic* < https://www.theatlantic.com/international/archive/2019/04/how-technology-could-revolutionize-refugee-resettlement/587383 > accessed 11 October 2019.

European borders[4] has made it more difficult for asylum seekers to use informal channels to reach Europe and apply for asylum, raising concern amongst human rights advocates, and sparking debates about the appropriate form of refugee protection that would slow the tide of death of people risking their lives across the Mediterranean sea to reach the West. Scholarly debates on humanitarian admission and how it would be implemented contrast sharply with politicians who see development as the main solution or realistic channel to solve the current migration crisis. The two options are contradictory because while proponents of humanitarian admission aim to find ways to enable legal and safe access to Europe, a focus on addressing development issues aims at keeping migrants in their home countries. The latter option erroneaously assumes that the root cause of migration can be resolved by addressing development issues alone. In so doing it ignores the causes of war and conflict and the role of West in pertuating these for their own benefit. Proponents of the developmental approach aim to tame the tide of population flows leaving countries on the African continent and risking their lives in search of safer spaces or better economic opportunities in Europe. The situation is particularly dire for African refugees majority of whom continue to lose their lives in desperate efforts to reach Europe through the Mediterranean sea while others have fallen victims of modern slavery in Libya.[5]

The answer as I argue here, does not lie in creating more legal protection or new policy models for reaching Europe safely and legally but, rather, in addressing the implementation gaps of current resettlement programmes. I show the limits of the criteria used by UNHCR by focusing on the challenges encountered in implementing the resettlement programme through an ethnographic account of the 'on-the-ground' realities of how UNHCR's resettlement policy is experienced by refugees in one settlement in Uganda. It is crucial to examine resettlement as a 'bureaucratic-legal arrangement'[6] because critical scholarship on this policy is scant despite it

---

4 A Betts and J Milner, 'The Externalisation of EU Asylum Policy: The Position of African States' (2006) 36 *Working Paper of the Centre on Migration, Policy and Society, University of Oxford*. Also see M Maes, M-C Foblets and P De Bruycker, *External Dimensions of European Migration and Asylum Law and Policy / Dimensions Externes du Droit et de la Politique d'Immigration et d'Asile de l'UE* (Brussels, Bruylant, 2011).

5 R Sherlock and L Al-Arian,'Migrants Captured In Libya Say They End Up Sold As Slaves' <https://www.npr.org/sections/parallels/2018/03/21/595497429/migrants-passing-through-libya-could-end-up-being-sold-as-slaves?t=1572517711075> accessed 31 October 2019.

6 K Bergtora Sandvik (2018) (n 2).

being widely implemented in Africa. The term bureaucratic-legal arrangement is used by Skandiv to describe the guidelines that agencies use when assessing refugees' eligibility for resettlement. A critical examination of resettlement as a legal tool or 'bureaucratic legal arrangement' is conspicuously absent from legal scholarship and critical legal studies.[7]

1 A Word on Method

The empirical data from which interpretations for this chapter are drawn were collected over seven months cumulatively. By empirical data I broadly refer to observations in the refugee settlement, interviews with aid workers and refugees including an analysis of documents circulated by diverse agencies within the settlement. I expound on the details of data collection (below in this section). The initial data collection took five months in 2017 and another two months in 2018. In both periods, I shadowed Refugee Law Project (RLP) – an organisation that offers legal services to refugees in various settlements. I followed their activities in the field and observed their interaction with refugees and other aid workers. Through RLP, I got (limited) access to other aid offices and open access to refugees who came to inquire about their cases or file complaints. I attended many official meetings, community sensitisation programmes and training sessions of refugee leaders, media and other personnel. My time during the fieldwork was divided between aid offices and refugee living quarters, court sessions, churches, prisons or trading spaces. Thus, I was able to collect data through participant observation, informal conversations, formal interviews, which were conducted in a semi-structured as well as unstructured manner. Owing to the lengthy period I spent in the diverse spaces in the refugee settlement and aid workers' offices and social spaces, I was able to get in-depth information, and as a result was well acquainted with how aid workers and refugees conducted their daily activities in executing their tasks or accessing aid services, particularly in pursuit of 'resettlement'. Formal and informal interviews were made with aid workers from different agencies and refugees from diverse countries. Using an ethnographic approach, I oscillated between the world of aid workers and refugees, maintaining enough distance as an insider and outsider to understand how they perceived their respective spaces. Shore and Wright posit that it is important to keep a balance as an 'insider' and outsider' in the field. They argue

7 ibid.

that, as an insider, an anthropologist should appreciate 'the beliefs, values and ritualised practices'[8] of the actors' world. Explaining the benefits of keeping a distance as an outsider, they posit that this allows one to ask important questions about how actors perceive their worlds and the implications for theory.[9] In this particular settlement, observations, conversations, interviews, documents and interactions with aid workers and refugees were triangulated in ways that exposed how these actors viewed their worlds. The empirical data allowed me to understand the world of the implementers of the policy as well as the experiences of refugees in respect to the resettlement program. The result is hopefully a nuanced understanding of the difficulties of implementing the resettlement policy.

Scholarship on resettlement that has been conducted in Uganda has focused on the distribution of resettlement spaces and centred on urban refugees in Kampala and the 'formal, informal and illegal'[10] systems into which these refugees enrol in efforts to attain resettlement slots. In her article, 'Blurred Boundaries', Sandvik argues that rather than create homogeneity, 'the regularization of resettlement has engendered a pluralist system that draws on and combines multiple sources and levels of legal and bureaucratic norms'.[11] This chapter builds on existing research by going beyond the procedural and administrative ambiguities that are reported to emanate from the transnational soft law system created by the resettlement handbook of 2004, as identified by Sandvik in the highlighted work. Transnational soft law in this context refers to the guidelines stipulated in the resettlement handbook and which are meant to be applied in assessing the resettlement eligibility of refugees in various contexts. I argue that although the legal and procedural ambiguities identified are important, they are only a part of the implementation problem. Thus, this chapter contributes to legal and anthropological scholarship by analysing how resettlement is implemented in a refugee camp in rural southwestern Uganda – thereby showing the effects of the policy's implementation in a rural con-

---

8 C Shore and S Wright, 'Conceptualising Policy: Technologies of Governance and the Politics of Visibility' in C Shore et. al. (eds), *Policy Worlds: Anthropology and the Analysis of Contemporary Power* (New York, Berghahn Books, 2011) at 15.

9 ibid.

10 K Bergtora Sandvik, 'Blurring Boundaries: Refugee Resettlement in Kampala—between the Formal, the Informal, and the Illegal' (2011) *PoLAR* 34 1. Sandvik explores the variegated strategies strategies that refugees use in their attempts to acquire resettlement slots. This includes legal and illegal ways as well as informal avenues (which may not encompass any illegality).

11 ibid.

text. Second, it starts with the premise that there is an inherent problem with the definition of who warrants international protection, which raises issues of who defines 'vulnerability' and whether the current definition and categories suffice, given evolving and contextual forms of threats to human security. I posit that although international protection mechanisms such as the resettlement policy and other forms of humanitarian admission are well intended, their translation on the ground may have adverse effects, and the implementation of protection mechanisms may be hindered by factors that may not have been envisioned by the policy nor can be easily addressed by laws. Thus, although the focus of this chapter is on the challenges of implementing resettlement programmes, it is also motivated by a broader goal of illuminating on what these challenges teach us about humanitarian aid or developmental programes more broadly.

Therefore, inspired by Shore and Wright 's explanation of the importance of conducting an ethnographic account of consequences of policy implementation, which they refer to as an anthropology of policy[12], this chapter examines the resettlement programme as an international protection mechanism and its implications for protecting the most vulnerable in a refugee settlement in Uganda. In essence then, this chapter is simultaneously an 'anthropology of the resettlement programme' as well as a critique of the execution of the this programme. In problematising this policy, it asks the following empirical questions: How do refugees relate to or experience the resettlement programme as a protection mechanism? What meaning does resettlement take on in a refugee settlement? By the preceding question I aim to investigate the significance of resettlement to the lives of refugees and those who implement the resettlement program. Examing the role that resettlement plays in the lives of the implementers and subjects of this policy will reveal the (unintended) consequences that arise from the implementation of the resettlement program and its implication as a tool of protection for refugees.

2 *Problematising Vulnerability*

As will be shown below, the concept of vulnerability used by UNHCR vulnerability criteria, does not capture in entirety the various social, economic and political factors as lived in the everyday lives of refugees in Nakivale

12 C Shore and S Wright (2011) (fn 1) at p 8.

settlement. In fact social science scholars such as Bakewell[13] and Clark[14] have questioned the usefulness of the concept of vulnerability pointing out that it is 'essentialist, paternalistic and reductionist'.[15] Although, as my findings show, the concept of vulnerability is mainly drawn upon by refugees in the refugee settlements in efforts to fit into UNHCR's vulnerability criteria, some scholars assert that it has little meaning to refugees beyond humanitarian contexts.[16] Moroever, its worth noting that for or a long time, no country had any allocated slots for African refugees, and resettlement was not favoured in policy or practice.[17] Developed countries did not have any quotas for African refugees because they were regarded as too numerous to render the refugee term applicable.[18] Moreover, when resettlement was considered, selection was based on educated or skilled refugees. Thus at at the insistence of African leaders who feared that this might lead to brain drain of Africa's elite, refugees fleeing conflict regions in Africa were placed in other parts of the continent (and not in developed countries).[19] It was not until the 1990s that things began to change, when UNHCR advocated for resettlement out of Africa by putting an emphasis on *suffering* as a requirement for resettling the deserving refugee.[20] The disadvantage of the emphasis on suffering as a criteria for resettlement, is that although international protection is intended as a 'durable solution', it has created a competition based on the metrics of vulnerability where a refugee with the most traumatic experience of suffering is rewarded with resettlement.

It is the turn to 'vulnerability' that led to the inclusion of African refugees as candidates for resettlement to the West.[21] In spite of this, only a small percentage of people from the continent get resettled. For example, according to the Resettlement Factsheet for Uganda, at the end of August 2018, out of the submission target of 5,426 refugees for resettlement only 2,937 submissions were made. Of that number only 1,787 refugees depart-

---

13 O Bakewell, 'Research Beyond the Categories: The Importance of Policy Irrelevant Research into Forced Migration' (2008) 432 *Journal of Refugee Studies* 21 4.

14 C Christina, 'Understanding vulnerability: From categories to experiences of Congolese young people in Uganda' (2007) 21 *Children & Society* 4 284 at 296.

15 M-T Schueler, *Disability and Logics of Distribution in a Refugee Settlement* (PhD Dissertation, University of Zurich, 2018) at 18.

16 ibid.

17 K Bergtora Sandvik (2018) (n 2) at 47.

18 ibid.

19 ibid.

20 ibid at 48.

21 ibid.

ed the country. This suggests logistical problems in meeting submission targets (UNHCR, 2018) and that third countries take only those few refugees that meet the resettlement criteria.

2.1 *Conforming to Vulnerability Categories*

UNHCR's vulnerability categories create sub-classes of subjectivity that are intended to offer more protection to refugees based on a 'hierarchy of suffering'.[22] In this respect, the resettlement policy attempts to 'define' and 'manage' refugee populations as subjects.[23] To this end, refugee settlements become 'disciplinary spaces'[24] in which refugees as subjects are managed by a set of institutions, bureaucratic processes, laws and policies. The unintended consequence of this subjectivity is that in a context where majority of the refugees are de facto and ab initio vulnerable (given the fact that they are exiled in an underdeveloped country with no real prospects of becoming economically independent), this incentivises refugees to construct their identities in a manner that is legible to the humanitarian system. In the case where certain subjectivities are rewarded with a chance at resettlement to a developed country, this incentivises refugees to construct vulnerable identities to fit into pre-conceived categories of vulnerability, especially if their identities do not neatly fit into UNHCR criteria for resettlement.

An understanding of the history of the inclusion of African refugees in the resettlement scheme is crucial for managing expectations of what the future holds for the protection of vulnerable populations in the current era. Sandvik argues that African refugees were not even considered political subjects to begin with but 'subjects of development'.[25] It is said that the reluctance to 'endow African refugees with the capacity to have legal problems' was because African refugees were considered too numerous, dis-

---

22 J Betsy, 'Trauma as Hierachy in The resettlement Process' (2018) *News Deeply: Peace Building* <https://www.newsdeeply.com/peacebuilding/articles/2018/08/08/hierarchy-of-suffering-trauma-as-currency-in-the-resettlement-process> accessed 10 Match 2019.

23 C Shore and S Wright (2011) (fn 1) at 11.

24 ibid citing D Hubert and P Rabinow, *Michel Foucault: Beyond Structuralism and Hermeneutics* (Chicago, University of Chicago Press, 2nd Edition, 1983) at 121.

25 K Bergtora Sandvik (2018) (n 2) at p 55 citing L Robyn, 'The international government of refugees', In W William and LWendy (eds), *Global Governmentality: Governing International Spaces* (London/New York, Routledge, 2004).

persed, premodern, and poor to make individual assessments to establish the elements of the refugee definition possible or necessary.[26] Thus due to 'the emphasis on material assistance, overseas resettlement was rarely offered to Africans'.[27]

This exclusion had implications for how they were protected. Humanitarian assistance was based on a developmental approach as it was assumed that Africans needed 'emergency assistance, rather than international legal protection'.[28] The argument made by the West for excluding Africans, despite the numerous conflicts that had resulted in the displacement of many populations on the continent, was that they were too numerous to render the application of the 'refugee' definition useful.[29] Moreover, despite the realities on the ground, flawed assumptions about Africans were premised on a homogeneous African culture that would render assimilation in any African country they were resettled in 'spontaneous'.[30] Assertions were made that refugees did not want to be resettled out of Africa and that if they were, they would not be in position to integrate.[31]

While great strides have been made since the 1980's – when such assumptions prevailed – and some countries have made provisions for resettling refugees from Africa, participating countries are few. Many challenges that were faced early on in implementing the resettlement programme prevail to date albeit not on the same scale. For instance, the logistics of running of humanitarian assistance programmes in poor countries in Africa continues to take up a lot of the UNHCR budget.[32] And developmental programmes based on 'self-sufficiency' continue to be implemented in settlements despite the fact they often do not yield the intended results. And assumptions about local integration as a durable solution made in the 1970's continue to prevail. This is not to argue that these are not

26 W. Holborn Louise, *Refugees, a Problem of Our Time : The Work of the United Nations High Commissioner for Refugees, 1951-1972*, (Metuchen, N.J., Scarecrow Press, 1975) at 836; K Bergtora Sandvik (2018) (n 2) at 55-56.

27 ibid.

28 K Bergtora Sandvik (2018) (n 3) at 55 citing G Loescher, 'The UNHCR and World Politics: State Interests vs. Institutional Autonomy' (2001) 35 *The International Migration Review* 1, 50.

29 K Bergtora Sandvik (2018) (n 3) at 55.

30 ibid.

31 C Shore and S Wright (2011) (fn 1) at 58 citing R John, 'Africa's Displaced Population: Dependency or Self Sufficiency?' in C John et al. (eds), *Population and Development Projects in Africa* (New York, Cambridge University Press, 1985) at 68-83.

32 K Bergtora Sandvik (2018) (n 3) at 47.

good long term solutions, rather I posit that they are idealistic at best as practical challenges make them difficult to be achievable.

Currently, one of the main challenges UNHCR faces is implementing the resettlement programme in an era when politicians are advocating the closing of borders in America and elsewhere in Europe. While there are many countries contributing to the running of refugee settlements,[33] very few are partners in resettlement. In the case of Uganda, according to UNHCR's Resettlement Factsheet, there are only six Resettlement Countries, namely USA, Norway, Canada, Sweden, Australia and the Netherlands.[34] Although France and Finland have since taken refugees, as of December 2018, they had taken five and two refugees respectively.[35]

Marfleet argues that large numbers of refugees are *produced* by overlapping factors such as 'economic, political, social, cultural and environmental'.[36] Yet proponents of migration use securitisation frameworks to vilify victims of war as potential terrorists. Moreover, when it comes to refugees from Africa, they are labelled as 'mere' economic migrants looking for better opportunities, instead of *forced migrants*. This labelling is problematic when viewed in light of Marfleet's argument that forced migration is caused by a multitude of factors.[37] The 'securitisation of migration'[38] started after 9/11, but particularly in the Trump era, which saw the banning of Muslims from select countries two months after he got into office, the increase in this trend has been palpable. The travel ban has not only had adverse effects on Muslims from blacklisted countries, but it has particularly affected refugees from Somalia who had been living in this settlement for a protracted duration and who were themselves victims of war. One has to understand the lengthy and drawn out process of resettlement to appreciate the effects of this travel ban on Somali refugees who had been "processed" and approved for resettlement only to be banned from entering America.

---

33 A noticeboard at the entrance of the shows lists Belgium, Switzerland, Germany, Japan, as donors to the resettlements programmes but many of them are not listed on UNHCR's resettlement countries in the resettlement Fact Sheet. United Nations High Commissioner for Refugees, *Uganda Resettlement Factsheet* (2018; 1) <https://reliefweb.int/sites/reliefweb.int/files/resources/67858_0.pdf> accessed 5 May 2019.

34 ibid.

35 ibid.

36 P Marfleet, *Refugees in a Global Era* (New York, Palgrave Macmillan, 2006) at 7.

37 ibid.

38 H CC García, 'Deconstructing Crimmigration' (2018) 52 *University of California, Davis Law Review* 197, 253.

Additionally, it should be noted that not all those who are selected for resettlement interviews get effectively resettled. In principle, refugees cannot apply for resettlement. One can only be recommended for resettlement if one fits the specific criteria laid out in the UNHCR Resettlement Handbook and this recommendation is exercised at the discretion of particular protection officers in certain aid agencies. Criteria for being considered include refugees in need of 'Legal and physical protection', 'Survivors of Violence and Torture', refugees in need of medical treatment that cannot be offered in Uganda; Women-At-Risk, e.g. single mothers; elderly refugees or refugees with 'lack of integration prospects'.[39]

UNHCR projected that 153,000 refugees in Uganda would be in 'need of resettlement in 2019'.[40] This is a modest number in relation to the 1,350,504 refugees that were registered as of January 2018.[41] In fact, statistics show that less than one per cent of the refugees who meet the criteria for resettlement get effectively resettled to a third country.Thus many of the refugees looking to be resettled try to tell their stories and emphasise their suffering in ways that could make them legible to the vulnerability-sensibilities of aid agencies. The aid agencies are specifically chosen by the refugees because of their ability to recommend solutions for 'the suffering refugee' of which resettlement is but one option. The other options range from counselling, referral to another agency or technical support within the mandate of the agency in question.

These categories are so broad that they could easily be applied to majority of the refugees, yet, simultaneously, so narrow that they exclude other forms of vulnerability. Thus, given the limited slots for resettlement, refugees' stories of suffering reveal diverse layers of trauma or insecurity, suggesting that refugees try to fit their traumatic experiences into multiple layers of UNHCR's vulnerability categories. Thus, the resettlement policy has not only created a system that rewards the most vulnerable refugee but has produced immense distrust between aid workers and refugees because of the lack of transparency in how refugee slots are distributed.

---

39 United Nations High Commissioner for Refugees, '*Resettlement Submission Categories*' <https://www.unhcr.org/558bff849.pdf> accessed 11 October 2019.

40 ibid at 2.

41 ibid.

2.2 Multiplying Soft Law Regimes

Based on ethnographic research in Kampala, Sandvik posits that there is not much ethnographic engagement on the legal pluralism linked to 'soft law regimes' nor the manner in which 'such regimes shape everyday interactions between humanitarian workers and their clients'.[42] In this section, I contribute to the legal pluralism scholarship by showing how aid agencies' guidelines act as soft law and how the adherence to these guidelines shapes implementation of resettlement scheme on the ground. In so doing, it becomes clear that diverse agencies, each with its own norms and way of assessing vulnerability, are central to the implementation of the refugee resettlement programme.

There are several aid agencies in Nakivale refugee settlement that cater to diverse refugees needs – ranging from food rations, counselling services, education programs, legal aid, farming needs, security provision, housing and livelihood and so forth. All these agencies, as one aid worker explained to me, describe what they do to ensure refugee 'protection'. One could argue that this broad view of providing aid services recognises the diverse but overlapping issues that constitute human security. However, in executing their mandates, these different agencies have their own respective guidelines to which they must adhere when providing services or solutions to problems that refugees who interface with them. I argue that these guidelines are *akin* to normative orders or soft laws that aid workers must follow in screening or assessing refugees. The result of strict adherence to these guidelines is that this creates plural normative orders, which sometimes compete or contest with different notions of 'vulnerability' of other agencies providing aid services within the same physical space. This is because each agency, depending on its mandate in the settlement, has developed its own distinct method for assessing vulnerability or protection needs. In doing so, aid agencies invariably influence the resettlement process in the screening of refugees for protection needs.

The strict adherence to these guidelines in service provision results in what some have argued as the prioritisation of 'procedure and consistency to the detriment of humanitarian goals'.[43] Extending this argument, I posit that in the context of the Nakivale refugee settlement, strict adherence to guidelines was due to a combination of several factors. First, it was a result of a mistrust of refugees' narratives of suffering by aid workers with whom

---

42 K Bergtora Sandvik (2011) (n 10) at 12.
43 Cited in K Bergtora Sandvik (2018) (n 3) at 204.

they interfaced. Second, aid agencies' forms often had prescribed solutions that did not leave much room for flexible or creative ways to respond to specific needs. Third, there was an inherent contradiction in the recommendation of resettlement by an agency and accepting that would amount to an implicit admission that that the agency recommending resettlement has failed to address the problem faced by the refugee. As one refugee told me, 'this place is insecure but government don't want to admit that because it would mean that it cannot keep us safe. So if you report any incident of insecurity, they can never recommend resettlement'.[44] The same interlocutor said that the main problem that they [refugees] face is that the 'aid agencies do not understand our problems'.[45] These problems, which sometimes did not fall within the exact frames of vulnerability as defined by the mandate of a specific agency were either relegated to a less critical category or excluded altogether. In the context of resettlement, this means that a refugee claiming to be suffering or facing a protection need that is outside the UNHCR criteria of vulnerability may not be eligible for resettlement even if the effect of said suffering culminates in a serious form of vulnerability. A common example that was often brought up by refugees of Congolese descent included instances of suspicions or accusations of witchcraft.[46] Many refugees I interviewed or held informal conversations with claimed that witchcraft was a serious problem in the settlement. Many believed that the delay in their resettlement cases, or the rejection of their resettlement cases, was the result of evil effects of witchcraft from envious neighbours.[47] The effects of such accusations are serious and could have dire consequences for those who are accused. In one particular village, it led to the burning down the house of a woman suspected of witchcraft.[48] However, allegations of witchcraft, despite having life threatening effects for the accused, fall outside UNHCR's vulnerability criteria. Moreover, as some of my interlocutors explained to me, when they reported to the police, they were often told that the police did not deal with

44 Informal conversation, October, 2018.

45 ibid.

46 N Sophie, 'The Politics of Accusations Amidst Conditions of Precarity in the Nakivale Resettlement Camp' (2019) 37: 2 *The Cambridge Journal of Anthropology* 39, 56.

47 ibid.

48 ibid.

witchcraft. In their earlier work, Comaroff and Comaroff[49] noted that accusations of witchcraft in South Africa increased at a time when the effects of global processes could not be understood by the locals.

I argue that delays in processing resettlement cases or the rejection of resettlement claims create the very conditions that the resettlement policy aims to alleviate. By taking a long time to process claims, the resettlement programme further exacerbates vulnerability not only for those who are 'in the process' but also of those suspected to be the cause of delaying the resettlement process because they are consequently accused of witchcraft. Moreover, that the latter cannot rely on the police (or other agencies in the camp) to protect them, given that witchcraft allegations do not fall within the mandate of the diverse agencies, not only shows a lack of contextual understanding of security threats but also highlights the limits of the law. The fact that the police as law enforcers are not equipped to deal with crimes involving witchcraft is crucial to understanding the limits of Ugandan criminal law since it does not address how to deal with the supernatural.

This suggests that in assessing resettlement claims, what counts as vulnerable should be broadened to include traditional beliefs. Belief in witchcraft and its evil effects is particularly common in Africa, and while in this specific settlement accusations and precautions against witchcraft were mainly prevalent among Congolese refugees, scholars have noted that the difficulty in policing or enforcing witchcraft allegations are very common. Sandvik argues that UNHCR recognises witchcraft as a security threat[50], however interviews conducted with refugees as well as some aid workers suggested that it is not recognised as a vulnerability criteria for resettlement.

UNHCR acknowledges three key challenges in implementing resettlement programmes. The first is the necessity for more 'resettlement submission opportunities to meet increasing needs'. The second is a logistical issue. Resettlement is an arduous process that requires more personnel just to meet the submission targets. For instance, as mentioned earlier, according to the UNHCR Resettlement Factsheet for Uganda, the submission tar-

---

49 J Comaroff and L John Comaroff, 'Occult Economies and the Violence of Abstraction: Notes from the South African Postcolony', (1999) 26:2 *American Ethnologist* 279, 303.

50 K Bergtora Sandvik, 'The Physicality of Legal Consciousness: Suffering and the Production of Credibility in Refugee Resettlement' in A Richard Wilson & D Richard Brown (eds), *Humanitarianism and Suffering: The Mobilization of Empathy* (Cambridge, Cambridge University Press, 2008) at 225.

get was 5,426 but only 2,937 applications were submitted and only 1,787 of that number were resettled to the respective Resettlement Countries[51]. Lastly, one of the main challenges that UNHCR faces is 'managing refugees' expectations' owing to the low number of slots.[52] As one interlocutor who has been in the resettlement process since 2013 explained to me, 'we were told that resettlement is not a right.' This response could have been elicited because aid workers state that most refugees consider resettlement as the only durable solution available to them. Consequently, aid workers try to manage refugees' expectations by offering counselling or other practical solutions to complaints that refugees report to them. These solutions are not always well received by some refugees who perceive resettlement as the only durable solution to their problems. One refugee working in one of the aid agency explained that as male survivor of sexual violence, remaining in the settlement was not an option because he endured homophobic slurs regularly.[53]

In the section that follows, I discuss UNHCR's vulnerability categories and show the specific ways in which refugees seeking resettlement in Nakivale experience vulnerability, or make vulnerability claims, in order to demonstrate how the disjuncture between these categories and refugees' experiences presents a challenge for implementing the resettlement programme.

3 *Unpacking UNHCR's Categories of Vulnerability*

Various scholars have noted the ubiquity of labels and categories in humanitarian contexts.[54] Glasman argues that UNHCR's interventions and distribution of resources are inherently premised on specific categories.[55] This is particularly evident in the implementation of the resettlement programme, and also in the ways diverse agencies in Nakivale refugee settlement allocate resources such as food rations, education scholarships, housing material and other services. Aid services are provided by multiple agen-

---

51 United Nations High Commissioner for Refugees (n 28) at 1.

52 ibid at p 2.

53 Informal conversation, November, 2019.

54 See for instance R Zetter, 'Labelling refugees: Forming and transforming a bureaucratic identity' (1991) 4:1 *Journal of Refugee Studies* 39, 62; J Glasman, 'Seeing Like a Refugee Agency: A Short History of UNHCR Classifications in Central Africa (1961–2015)' (2017) 30 *Journal of Refugee Studies* 2 337-362.

55 ibid J. Glasman (2017).

cies in Nakivale refugee settlement. The pluralisation of aid services is aimed at the broader goal of protecting refugees in this settlement and is overseen under the auspices of United Nations High Commissioner for Human Rights (UNHCR) and the Office of the Prime Minister (OPM). The aid agencies offer different but complimentary forms of protection that are aimed at providing refugees with food, housing, education, legal aid, medical treatment and identification cards.

In line with anthropological scholarship, UNHCR vulnerability categories centre on the 'suffering body',[56] suggesting that in many ways suffering is the 'most legitimate source for claim-making and legal and political recognition'[57]. I argue that as valid as these categories are, they only capture a small fraction of the varied ways in which refugees experience vulnerability. The result is that other forms of suffering are framed differently and thus addressed in ways that do not solve the problem in reality.

This results in a reframing of these problems and their repackaging by refugees in efforts to make them legible to the humanitarian system. The effect of this is forum shopping, as refugees attempt to make their claims to as many aid offices that will recognise their claims. I argue that the use of UNHCR categories in the implementation of the resettlement programme is an attempt at having a uniform standard,[58] while efforts by refugees to bypass these mechanisms of bureaucratic control through reframing of their problems and forum shopping should be understood as an exercise in agency.

In the following section, I discuss the many ways in which many refugees experience vulnerability in their everyday life in Nakivale. In doing so, I show the extent to which these categories are not encapsulated by the UNHCR criteria of vulnerability for resettlement. I argue that refugees' experiences of other forms of suffering outside those recognised by UNHCR exacerbate the harsh living conditions in the settlement in ways that enhances their vulnerability. Below are some examples of the factors that further exacerbate vulnerability in ways that international and resettlement policies do not anticipate or address on the ground.

---

56 K Arthur et. al. (eds), *Social suffering* (Berkeley, University of California Press, 1997).

57 T Miriam, 'Transnational Humanitarianism' (2014) 43 *Annu. Rev. Anthropol* 89 273, at 276.

58 K Bergtora Sandvik (2011) (n 9) at p 12. M Liisa, 'Speechless Emissaries: Refugees, Humanitarianism, and Dehistoricization' (1996) 11 *Cultural Anthropology* 3 377 at 404.

3.1 Dependency on aid system

Refugees come from different countries and constitute different ethnic groups, which makes adapting to their current reality difficult without any assistance.[59] Not only are many of them impoverished, coping in their new spaces is hindered by lack of resources, language skills or other forms of knowledge that would potentially enable them to engage in economic activities outside the settlement. Moreover, the structure of assistance constructs refugees as the 'needy' recipients of humanitarian assistance and aid workers as the benevolent providers of humanitarian aid.[60] Thus, from an anthropological perspective, humanitarian assistance is 'but a moral transaction which defines status and power relations between the giver and the recipient'.[61] Quoting Mauss' famous work Benoist, et al equate humanitarian assistance with 'the gift'. Maus argued that '[the gift] not yet repaid debases the man who accepted it'.[62] Thus, the way in which refugees are helped places them 'at a structural disadvantage with respect to their helpers'.[63] This makes refugees vulnerable in ways that might not be envisioned or recognised in UNHCR's categories of suffering.

3.2 Climate Change

When refugees come to Uganda they are given a small plot of land as part of the self-sufficiency strategy developed by UNHCR and Uganda. The idea behind this strategy is that refugees can, with time (within a period of 6 months), be expected to supplement their aid supplies with food they have grown. While well intended, especially in light of dwindling donor support to aid programme, climate change has affected the farming seasons and people can no longer predict the rainy season accurately so as to know when to plant their crops. The long dry spells in Nakivale often end up scorching the earth. In 2016, for instance, the drought caused the death of several animals and people, affecting both the host community and

---

59 B Jacques et al, *Anthropology in Humanitarian Assistance* (Brussels, European Commission, vol 4, 1998).

60 ibid B Jacques et al (1998) at 50; Z David, 'Vernacularising Asylum Law in Malta' in R Arnold and V Colcelli (eds), *Europeanization through Private Law Instruments* (Regensburg, Schnell & Steiner, 2016).

61 ibid B Jacques et al (1998) at 50.

62 Cited in ibid B Jacques et al (1998) at 50.

63 ibid B Jacques et al (1998) at 50.

refugees indiscriminately. The effects of climate change make both the refugees and the host community vulnerable since refugees are expected to rely on the land they are given for subsistence farming, while the host community is not entitled to food aid. Thus, it is worth noting that climate change has serious implications for diverse experiences of vulnerability on the ground – not only among refugees but owing to human security issues, also among those generally not identified as needing international protection.

As Imana, one of my interlocutors explained to me in 2017 when complaining about the small food portions, most of the health problems people complain about are stomach related. This is because 'security starts with the stomach.' In their chapter on 'Vulnerability and Human Security', Robin Leichenko and Karen O'Brien not only argue but also show how '…climate change can contribute to food, water and health insecurities, particularly for vulnerable populations that are burdened by poverty or face other social, economic, political or environmental constraints'.[64] This is especially true in the case of many of the refugees living in Nakivale refugee settlement who relied on subsistence farming to supplement their food aid. Leinchenko and O'Brien posit that in the context of climate change, the concept of vulnerability highlights the 'social, economic and political factors that expose specific 'nations, communities, individuals and groups'[65] to more risks. To this end, we see that their definition broadens the concept of vulnerability to acknowledge other factors that make people more susceptible to threats other than those stipulated in UNHCR's vulnerability criteria for resettlement. In the case of Nakivale, climate change contributes to the reasons why some people want to leave the settlement.

Scholars in the environmental field have acknowledged that vulnerability can also arise from what people depend on for survival. Those whose livelihood depends on naturally and locally available resources and are thus sensitive to environmental changes, such as farmers, fishers or those who engage in forest-based activities, are more prone to the effects of climate change.[66] In the context of refugees fleeing conflict zones in neighbouring regions to Uganda, vulnerability is further exacerbated by their dependency on environmentally sensitive livelihoods if their livelihood is subsistence-oriented. This is because even when they flee to countries of

---

64 R Leichenko and K O'Brien, *Climate and Society: Transforming the Future* (Hoboken, John Wiley & Sons, 2019) at 139.

65 ibid at 140.

66 ibid.

first asylum, they are unlikely to have the capacity to recover from climate change. This is already the case for subsistence farmers and informal workers who have remained in their own countries, as research shows.[67]

3.3 Economic Dimension

A review of literature in the Great Lakes region clearly shows a bias in migration scholarship by its focus on 'conflict-related refugee migration'.[68] This bias ignores labour migrants within and between these countries.[69] I argue that whilst the 1951 convention excludes economic migrants from its definition of a refugee, the reasons for moving render such distinctions meaningless in practice, as one could argue that economic migrants have been forced to move to find a means to make a living outside their home country. If one agrees that people fleeing wars, political or religious persecution or displacement are in need of protection, then economic factors have to be regarded as an inevitable effect. One can still advocate for a narrow view of vulnerability for the sole purpose of precluding a majority of economically vulnerable groups from resettlement and also recognise the connection between these processes and their economic and social effects on those who flee. In the case of Nakivale Refugee Settlement in Uganda, as is indeed the case for most people who live in post-conflict conditions, there is a thin line between forced migration and economic migration.[70] Castles et al posit that 'efforts for prevention of conflicts and for protection and assistance of forced migrants are far from adequate, since conflict and impoverishment often go together'.[71] This, they contend, makes it hard for UNHCR to respond to appropriately to 'mixed flows',[72] particularly be-

---

67 ibid at 143, citing R Leichenko and A Julie Silva, 'Climate change and poverty: vulnerability, impacts, and alleviation strategies' (2014) 5 *Wiley Interdisciplinary Reviews: Climate Change* 4, 539-556.

68 S Castles et. al., *The Age of Migration: International Population Movements in the Modern World* (New York, Guilford, 5th ed., 2014) at 186.

69 ibid.

70 ibid at 185.

71 S Castles, *Migration, Citizenship and Identity: Selected Essays* (Londong, Edward Elgar Publishing, 2017) at 229.

72 C Jeff, *Beyond the nexus: UNHCR's evolving perspective on refugee protection and international migration* (Geneva, UNHCR Research Paper No. 155, 2008) <http://www.unhcr.org/en-us/ research/working/4818749a2/beyond-nexus-unhcrs-evolving-perspective-refugee-protection-international.html> accessed 14 October 2019.

cause lines between economic migrants and forced migrants are blurred.[73] I argue that rather than focus on labels to distinguish between these two categories, a more appropriate approach would be to assume that any asylum seeker or forced migrant is by nature an economic migrant. This approach recognises the indivisibility of human security and would allow for a more realistic approach to address population flows.

3.4 Poor Infrastructure

Uganda has great legal infrastructure and its refugee laws have been hailed as the 'most compassionate' laws in the world because of its welcoming refugee policies. Theoretically, refugees in Uganda are allowed to work, have freedom of movement, free education, the right to health, and they are given land on which they can farm and build a small house. However, these services have often remained hard to access, for refugees and citizens alike. In particular, healthcare remains a challenge in the settlement, which has a small health centre that caters to a large population of over 100,000 refugees. Refugees complained that the health centre was equipped with only one doctor and that they often had to queue up for long periods before they could be attended to. While interlocutors complained about not having money to pay for the 'free' education, they also cited the long distance that high school students had to walk to attend the only school catering to refugees from different villages. One Somali interlocutor said that he could never allow his daughter to walk that far from home because he could not guarantee her safety. These few examples show the limits of law. While it is true that the laws provide for adequate refugee protection on paper, accessing services such as health, education and work remains a challenge in practice. While many interlocutors gave 'hard life' or lack of employment as the reason they wanted to be resettled to a country in the West, majority of them complained that the lack of good healthcare and seeing no future in Uganda were the main reasons for wanting to leave. Thus, the presence of an ever-increasing refugee population due to conflict in the neighbouring countries compounds the problem of poor public service provision. This is the case not only for Uganda's citizens with whom refugees have to share already strained, poor infrastructure but as research by other scholars has shown elsewhere '...vulnerability of poorer populations is sometimes tied to infrastructure and provision of public

73 S Castles, et. al. (2014) (n 62) at 229.

services'.[74] This is the case for most refugees who live in refugee settlements and neighbouring host community which are often situated in rural areas, thus presenting Uganda with a whole new set of social and economic challenges. Socially, host communities around areas near refugee settlements that are comparatively poor have expressed their frustration at being evicted from land to make space for more refugees. Host communities have at times been hostile towards refugees because of what they interpret as preferential treatment of foreigners by the aid system, which gives food rations and other provisions to refugees but not to the local community. As one interlocutor told me, the 'nationals' sometimes destroy their crops. Another interlocutor, who is a chairperson for one of the zones in the refugee settlement, told me that many of the cases or complaints that are brought to him are conflicts between 'nationals' and refugees, with the latter reporting that the locals had destroyed their crops. This suggests that the aid system creates vulnerable conditions for refugees through the preferential allocation of land and other resources, thus making them potential targets to hostile attacks from those who feel excluded and perceive themselves as equally vulnerable and deserving of help from the aid system or the government.

3.5 Contested Concept of 'Family'

Customarily, in most African countries, cultural definitions of family often go beyond the nuclear family. For the purposes of attaining refugee status within the country of asylum, any relative that joins an asylum seeker that is granted refugee status in Uganda is welcomed. However, for the purposes of resettlement, the idea of family takes on a different meaning. In line with UNHCR's principles of keeping families united, those who are approved for resettlement are often resettled with their close relatives. However, it is up to the receiving country to decide whether or not they will accept the family size. In an informal interview with UNHCR officer in charge of resettlement, she gave a hypothetical example, elucidating that houses in Finland are small and that it was unlikely that a large family would be resettled in Finland because if a refugee has a large family. Thus, although UNHCR tries to keep families together, the idea of family is narrowly defined as it excludes married adults. A western conception of family in a refugee context disregards the refugees' histories and the bond they

74 R Leinchenko and K O'Brien (2019) (n 58) at 144.

share with family members with whom they have endured so much suffering while fleeing their countries of origin.

3.6 *Conflict of Interest in the Provision of Aid Services*

As explained above, humanitarian services in Nakivale refugee settlement are provided by diverse aid agencies that cater to refugees' diverse needs. This is in line with many other refugee and asylum centres where non-governmental organisations have taken on governance responsibility under the auspices of UNHCR and the host countries. In the case of Uganda, funding for the operations of Nakivale refugee settlement hails mainly from donor countries in Europe as well as America and a few Asian countries. While there are many countries that donate to the aid programmes, very few of them participate in the resettlement scheme. I argue that the aid agencies in this specific settlement perform a dual role that is inherently contradictory. These agencies' very existence depends on funds donated by States because of their demonstrable expertise in the aid service provision or capacity to solve protection needs of refugees in the country of asylum. Therefore, they are important actors in constraining or enabling refugee outflows. In essence then, these agencies act as gatekeepers by ensuring that refugees' needs are addressed in the country of asylum and that only the most vulnerable refugees are recommended for resettlement.[75]

This results in gatekeeping practices as aid agencies have to write reports and keep records that account for provision of protection solutions to refugees in the country of asylum. Consequently, aid offices are effectively transformed into 'borders' of first instance, where refugees make their 'vulnerability' claims. Viewed from a broader perspective, aid agencies are important actors in the externalisation process in which undesirable populations are screened and documented before a decision can be made on their desirability as potential immigrants to developed countries in the Global North. This is because the bureaucratic process of making a vulnerability claim warrants admission on the part of the agency recommending resettlement that it cannot provide the service, or address the needs required to keep the refugee in the country of asylum. It is no surprise then that few

75 S Nakueira, 'Governing through Paperwork: Examining the regulatory effects of documentary practices in a refugee settlement' (forthcoming 2020) *Journal of Legal anthropology*.

agencies would be ready to recommend resettlement given the implication of such a recommendation. As noted by Sandvik,[76]

> access to third-country resettlement is in essence a question of administrative discretion about whether to grant admission to the First World. Legal bureaucrats, not judges, therapists, political leaders, human rights researchers or journalists, are in charge of determining the adequate threshold of suffering.

This raises issues of justice in the discretion exercised by agencies in the screening process. The section below will explore how this discretion affects the implementation of the resettlement programme.

3.7 *The Exercise of Discretion by Aid Agencies*

Discretion has been a key issue of contention in administrative law, with some scholars arguing that the exercise of discretion can lead to injustice.[77] While acknowledging the need for discretion, Davis argues that it has a high risk of leading to injustice.[78] In the context of implementing the resettlement policy, the exercise of discretion has grave implications for the protection of extremely vulnerable refugees who may be eliminated by a system that positions legal protection officers as objective assessors of vulnerability.[79] Thus, Sandvik urges us to 'scrutinize these processes of administrative humanitarian interventionism, and the technologies of control that the machineries for human rights protection provide for legal bureaucrats'.[80]

In many of the forms I analysed, the exercise of discretion was structured and confined to pre-conceived solutions on many of the agency forms. Therefore, aid workers could choose which solution to recommend

---

76 K Bergtora Sandvik , 'The Physicality of Legal Consciousness: Suffering and the Production of Credibility in Refugee Resettlement' in A Richard Wilson & D Richard Brown (eds), *Humanitarianism and Suffering: The Mobilization of Empathy*, (Cambridge, Cambridge University Press, 2008) at 225.

77 DKenneth Culp, 'Confining and Structuring Discretion: Discretionary Justice (1970) 23 *Journal of Legal Education* 1 62 at 56.

78 ibid.

79 T Marnie Jane, '"Giving Cases Weight": Congolese Refugees' Tactics for Resettlement Selection' in A Garnier et al. (eds), *Refugee resettlement: power, politics, and humanitarian governance* (New York, Berghahn Books, Studies in Forced Migration, vol. 38, 2018).

80 K Bergtora Sandvik, (n 44) at 225.

based on limited choices stipulated on these forms. However, there is an inherent distrust of refugees' stories among aid workers. Many aid workers I interviewed complained that many of the refugees who sought their help were mainly looking for resettlement and would do anything (including making false accusations of rape or defilement) so as to get in the resettlement process. These real or perceived bogus claims are often accompanied with equally dubious papers meant to support their claims that have been acquired from an illicit market of actors seeking to capitalise on the desperation of refugees seeking to circumvent the formal resettlement process. It is mainly due to this distrust of refugees' narratives of suffering that many aid workers do not recommend resettlement but often refer the refugee for counselling – an option that is already provided for on many agency forms. This issue of distrust raises important questions on how aid workers make decisions, how they distinguish between true and bogus claims, and the resulting consequences for refugee protection. This problem is compounded by the fact that not all those who have acquired supporting documents illicitly are making bogus claims. Rather, many genuinely vulnerable refugees are often victims of an illicit market that capitalises on their despair and solicits bribes in return for fake 'supporting' documents.

The screening process embedded in the documents of aid agencies reveals not only power relations between aid workers and refugees, but also another aspect that may not be so apparent, namely 'governing at a distance'.[81] Since the selection or recommendation by aid agencies in the settlement results in the resettlement of a few of the most deserving suffering refugees to participating resettlement countries in the Global North, this raises two interrelated key issues. First, aid agencies become de facto 'gatekeepers' or external migration control officers for resettlement countries. As inadvertent policing agents of resettlement countries, aid agencies become conduits through which migration control is exercised in a humanitarian context. This image invokes Osborne and Gaebler's popular image of 'steering' and 'rowing'[82] with resettlement countries doing the steering and aid agencies doing the rowing of migration control. This transforms not only the resettlement programme into a regulatory tool that controls refugee outflows from the Global South to the Global North but also

81 N Rose and PMiller, 'Political power beyond the State: problematics of government' (1992) 61 Suppl 1 *The British Journal of Sociology* 271 at 303.

82 D Osborne and T Gaebler, *Reinventing Government: How the Entrepreneurial Spirit is Transforming the Public Sector* (Melbourne, Addison-Wesley Publishing, 1993) at 28.

refugee settlements into complex spaces. For they are at once refugee settlements and transit spaces where the management of population outflow is exercised through humanitarian protection regime.

This externalisation of migration control on the part of countries in the Global North in humanitarian spaces makes aid workers key decision makers in the implementation of resettlement programmes. Through bureaucratic documents, each agency in the settlement fills out a form in which refugees are classified and offered preconceived solutions. This leads to a type of 'governmentality' in which settlements are transformed into spaces in which refugees are 'classified and managed'.[83] These documents become important testimonies that attest to refugees' vulnerability, thereby positioning aid workers and refugees in asymmetrical power relations. The latter has consequences for how aid workers interact with refugees in a context where the process of selecting the most vulnerable among a broad population of vulnerable refugees is not transparent.

This highly intransparent bureaucratic process creates room for exploitation of already vulnerable populations and gives aid workers a wide range of discretionary powers, whether real or imagined. This gives unscrupulous aid workers the capacity to take advantage of refugees who seek to influence the resettlement selection process. It is this imagined power over the selection process and the opacity in the allocation of resettlement slots to refugees that fuels accusations of corruption. One aid worker declared that the system has the potential to exploit refugees seeking resettlement, 'It is easy to exploit them as they are all looking for resettlement and will give anything to get it.' However, he was quick to add that not all agencies can recommend resettlement as a durable solution and that his agency was one of those that do not. The allegations that one has to pay money in order to be shortlisted was often cited as a reason for self-exclusion on the part of some refugees, since they were of the opinion that they stood no chance of being selected even though they felt that they qualified for resettlement. Despite well-positioned noticeboards cautioning people not to engage in resettlement fraud, there was a persistent belief that the system favoured those with money and not people with genuine protection needs.

Moreover, the Initiative for Enhanced Resettlement of Congolese Refugees which was introduced in 2012 to resettle Congolese refugees due to the protracted nature of the war in DRC[84] remains ambiguous to many Congolese refugees. It is unclear whether all refugees from Congo in the

83 C Shore and S Wright (2011) (fn 1) at 16.
84 United Nations High Commissioner for Refugees (n 28) at 2.

settlement are eligible for resettlement, or only those who came in the 1990's referred to as 'old case'. In a conversation with a UNHCR official, she mentioned that they cannot reveal some information about the selection process to the refugees, as much of it remains at the discretion of the Resettlement countries. Therefore, it was not uncommon for interlocutors to complain that some Congolese refugees who came recently were being resettled while those who have spent several years in the settlement are still waiting for their turn. Such complaints suggest that lack of opacity can spark a lot of distrust in the system and in the aid workers themselves who are deemed by refugees to have power to influence the selection process. Moreover, confusion and distrust is made worse by the shortlisting of Congolese refugees of Tutsi ethnicity on UNHCR noticeboard, prompting further allegations that Rwandans are getting resettled or are posing as Congolese refugees, when in fact they are Congolese by nationality. This apparent misunderstanding is explicable. The shortlisted Rwandese ethnic surnames on the UNHCR noticeboards, which are in plain view for anyone to read, have no resemblance to other ethnic groups from Congo – thus causing speculation of corruption.

4 Escaping Vulnerability: Survival Strategies

Whilst interviews with refugees revealed that many of them fit the vulnerability criteria in one way or another, exasperation and motivation for wanting to be resettled was explained by the precarious nature of life in the settlement. Lack of economic opportunities, a poorly equipped health centre and 'no hope' in the country of asylum or Africa generally were the most cited reasons for the desire to 'look for survival' elsewhere. Looking for survival outside the settlement was also the reason that young people who had given up faith in the system are reported to have embarked on dangerous journeys through Libya to reach Europe or end up servitude in host communities. Servitude was one of the options for some refugees who worked as herders for 'nationals' – as Ugandans near the settlement are referred to. Payment was often through exchange of labour for food or small wages, given that the Ugandan villagers that employed them are themselves usually poor.

While many refugees adapt to life in the settlements, others do not see settlements as permanent homes. This is especially the case with educated refugees who cannot imagine spending the rest of their life in the rural spaces they now find themselves in. In thinking about the future for themselves or their children, many refugees spoke of an ideal life in the West, where they saw a better future for themselves and their children. Despite not being in the resettlement process, some refugees were waiting until they got abroad to start families, thus putting family life on hold.

Although many refugees queue outside aid offices and the UNHCR building, not all are looking for resettlement. Interviews I conducted with people waiting outside UNHCR offices revealed that many of the refugees were already in the resettlement process, but had been waiting for years to leave the settlement. One of my interlocutors, who was finally resettled to Sweden in August 2018, had been in the resettlement process for six years.

Those who had resettlement claims approved on grounds of medical needs were afraid that their relative would not make it out of the settlement alive. One refugee, whose sister had been approved for resettlement on medical grounds told me that his sister had died before getting resettled and he was now seeking resettlement on grounds of security – having missed the chance to get resettled by default on account of his sister's death.

In general, some refugees find it hard to integrate in settlements – they deem them unsympathetic to their needs for survival. Specifically, inadequate healthcare and unemployment were the most cited reasons for refugees desiring to leave the settlement. Many refugees that were interviewed saw no future in a third-world rural settlement, which lacks basic institutions to make permanent arrangements thinkable. In Uganda, the Self Reliance Programmes, which assume that refugees that have been given plots of land will grow their own food and be self-sufficient and consequently less dependent on aid, render the idea of local integration impossible for refugees that are not from agricultural backgrounds. Moreover, this is not discounting the fact that even for those refugees that have an agriculture background, yielding crops in a changing climate make it difficult for them to anticipate when best to plant food crops on account of long spells of dry seasons. It is for this and many other reasons that resettlement remains the most desired durable solution for many, and it is also why the broad overlapping conditions which structure vulnerability make it difficult for the programme to be implemented in a context where there are multiple and overlapping layers of vulnerability, some of which are produced by the resettlement policy itself.

Conclusion

This chapter set out to show how refugees engage with the resettlement programme in a refugee settlement in Uganda and the meaning resettlement takes on in this refugee settlement.

In doing so, this chapter exposed the shortcomings of the resettlement policy by extrapolating in detail the challenges of implementing the resettlement programme on the ground. It showed that while international humanitarian law attempts to offer protection to displaced people, the translation of international law on the ground does not offer adequate protection in a meaningful way. Moreover, as the chapter has illustrated, the resettlement policy offers protection to only a limited number because admission to third country States is discretionary. I have argued that the vulnerabilitiy criteria used in assessing resettlement cases privileges specific taxonomies of suffering over others. That leads refugees to reconstruct legal personhood in ways that fit forms of suffering required in the country of asylum as well as for the purposes of resettlement. Additionally, by describing the discretion exercised by aid actors involved in screening or the selection of vulnerable refugees, I show that, in essence, while the resettlement programme is meant to protect the most vulnerable refugees, it promotes interests of third countries as an effective regulatory tool of refugee outflow. For those refugees looking for a way out of the precarious conditions of the settlement, the resettlement policy is a means through which they aim for a chance for a better life in America, Europe or elsewhere in the West. This not only creates opportunities for exploitation by aid workers who do the screening process, but in a context where majority of the refugees are vulnerable, the system creates potential for excluding those refugees who may not adequately or credibly meet indeterminate performative standards of vulnerability.[85]

By taking an anthropological approach in unpacking the resettlement policy, I have shown the 'messiness and complexity' as well as the 'ambiguous and often contested manner' in which the resettlement policy is implemented. In the context of Nakivale settlement, the resettlement policy, in essence, is a regulatory tool that controls refugee outflows from the Global South to the West, as well as a protection tool. The difficulty is not only in discerning how it manages to select the most vulnerable in a context where majority of the refugees are vulnerable because of the broad and overlapping conditions which shape vulnerability and precarity in the settlement.

---

85 K Bergtora Sandvik (2018) (n 3) at 227 .

As may have been obvious to the perceptive reader, not all the issues can be remedied by the resettlement policy. For many of the problems faced on the ground are beyond what the protection regime of resettlement is intended to achieve. Yet the paradox is that if not remedied, these problems will render the majority of refugees suitable for the resettlement programme. It is for this reason that I suggest that any discussion of another kind of humanitarian admission to Europe– in spite of its well-intended objectives – would do well to anticipate how to address existing challenges such as the ones mentioned above

Chapter 8:
Making the Case X&X for the Humanitarian Visa

Tristan Wibault[1]

This chapter aims to introduce the perspective of a legal practitioner who represented the interests of a Syrian family that applied for a humanitarian visa to Belgium, in a case that led to the *X. and X.* ruling of the CJEU. It will answer the following questions: Did I have any specific intentions before initiating such a visa request? Is it related to what is usually called 'strategic litigation'?

Strategic litigation may be used with different intentions, but it is essentially about effecting enduring systemic change in the fabric of law through path-breaking precedents in Courts. The repressive turn in immigration law has driven many actors to assume that strategic litigation is one of the best tools to achieve a progressive agenda in the legal field. History shows nonetheless that movements relying on judges to move social norms are weak if they are not aligned with grassroots political movements.[2] Actions in the interest of the public, appeals against the law at Constitutional Courts, there are many kind of actions where lawyers, representing collectives may try to use the law strategically. But what about the defence of individual cases?

I have my doubts about the fact that, as an asylum and migration lawyer, I could be in a position to be strategic. Michel de Certeau, in the *Practice of Everyday Life*, claims that any use is a creative appropriation. In his analysis of the user, de Certeau brings the distinction between a strategic position and a tactical position.[3]

Strategy is the prerogative of those in a position of power to manage relations with external targets. A tactic is an art practised by those not in power to move on the territory controlled by others, and in that sense a tactic is an art practised by the 'weak'.

1 Lawyer at the Bar of Brussels.
2 S Moyn, Human rights and the use of History (London & New-York, Verso, 2014, 2017) 178.
3 M de Certeau, L'invention du quotidien, 1. Arts de faire (Paris, Gallimard, 1980 and Paris, Poche, 1990) 60-61.

My clients definitively adopt tactics. Their attempts to enter the European Union's territory, for instance, when they bypass border control, can be characterised as tactics. Their tendencies to adapt their life story to the expectations of an inquisitorial assessment of their 'refugee quality' are again tactical moves. And the sphere is changing all the time. Regularly, clients share information they gain about new administrative practices, new pathways, or new means, which points to their reactivity to structural changes that might affect them. Especially the last years have witnessed new tensions in the relations between newcomers and the authorities. As a direct consequence of that, there are now refugees who refuse to ask for asylum, as in Brussels, in Calais and in other places around Europe. That raises questions for which there is no straight answer, and it is important at this juncture to consider this new reality of the refugees, earn their confidence, and defend them against oppression.

As a lawyer, the first step involves listening to the problems of the clients, in order to appropriately respond in light of the changes in the legal and policy landscape. In my view, giving legal advice is not a prescription on the conduct of the client. Such a response is not compatible with a purely analytical approach of the law. But its potential must be tapped into because anticipating, tracking, and understanding those tactical moves often highlights sensitive zones of friction in the law.

In reality, for a lawyer, it is never about building a single case. A lawyer is involved in repetitiveness, and in many different relations at any given time: with clients, social workers, activists, other lawyers, with the administration, and with judges. From time to time, there will be cases that bring to light the evidence before the Court of a new reality, where what can be considered as the truth must be redefined. All of a sudden, the definition of truth can change radically. Every lawyer has experienced this sudden shift of the truth when, for instance, the Supreme Court overturns an interpretation of the law widely accepted over many years.

Having worked for years at the Belgian Refugee Council,[4] a Belgian NGO providing legal assistance to asylum seekers and refugees and acting as the representative of UNHCR in Belgium, I am aware of the huge impact of networks and the collective nature of legal work. A judgment like *MSS*,[5] for instance, is the result of hammering on the same nail for more

---

4 The Comité Belge d'Aides aux Réfugiés (CBAR) has been dissolved in 2016. A new NGO named NANSEN is now assisting asylum seekers in Belgium, see: < https://nansen-refugee.be/> (accessed 25 November 2019).

5 M.S.S. v. Belgium and Greece (App. No. 30696/09)ECHR GC 21 January 2011.

than three years by hundreds of lawyers all over Europe. While most EU countries, insisting on their duties under EU Regulation, were wont to transferring asylum seekers to Greece despite alarming reports from human rights bodies, hundreds of complaints were finally made to the ECtHR denouncing these transfers.[6] In a lead judgment, the Court found that the terms of European cooperation within the asylum system had to take into account the responsibility of the States to protect fundamental rights.[7] If *MSS* has turned out to be a highly strategic case, one must not forget that it is the result of a very long collective fight.

X. and X. suddenly became highly sensitive and strategic following the decision of the Belgian Court to refer to the Court of Justice. Many important cases have this same pattern. In such situations, the lawyer and the clients become part of a larger and more complicated cause.[8]

In Belgium, visas usually do not represent a rich field of litigation. The Belgian Refugee Council was among very few with expertise on the issuance of family reunification visas for refugees. When the war started to rage in Syria, no week went by without phone calls from Syrians asking for support for family members in Syria and how to bring them safely to Europe. This led to new reflections and new practices on humanitarian visas.

In January 2015, I left the Belgian Refugee Council and started to work as a lawyer registered at the Brussels bar. Soon I had to deal with requests for humanitarian visas and the ensuing proceedings. My first client was a Christian Syrian with a mental disability. While his entire family had come to Belgium over the last three years, and he was the last one remaining in Syria, because he was the only one not able to travel with a smuggler.

In Belgian law, there is no specific provision on humanitarian visa under a specific legal framework. Basically the law says that if a foreigner does not have the right to remain more than three months on the territory on a specific ground foreseen by the law, he or she may be authorised to do so by the minister in charge.[9] Beyond that, the law does not establish the cri-

6 For Belgium alone, there were 97 pending applications before the ECtHR against the transfer of asylum seekers to Greece.

7 M.S.S. v. Belgium and Greece (n 5) at para. 338.

8 M Baumgärtel, Demanding Rights. Europe's Supranational Courts and the Dilemma of Migrant Vulnerability (Cambridge, Cambridge University Press, 2019) at 136.

9 Article 9 of the Law of 15 December 1980 on the Stay, the Establishment and the Removal of Aliens from the Belgian territory (Aliens Act).

teria to be fulfilled to obtain a humanitarian visa and every application is examined on a case-by-case and discretionary basis.

These experiences allowed me to draw the following conclusions on the problems faced by those trying to flee from conflict zones by means of humanitarian visas and by those who represent their interests:

- These cases are time consuming.
- Most of the time, there is no direct contact with the client, owing among others to such diverse factors as the distance, the conflict, and the language.
- There are challenges to getting the legal fees covered by legal aid. Since the client resides abroad, it is difficult to prove lack of sufficient income.
- There is no functioning Belgian embassy in Damascus. A Syrian client faces the challenge of crossing the borders. It is very dangerous to cross the Turkish borders. Procurations are accepted at the Belgian consulate of Ankara, but reaching Ankara to get the visa is not as easy.
- Establishing the facts to build the case on humanitarian grounds is yet another challenge. The expectation of the administration is that the full scope of information will be made available. Very often, the situation demands an external assessment. Who is to be entrusted with this task? This is when contact with international NGO's, the UNHCR, and other bodies, and bureaucracies comes into play.
- Once the request is completed, one remains at the mercy of a discretionary procedure. First, there is no time limit for the treatment of your request. Second, it is difficult to anticipate the grounds that may be invoked to justify the rejection of the request, as there is no right to be heard before the decision is made.
- There is no effective remedy. The appeals procedure may be very slow. Lawyers attempt to overcome this problem by using the extreme urgency procedure, which allows the competent judge, the Council for Aliens Law Litigation (hereinafter: the Council) to suspend the decision awaiting a decision on the merits; but for obvious reasons, this procedure is not fit for the purpose. What does it mean to get the suspension of a decision to deny a visa?
- The administrative nature of the proceeding makes it hazardous. You may get the suspension of the visa refusal, you may even get it cancelled, the risk of a new refusal with a modified motivation is high, making the process more lengthy.

The idea to invoke the EU Visa Code[10] thus came with the objective of obtaining better safeguards, less discretionary decisional processes and quicker decisions, namely by connecting the issue of humanitarian visa to general principles of the EU law and the Charter of Fundamental Rights of the European Union (hereinafter: the Charter).

The possibility of working with the Visa Code to get a better access to humanitarian visa was in the air at that time. The European Parliament had issued a report on humanitarian visas[11] with recommendations for clear safeguards for protection seekers when asking for a visa on humanitarian grounds. Professor Steve Peers wrote a blogpost on the *Koushkaki*[12] ruling,[13] from which he deduced an obligation on the part of EU Member States to issue visas with limited territorial validity if such a visa became necessary on humanitarian grounds. There were also many political calls for a stronger use of humanitarian visas. The European Parliament voted for a resolution where Member States were asked to deviate from the normal admissibility criteria for a visa application 'on humanitarian grounds' and to the create new safe and lawful routes for asylum seekers.[14] Even the European Commission stated that Members States should use the other legal avenues available to persons in need of protection, including private/non-governmental sponsorships and humanitarian permits, and family reunification clauses.[15] The UNHCR[16] and many others, made calls for the use of the humanitarian visa to respond to the Syrian refugee crisis. There were many references to Article 25 of the Visa Code as one possible legal

---

10 Regulation No 810/2009 of the European Parliament and of the Council of 13 July 2009 establishing a Community Code on Visas (Visa Code) [2009] OJ L 243.

11 U I Jensen, Humanitarian Visas: Option or Obligation? (Brussels, European Parliament, Study for the LIBE Committee, 2014).

12 Case C-84/12 Koushkaki [2013] EU:C:2013:862.

13 S Peers, 'Do potential asylum - seekers have the right to a Schengen visa?' (2014) EU Law Analysis <http://eulawanalysis.blogspot.com/2014/01/do-potential-asylum-seekers-have-right.html> (accessed 25 November 2019).

14 European Parliament resolution of 12 April 2016 on the situation in the Mediterranean and the need for a holistic EU approach to migration, 2015/2095(INI).

15 COM (2015) 240 final, Communication from the Commission to the European Parliament, the Council, the European Economic and Social Committee and the Committee of the Regions. A European Agenda on Migration.

16 UNHCR, UNHCR highlights dangers facing Syrians in transit, urges countries to keep borders open (Press Release, 18 October 2013) <http://www.unhcr.org/526114299.html> (accessed 25 November 2019); UNHCR, UNHCR Reports Progress on Resettlement, Aid for Syrian Refugees (Press release, 30 March 2016) <http://sd.iisd.org/news/unhcr-reports-progress-on-resettlement-aid-for-syrian-refugees/> (accessed 25 November 2019).

frame for issuing humanitarian visa to asylum seekers, but there was no legal consensus on whether the EU Visa Code was indeed applicable. All these views on the application of the Visa Code were remaining prospective, trying to fill a gap in the legal framework.

Then came a specific request from a family with three children, who were Christians from Aleppo and had friends in Belgium. They knew that Belgium had taken in some Christians from Aleppo and had personal relationships with some of those who have been exfiltrated out of Aleppo during a humanitarian operation organised by the Belgian government in July 2015.[17]

The personal situation of the family was well documented – not just that they lived in Aleppo or that they were Christians, but also that the father had been kidnapped by the militias and his car business has been ransacked and then taken over.

Without any strong ties with Belgium, in practice, they had no chance of obtaining a visa under the purely discretionary procedure.[18] Under these circumstances, this was maybe a fitting case to make a request under the Visa Code.

The visa request was prepared in July 2016. At that time, Aleppo was under siege and the UN was regularly publishing news about the humanitarian needs in the city. On different occasions, the Belgian State Secretary for Asylum and Migrations, Mr Theo Francken, had declared his willingness to 'save Christians from hell' in Syria and two operations were organised in 2015 to bring Christians from Syria to Belgium. The family relied on these declarations and actions of the State Secretary to argue that their personal case could not be treated in a different manner.

While these rescue actions were politically motivated by the State Secretary to oppose different categories of refugees,[19] they were used by us here to demonstrate that the same administration could not reject the absolute necessity of issuing such visas for other categories of people living under

---

17 De Morgen, België redt 250 omsingelde christenen uit Aleppo (8 Juli 2015) <http://www.demorgen.be/buitenland/belgie-redt-250-omsingelde-christenen-uit-aleppo-a2388752/> (accessed 25 November 2019).

18 There ar no clear criteria for the issuance of humanitarian visa, but the practice shows that a personal link to Belgium is often requested, beyond the sole humanitarian needs. See : MYRIA, Les visas humanitaires, Frontières et droits fondamentaux (Brussels, MYRIA, Myriadocs 4, May 2017) <https://www.myria.be/fr/publications/myriadocs-4-visa-humanitaire> (accessed 25 November 2019).

19 The State Secretary has been accused of favouring Christian refugees in the Syrian context.

the exact same conditions, experiencing the same vulnerabilities. If the administration cannot but confirm the state of necessity, the conditions for the issuance of an humanitarian visa should be met. A reference was made to Article 18 of the Charter, under the consideration that the claimants are *prima facie* refugees.[20]

After the reservation of an appointment to the embassy online, the organisation of the travel of the family, the request for a visa to claim asylum in Belgium was finally registered at the Embassy in Beirut in September 2016.

Another similar case was already introduced in Belgium a few weeks ago, which very quickly drew the attention of the national press. After several positive judgments in the extreme urgency procedure, and owing to the unwillingness of the administration to confront its reasoning to those judgements, a judge decided to order in favour of the issuance of the visas, but the State Secretary refused to execute this judgement.[21]

Our visa request very quickly received a negative answer. The Belgian Consulate in Beirut sent an alarming signal to the ministry. The Consul wrote to the ministry that such visa requests could not be possible because it would mean that people would no longer need to take makeshift boats to reach Europe.

In a media war on humanitarian visas, the State Secretary was accusing disconnected judges of fuelling a no-border policy. This situation probably motivated the Council for Alien's Litigation to process our appeal within the General Assembly of the Council.[22] After a first audience, this Assembly of the Council decided on its own move, within the framework of urgent procedure, to refer the case to the EU Court of Justice.

The referral of the Council came in a judgment on 8 December 2016. On 12 December 2016, the case was registered at the Court of Justice and communications to the parties were sent on 16 December 2016. The case

---

20 A prima facie approach means the recognition by a State or UNHCR of refugee status on the basis of readily apparent, objective circumstances in the country of origin. See: UNHCR, Guidelines on International Protection No. 11: Prima Facie Recognition of Refugee Status(Geneva, UNHCR, 5 June 2015).

21 This case is now pending before the Grand Chamber of the ECtHR (M.N. & others v. Belgium, App. No. 3599/18). The case raises the issue of the applicability of the ECHR within the assessment of humanitarian visa requests, but also the effectivity of the remedies offered to the claimants in their contestations of the visa refusal.

22 The General Assembly may be summoned to preserve the unity of the case law or to develop the case-law (Article 39/12 of the Alien's Act). It gathers minimum 10 judges.

would be treated in the fast track procedure and written observations of maximum 15 pages have to be delivered on 4 January 2017.

I had to send in written observations to the Court in a very short timeframe (19 days). There would be no Christmas break that year. *X. and X.* needed exclusive attention and that meant leaving aside all other clients and finding the means to assume this workload.

Legal aid is no longer an option. The fee for a proceeding at the CJEU is three points for the written observations and three points for the audience, for an estimated retribution of 450 euros. This is grossly undervalued when, for example, an appeal against an order to leave the territory would be rewarded with nine to eleven points. This amount would not even cover the expenses incurred over one month, and a month was required to establish a proper defence. Financial alternatives had to be found quickly to be able to work seriously on the case. Fortunately, the fundamental issues raised in the course of *X. and X.* helped me to find sponsors for the legal work.

Being an autonomous lawyer without significant internal resources, building up a work team has become a central issue for preparing the written observations. Access to academic literature on extraterritorial asylum, on diplomatic asylum, and on the right to enter was an essential part of the preparatory work to gain an overarching view of the state of international law and its prospective developments. Academics were generous in sharing their work with me. I hired a colleague, Pierre Robert to collaborate on the drafts. Different lawyers, legal researchers, NGO staff gave interesting feedback on the drafts. Universities seemed very accessible in their sharing knowledge with me. The EDEM Center of the Université Catholique de Louvain[23] and the Vrije Universiteit Amsterdam[24] were particularly helpful in making their research available to me at the time of the redaction, either by making publications accessible or by commissioning new relevant articles.

23 J-Y Carlier and L Leboeuf, 'The X. and X. case: Humanitarian visas and the genuine enjoyment of the substance of the rights, towards a middle way?' (2017) EU Immigration and Asylum Law and Policy <https://eumigrationlawblog.eu/the-x-and-x-case-humanitarian-visas-and-the-genuine-enjoyment-of-the-substance-of-rights-towards-a-middle-way/> (accessed 25 November 2019).

24 T Spijkerboer, E Brouwer and Y Al Tamimi, Advice in Case C-638/16 PPU on Prejudicial Questions Concerning Humanitarian Visa(VU University Amsterdam, 5 January 2017) <https://www.refworld.org/docid/5874ee484.html> (accessed 25 November 2019).

Beyond strict legal work, much time was also spent on meetings with NGOs, people working on recasting the Visa Code, on possible interventions of the European Parliament in the case, and on correspondence with journalists from the Belgian and European press whose questions needed immediate response.

What did we try to achieve and avoid in our written observations ?

First of all, we wanted to avoid turning the scope of Article 4 of the Charter (Article 3 of the ECHR) into the central focus of the interpretation. Given the absolute nature of those dispositions, there was the risk of making a positive obligation to issue a visa under Article 4 of the Charter an unsustainable and unrealistic goal. What if the person at risk of torture and requesting a visa is a criminal?[25]

We also avoided any request for an externalised asylum procedure within the embassies. The aim here was to confirm the refugee status via regular procedure in Belgium according to the Directive 2013/32/EU of the European Parliament and the Council of 26 June 2013 on common procedures for granting and withdrawing international protection (recast)[26] and not to claim the refugee status from abroad.

In the practice, visa requests were made in Lebanon, a third country. So that the persons in question here, no longer living in their country of origin, were already refugees. Considering the situation in Syria at the time of processing, they were indeed *prima facie* refugees. The fact that no authority is ready to recognise them as such in Lebanon forms no obstacle to this reasoning while the refugee status is a declarative one.[27] All issues here are very easy to assess. Just the knowledge of the most common facts is enough to assess the protection needs. At the root of the case, of course, were the reasons to flee Syria, but equally relevant were the reasons not to remain in Lebanon. The country cannot be considered a first country of asylum as it

---

25 Abdul Wahab Khan v the UK (App No 11987/11) ECHR (dec.) 28 January 2014.

26 Art 3.2 of the Directive 2013/32/EU states that the Directive shall not apply to requests for diplomatic or territorial asylum submitted to representations of Member States.

27 UNHCR, Handbook and Guidelines on Procedures and Criteria for Determining Refugee Status under the 1951 Convention and the 1967 Protocol Relating to the Status of Refugees (Geneva, UNHCR, December 2011) at para. 28: 'A person is a refugee within the meaning of the 1951 Convention as soon as he fulfils the criteria contained in the definition. This would necessarily occur prior to the time at which his refugee status is formally determined. Recognition of his refugee status does not therefore make him a refugee but declares him to be one. He does not become a refugee because of recognition, but is recognized because he is a refugee.'

was common knowledge at that time that Syrian refugees were no longer allowed to register as refugees in Lebanon.[28]

If we agree that the visa requests are made by refugees, we can draw a positive obligation under the institution of asylum to secure access to refugee rights when Article 18 of the Charter is meant to protect the institution of asylum.

Article 18 of the Charter can be the perfect safeguard of the asylum institution within EU law. Unfortunately, asylum remain the 'invisible right'[29] within EU law. So far, the CJEU has not declared its position on the scope of Article 18 of the Charter, the right to asylum and its distinction from Article 19 of the Charter, the protection against *refoulement*.[30] Contrary to the ECHR, EU law and the Charter are not connected to any territorial definition of the jurisdiction. The sole application of EU law makes the Charter compulsory.[31] Article 18 of the Charter might also apply when the Visa Code is at play.

Access to asylum may also be directly connected to protection against *refoulement*. In practice, the action to prevent a departure may constitute a *refoulement*. Under Article 33 of the Geneva Convention, *refoulement* is forbidden '*by any means what so ever*'. How do you conceive the notion of *refoulement* in the context of blurring of borders and of public policies that tend to externalise border management to other spaces and authorities. Following some ExCom statements, the limitation to access to the territory may amount to *refoulement*, even within visa policy.[32] How can we accept

28 The claimants were not able to obtain the recognition of their refugee status because of the suspension of the registration of Syrian refugees by the UNHCR as of 6 May 2015, following an order from the Lebanese authorities. See: M Janmyr, 'The fragile legal order facing Syrian refugees in Lebanon' (24 July 2018) EU Migration Law Blog <https://eumigrationlawblog.eu/the-fragile-legal-order-facing-syrian-refugees-in-lebanon/> (accessed 25 November 2019).

29 This expression was used in M-T Gil-Bazo, 'The Charter of Fundamental Rights of the European Union and the Right to be Granted Asylum in the Union's Law' (2008) 27 Refugee Survey Quarterly 3 at 37.

30 In a recent judgment, Article 18 of the EU Charter of Fundamental Rights is interpreted as safeguarding the right to asylum within EU law, see: Case C-391/16 M & Others [2019] EU:C:2019:403. In this judgment, the CJEU examines the validity of the exclusion from the international protection under article 14.4 to 14.6 of the Directive 2011/95 with the Geneva Convention.

31 Case C-617/10 Akerberg Fransson [2013] EU:C:2013:105 at para. 21.

32 UN, ExComm No. 87 (L) – 1999 – General Conclusion on International Protection; UN ExComm, No. 97 (LIV) – 2003 – Conclusion on Protection Safeguards in Interception Measures.

the paradox that Europe may try to make its territory inaccessible and at the same time claim that it still respects the principle of *non refoulement*?

In the beginning of January, our observations were sent to the Court and we received the written observations of the Belgian State and the EU Commission.

The main counter-argument put forth by both the Belgian State and the Commission was to disqualify all claims as being outside the scope of EU law, because, concretely, the claimants wished to get a long-term visa, and not a short-term visa under the Visa Code.

The public audience gave us the opportunity of contesting this legal interpretation of the facts. Following the official statistics of Eurostat, European Member States issued about 30,000 Schengen visas to Syrians in 2010. In 2013, when the war was raging, this number was near to zero. This is precisely the paradox the Court had to answer in *X. and X*. The EU policy on the border control aims to fight illegal migration but at the same time forces refugees to rely on the same illegal migration networks that they are fighting.

The cohesion duty seeks to ensure that the border control policy is compatible with refugee protection. Obviously, you may always doubt the willingness of a *prima facie* refugee to leave the Schengen space when the visa expires. This essentially means that no Schengen visas will be issued to Syrian citizens since the recognition rate is above 95 %.

While Article 21 of the Visa Code stipulates that particular consideration shall be given to assessing whether the applicants present a risk of illegal immigration, *X. and X* gave an humanitarian explanation to a foreseeable refusal ground by admitting already at the stage of their request that they would apply for asylum once they arrived in Belgium.

The opinion of Advocate General Mengozzi came as a big surprise, especially because the same Advocate General had ruled in *Kouskhaki* that the Visa Code was barely EU law, leaving a very important margin of appreciation to the Member States.

Advocate General Mengozzi came to the same conclusion as the claimants by stating that the refusal to issue the visa sought has the direct consequence of encouraging the applicants in the main proceedings to put their lives at risk, including those of their three young children, to exercise their right to international protection.[33] He insisted that careful consideration be given to his reasoning in reaching a decision, as this pertained to a

33 Case C-638/16 PPU X and X [2017] EU:C:2017:93 Opinion of AG Mengozzi at para. 159.

matter of law and not of emotions. This opinion will continue to be brought to bear for its strong arguments in favour of legal access to asylum seekers and may inspire other legal actions in the future.

Unfortunately, the Court found a consensus on a shorter track. Even if formally submitted on the basis of Article 25 of the Visa Code, the request falls outside the scope of that Code and the situation at issue in the main proceedings is not governed by EU law.[34] Imagine for a second that my clients would have said that they wanted to buy some chocolate in Brussels to bring them back in Aleppo, then, following the reasoning of the Court, the Visa Code would have applied.[35]

Made on the wrong legal basis, following the EU judgement, the appeals in the Belgian Courts would be declared without object and the case would be definitively closed.

The State Secretary praised this judgment for helping him to consolidate his discretionary power with respect to the issuance of the humanitarian visa. In that sense, the legal frame has remained unchanged.

Ironically, two years later, intermediaries of the State Secretary have been charged with corruption in the possible sell-out of humanitarian visas to Christians from Syria, and Mr Theo Francken has been accused of promoting a system of humanitarian visas that feeds corruption and clientelism.

---

34 Ibid. at para. 43-45.

35 See M Zoeteweij-Turhan and S Progin-Theuerkauf, 'CJEU Case C-638/16 PPU, X and X – Dashed hopes for a legal pathway to Europe' (10 March 2017) European Law Blog <https://europeanlawblog.eu/2017/03/10/cjeu-case-c-63816-ppu-x-and-x-dashed-hopes-for-a-legal-pathway-to-europe/> (accessed 25 November 2019).

Part 4.
Some Future Prospects on Humanitarian Admission to Europe

Chapter 9: The Objective of Resettlement in an EU Constitutional Perspective

Catharina Ziebritzki[1]

Contents

1 PhD candidate. Research fellow at the Max Planck Institute for Comparative Public Law and International Law in Heidelberg, member of the research initiative 'The Challenges of Migration, Integration and Exclusion' of the Max-Planck Society. I would like to thank Christoph Krenn, Michael Ioannidis, Constantin Hruschka, Luc Leboeuf, Pauline Endres de Oliveira and the *Dienstagsrunde* for their criticism and suggestions. I would also like to thank Gita Rajan for her language review.

Introduction

Resettlement means the organised movement of pre-selected refugees from the State where they initially sought protection to a destination country in which their settlement is expected to be permanent.[2] In the EU context, resettlement more specifically refers to the transfer of persons in need of international protection from a third country to an EU Member State.[3]

Global resettlement needs are increasing in accordance with the continuous rise of the number of forcibly displaced persons. UNHCR estimates that in 2020, about 1.4 million persons will be in need of resettlement, which represents a 20 per cent increase from 2018.[4] Nevertheless, global resettlement has decreased in the past years, both in absolute numbers as well as in proportion to the needs.[5] Traditionally, Europe is considered a side stage for global refugee resettlement. In the past decades, EU Member States have continuously offered less than ten per cent of global resettle-

2 J Van Selm, 'Refugee Resettlement' in E Fiddian-Qasmiyeh, G Loescher, K Long and N Sigona (eds), *The Oxford Handbook of Refugee and Forced Migration Studies* (Oxford University Press, 2014) 512.

3 Art 2 lit. a Regulation (EU) No 516/2014 of the European Parliament and of the Council of 16 April 2014 establishing the Asylum, Migration and Integration Fund [hereinafter: *AMIF Regulation*], see however n 17712. The organised movement of pre-selected asylum seekers from one Member State to another member state is termed *relocation* and differs fundamentally from resettlement. The Relocation Programme was established by Council Decision (EU) 2015/1523 of 14 September 2015 and Council Decision (EU) 2015/1601 of 22 September 2015 resp. establishing provisional measures in the area of international protection for the benefit of Italy and of Greece. The Relocation Programme expired in September 2017.

4 UNHCR, Projected Global Resettlement Needs 2020, published in the context of the 25th Annual Consultations on Resettlement (2019), available online: https://www.unhcr.org/protection/resettlement/5d1384047/projected-global-resettlement-needs-2020.html [all links last accessed on 02 Sept 2019].

5 While in 2016, about 125,000 persons were resettled globally with the assistance of UNHCR, in 2018 only about 80,000 persons benefitted from resettlement through UNHCR. Cf UNHCR, Resettlement Data, available online: https://www.unhcr.org/resettlement-data.html; M Engler, 'Versprechen gegeben, Versprechen gebrochen – Resettlement-Zahlen seit 2016 mehr als halbiert' (2019) *Fluchtforschungsblog* 28 Feb 2019. This coincides with a sharp reduction of the US resettlement programme due to its recent anti-migration politics. UNHCR data, referred to here, however, only includes resettlement with assistance by UNHCR, and the US programme much less relies on UNHCR, see J Van Selm (n 2) 512.

ment capacity.[6] Since the early 2000s however, a renewed European interest in resettlement has been noted.[7] Resettlement not only provides protection and a durable solution to refugeehood, it is also a means of sharing international responsibility for refugee protection.[8] The 2018 UN Global Compact on Refugees, hence, explicitly calls on the emerging destination countries to intensify their efforts.[9] And, indeed, Europe is slowly becoming more important for global resettlement in terms of numbers.[10] But not only Europe as a region, also the EU as an actor is becoming increasingly relevant for resettlement.

EU resettlement policy has gained new momentum, in particular since the crisis of the Common European Asylum System. The EU-Turkey Statement of March 2016 prominently provides for the resettlement of Syrian nationals through the '1:1 scheme'.[11] In the same year, the Commission put forward a proposal for a comprehensive Union Resettlement Framework.[12] The emphasis on resettlement in the context of crisis might be explained by the fact that resettlement is particularly well suited to deal with

---

6 The USA, Canada and Australia together provided for the other about ninety per cent. Even though Sweden, Finland, Denmark, Netherlands, and the UK have well-established resettlement programmes, their capacity is relatively small in the global context, see J Van Selm (n 2) 512; A Cellini, 'Annex: Current Refugee Resettlement Program Profiles' in A Garnier, LL Jubilut and KB Sandvik (eds), *Refugee Resettlement. Power, Politics, and Humanitarian Governance* (Berghahn, 2019) 253 ff.

7 J Van Selm, 'The Strategic Use of Resettlement: Changing the Face of Protection?' (2004) 22 *Refuge* 39.

8 J Van Selm (n 2) 512. Further, resettlement is generally understood as one of the three durable solutions to refugeehood alongside local integration in the first host state and voluntary return to the country of origin, see BN Stein, 'The Nature of the Refugee Problem' in AE Nash (ed) *Human Rights and the Protection of Refugees under International Law* (Montreal Institute for Research on Public Policy, 1988) 47, 50 ff.

9 UNHCR Report, Global compact on refugees, A/73/12 (Part II), affirmed by the UN General Assembly on 17 December 2018, 73rd Session Supplement No. 12, [in the following: *2018 Global Compact*], para 90 ff.

10 However, the decline of US resettlement capacity can by far not be balanced out, see M Engler (n 5).

11 European Council, Press Release of 23 April 2015, available online: https://www.consilium.europa.eu/en/press/press-releases/2015/04/23/special-euco-statement/ [in the following: *EU-Turkey Statement*].

12 European Commission, Proposal for a Regulation of the European Parliament and of the Council establishing a Union Resettlement Framework and amending Regulation (EU) No 516/2014 of the European Parliament and the Council, 13 July 2016, COM(2016) 468 final [in the following: *Union Framework Proposal*].

the challenge of complying with contradicting demands of different political groups, which are increasingly drifting apart.[13] Some appreciate resettlement as a means of providing international protection to third country nationals and preventing loss of life, or severe harm to life, during attempts to irregularly cross borders.[14] Others praise resettlement rather as a means of enhancing state control in the realm of forced migration, as an immigration management tool, or even as a foreign policy instrument serving the political and economic interests of the EU beyond the realm of migration.[15] While both positions agree on increasing the use of resettlement, the respective answers to the question of 'why' are obviously quite different. This question is far from being only conceptual. Quite to the contrary, addressing the question of why – the objective of resettlement – is a precondition for answering the equally contentious questions of how and whom to resettle.[16] In other words, defining the objective of resettlement has direct practical implications for the concrete design of a resettlement scheme.

The controversies over the objective of resettlement in particular concern two issues: *First*, is the purpose of resettlement to complement the traditional territorial asylum procedures, or can it be understood as eventual-

---

The Proposal extends the definition of resettlement so as to include internally displaced persons as eligible for resettlement, see Art 2, 5 Union Framework Proposal.

13 *cf* M Savino, 'Refashioning Resettlement: from Border Externalization to Legal Pathways for Asylum' in S Carrera, L den Hertog, M Panizzon and D Kotsakopoulou (eds) *EU External Migration Policies in an Era of Global Mobilities: Intersecting Policy Universes* (Brill, 2019) 81, 94 similarly refers to the 'Commission's attempt to reconcile humanitarian goals with the deterrence of irregular immigration'; similarly: Forschungsbereich beim Sachverständigenrat deutscher Stiftungen für Integration und Migration (SVR), 'Die Zukunft der Flüchtlingspolitik? Chancen und Grenzen von Resettlement im globalen, europäischen und nationalen Rahmen', authored by K Popp (2018) 4.

14 *cf* Caritas Europa, Churches' Commission for Migrants in Europe (CCME), European Council for Refugees and Exiles (ECRE), International Catholic Migration Commission (ICMC Europe), International Rescue Committee (IRC), Red Cross EU office (2016) Joint Comments Paper on the [Union Framework Proposal], available online: https://www.asylumlawdatabase.eu/en/content/ngo-comments-european-commission-proposal-regulation-establishing-union-resettlement.

15 The renewed European interest in resettlement can indeed be traced back, at least inter alia, to 'security concerns'. See J van Selm (n 7) 43 who notes that, while European politics understand resettlement as a way to control forced migration, the US reduced its resettlement capacity due to 'security concerns'.

16 *cf* J Van Selm (n 2) 514 who identifies the questions of who, why and how to resettle as the central issues of global resettlement.

ly replacing them in the long term? *Second*, should resettlement ensure fair sharing of international responsibility for refugee protection, or is it an instrument which may as well be used for the purpose of externalising responsibility to third States? While the Common European Asylum System has for long not taken a position on these questions due to its traditional silence on legal access to protection, the increasing EU involvement in the regulation of resettlement requires answers.[17] However, and despite these pressing questions, resettlement is currently surprisingly underrepresented in the almost omnipresent public debate on asylum in Europe.[18] Legal scholarship on resettlement to Europe is emerging slowly.[19] Nevertheless, the discussion on resettlement still seems to be characterised by a certain

---

17 *cf* J Van Selm (n 7) 44 who already observed that 'the relationship [...] between asylum and resettlement is perhaps one of the most confusing points for European policy making.'; SVR (n 13) at 5, 9 ff. stresses that the relation between territorial asylum and resettlement is one of the principal questions with regard to a common EU resettlement policy; M Savino (n 13) 95 identifies as 'the crucial question [...] whether the proposed Union resettlement mechanism is meant to create a stable and meaningful legal pathway [...] or whether, by contrast, it is rather meant to become a new piece of the EU non-entrée strategy'.

18 Even the term 'resettlement' seems, generally, not to be very well known, a not irrelevant detail, since words matter, and particularly so in the current debate on migration and asylum. The picture changes when turning to the more specialised policy discourse, in particular since the Union Resettlement Framework was proposed in 2016: Caritas et al. (n 14); Amnesty International, European Institutions Office (2016) Position Paper: The Proposed EU resettlement framework, available online: https://www.amnesty.eu/news/amnesty-international-position-paper-on-the-proposed-eu-resettlement/; European Council on Refugees and Exiles (ECRE) (2016) Policy Note: Untying the EU Resettlement Framework, available online: https://www.ecre.org/policy-note-untying-the-eu-resettlement-framework/; UNHCR, 'Proposal for a Regulation of the European Parliament and of the Council establishing a Union Resettlement Framework and amending Regulation (EU) No 516/2014 of the European Parliament and of the Council. UNHCR's Observations and Recommendations' (2016), available online: https://www.refworld.org/docid/5890b1d74.html. For an overview of the policy debate see: European Parliament Research Service (2016) Briefing EU Legislation in Progress. Resettlement of refugees: EU Framework, available online: http://www.europarl.europa.eu/legislative-train/theme-towards-a-new-policy-on-migration/file-jd-eu-resettlement-framework.

19 See P De Bruycker and EL Tsourdi, 'Building the Common European Asylum System beyond Legislative Harmonisation: Practical Cooperation, Solidarity and External Dimension' in V Chetail, P de Bruycker and F Maiani (eds) *Reforming the Common European Asylum System* (Brill, 2016) 473, 516; M Savino (n 13). The emerging (legal) scholarship on resettlement to Europe seems to be influenced by scholarship on resettlement to established resettlement countries such as Aus-

scarcity of legal arguments. Due to the absence of an international legal framework on resettlement, it is generally understood as an entirely discretionary act, qualifying the questions of why, how and whom to resettle as subject to political preference solely.[20] The discussion, therefore, generally speaking, refers to the international policy framework as the normative yardstick.[21] The international policy framework on resettlement is shaped mainly by UNHCR and consists of non-binding guidelines and recommendations to States.[22] Accordingly, resettlement has been described as 'at law's border'.[23] With regard to the international level, this might be an ap-

---

tralia, *cf eg* J McAdam, 'Extraterritorial Processing in Europe. Is 'regional protection' the answer, and if not, what is?' (2015) Policy Brief, Kaldor Centre for International Law.

20 European Commission, Study on the Feasibility of setting up resettlement schemes in EU member states or at EU Level, against the background of the Common European Asylum system and the goal of a Common Asylum Procedure (2003), carried out by the Migration Policy Institute, authored by J Van Selm [hereinafter: *COM Resettlement Feasibility Study*] 112.

21 See UNHCR, Observations and Recommendations on the Union Framework Proposal (n 18) passim; SVR (n 13) 9 ff; Caritas et al (n 14) 4 ff.; Amnesty International (n 18) 3 ff; ECRE (n 18) 1 ff; K Bamberg, 'The EU Resettlement Framework: From a humanitarian pathway to a migration management tool?' *European Policy Center Discussion Paper* (2018) passim; SVR (n 13) 9 ff. The EU constitutional framework, again, generally speaking, is mainly referred to concerning questions of competences: COM Resettlement Feasibility Study (n 20). However, with reference to the EU constitutional framework concerning the complementarity of resettlement to traditional asylum procedures: B Kowalczyk, 'Resort to Resettlement in Refugee Crisis in Europe' in J Jurníková and A Králová (eds) *Společný evropský azylový systém v kontextu uprchlické krize. Sborník z konference* (Masaryk University, 2016) 135, 147. However, with reference to the EU constitutional framework concerning the relevance of fundamental rights relating to the procedure: UNHCR Observations and Recommendations on the Union Framework Proposal (n 18) 8 ff; M Savino (n 13) 95.

22 The international policy framework on resettlement is considered here as consisting of: The UNHCR Resettlement Handbook (2011), available online: https://www.unhcr.org/protection/resettlement/46f7c0ee2/unhcr-resettlement-handbook-complete-publication.html); UNHCR position and policy papers including those adopted by the UNHCR Executive Committee (ExCom) or its Standing Committee (overview available online: https://www.refworld.org/docid/4607d5072.html); the positions of the Annual Tripartite Consultations on Resettlement ('ATCR', *cf* https://www.unhcr.org/annual-tripartite-consultations-resettlement.html2017); the UNHCR Projected Global Resettlement Needs (n 4); and the 2018 Global Compact (n 9).

23 S Labman, *At Law's Border: Unsettling Refugee Resettlement* (2012), available online: https://open.library.ubc.ca/cIRcle/collections/ubctheses/24/items/1.0071854.

propriate characterisation. In the context of the EU, however, EU constitutional law cannot be disregarded.[24]

The EU is increasingly regulating resettlement and can only do so in compliance with its constitutional framework. This article thus explores the objective of resettlement from an EU constitutional perspective. To be sure, EU constitutional law does not contain explicit rules on resettlement. And yet, the relevance of its constitutional framework is undeniable: Depending on whether resettlement forms part of EU asylum law, or, for instance, of EU immigration policy, or even EU foreign policy, its rationale is governed by the constitutional framework of the respective area of EU law. This article thus proceeds as follows: *First*, it describes and defines the emerging EU resettlement law (1). *Second*, it shows that the objective of resettlement is controversial and that the conceptualisation of the objective as reflected in the emerging EU resettlement law partly contradicts the international policy framework (2). *Third*, it argues that the emerging EU resettlement law is governed by the constitutional framework of the Common European Asylum System, and that therefore, the objective of resettlement is to provide international protection to third country nationals, thereby complementing territorial asylum and ensuring fair sharing of responsibility with third States (3).

1. The emerging EU resettlement law

For decades, granting asylum has been conceptualised as an expression of State sovereignty.[25] This understanding has been based on the 'undisputed

24 For the understanding of the EU primary law as EU constitutional law see M Zuleeg, The Advantages of the European Constitution in A von Bogdandy and J Bast (eds) *Principles of European Constitutional Law* (Hart Publishing & C.H. Beck, 2nd edition, 2010) 763. The increasing relevance of the EU constitutional framework for the external dimension of EU migration policy is often referred to as 'constitutionalisation', see S Carrera, JS Vara and T Strik (eds) *Constitutionalising the External Dimensions of EU Migration Policies in Times of Crisis. Legality, Rule of Law and Fundamental Rights Reconsidered* (Elgar Publishing, 2019); L Leboeuf, 'La Cour de justice face aux dimensions externes de la politique commune de l'asile et de l'immigration. Un défault de constitutionnalisation?' (2019) 55 *Revue trimestrielle de droit européen* 55.

25 GS Goodwin-Gil and J McAdam, *The Refugee in International Law* (Oxford University Press, 3rd edition, 2007), 357: 'From the point of view of international law, therefore, the grant of protection to its territory derives from the State's sovereign competence, a statement of the obvious.'.

rule of international law' that every State has exclusive control over its territory.[26] In Europe, more specifically in the EU, both are changing.[27] The consolidation of a genuine Union territory has advanced to a certain extent.[28] The Common European Asylum System is a highly integrated regional system in which access to and content of protection status are mainly determined by the EU.[29] EU asylum law sets common standards,[30] including on eligibility and status accorded to persons in need of international protection,[31] and provides for an internal allocation mechanism,[32] as

---

26 F Morgenstern, 'The Right of Asylum' (1949) 26 *British Yearbook of International Law* 327; P Kirchhof, 'Staatliche Souveränität als Bedingung des Asylrechts' in G Jochum, W Fritzemeyer and M Kau (eds), *Grenzüberschreitendes Recht - Crossing Frontiers Festschrift für Kay Hailbronner* (2013) 105.

27 Clearly reflected in the Opinion of Advocate General Cruz Villalón, delivered on 11 July 2013 in the case C-394/12, Shamso Abdullahi v Bundesasylamt, para 41.

28 Cf U Jureit and N Tietze 'Postsouveräne Territorialität. Die Europäische Union als supranationaler Raum' (2016) 55 *Der Staat* 353; J Bast 'Völker- und unionsrechtliche Anstöße zur Entterritorialisierung des Rechts' in *Grenzüberschreitungen: Migration. Entterritorialisierung des Öffentlichen Rechts. Referate und Diskussionen auf der Tagung der Vereinigung der Deutschen Staatsrechtslehrer in Linz vom 5. bis 8. Oktober 2016*, 76 (2017) 227.

29 E Guild, 'The Europeanisation of Europe's Asylum Policy' (2006) 18 *International Journal of Refugee Law* 630. For the Europeanisation on legislative level, see eg J Bast, 'Ursprünge der Europäisierung des Migrationsrechts' in G Jochum, W Fritzemeyer and M Kau (n 26) 201. For the Europeanisation on administrative level see J Bast, 'Transnationale Verwaltung des europäischen Migrationsraums: Zur horizontalen Öffnung der EU-Mitgliedstaaten' (2007) 46 *Der Staat* 1; C Costello, 'Administrative Governance and the Europeanisation of Asylum and Immigration Policy' in HCH Hofmann and AH Türk (eds) *EU Administrative Governance* (Elgar Publishing, 2006) 287; EL Tsourdi, 'Bottom-Up Salvation? From Practical Cooperation Towards Joint Implementation Through the European Asylum Support Office' (2017) 1 *European Papers* 997.

30 Directive 2013/32/EU of the European Parliament and of the Council of 26 June 2013 on common procedures for granting and withdrawing international protection [hereinafter: *Asylum Procedures Directive*]; Directive 2013/33/EU of the European Parliament and of the Council of 26 June 2013 laying down standards for the reception of applicants for international protection [hereinafter: *Reception Conditions Directive*].

31 Directive 2011/95/EU of the European Parliament and of the Council of 13 December 2011 on standards for the qualification of third country nationals or stateless persons as beneficiaries of international protection, for a uniform status for refugees or for persons eligible for subsidiary protection, and for the content of the protection granted [hereinafter: *Qualification Directive*].

32 Regulation (EU) No 604/2013 of the European Parliament and of the Council of 26 June 2013 establishing the criteria and mechanisms for determining the Mem-

well as an increasingly integrated administration.[33] However, in accordance with the constitutional tradition of most Member States, EU asylum law has long been characterised by relative silence on *legal access*.[34] Legal access instruments, such as humanitarian visa or resettlement, in contrast to the traditional territorial asylum procedures, do not require irregular border-crossing as a pre-condition for access to protection.[35] The traditional 'legal access gap' of the Common European Asylum System is slowly being closed by the increasing involvement of the EU in regulating and implementing resettlement, a development confirming and reinforcing the evolution of the notions of asylum, sovereignty and territory in the EU.[36]

In the following, the developments leading to the EU's focus on resettlement as legal access instrument will be shortly set out (1.1), before the elements of the emerging EU resettlement law will be defined (1.2).

---

ber State responsible for examining an application for international protection lodged in one of the Member States by a third-country national or a stateless person [hereinafter: *Dublin III Regulation*].

33 Regulation (EU) No 439/2010 of the European Parliament and of the Council of 19 May 2010 establishing a European Asylum Support Office [hereinafter: *EASO Regulation*]; AMIF Regulation.

34 M Savino (n 13) 81; FL Gatta, 'Legal Avenues to access to international protection in the European Union: past actions and future perspectives' (2018) *European Journal of Human Rights* 163, 185 ff, 199 with further references.

35 This article is limited to legal pathways, which are based on the need for protection as central eligibility criterion and refers to these as '*legal access instruments*'. Legal pathways further include various instruments such as visa for the purpose of family reunification, education, or employment in particular. The status accorded to persons who are admitted under those instruments is not based on the need for protection as central eligibility criterion. Such legal pathways are, therefore, usually referred to as '*complementary pathways*', see 2018 Global Compact, para 90 ff.

36 In order to comprehensively understand resettlement to Europe, the national resettlement programmes would have to be analysed in addition, since the emerging EU resettlement law is indeed mainly implemented through national schemes. The emerging EU resettlement law together with the national resettlement programmes could be described as 'European resettlement law'. As this would, however, go beyond the scope of this article, see on the national schemes D Perrin and F McNamara, Refugee Resettlement in the EU: Between Shared Standards and Diversity in Legal and Policy Frames, *KNOW RESET Research Report* 2013/03; E Bokshi, Refugee Resettlement in the EU: The capacity to do it better and to do it more, *KNOW RESET Research Report* 2013/04, both studies carried out by the Migration Policy Centre, EUI, in cooperation with ECRE, co-financed by the EU.

1.1. Emphasis on resettlement in the context of crisis

The EU policy debate on resettlement dates back to the early 2000s.[37] The European Commission advocated for increased resettlement to the EU,[38] and the UK and Germany proposed establishing extraterritorial processing centres.[39] In response, beyond launching a study on the feasibility of extraterritorial processing of asylum claims,[40] the Commission also ordered an extensive study on the feasibility of resettlement on EU level.[41] While the first study focused on the international and EU legal framework,[42] the second study, by contrast, characterised resettlement as a discretionary measure with little legal stipulation.[43] In 2004, the Commission concluded that the concept of resettlement should be explored with a view to creating a common EU scheme.[44] The Hague Programme, adopted by the Council

37 For a comprehensive overview of the policy debate on legal access on EU level, see: FL Gatta (n 34) 184; P De Bruycker and EL Tsourdi (n 19) 473, 512 ff.

38 European Commission, Communication to the Council and the European Parliament 'Towards a common asylum procedure and a uniform status, valid throughout the Union, for persons granted asylum', 22 Nov 2000, COM(2000) 755 final, p 9.

39 In 2003, the UK proposed extraterritorial centres including a 'screening' system with the possibility of resettlement. In 2004, Germany proposed to intercept potential applicants in international waters in order to transfer them to extraterritorial centres where a 'screening process' would be carried out, with the exceptional possibility of resettlement through 'humanitarian admission programmes'. The European Commission explored these proposals in its Communication 'Towards more accessible, equitable and managed asylum systems', 3 June 2003, COM(2003) 315 final. On these discussions and the ensuing legal questions, see: G Noll, 'Visions of the Exceptional: Legal and Theoretical Issues Raised by Transit Processing Centers and Protection Zones' (2003) 5 *European Journal of Migration and Law* 30; M Garlick, 'The EU Discussions on Extraterritorial Processing: Solution or Conundrum?' (2006) 18 *International Journal of Refugee Law* 601, 623 ff.

40 European Commission, Study on the Feasibility of Processing Asylum Claims outside the EU against the Background of the Common European Asylum System and the Goal of a Common Asylum Procedure (2002), carried out by the Danish Centre for Human Rights, authored by G Noll, J Fagerlund and F Liebaut [hereinafter: *COM Protected Entry Procedures Feasibility Study*].

41 COM Resettlement Feasibility Study (n 20).

42 COM Protected Entry Procedures Feasibility Study (n 40) 30 to 60, and 212 to 252.

43 COM Resettlement Feasibility Study (n 20) viii, 146, passim.

44 European Commission, Communication to the Council and the European Parliament, 'On Managed Entry in the EU of Persons in Need of International Protection and Enhancement of the Protection Capacity of the Regions of Origin: Improving Access to Durable Solutions', 4 June 2004, COM(2004) 410 final. The

in the same year, reinforced the political emphasis on resettlement.[45] Since then, resettlement has incrementally become the politically most relevant means of providing legal access to the Common European Asylum System. In 2009, the Commission put forward an initiative for a Joint Resettlement Programme.[46] Even though this proposal was not adopted, the idea was taken up in the Global Approach on Migration and Mobility of 2011.[47]

The focus on resettlement has gained new momentum in the context of the crisis of the Common European Asylum System.[48] In April 2015, the European Council emphasised that resettlement would be an option to cope with the tragedy in the Mediterranean and prevent further loss of life at sea.[49] This impetus is clearly reflected in the European Agenda on Migration of May 2015, which is the overarching document guiding EU poli-

---

idea of 'protected entry procedures' was not further pursued by the Commission due to a lack of Member State commitment, *cf* M Den Heijer, Europe and Extraterritorial Asylum (Oxford University Press, 2012) 187; M Savino (n 13) 90.

45 Council, The Hague Programme: Strengthening Freedom, Security and Justice in the European Union (2005) OJ No C 53/01, in particular proposed 'Regional Protection Programmes', which would include strengthening protection capacity of third countries on the one hand, and limited voluntary resettlement schemes on the other hand. The Proposal was further elaborated by the European Commission: Communication from the European Commission to the Council and the European Parliament on Regional Protection Programmes, 1 Sept 2005, COM(2005) 388 final.

46 European Commission, Communication from the Commission to the European Parliament and the Council. On the Establishment of a Joint EU Resettlement Programme, 2 September 2009, COM(2009) 447 final, and accordingly: European Commission, Proposal for a Decision of the European Parliament and of the Council, 2 Sept 2009 COM(2009) 456 final.

47 European Commission, Communication from the Commission to the European Parliament, the Council, the European Economic and Social Committee and the Committee of the Regions. The Global Approach to Migration and Mobility, 18 November 2011, COM(2011) 743 final [hereinafter: *GAMM*]. The Global Approach on Migration – adopted by the European Council in 2005, confirmed by the Council in 2006, and then further elaborated on by the European Commission in the following years – already mentioned the need for legal pathways to the EU, without, however, putting an emphasis on legal access to protection yet, *cf* European Commission, Global Approach to Migration, 5 December 2007, MEMO/07/549 [hereinafter: *GAM*].

48 B Kowalczyk (n 21) 141; M Savino (n 13) 82 ff.

49 European Council, Press Release of 23 April 2015, available online: https://www.consilium.europa.eu/en/press/press-releases/2015/04/23/special-euco-statement/.

cy since the crisis.[50] Drafted as a response to the intolerable situation in the Mediterranean, resettlement was designed as a policy for immediate action, but not yet as long-term strategy. In the same year, the European Union Agency for Fundamental Rights (FRA) called upon the EU and its Member States to increase their efforts in providing legal access to international protection in the EU.[51] In April 2016, the European Parliament expressed its view that resettlement is one of the preferred options for granting safe and lawful access for those in need of protection.[52]

Two developments were particularly relevant for the development towards a common EU resettlement policy: *First*, the EU-Turkey Statement was published as press release in March 2016,[53] and represents the EU's immediate response to the crisis.[54] The objective of the Statement is to 'end irregular migration from Turkey to the EU'.[55] In order to achieve this goal, several measures were agreed upon, inter alia the provision of considerable financial support to Turkey, the return of applicants who entered the EU

50 European Commission, Communication from the Commission to the European Parliament, the Council, the European Economic and Social Committee and the Committee of the Regions. A European Agenda on Migration, 13 May 2015, COM(2015) 240 final [hereinafter: *EAM*].

51 European Union Agency for Fundamental Rights, 'Legal entry channels to the EU for persons in need of international protection: a toolbox' (2015) FRA Focus 02/2015.

52 European Parliament, Resolution of 12 April 2016, available online: http://www.europarl.europa.eu/sides/getDoc.do?pubRef=-//EP//TEXT+TA+P8-TA-2016-0102+0+DOC+XML+V0//EN&language=EN.

53 See n 11.

54 According to the General Court, the Statement cannot be attributed to the EU. *Cf* General Court, orders of 28 Feb 2017, T-192/16, T-193/16 and T-257/16, NF, NG and NM v European Council: 'the EU-Turkey statement [....] cannot be regarded as a measure adopted by the European Council, or, moreover, by any other institution, body, office or agency of the European Union' (T-192/16, para 71). The judgment, however, disregards the jurisprudence of the Court of Justice, in particular: European Court of Justice, judgment of 31 March 1971, 22/70, Commission v Council, 'AERT', para 5. See E Cannizzaro, 'Denialism as the Supreme Expression of Realism. A Quick Comment on NF v European Council' (2017) 2 *European Papers, European Forum* 251; J Bast, 'Scharade im kontrollfreien Raum: Hat die EU gar keinen Türkei-Deal geschlossen?' (2017) *Verfassungsblog* 03 March 2017. The EU-Turkey Statement is therefore considered here as reaction of the *EU* to the crisis.

55 EU-Turkey Statement (n 11): 'the EU and Turkey today decided to *end the irregular migration from Turkey to the EU. In order to achieve this goal*, they agreed on the following additional action points. [...]' [emphasis added].

irregularly via the Greek Aegean islands,[56] and the resettlement scheme providing for legal access to Member States.[57] *Second*, the Commission proposed a Regulation on a Union Framework on Resettlement in July 2016.[58] This proposal is part of the endeavour to comprehensively reform the Common European Asylum System, in the context of which establishing a structured resettlement system is one of the main strategies.[59]

In March 2017, the Court of Justice decided in the case 'X and X' that the grant of humanitarian visa with a view to applying for international protection upon arrival falls solely within the scope of national law,[60] which can be seen as a confirmation of the traditional 'legal access gap' of the Common European Asylum System. The following attempts by the European Parliament to include a provision on humanitarian visa in the Visa Code seem to have failed for now.[61] At least for the time being, the discussion on harmonised rules on humanitarian visa has come to a standstill. The focus of the legal access debate clearly lies on resettlement.[62] And, indeed, the proposal by the European Council of June 2018 to establish ex-

---

56 EU-Turkey Statement (n 11) points 1 and 6. Less explicitly agreed upon was the effective increase of departure-preventing measures by Turkey, which, in fact, seems to be crucial for the substantial and sustainable decrease in arrivals. *Cf* European Commission, Sixth Report on the Progress made in the implementation of the EU-Turkey Statement, 13 July 2017, COM(2017) 323 final, p 4: '*On its side, the Turkish Coast Guard has continued active patrolling and prevention of departures* from Turkey.' [emphasis added].

57 EU-Turkey Statement (n 11) points 2 and 4.

58 European Commission, Proposal for a Regulation of the European Parliament and of the Council establishing a Union Resettlement Framework and amending Regulation (EU) No 516/2014 of the European Parliament and the Council, 13 July 2016, COM(2016) 468 final [hereinafter: *Union Framework Proposal*].

59 The Union Framework Proposal relies on the comprehensive reform proposal of April 2016: European Commission, Communication from the Commission to the European Parliament and the Council. Towards a Reform of the Common European Asylum System and Enhancing Legal Avenues to Europe, 6 April 2016, COM(2016) 197 final.

60 European Court of Justice, judgment of 7 March 2017, C-638/16 PPU, X and X v Belgium, para 44. See E Brouwer, 'The European Court of Justice on Humanitarian Visa: Legal integrity vs. political opportunism?' (2017) *CEPS Commentary*, 16 March 2017; see the contributions of Dirk Hanschel, Stephanie Law and Sylvie Sarolea in this volume.

61 See the contribution of Eugenia Relano Pastor in this volume.

62 M Savino (n 13) 82, 90 ff; FL Gatta (n 34) 175 ff.

traterritorial processing centres foresees possible resettlement to the EU, without considering other legal access instruments as an option.[63]

1.2. Elements of the emerging EU resettlement law

These developments are geared towards establishing a comprehensive EU resettlement framework, which, to be sure, is not in place as of yet. There are, however, already several legal and non-legal instruments regulating resettlement on the EU level. Taken together, they consolidate EU regulation of resettlement to an extent that they represent a new component of the Common European Asylum System and can be described as the 'emerging EU resettlement law'.[64]

As will be shown in the following, the emerging EU resettlement law, as it currently stands, is defined firstly by the Regulation on the Asylum, Migration and Integration Fund (AMIF), the Regulation on the European Asylum Support Office (EASO), and several 'common resettlement goals' laid down in different legal and non-legal instruments. Secondly, the EU-Turkey Statement provides for a crisis-driven ad hoc implementation of a certain approach to resettlement currently under discussion. Indeed, the Standard Operating Procedures regulating the implementation of the '1:1 resettlement scheme' under the EU-Turkey Statement represent the more

---

63 European Council, Conclusions, 28 to 29 June 2019, available online: https://www.consilium.europa.eu/en/press/press-releases/2018/06/29/20180628-euco-conclusions-final/; European Commission, Factsheet 'Migration: Regional Disembarkation Arrangements', available online: https://europa.eu/rapid/press-release_IP-18-4629_en.htm. Note the similarity to the 2003 and 2004/5 proposals (n 39), and that those proposals were based on the Australian example, see O Lynskey, 'Complementing and completing the Common European Asylum System: a legal analysis of the emerging extraterritorial elements of EU refugee protection policy' (2006) 31 *European Law Review* 230, 240 note 51.

64 M Savino (n 13) 9 ff. similarly refers to the 'The Evolution of the EU Legal Framework', and analyses 'the current legal framework as defined by [the AMIF Regulation]' in close connection with the 'July 2015 scheme' and the '50,000 scheme' as well as resettlement under the EU-Turkey Statement. In the same vein, the European Parliament describes the current EU regulation of resettlement as defined by the AMIF Regulation, the relevant Commission Recommendations and Council Conclusions, and refers to the EU Turkey Statement in addition, *cf* European Parliament, European Parliamentary Research Service, 'Briefing. EU Legislation in Progress. Resettlement of refugees: EU framework', 29 March 2019, available online: www.europarl.europa.eu/RegData/etudes/BRIE/2016/589859/EPRS_BRI%282016 %29589859_EN.pdf.

recent developments of the emerging EU resettlement law. The implementation of the '1:1 scheme' has served as a blueprint for the Union Framework Proposal.[65] The practical implementation of resettlement under the EU Turkey Statement is, hence, particularly useful for understanding the emerging EU resettlement law.[66] The Union Framework Proposal in turn, thirdly, provides a model of what a codification of such an approach could look like and shows the direction in which the emerging EU resettlement law is potentially evolving.[67]

The EU asylum *acquis*, in a strict sense, contains a definition of resettlement, sets priorities on from where and whom to resettle, and provides for financial and operational support to the Member States. A binding definition of resettlement in EU law is found in the *AMIF Regulation*: '[R]esettlement means the process whereby, on a request from [...] "UNHCR" based on a person's need for international protection, third-country nationals are transferred from a third country and established in a Member State where they are permitted to reside with [...] [either] "refugee status" [...] "subsidiarity protection status" [...] or any other status which offers similar rights and benefits [...]'.[68] The Regulation further lays down the Union re-

---

65 Union Framework Proposal, p 7: 'The Proposal is 'building on the experience with existing resettlement initiatives in the EU framework and existing resettlement practices of the member states, in particular the Standard Operating Procedures guiding the implementation of the resettlement scheme with Turkey set out in the EU-Turkey Statement of 18 March 2016'. The reform paper of April 2016 (n 59) already mentions that future initiatives should build on the 'July 2015 scheme' and resettlement under the EU-Turkey Statement.

66 In order to understand the practice of resettlement under the EU-Turkey Statement, the following interviews were conducted via phone, in the form of qualitative semi-structured interviews, and are on file with the author: (1) interview with a former staff member of a German representation in Turkey, conducted on 18 February 2019, (2) interview with a staff member working for an NGO in Germany in the camp Friedland where all persons resettled from Turkey arrive, conducted on 20 February 2019, (3) interview with a staff member working for another NGO in Friedland, conducted on 26 February 2019, (4) interview with a high-level staff member of UNHCR in Ankara, Turkey, conducted in two sessions on 13 and 22 March 2019, (5) interview with a staff member of a NGO supporting resettlement procedures from Turkey, conducted on 13 March 2019, (6) interview with another staff members of the same NGO supporting resettlement procedures from Turkey, conducted and 22 March 2019. All information purely based on these expert interviews is indicated as such. I would like to thank all interview partners for their time and openness.

67 *cf* M Savino (n 13) 92 ff.

68 Art 2 lit. a AMIF Regulation.

settlement priorities, which may be amended by the Commission.[69] On the administrative level, the AMIF provides for financial incentives to the Member States, which shall implement the Union priorities through their respective national schemes.[70] In addition, the *EASO Regulation* provides for a rather limited mandate of the agency to coordinate exchanges of information and other actions on resettlement taken by Member States.[71]

While there is currently no binding EU law obliging Member States to resettle a certain number of persons, several instruments which can be classified as EU soft law do provide for targets in terms of common resettlement capacity.[72] *First*, in July 2015, the Council endorsed a Recommendation by the Commission providing for a single European pledge of 20,000 resettlement places in a timeframe of two years.[73] This *'July 2015 scheme'* was the first common EU resettlement capacity goal. Even though it was obviously based on voluntary participation by the Member States, implementation has effectively been monitored by the European Commission,

69 The Commission is empowered to adopt delegated acts to amend the priorities, and implementing acts concerning implementation conditions, see Art 17 para. 4, 8 and 10 AMIF Regulation, recital 40 AMIF Regulation.

70 The AMIF Regulation provides 'resources for the Union Resettlement Programme' including a lump sum for resettlement under national schemes, and an increased lump sum for resettlement in accordance with the Union priorities, see Art 7, and Art 17 para. 1 and 2 in conjunction with Art 15 para. 1 lit. b and para. 2, Art 17 para. 3, Annex III, and Art 17 para. 5 AMIF Regulation.

71 Art 7 EASO Regulation, see recital 12 AMIF Regulation. *See* P De Bruycker and EL Tsourdi (n 19) 491 ff.

72 EU soft law is understood here as 'rules [...] which, in principle, have no legally binding force but which nevertheless may have practical effects', following the definition of F Snyder, 'The Effectiveness of European Community Law: Institutions, Processes, Tools and Techniques' (1993) 56 *The Modern Law Review* 19, 32; F Snyder, 'Soft Law and the Institutional Practice in the European Community' in S Martin (ed) *The Construction of Europe* (Kluwer Academic Publishers, 1994) 197, 198. *Cf* J Schwarze, 'Soft Law im Recht der Europäischen Union' (2011) 46 *Europarecht* 3, 6 ff; F Terpan, 'Soft Law in the European Union – The Changing Nature of EU law' (2015) 21 *European Law Journal* 68, 70.

73 European Commission, Recommendation on a European resettlement scheme, 8 June 2015, C(2015) 3560 final; Council, Conclusions of the Representative of the Governments of the member states meeting within the Council on resettling through multilateral and national schemes 20,000 persons in clear need of international protection, 22 July 2015, available online: https://www.consilium.europa.eu/media/22985/st11097en15.pdf. This scheme constitutes the immediate action under the EAM (n 49).

and the scheme has been completed in the meanwhile.[74] *Second*, in the context of the EU-Turkey Statement, the Relocation Programme has been amended with a view to re-assigning 18,000 places from relocation to resettlement. The relevant Council Decision ('*Amending Council Decision*') allowed Member States to fill their remaining obligation concerning intra-EU relocation through resettlement from Turkey instead.[75] Even though the Decision has already expired,[76] it is worth taking note of it, because it arguably legally obliged Member States to resettle: The Decision is a non-legislative measure imposing a binding mechanism under Art. 288 TFEU.[77] *Third*, because the Union Framework Proposal was not adopted as swiftly as expected, the Commission in 2017 put forward another ad hoc scheme in the form of a Recommendation, providing for the aim of resettling 50,000 persons in need of international protection within two years ('*50,000 scheme*').[78] The Commission is monitoring the implementation, and as of June 2019, about 30,000 persons were resettled under this scheme.[79] The Recommendation focuses on resettlement from Turkey, which means that resettlement under the '1:1 scheme' is now counted under the '50,000 scheme'.[80]

---

74 European Commission, Communication from the Commission to the European Parliament, the European Council and the Council, Progress Report on the Implementation of the European Agenda on Migration, 16.5.2018, COM(2018) 301 final, Annex 4 – Resettlement, State of Play as of 4 May 2018; European Commission, 'Factsheet: Delivering on Resettlement', on the occasion of the World Refugee Day 20 June 2019, available online: https://ec.europa.eu/commission/presscorner/detail/sl/statement_19_3056.

75 Council Decision 2016/1754 of 29 September 2016 amending Decision (EU) 2015/1601 establishing provisional measures in the area of international protection for the benefit of Italy and Greece [hereinafter: *Amending Council Decision*].

76 The Amending Council Decision expired in September 2017 according to its Art 2.

77 However, its binding effect is limited since it leaves member states the choice whether to engage in relocation or in resettlement instead, Art 1 Amending Relocation Decision. *Cf* European Court of Justice, judgment of 6 Sept 2017, C-643/15 and C-647/15, Slovak Republic and Hungary v Council, 'Relocation Judgement', para 66, 244 to 253. The reasoning applies accordingly.

78 European Commission, Commission Recommendation of 27 September 2017 on enhancing legal pathways for persons in need of international protection, 27 September 2017, C(2017) 6504.

79 European Commission, 'Factsheet: Delivering on Resettlement', on the occasion of the World Refugee Day 20 June 2019 (n 74).

80 European Commission, 'Factsheet: Delivering on Resettlement', on the occasion of the World Refugee Day 20 June 2019 (n 74); European Commission, Commission Recommendation of 27 September 2017 on enhancing legal pathways for

The *EU-Turkey Statement* of March 2016, hence, does not amend the common resettlement capacity goal, but simply shifts the priority towards resettling Syrians from Turkey.[81] The Statement provides for two resettlement schemes. *First*, the '1:1 scheme', which provides that 'for every Syrian being returned to Turkey from Greek islands, another Syrian will be resettled to the EU […]'.[82] Remarkably, the '1:1 scheme' has never been implemented as such. To date, only about 2,400 persons have been deported from the Greek islands to Turkey, while about 20,000 persons have been resettled from Turkey to EU Member States under the '1:1 scheme'.[83] The scheme is, however, still referred to as such by the relevant actors.[84] The *second* resettlement mechanism is the Voluntary Humanitarian Admission Scheme ('V-HAS'), which shall be activated in the event 'irregular crossings between Turkey and the EU are ending or at least have been substantially and sustainably reduced'.[85] Even though this condition was met immediately after the Statement entered into force,[86] the V-HAS has not yet been activated. The legal nature and the legality of the EU-Turkey Statement are disputed.[87] Insofar as resettlement is concerned, the stronger arguments support the conclusion that the Statement provides for legally

persons in need of international protection, 27 September 2017 (n 78), para (3) (a).

81 The EU-Turkey Statement does not increase EU resettlement capacity but determines that the existing schemes focuses on resettlement of Syrians from Turkey. The capacity of the '1:1 scheme' was set at 72,000 persons: This number consists of 18,000 places which are taken from the original relocation programme (*cf* Amending Council Decision) as well as 'an additional 54,000 persons'. The latter places are, however, not additional in a strict sense either but are counted under the 'July 2015' or the '50,000 scheme' respectively, see European Commission, Recommendation establishing the '50,000 scheme' (n 78) p 5.

82 EU-Turkey Statement (n 11) point 2.

83 European Commission, 'Factsheet. The EU-Turkey Statement, Three years on', March 2019, available online: https://ec.europa.eu/home-affairs/what-we-do/policies/european-agenda-migration/background-information_en.

84 Information based on expert interviews (n 66).

85 EU-Turkey Statement (n 11) point 4. The V-HAS is based on the at the time unsuccessful Commission Recommendation for a voluntary humanitarian admission scheme with Turkey, 15 December 2015, C(2015) 9490.

86 While the daily average of arrivals on the Greek islands at the end of 2015 was between 6,000 and 3,000 persons, the daily average since 21 March 2016 when the Statement 'entered into force' is consistently about 80 arrivals. European Commission, Factsheet. The EU-Turkey Statement, Three years on, March 2019 (n 83).

87 See UNHCR, 'Legal Considerations on the Return of Asylum Seekers and Refugees from Greece to Turkey as Part of the EU–Turkey Cooperation in Tackling the Migration Crisis under the Safe Third Country and First Country of Asy-

binding international obligations.[88] Nevertheless, it is difficult to consider the EU-Turkey Statement as part of the emerging EU resettlement law in a strict sense because, according to the European Court, the Statement cannot be attributed to the EU.[89] Nevertheless, resettlement, as implemented under the EU-Turkey Statement, is key to understanding the emerging EU resettlement law, as explained above.[90] The details of the implementation of the '1:1 resettlement scheme' are laid down in the *Standard Operating Procedures* ('SOP Resettlement-EuT'), which were drafted by the Commission, subsequently endorsed by the Council, and then 'formalised' by way of an exchange of letters between the Commission and the Turkish authorities in May 2016.[91] The SOP Resettlement-EuT contains rules on eligibility criteria and on the procedure. The scheme is implemented through national programmes, the respective design of which differs. Operational support for the resettlement procedure is still mainly provided by UNHCR, and by IOM with regard to travel arrangements. A pilot project providing for enhanced operational support through EASO is envisaged.[92]

---

lum Concept' (2016), available online: https://www.refworld.org/docid/56f3ee3f4.html; D Thym, 'Why the EU-Turkey Deal is Legal and a Step in the Right Direction' (2016) *Verfassungblog* 09 March 2017; R Hofmann and A Schmidt, 'Die Erklärung EU-Türkei vom 18.3.2016 aus rechtlicher Perspektive' (2016) 11 *Neue Zeitschrift für Verwaltungsrecht* 1. The dispute on the legal nature and the legality was not solved by the orders of 28 Feb 2017, T-192/16, T-193/16 and T-257/16, NF et al (n 54). The appeal to the European Court of Justice was rejected as inadmissible: European Court of Justice, order of 12 Sept 2018, Joined Cases C-208/17 P to C-210/17 P, NF and Others v European Council.

88 Convincingly in favour of an international obligation on resettlement: R Hofmann and A Schmidt (n 87) 5.

89 European Court, orders of 28 Feb 2017, T-192/16, T-193/16 and T-257/16, NF et al (n 54).

90 See n 65 ff. Another reason why the implementation of resettlement under the EU-Turkey Statement is key to understanding resettlement on EU level, is that almost all elements of the emerging EU resettlement law are of relevance to the implementation of the '1:1 scheme': The procedures are guided by the 'Standard Operating Procedures', the capacity is counted under the 'July 2015 scheme' and the subsequent '50,000 scheme', and the relevant provisions of the AMIF Regulation and the EASO Regulation are obviously applicable.

91 Council of the European Union, Annex to the Note from the Presidency to the Representatives of the Governments of the member states, Subject: Standard Operating procedures implementing the mechanism for resettlement from Turkey to the EU as set out in the EU-Turkey Statement of 18 March 2016 – Endorsement, Brussels, 27 April 2016, 8366/16.

92 Information based on expert interviews (n 66).

Finally, the Commission's *Proposal for a Union Resettlement Framework* of 2016 provides a model codification of resettlement as implemented under the EU Turkey Statement.[93] The Proposal must be seen in context of the proposals addressing a comprehensive reform of the Common European Asylum System, in particular, the proposal for a European Union Asylum Agency (EUAA) and the AMIF reform proposal,[94] providing for enhanced administrative support to Member States. The proposal aims at the establishment of common rules on admission through resettlement, including rules on eligibility criteria and exclusion grounds, standard procedures, the status to be accorded to the resettled person, and conditionality clauses towards third States.[95] With regard to the administrative level, the Proposal still focuses on financial support to the Member States. It thus not only upholds the central role of UNHCR, but also provides for the possibility of enhanced operational support through the EU agency.[96] The Proposal – which, as explained, reflects the recent EU approach to resettlement, as implemented in an ad hoc manner under the EU-Turkey Statement – has been met with widespread criticism, including from UNHCR, academia and the relevant policy actors.[97] The European Parliament has proposed numerous amendments to generally realign resettlement with the international policy framework.[98] Interestingly, however, it mainly seems to be due to the lack of a common political position concerning internal allocation that the Proposal has not yet moved forward.[99]

---

93 See n 12.

94 European Commission, Amended Proposal for a Regulation of the European Parliament and of the Council on the European Union Agency for Asylum and repealing Regulation (EU) No 439/2010. A contribution from the European Commission to the Leaders' meeting in Salzburg on 19-20 September 2018, 12 September 2018, COM(2018) 633 final; European Commission, Proposal for a Regulation of the European Parliament and of the Council establishing the Asylum and Migration Fund, 12 July 2018, COM(2018) 471 final.

95 Union Framework Proposal, p 9.

96 In particular, Art 10 para 8 Union Framework Proposal.

97 FL Gatta (n 34) 184 ff provides a good overview of the criticism. See in more detail below, n 123 and n 150.

98 European Parliament, Report on the proposal for a regulation of the European Parliament and of the Council establishing a Union Resettlement Framework and amending Regulation (EU) No 516/2014 of the European Parliament and the Council, 19 October 2017. The amendments proposed by the Council are much less numerous: Council of the European Union, Note from the Presidency to the Delegations on the [Union Framework Proposal], Brussels, 22 Feb 2017, 5332/17.

99 M Savino (n 13) 89. It seems somehow ironical that what is blocking international responsibility-sharing is the disagreement on EU internal solidarity.

The emerging EU resettlement law, as it currently stands, shows that most aspects of resettlement are increasingly provided for on EU level, in particular, resettlement capacity, eligibility criteria, procedure and conditionality clauses. While there is a tendency towards a binding harmonisation of eligibility criteria, procedure and conditionality, this seems to not be the case when it comes to capacity. Even though Member States are implementing the EU schemes through their respective national programmes, the relevance of the EU on the legislative level is clearly on the rise. On the administrative level, however, the role of the EU has not increased at the same pace. The latter becomes clear from the fact that the EU support continues to focus on financial incentives, while operational support is still mainly provided by UNHCR, which indeed is the global key actor, and the decade-long partner of Member States for implementing resettlement. It does not seem clear yet whether attempts to strengthen EU operational support through the responsible EU agency would be practically and politically feasible.

2. *The controversies on the objective of resettlement*

While there seems to be a broad agreement that the emergence of an EU resettlement law is a welcome development, the rationale and the very objective of resettlement is subject to debate. Undoubtedly, resettlement provides legal access to international protection. However, is this the main objective of resettlement? Or can the provision of international protection be considered as the side effect of a policy that pursues first and foremost other objectives, such as 'managing migration' or even strengthening the bargaining position of the EU with regard to the achievement of foreign policy goals in other areas? The answer to this question has repercussions on two more specific controversies concerning the purpose of resettlement. *First*, the relation of resettlement to territorial asylum procedures is contentious: Should resettlement complement or, in the long term, eventually replace territorial asylum? *Second*, the purpose with regard to the concerned first host countries is disputed: Should resettlement primarily ensure fair sharing of international responsibility for refugee protection, or can it instead be used to achieve the externalisation of such responsibility? Defining the objective of resettlement is of practical relevance, since it has direct implications for the concrete design of a certain resettlement scheme, including eligibility criteria, procedure and conditionality clauses.[100]

In the following, the objective underlying the emerging EU resettlement law will be analysed. It will be shown that the emerging EU resettlement recently seems to reflect a certain tendency towards the controversial conceptualisation of resettlement as eventually replacing territorial asylum procedures (2.1) and that it increasingly seems to reflect the contentious understanding that resettlement may be employed to externalise responsibility for refugee protection to third countries (2.2). Such an approach stands in contradiction to the international policy framework and has accordingly been met with harsh criticism.[101]

2.1. Towards replacing territorial asylum procedures?

The relation of resettlement to territorial asylum is controversial. The question is whether resettlement as a form of extraterritorial status determination in the long term has the objective of eventually replacing traditional territorial asylum procedures, which require spontaneous, and hence usually irregular, arrival.[102]

The international policy framework conceives resettlement and territorial asylum as complementary parts of an effective protection system, as

---

100 See below 2. To give an example: If the objective of resettlement is to eventually replace territorial asylum, this could be reflected in corresponding incentives for the individuals and the Member States, such as an exclusion clause precluding from resettlement those who have attempted to irregularly cross the border, and a conditionality clause, making resettlement dependent upon the Member State's effective prevention of border-crossings towards the destination State.

101 See n 97 and n 98, as well as in more detail n 123 and n 150.

102 The term 'territorial asylum' is being used here as abbreviation of 'territorial asylum procedures', ie in the sense of 'granting protection to persons who have arrived spontaneously' – thus referring to the *means of access* to protection; for the use of the term in this sense, see: J Van Selm (n 7) 43 ff. The term 'territorial asylum' is hence not used here in the sense of the Draft Convention on Territorial Asylum; for the use of the term in that sense, see: R Plender, 'Admission of Refugees: Draft Convention on Territorial Asylum' (1977) 15 *San Diego Law Review* 45 and further P Weis, 'Territorial Asylum' (1966) 6 *Indian Journal of Refugee Law* 173. The term 'asylum' is hence also not used to refer to the *content* of protection; for the use of the term in that sense, see: GS Goodwin-Gil and J McAdam (n 25) 355 ff; S Meili, 'The Constitutional Right to Asylum: The Wave of the Future in International Refugee Law?' (2018) 41 *Fordham International Law Journal* 383.

stressed by UNHCR as well as by scholarship.[103] The understanding of resettlement as complementary even represents the very argumentative basis for its generally accepted conceptualisation as discretionary act.[104]

In order to identify the provisions reflecting the conceptualisation of the relation between resettlement and territorial asylum, it is useful to have a closer look at the argument underlying the idea of resettlement as eventually *replacing* traditional territorial asylum procedures.[105] The Australian protection system is the most prominent example of a consistent implementation of the 'replacement approach' to resettlement, resulting in a system which is in breach of international refugee and human rights law.[106] Indeed, the 'replacement argument' is central to the Australian discussion on resettlement.[107] The Australian discourse shows that the 'replacement argument' actually appears in two variations.[108] On the one hand, the 'wait-in-the-line argument' suggests that persons irregularly arriving are 'illegitimately jumping the queue' instead of waiting in the country of first

---

103 UNHCR, Observations on the Communication from the European Commission to the Council and the European Parliament on Regional Protection Programmes (COM (2005) 388 final, 1 Sept 2005), 10 Oct 2005; J Van Selm (n 7) 44 ff; SVR (n 13) 4.

104 COM Resettlement Feasibility Study (n 20) v, xxiii, passim.

105 Similarly, SVR (n 13) 20 ff identifies the arguments underlying the Australian 'replacement approach' and shows that this approach is reflected in the Union Framework Proposal. *Cf* J Van Selm (n 2) 517 ff who identifies the question as crucial on the global level.

106 *cf* S Kneebone, 'The Australian Story: Asylum Seekers Outside the Law', in S Kneebone (ed) *Refugees, Asylum Seekers and the Rule of Law: Comparative Perspectives* (Cambridge University Press, 2009) 17; J McAdam and F Chong, *Refugees: Why seeking asylum is legal and Australia's policies are not* (University of New South Wales Press, 2014).

107 See Parliament of Australia, Department of Parliamentary Services, Research Paper Series, 2014-15, 3 February 2015, 'Refugee Resettlement to Australia: what are the facts?', available online: https://www.aph.gov.au/About_Parliament/Parliamentary_Departments/Parliamentary_Library/pubs/rp/rp1617/RefugeeResettlement.

108 The potential 'export value' of the Australian discourse has already been noted before the crisis of the Common European Asylum System, see J van Selm (n 2) 516. The 'export value' of certain discourses on resettlement can be noted more generally because, in the absence of an international binding framework, States justify their practice with reference to practice of other States, *cf* D Ghezelbash, 'Lessons in Exclusion: Interdiction and Extraterritorial Processing of Asylum Seekers in the United States and Australia' in J-P Gauci, M Guiffré and EL Tsourdi (eds) *Exploring the Boundaries of Refugee Law* (Brill, 2015) 90.

refuge for their time to be resettled.[109] The first variation of the argument is thus: 'there should be a preference for resettlement'. On the other hand, the 'see-saw hypothesis' assumes that the overall number of persons who are 'legitimately' entitled to receive protection by a particular country is stable.[110] The second variation of the argument is thus: 'the more resettlement, the less territorial asylum'. Quite apart from the fact that both variations of the argument lack an empirical basis and that the assumptions about what is 'legitimate' do not seem to be substantiated with any arguments,[111] it should be noted from a conceptual point of view that the combination of both variations amounts to an argument in favour of abolishing territorial asylum.[112]

In the early 2000s, the European Commission, in line with the international policy framework, still stressed that 'any resettlement scheme must be complementary to and not alternative to the processing of spontaneous asylum claims'.[113] Both the EU asylum *acquis* in a strict sense, in particular the AMIF Regulation and the EASO Regulation, as well as the legal and non-legal instruments providing for common EU resettlement goals, remain silent on the issue.[114] The more recent developments in the emerging EU resettlement law, in particular the EU-Turkey Statement and the Union Framework Proposal, however, do address the relation of resettlement to territorial asylum both explicitly and implicitly.

The explicit references in the respective elements of the emerging EU resettlement law are not entirely consistent in this regard. On the one hand, the SOP Resettlement-EuT underline that the implementation of resettle-

---

109 J Van Selm (n 7) 40; M O'Sullivan, 'The ethics of resettlement: Australia and the Asia-Pacific Region' (2016) *The International Journal of Human Rights* 241, 246, 249.

110 J Van Selm (n 7) 40; M O'Sullivan (n 109) 246 with different terminology.

111 M O'Sullivan (n 109) 246: 'there is no 'resettlement queue'' with reference to J McAdam, 'Editorial: Australia and Asylum Sekers' (2013) 15 *International Journal of Refugee Law* 435, 439; J Van Selm (n 7) 41: 'No country that carries out resettlement in significant numbers has seen spontaneous arrivals of asylum-seekers disappear or dwindle as a result'.

112 Giving preference to resettlement, while at the same time reducing territorial asylum proportionally, amounts to aiming at reducing territorial asylum to zero. As exemplified by the Australian example, this is actually the practical consequence of an approach based on the 'replacement argument', *cf* n .

113 European Communication, 2004 Communication on Managed Entry (n 44) para 12; COM Resettlement Feasibility Study (n 20) v.

114 Even though it stresses the complementary function of, for instance, voluntary and forced return as two forms of return management, *cf* AMIF Regulation, recital 28.

ment under the EU-Turkey Statement is 'without prejudice to apply for asylum'.[115] The Union Framework Proposal along the same lines stresses that it is 'without prejudice to the right to asylum and the protection from refoulement'.[116] On the other hand, however, the EU-Turkey Statement explicitly conceives resettlement as a measure which has been agreed upon in order to 'end irregular migration from Turkey to the EU', and thus reflects the 'wait-in-the-line argument'.[117] The Union Framework Proposal for the first time explicitly states that 'resettlement should be the preferred avenue to international protection in the territory of the Member States'.[118]

This latter understanding indeed seems to be reflected in the concrete design of resettlement, as conceived by the EU-Turkey Statement and the Union Framework Proposal. First, both contain 'punitive exclusion clauses', precluding from resettlement those who have attempted to irregularly cross the border towards the EU.[119] These clauses reflect the 'wait-in-the-line argument'.[120] Second, the emerging EU resettlement law increasingly tends towards conditionality clauses, reflecting the 'replacement argument'. The '1:1 scheme', as conceived under the EU-Turkey Statement, is a clear reflection of the 'see-saw hypothesis'. In the same vein, the activation of the V-HAS was made dependent upon the ending, or at least a substantial and sustainable reduction, of irregular border-crossings from Turkey to the EU. To be sure, neither of those schemes has been implemented as

---

115 SOP Resettlement-EuT, Step 5.

116 Union Framework Proposal, p 8.

117 EU-Turkey Statement (n 11). It could only be understood differently if, at the same time, policies to reduce visa requirements or carrier sanctions were pursued, this is, however, not the case.

118 Union Framework Proposal, p 13: 'Resettlement should be the preferred avenue to international protection in the territory of the member states and should not be duplicated by an asylum procedure.' It seems that the last part of the sentence cannot be understood as limiting the content of the first part so as to mean that territorial asylum should only be de-prioritised for those who have already benefitted from resettlement, since the Proposal – in contrast to earlier policy documents of the early 2000s – does not mention anywhere that resettlement is to be understood as 'complementary' to territorial asylum.

119 SOP Resettlement-EuT, 'Selection Criteria': 'Priority will be given to eligible persons who have not previously entered or tried to enter the EU irregularly'; Art 6 Union Framework Proposal, 'Grounds for Exclusion': '[…] shall be excluded […] persons who have irregularly stayed, entered, or attempted to irregularly enter the territory of the member states during the five years prior to resettlement'.

120 *cf* O'Sullivan (n 109) 242, 247 ff.

foreseen in the letter of the Statement itself.[121] The argument underlying these schemes, however, seems to have had a lasting effect on the understanding of resettlement, as it is taken up in the Union Framework Proposal. The Proposal namely makes resettlement dependent upon several factors, including the third country's effective 'cooperation with the Union' in terms of reducing the number of irregular border-crossings towards the EU.[122] This condition determines that an increase in resettlement capacity depends on a decrease in numbers of persons applying for territorial asylum, in other words, it reflects the 'see-saw hypothesis'.

To conclude, the emerging EU resettlement law recently seems to be tending towards the 'replacement approach'. This approach seems to underlie the EU-Turkey Statement and the Union Framework Proposal in particular. The international policy framework, however, conceives resettlement as complementary to territorial asylum procedures. The provisions of the Union Framework Proposal reflecting the 'replacement approach' have accordingly been criticized by the relevant policy actors with reference to the international policy framework.[123]

2.2. Towards externalising responsibility?

In analysing the objective underlying a resettlement scheme, not only the relation of the destination state to the concerned individuals, but also the relation of the destination State to the first host country must be taken into account. In this regard, the function of resettlement for the allocation of international responsibility is controversial.

The international policy framework clearly conceptualises resettlement as a tool for ensuring fair sharing of international responsibility for refugee

121 See n 85 and 86.

122 Art 4 lit d Proposal Union Framework Proposal.

123 Caritas et al. (n 14) at 2 specifically stressing that resettlement must be regarded as complementary to territorial asylum procedures and at 5 recommending to remove the punitive exclusion clauses; ECRE (n 18) 3 and Amnesty International (n 18) at 2 ff criticising the 'punitive exclusion clause'; SVR (n 13) 19 ff, 25, clearly identifying the 'replacement approach' and stressing the complementary function of resettlement.

protection.[124] The 2018 Global Compact puts even greater emphasis on resettlement as a way of ensuring international responsibility sharing.[125]

Before analysing which conceptualisation underlies the emerging EU resettlement law, the meaning of responsibility for refugee protection and its externalisation must be briefly clarified. States have recognised that the responsibility to protect refugees is common to all States.[126] This seems consequential, given that the situation of refugeehood is characterised by the loss of protection by the home country, and that this situation should be remedied by another State.[127] Which State is to be held responsible, however, is not that obvious. And indeed, the question of the allocation of responsibility for refugee protection remains, to a large extent, unsolved on the international level.[128] In the absence of an international allocation mechanism, one can distinguish between State policies primarily aiming at ensuring fair sharing of international responsibility,[129] and those designed to avoid the concerned State's own responsibility.[130] The former policies are increasingly referred to as an expression of international solidarity.[131] The latter policies can be described as externalisation policies.[132] Indeed,

---

124 UNHCR, Observations and Comments on the Union Framework Proposal (n 18) 1 ff; UNHCR, Position Paper on the Strategic Use of Resettlement, Annual Tripartite Consultations on Resettlement, Geneva, 4 June 2010, available online: https://www.refworld.org/docid/4c0d10ac2.html, passim; J Van Selm (n 7) 40 ff.

125 2018 Global Compact (n 9) para 90 ff.

126 2018 Global Compact, v: 'The predicament of refugees is a common concern of humankind.', *cf* A Hurwitz, *The Collective Responsibility of States to Protect Refugees* (Oxford University Press, 2009). This kind of 'common responsibility' is not to be confused with 'shared responsibility' in the legal sense, *cf* on the question of shared responsibility in the legal sense A Nollkaemper and D Jacobs, 'Shared Responsibility in International Law: A Conceptual Framework' (2012) 34 *Michigan Journal of International Law* 359, 362.

127 *cf* J Hathaway and H Storey, 'Opinion. What is the Meaning of State Protection in Refugee Law? A Debate' (2016) 28 *International Journal of Refugee Law* 480 ff.

128 GS Goodwin-Gil and J McAdam (n 25) 149.

129 Yet another question is what could be considered 'fair' in this context, see n 233.

130 These are obviously rough categories.

131 2018 Global Compact, 1: 'The global compact emanates from fundamental principles of humanity and international solidarity [...]'. For the purpose of this paper, however the less ambitious understanding as international responsibility-sharing is sufficient.

132 J Hyndman and A Mountz, 'Another Brick in the Wall? Neo-Refoulement and the Externalization of Asylum by Australia and Europe' 43 *Government and Opposition* 249; T Gammeltoft-Hansen, 'Outsourcing Asylum: The Advent of Protection Lite' in L Bialasiewicz (ed) *EU Geopolitics and the Making of European Space* (Routledge, 2011) 129.

not all externalisation policies in this sense entail the transfer of *legal* responsibility for protection.[133] Externalisation policies can rather be understood as encompassing both policies aiming at the prevention of the emergence of legal responsibility, in particular so-called non-entrée policies,[134] as well as policies aiming at the transfer of legal responsibility, in particular, so-called protection-elsewhere policies.[135] As States currently generally seem to have an interest in reducing the number of persons in need of protection present on their territory,[136] resettlement policy gives political leverage to the destination State, which can make resettlement dependent

---

133 Legal responsibility for protection, generally speaking, emerges in case of territorial or jurisdictional contact, *cf* ECtHR, Grand chamber judgment of 23 Feb 2012, Hirsi Jamaa and Others v Italy, Application No 27765/09; *cf* Art 31 of the 1951 Convention Relating to the Status of Refugees [hereinafter referred to as: *Geneva Convention*]. In the case of the EU however, legal responsibility for protection might arise due to Art 4, 18, 19 ChFR under less demanding preconditions, *cf* V Moreno-Lax and C Costello, 'The Extraterritorial Application of the EU Charter of Fundamental Rights: From Territoriality to Facticity, the Effectiveness Model' in S Peers, T Hervey, J Kenner and A Ward (eds) *The EU Charter of Fundamental Rights. A Commentary* (Oxford University Press, 2014) 1658; cf M Savino (n 13) 88.

134 See on the notion of non-entrée policies: J Hathaway, 'The Emerging Politics of Non-Entrée' (1992) 91 *Refuge* 40; J Hathaway and T Gammeltoft-Hansen, 'Non-Refoulement in a World of Cooperative Deterrence' (2014) 8 *University of Michigan Law School, Law and Economics Working Papers*. The effective application of non-entrée policies seems to consist of visa requirements and carrier sanctions, increasingly combined with externalization of entry-preventing border control to third states, cf. V Moreno-Lax, Accessing Asylum to Europe. Extraterritorial Border Control and Refugee Rights under EU Law (Oxford University Press, 2017), 39ff.

135 See on protection-elsewhere policies M Foster, 'Responsibility Sharing or Shifting? "Safe" Third Countries and International Law' (2008) 25 *Refuge* 64; C Costello (2005) 'The Asylum Procedures Directive and the Proliferation of Safe Country Practices: Deterrence, Deflection and the Dismantling of International Protection?' 7 *European Journal of Migration and Law* 35. The effective application of protection-elsewhere policies requires two components: First, a situation in the third country with regard to which the 'safe third country concept' or the 'first country of asylum concept' as laid down in eg Art 35, 38 Asylum Procedures Directive can be applied ie, cooperation of the third State with regard to the 'creation of a protection elsewhere situation', and second, the willingness of the third country to accept the forced transfer of persons who do not have the nationality of the state to where they are transferred ie, cooperation of the third State with regard to readmission.

136 As, for instance, reflected in the language of '*burden*-sharing'. *Cf* 2018 Global Compact, v: 'There is an urgent need for more equitable sharing of the burden and responsibility for hosting and supporting the world' refugees […]'; in the

upon the cooperation of the first host State, for instance, with regard to the destination State's externalisation policies. As such, this approach has the consequence that resettlement is conceived as a measure for supporting externalisation of responsibility, and can thus be described as 'externalisation approach' to resettlement.

The explicit references in the emerging EU resettlement law, as it currently stands, seem to reflect, in line with the international policy framework, the objective of ensuring fair sharing of international responsibility. The EASO Regulation explicitly refers to the support of resettlement 'with a view to meeting the international protection needs of refugees in third countries and showing solidarity with their host countries.'[137] The AMIF Regulation is not entirely clear on this point as it differentiates between 'responsibility-sharing between member states' and 'cooperation with third countries' without clarifying what is meant by cooperation.[138] The 'July 2015 scheme' more clearly refers to the aim of a more equitable sharing of responsibility, and at the same time puts an emphasis on the objective of resettlement to admit and grant rights to those in need of interna-

---

same vein already New York Declaration for Refugees and Migrants, Resolution adopted by the General Assembly on 19 September 2016, A/RES/71/1 [hereinafter: *2016 New York Declaration*], para 68: 'We underline the centrality of international cooperation to the refugee protection regime. We recognize the burdens that large movements of refugees place on national resources, especially in the case of developing countries [...] we commit to a more equitable sharing of the burden and responsibility of hosting and supporting the world's refugees [...].' The situation was entirely different during the Cold War, when resettlement was rather seen as economic and ideological advantage by 'Western' destination states. See on the ensuing shifts in the 'hierarchy' between the three durable solutions in the aftermath of the Cold War: TA Aleinikoff, 'State-Centered Refugee Law: From Resettlement to Containment' (1992) 14 *Michigan Journal of International Law* 120. However, it must be noted in this context that Turkey, while party to the Geneva Convention, maintains the geographical limitation ie, is bound by the Convention only with regard to persons originating from Europe. Therefore, resettlement is still considered the preferred durable solution for refugees in Turkey arriving due to events occurring outside of Europe, see UNHCR, 'Refugees and Asylum Seekers in Turkey', available online: https://www.unhcr.org/tr/en/refugees-and-asylum-seekers-in-turkey; and in more detail M Ineli-Ciger, 'Protecting Syrians in Turkey: A Legal Analysis' (2017) 29 *International Journal of Refugee Law* 555, 564.

137 Art 7 para 2 EASO Regulation.

138 See recitals 2, Art 3 para 2 lit d, Art 18 para 1 and 4 AMIF Regulation for 'responsibility-sharing between member states' and 'cooperation with third states' and see recital 7 for 'sharing responsibility and strengthening cooperation with third countries'.

tional protection.[139] Similar references are made in the '50,000 scheme'.[140] Remarkably, the EU-Turkey Statement is silent on the issue of international responsibility sharing. The Union Framework Proposal again stresses the objective of 'international solidarity and responsibility sharing with third countries'.[141]

Nevertheless, the concrete design of the resettlement schemes under the EU-Turkey Statement, as well as under the Union Framework Proposal, seem to increasingly reflect the understanding that resettlement might be used for the purpose of externalising responsibility. This is suggested by the factors determining which third countries or regions EU Member States shall focus on with regard to resettlement. These factors increasingly require the third country's effective cooperation on the prevention of irregular border-crossing towards the EU, on the creation of conditions which allow for the application of 'protection elsewhere clauses' such as, in particular, the 'safe third country concept',[142] and on readmission to the third country.[143] The EU-Turkey Statement, for the first time, comprehensively relies on externalisation through this combined conditionality in the context of resettlement.[144] The '1:1 scheme', as implemented in practice, seems to be based on an implicit conditionality clause, making resettlement dependent upon cooperation in terms of entry-preventing border control

139 European Commission, Recommendation establishing the 'July 2015 scheme' (n 73), point 2 referring to the 2016 New York Declaration.

140 European Commission, Recommendation establishing the '50,000 scheme' (n 78), recital 6 ff referring to the 2016 New York Declaration.

141 Union Framework Proposal, 1, 2, 6, 8.

142 See M Savino (n 13) 84 ff.

143 See M Garlick (n 45) 603 who already in 2006 identified these three elements. Concerning the 'creation of a protection elsewhere situation' she notes that with regard to 'EU's expressed desire […] to help states improve their refugee protection record […] a link is sometimes made to the EU's emphasis on [safe third country] rules'.

144 Even though the 'July 2015' scheme already aimed at externalisation through resettlement, it still relied on a slightly different approach, focusing on the application of so-called 'Regional Development and Protection Programmes', see GAMM (n 47). *Cf* UNHCR, 'Note on Legal Considerations for Cooperation between the European Union and Turkey on the Return of asylum Seekers and Migrants, 10 March 2016' (2017) 29 *International Journal of Refugee Law* 492, criticising at 493 with regard to the EU Turkey Statement that '[s]uch arrangements would be aimed at enhancing the sharing, rather than shifting of burdens and responsibilities', however, at 495 not noting the reflection of the externalisation approach in the design of the resettlement scheme.

and readmission.[145] At the same time, since, at least conceptually, resettlement is made directly conditional upon returns,[146] and return is conditional upon the application of 'protection elsewhere clauses',[147] resettlement is made indirectly conditional upon the 'creation of a protection elsewhere space'.[148] The Union Framework Proposal, for the first time, explicitly lays down this approach of externalisation through the combined conditionality. It provides that the criteria to be taken into account when determining from which countries or regions resettlement is to occur include 'the number of persons in need of international protection [...] within a third country', but puts a clear emphasis on 'a third country's effective cooperation with the Union in the area of migration and asylum', including effective entry-preventing border control, 'creating conditions for the use of the first country of asylum and safe third country concepts for the return of asylum applicants' and 'increasing the capacity for reception and protection', as well as effective cooperation in terms of readmission.[149]

---

145 As already mentioned, the '1:1 scheme' has never been implemented as such. According to information based on expert interviews (n 66), the reason for EU Member States to nevertheless engage in resettlement independent of the return numbers is the 'symbolic value' of resettlement: Resettlement is apparently politically relevant, regardless of the fact that resettling 20,000 refugees can hardly be considered effective 'international responsibility sharing' by a country hosting 3.6 million Syrian refugees along with over 365,000 persons of concern for UNHCR from other nationalities, *cf* UNHCR, 'Refugees and Asylum Seekers in Turkey', available online: https://www.unhcr.org/tr/en/refugees-and-asylum-seekers-in-turkey. The 'symbolic value' of resettlement according to information based on expert interviews consists in serving to show the 'goodwill' of EU Member States, which is in turn perceived as necessary for ensuring Turkey's continuous cooperation in terms of border control and readmission.

146 However, only on a conceptual level, under the '1:1 scheme'. As to the implementation, see n 145.

147 Since, obviously, the implementation of the return policy in the EU Hotspots in Greece depends on the recognition of Turkey as 'safe third country' or 'first country of asylum'. C Ziebritzki and R Nestler, 'Hotspots an der EU-Außengrenze. Eine rechtliche Bestandsaufnahme. Arbeitspapier' (2017) 17 *MPIL Research Paper* 28 ff.

148 However, as the financial support provided to Turkey has not led to the creation of conditions that make it possible to recognise Turkey as such, the return policy has failed. *Cf* O Ulusoy and H Battjes, 'Situation of Readmitted Migrants and Refugees from Greece to Turkey under the EU-Turkey Statement' (2017) 15 *VU Migration Law Series*; M Gkliati, 'The Application of the EU-Turkey Agreement: A Critical Analysis of the Decisions of the Greek Appeals Committee' (2017) 10 *European Journal of Legal Studies* 81.

149 The 'focus regions' shall be determined through an 'annual Union resettlement plan' adopted by the Council upon proposal from the Commission, on the basis

To conclude, the emerging EU resettlement law more recently seems to reflect the 'externalisation approach'. The EU-Turkey Statement and the Union Framework Proposal in particular reflect this trend towards employing resettlement for the purpose of externalisation. The international policy framework, however, conceives resettlement as an instrument ensuring international sharing of responsibility for refugee protection. The provisions of the Union Framework Proposal reflecting the 'externalisation approach' have thus been met with strong criticism, including from academia, the relevant policy actors, and UNHCR.[150]

3. *The constitutional objective of resettlement*

As shown, the emerging EU resettlement seems to be tending towards the controversial conceptualisation of resettlement as eventually replacing territorial asylum, while at the same time increasingly using resettlement as a tool for externalisation of responsibility for refugee protection through combined conditionality. This approach to resettlement in particular underlies the EU-Turkey Statement and the Union Framework Proposal, which have accordingly been described as reflecting a 'paradigm shift'.[151]

---

of which the Commission shall adopt 'targeted Union resettlement schemes', see Arts 7 and 8 Union Framework Proposal. These targeted schemes shall include the 'specification of the regions or third countries from which resettlement is to occur' in line with the mentioned criteria provided for in Art 4 lit. a and d Union Framework Proposal.

150 M Savino (n 13) at 92 ff speaks of a 'complete subjugation of resettlement to the priority of border control', and at 94 ff criticises 'the instrumentalisation of resettlement as an additional migration management tool and an exchange currency in negotiations with third countries'; UNHCR, Observations and Recommendations on the Union Framework Proposal (n 18) at 5 stressing that resettlement is not a migration management tool and therefore strongly objecting the conditionality clauses making resettlement dependent upon return or readmission; Caritas et al. (n 14) 3 ff, criticising the conditionality clauses towards third countries as transforming resettlement primarily into a migration management tool; ECRE (n 18) 1 ff, criticising the use of resettlement for the purpose of migration control, deterrence and readmission; Amnesty International (n 18) 1 ff, objecting to the conceptualisation of resettlement as instrumental to the objective of migration deterrence and return; K Bamberg (n18), arguing in favour of the conceptualisation as 'humanitarian pathway' instead of as a migration management tool; SVR (n 13) 7.

151 M Savino (n 13) 92 speaks of a 'paradigm shift' from the 'traditional humanitarian conception' to an 'instrumental conception' of resettlement. In the same

The Union Framework Proposal, modelling a possible codification of this resettlement practice, has therefore been met with strong criticism. The reaction to the Proposal is indeed only marginally concerned with the increasing EU involvement as such, but rather focuses on some specific provisions. As shown above, the contentious provisions can be identified as reflecting the 'replacement approach', respectively the 'externalisation approach'.[152] Surprisingly, however, resettlement under the EU-Turkey Statement is still not subject to much debate, even though it already implements, in an ad hoc manner, the approach codified in the Union Framework Proposal.

The criticism, generally speaking, refers to the international policy framework as the normative yardstick. The international *legal* framework is referred to only in some instances, while the EU *constitutional* framework seems to serve as an auxiliary yardstick concerning specific questions.[153] Referring primarily to the international policy framework as a normative benchmark, however, has certain disadvantages since this framework is binding only to a limited extent, and is to a certain degree unstable.[154] These disadvantages would be remedied by an increased reference to the EU constitutional framework as the normative yardstick.[155] And in any case, as the EU is increasingly regulating resettlement, it can only do so in compliance with its constitutional framework. The debate on the objective of resettlement, therefore, should take greater account of the EU constitutional framework.

The central question thus concerns what EU constitutional law says on the objective of resettlement.

---

vein, C Tometten, 'Resettlement, Humanitarian Admission, and Family Reunion' (2018) 37 *Oxford Refugee Survey Quarterly* 187, 190, 199 notes that the 'EU Turkey Deal […] transforms resettlement from a mechanism of protection into an instrument of containment. […] Resettlement is thus perverted into a tool for effective […] management and, concomitantly, containment of refugee flows instead of responsibility-sharing […].'.

152 See n 123 and n 150.

153 See n 21. For an assessment of the 'replacement approach' from an *ethical* perspective see M O'Sullivan (n 109) 247 ff, 258 who concludes that the approach is 'ethically unacceptable'.

154 As UNHCR is financed by the states, economic and political interest of potential destination states may lead to UNHCR adapting its positions. In particular, state practice during 'refugee crisis' seems to have a lasting influence on the positions of UNHCR, as shown by T Bessa, 'From Political Instrument to Protection Tool? Resettlement of Refugees and North-South Relations' (2009) 26 *Refuge* 91, 93.

155 Which could be seen as a beneficial side effect of the perspective of this article.

In order to answer that question, it is *firstly* necessary to understand where to locate the emerging EU resettlement law within EU law, in other words, to define the relevant constitutional framework and to identify into which area of EU law the emerging EU resettlement law is integrated. The more recent conceptualisation of resettlement, as eventually replacing asylum and as a tool supporting the externalisation of responsibility, could be understood as reflecting the view that the rationale of resettlement is governed by immigration policy or even foreign policy. However, as will be shown in the following, the emerging EU resettlement law is firmly integrated into the Common European Asylum System and therefore governed by the constitutional rationale of EU asylum law (3.1). This follows from the legal basis and the content of the emerging EU resettlement law, and is confirmed by explicit statements of the EU institutions.

Secondly, it is necessary to understand what the constitutional framework says on resettlement, that is, to analyse the relevant constitutional framework in regard to resettlement. To be sure, EU constitutional law does not contain explicit rules on resettlement. Nevertheless, as laid out in the following, the constitutional framework of the Common European Asylum System is indeed relevant to resettlement. In particular, Art. 78 TFEU and Art. 18 CHFR, which define the constitutional objective of the Common European Asylum System and provide for the incorporation of the international refugee law into the EU constitutional framework, are pertinent to the objective of resettlement.[156] As will be shown in the following, the constitutional framework of the Common European Asylum

156 *Further*, and going beyond the scope of this article, the pertinence of the constitutional framework to the emerging EU resettlement law is not limited the definition of its objective, *cf* n 21. In particular concerning the pertinence of the constitutional framework with regard to fundamental rights in the realm of resettlement, further analysis is required: On the one hand, it would have to be assessed whether the Charter of Fundamental Rights is applicable to resettlement, taking into account in particular European Court of Justice, judgment of 7 May 2013, C-617/10, Åklagaren v Hans Åkerberg Fransson, para 21; European Court of Justice, judgment of 20 Sept 2016, C-8/15 to C-10/15 P, Ledra Advertising Ltd and Others v European Commission and ECB, para 66 ff; European Court of Justice, judgment of 13 June 2017, C-258/14, Eugenia Florescu and Others v Casa Județeană de Pensii Sibiu and Others. If so, the debate on fundamental rights in extraterritorial asylum procedures cannot be circumvented simply by labelling a procedure as 'resettlement' instead of 'extraterritorial asylum procedure' or 'humanitarian visa'. On the other hand, the consequences of the external human rights commitment as arising from Art 3 para 5, Art 21 para 1 TEU would have to be assessed, taking into account in particular the human right to leave any country; see on the latter N Markard, 'The Right to Leave by Sea: Legal Limits

System defines that the principal objective of resettlement is to provide international protection to third country nationals (3.2), thereby complementing territorial asylum (3.3) and ensuring fair sharing of international responsibility with Member States (3.4). The constitutional perspective, thus, comes to the same conclusion as the positions criticising the approach recently underlying the emerging EU resettlement law. In other words, this criticism is undergirded by constitutional arguments.

3.1. Resettlement as a component of the Common European Asylum System

The question about the area of EU law into which the emerging EU resettlement law is integrated can be answered by assessing its legal basis and content, while taking into account the view of the EU institutions.[157]

First, the competence of the EU to adopt common rules on resettlement and to support national administrations with regard to implementation is found within the Common European Asylum System, namely in Art. 78 para 2, Art. 74 TFEU.[158]

---

on EU Migration Control by Third Countries' (2016) 27 *The European Journal of International Law* 591. As the aim of this article is, however, limited to the definition of the *objective* of the emerging EU resettlement law in a constitutional perspective, the constitutional requirements concerning fundamental rights will not be further examined within the scope of this contribution.

157 If the EU relies, for instance, on its broad competences in the Common European Asylum System in order to adopt common rules on resettlement, these rules must comply with the rationale of EU asylum law. In the same vein: If the content of the emerging EU resettlement law closely refers to the EU asylum *acquis*, it must be understood as forming part of the Common European Asylum System. If the EU institutions explicitly state that the emerging EU resettlement law forms part of the Common European Asylum System, this should imply the understanding that its rationale is governed by the constitutional framework of that system.

158 In light of the scope and content of the emerging EU resettlement law, it is no longer required to discuss 'whether or not a legal basis as such is even necessary' as was still discussed in the COM Resettlement Feasibility Study (n 20) 139. As a shared competence, EU legislation on resettlement must comply with the principles of proportionality and subsidiarity, see Art 5 TEU, Art 4 lit j TFEU. In cases of doubt, the objective of Art 78 para 1 TFEU speaks for harmonisation, see K Hailbronner and D Thym, 'Legal Framework for EU Asylum Policy' in K Hailbronner and D Thym (eds) *EU Immigration and Asylum Law. A Commentary* (CH Beck, 2nd edition, 2016) 1030 ff.

Art. 78 para 2 TFEU confers upon the Union the competence to harmonise resettlement rules.[159] Art. 78 para 2 lit. g TFEU allows the Union to adopt measures concerning 'partnership and cooperation with third countries for the purpose of managing inflows of people applying for asylum or subsidiary or temporary protection'.[160] Resettlement is a measure enhancing State control in the realm of forced migration through extraterritorial activities and is hence generally understood as falling under Art. 78 para 2 lit. g TFEU.[161] The provision contains an internal competence, even though it implies the external competence to conclude international agreements in order to achieve this objective.[162] The emerging EU resettlement law, however, mainly consists of common rules for the Member States, and insofar, Art. 78 para 2 lit. g TFEU is not sufficient as such. Common rules on resettlement procedures can be adopted on the basis of Art. 78 para 2 lit. d TFEU.[163] It becomes clear from the wording as well as from the drafting history of Art. 78 para. 2 lit. d TFEU that the competence is not limited to procedures conducted on the territory of the Member States. More generally, Art. 78 para 2 TFEU does not differentiate between the territorial and the extraterritorial dimensions of the Common European Asylum System and hence covers both. In other words, it is 'silent on the geographical scope'.[164] In the same vein, Art. 78 para 2 lit. a, b and e TFEU provide for the competence to adopt common rules on eligibility criteria, the status to be accorded to the person, and the internal allocation

159 See COM Resettlement Feasibility Study (n 20) 139 ff with regard to the corresponding provisions.

160 Note the limits of this competence, as 'managing forced migration' is per se only possible to a very limited extent due to the very nature of the phenomenon, see A Farahat and N Markard, 'Forced Migration Governance: In Search of Sovereignty' (2016) 17 *German Law Journal* 907.

161 V Moreno-Lax, 'Chapter 10. External Dimension' in S Peers, V Moreno-Lax, M Garlick and E Guild (eds) *EU Immigration and Asylum Law (Text and Commentary), Volume 3: EU Asylum Law* (Brill, 2nd edition, 2015) 617, 629; P De Bruycker and EL Tsourdi (n 19) 484; B Kowalczyk (n 21) 136; M Den Heijer (n 44) 206.

162 Following the 'AERT' jurisprudence (n 54), as codified in Art 216 para 1 TFEU. See G De Baere, 'The Basics of EU External Relations Law: An Overview of the Post-Lisbon Constitutional Framework for Developing the External Dimensions of EU Asylum and Migration Policy' in M Maes, M-C Foblets, and P de Bruycker (eds) *External Dimensions of EU Migration and Asylum Law and Policy* (Bruylant, 2011) 121, 168.

163 K Hailbronner and D Thym (n 158) 1037.

164 To be sure, the current EU secondary law does not contain rules on extraterritorial asylum procedures, see Art 3 para 1 Asylum Procedures Directive, as emphasised by the European Court of Justice, 'X and X' (n) para 49.

mechanism, regardless of whether the concerned persons have arrived spontaneously or through resettlement programmes.[165]

Art. 78 para 2, Art. 74 TFEU allow the Union to support the implementation of resettlement through financial or operational means.[166] Due to the mentioned parallelism between the EU's competences in the territorial and the extraterritorial dimensions, the questions concerning the administrative level pertaining to each of those dimensions seem not to fundamentally differ.[167] The EU does not have the competence to decide on individu-

---

165 See COM Resettlement Feasibility Study (n 20) 139 ff with regard to the corresponding provisions. Yet another question is whether the EU has the competence to set a binding resettlement capacity, which arises quite apart from the question of the political feasibility of such a scheme. An internal allocation mechanism, currently provided for in the Dublin III Regulation, obliges Member States to accept responsibility for a certain group of applicants. As the discussion on the Dublin reform confirms, an internal allocation mechanism may include obligations in terms of numbers. This is politically controversial but raises no issues with regard to the EU's competence. The overall number of applicants in this case cannot be regulated due to the very nature of spontaneous arrivals. In the context of the external dimension, however, the determination of the overall capacity is a precondition for the internal allocation due to very nature of extraterritorial admission procedures. Art 78 para 2 lit. e TFEU would hence be irrelevant with regard to the external dimension if it did not cover the competence to set the overall capacity as well. *Cf* COM Resettlement Feasibility Study (n 20)163 ff which also proposes that the EU could determine the overall capacity, even though without referring to a possible legal basis.

166 *cf* M Den Heijer (n 44) 206; F Comte, 'A New Agency is Born in the European Union: The European Asylum Support Office' (2010) 12 *European Journal of Migration and Law* 392 ff, 399.

167 The 2004 Hague Programme called for a study on 'the merits, appropriateness and feasibility of joint processing of asylum applications outside EU territory', see Hague Programme (n 45) para 1.3. However, this study was never published, in contrast to the study on the internal dimension of 2013: European Commission, Study on the Feasibility and legal and practical implications of establishing a mechanism for the joint processing of asylum applications on the territory of the EU, HOME/2011/ERFX/FW/04, authored by H Urth, MH Bausager, H-M Kuhn, and J Van Selm, available online: https://www.refworld.org/docid/524d5ba04.html [hereinafter: *COM Joint Processing Feasibility Study*]. Yet another question is whether national law sets limits to the extraterritorial administrative competences of the EU, see on this question eg Deutscher Bundestag, Wissenschaftliche Dienste, 'Extraterritoriale Verwaltungskompetenzen der Europäischen Union für Asylverfahren. Zu den rechtlichen Vorgaben aus nationaler Sicht' (2016) Ausarbeitung WD 3 – 3000 – 066/15.

al claims for international protection in territorial asylum procedures.[168] Therefore, it seems that 'replacing' UNHCR with the EU agency with regard to the assessment of the individuals' eligibility for resettlement would be compatible with Art. 78 para 2, Art. 74 TFEU only as long as the 'assessment' is not legally binding upon Member States, which must retain the competence to decide on admission in individual cases.[169]

Hence, the legal basis of the emerging EU resettlement law is found in Art. 74, Art. 78 TFEU. This is in line with the understanding of the institutions: The EASO Regulation is based on Art. 74 and Art. 78, para 1, 2 TFEU. Even though the AMIF Regulation is based not only on Art. 78, but also on Art. 79 para 2 and 4 TFEU, which form the legal basis for EU immigration policy, its relevant provisions explicitly state that resettlement is considered part of EU asylum policy.[170] The Amending Council Decision was adopted on the basis of Art. 78 para 3 TFEU. The Commission based

---

168 F Comte (n 166) 373, 392; EL Tsourdi, 'Bottom-Up Salvation? From Practical Cooperation Towards Joint Implementation Through the European Asylum Support Office' 1 *European Papers* 997, 999; K Hailbronner and D Thym (n 158) 1037.

169 Resettlement procedures under the emerging EU resettlement law, as it currently stands, can – in a simplified manner – be described as consisting of three steps: *First*, the 'assessment' by UNHCR, *second*, the 'decision' by the Member State, and *third* pre-departure arrangements by IOM. Art 10 para 8 Union Framework Proposal foresees that the EU agency would 'replace' UNHCR with regard to the first step. This would be in line with the Art 78 para 2, Art 74 TFEU. In the same vein, the third step could be conducted by an EU agency. Transferring the responsibility for the second step, the decision, to an EU agency would not be possible under Art 78 para 2, Art 74 TFEU. However, as can be observed in the practice in the EU Hotspots in Greece, the line between a 'non-binding decision' which is almost all the times followed by the Member States' authorities, and a 'binding decision' is rather difficult to draw: In the context of the implementation of the return policy under the EU-Turkey Statement, EASO is 'supporting' the national asylum administration by conducting interviews and issuing 'legal opinions' in which it assesses the individual's need for international protection in the EU. Even though these 'opinions' are not legally binding, the national asylum administration usually issues an according decision; this practice oversteps the competences provided for in the EASO Regulation; *cf* EL Tsourdi, 'Bottom-Up Salvation? From Practical Cooperation Towards Joint Implementation Through the European Asylum Support Office' (2017) 1 *European Papers* 997; C Ziebritzki and R Nestler (n 147) 48 ff; European Ombudsman, 'EASO's involvement in applications for international protection submitted in the 'hotspots' in Greece', Case 735/2017/MDC, decision of 05 July 2018; COM Joint Processing Feasibility Study (n 167) 78. Concerning a similar practice in extraterritorial resettlement procedures, this would have to be taken into account.

170 Art 2, 3 para 2 lit a, 7 AMIF Regulation, and its recitals.

the Union framework on Art. 78 para 2 lit. d and lit. g TFEU.[171] Even though the legal basis invoked by the Commission for the Union Framework Proposal can be considered incomplete, as has been shown, and invoking Art. 78 para 3 TFEU for the Amending Council Decision is not convincing for other reasons,[172] the invoked legal basis nevertheless confirms that the EU institutions consider the emerging EU resettlement as forming part of the Common European Asylum System.[173]

Second, and accordingly, the content of the emerging EU resettlement law is firmly integrated into the Common European Asylum System on a material level.

The definition of the status accorded to the resettled person is increasingly congruent with that accorded to persons who have been granted international protection in a territorial asylum procedure, and is, hence, increasingly defined by reference to the EU asylum *acquis* on the internal dimension. The AMIF Regulation already defines resettlement with refer-

---

171 Union Framework Proposal, p 17.

172 The provision allows the Council to adopt provisional non-legislative measures 'for the benefit of the member states concerned' in the event of an 'emergency situation characterised by a sudden inflow of nationals of third countries', *cf* European Court of Justice, 'Relocation Judgement' (n 77) para 66. Unless a resettlement scheme would somehow be conceived so as to relieve the member states under particular pressure due to a high number of asylum applications, Art 78 para 3 TFEU, hence, does not seem to be the appropriate legal basis.

173 As has been shown, this is convincing, but remarkable against the background that the Court of Justice in its judgement on *X and X* seemed to assume that 'the conditions governing the issue by member states of long-term visas and residence permits to third country nationals on humanitarian grounds' could only be based on Art 79 para 2 lit a TFEU, see European Court of Justice, *X and X* (n) para 44. Art 79 TFEU confers upon the Union rather limited competences in order to develop a 'common immigration policy'. However, as soon as extraterritorial procedures have the function of determining the need for international protection, these rules would not serve to 'develop a common immigration policy' as required by Art 79 para 2 TFEU, but would rather be conducted 'with a view to offering appropriate status to […] third-country nationals requiring international protection' in the sense of Art 78 para 1 TFEU, and would accordingly have to be based on Art 78 para 2 TFEU. Therefore, if the EU institutions decided to adopt a legal migration scheme which was not based on the central eligibility criterion of international protection, and which was accordingly not integrated into the EU asylum law *acquis*, Art 79 TFEU might indeed be the appropriate legal basis for such a scheme. These kinds of legal migration schemes are, however, not referred to as 'resettlement'. The statement of the Court is hence puzzling to the extent that it suggests that legal access based on 'humanitarian grounds' would fall under Art 79 TFEU. The analysis rather suggests that such schemes, forming part of resettlement, would be based on Art 78 para 1 TFEU.

ence to the status, namely the refugee status or the subsidiary protection status, as defined in the Qualification Directive, or any other status offering similar rights.[174] In the same vein, the 'July 2015' scheme provides that irrespective of whether international protection status or a national status is granted by the Member States, the 'resettled person [...] should enjoy [...] the rights guaranteed to beneficiaries of international protection by the [Qualification Directive] or similar rights'.[175] The '50,000 scheme' lays out its objective as being to 'admit [...] persons in need of international protection'.[176] The Union Framework Proposal provides for the same objective, and specifies that if a positive decision is taken, the Member State shall 'grant refugee status [...] or subsidiary protection status' and even that this decision 'shall have the same effect as a [corresponding] decision' in a territorial asylum procedure.[177]

The general references of the emerging EU resettlement as to its purpose are, however, not entirely unequivocal. Certainly, the emerging EU resettlement law does not contain any references suggesting that it forms part of EU foreign policy.[178] However, the AMIF Regulation and the Union Framework Proposal do include references to the 'management' of migration.[179] These could be understood either as references to the management of immigration in the sense of Art. 79 TFEU, or of *forced* migration in the sense of Art. 78 TFEU. The Common European Asylum System indeed encompasses instruments aimed at increasing state control in the realm of forced migration. This clearly follows from Art. 78 para 2 lit g TFEU.[180] A closer look at the emerging EU resettlement law reveals that the references to 'management' of migration indeed refer to the attempt to

---

174 Art 2 lit. a AMIF Regulation.

175 European Commission, Recommendation establishing the 'July 2015 scheme' (n 73) para 9.

176 European Commission, Recommendation establishing the '50,000 scheme' (n 78) para 1.

177 Art 10 para 7 lit. a Union Framework Proposal, recital 11 with regard to the objective of harmonisation of the status in resettlement procedures. Differently in the expedited procedure as foreseen under Art 11 Union Framework Proposal, in which only subsidiary protection status is assessed and can be granted.

178 To the best of the author's knowledge.

179 AMIF Regulation, recital 17, 25, 58, Art 3 para 1; Union Framework Proposal, pp 2, 5.

180 As this provision is a competence of the EU to achieve the objective laid down in Art 78 para 1 TFEU, the objective of 'managing migration' – the feasibility of which in the realm of forced migration is very doubtful anyways – can however not prevail over the objective to provide international protection to third country nationals. In other words, it seems that Art 78 para 2 lit. g TFEU can be un-

increase state control in the realm of *forced* migration.[181] The explicit references to the Common European Asylum System confirm this: The 'July 2015 scheme' refers to the resolution of the European Parliament in which it 'stressed the need to ensure safe and legal access to the Union asylum system'.[182] The '50,000 scheme' serves as ad hoc mechanism until the adoption of the Union Resettlement Framework and, accordingly, forms part of the Common European Asylum System.[183] The EU-Turkey Statement, along with the SOP Resettlement-T and the Amending Council Decision, confirm this understanding.[184] In the same vein, on the administrative level, support for the implementation of resettlement schemes is clearly defined as encompassed in the support for the implementation of the Common European Asylum System: Both the AMIF Regulation and the EASO Regulation explicitly define resettlement as subsumed under its external dimension.[185]

Third, the EU institutions explicitly take the position that the emerging EU resettlement law forms part of the Common European Asylum System, as becomes clear from the relevant policy documents.

While some of the early policy papers were not entirely unambiguous yet as to whether EU resettlement policy would form part of EU foreign policy or of EU asylum law,[186] policy documents, at the latest since 2009, have made clear – consistently, and indeed increasingly – that the emerg-

---

derstood as containing an auxiliary objective, which can, however, not prevail over Art 78 para 1 TFEU in case of conflict since the former serves the latter.

181 AMIF Regulation, recital 17, 58, Art 3 para 1; Union Framework Proposal, pp 2, 5.

182 European Commission, Recommendation concerning the 'July 2015 scheme' (n 73) recital 2, 12, 14 as well as point 12, 13. The term 'Union asylum system' can only be understood as referring to the Common European Asylum System.

183 European Commission, Recommendation concerning the '50,000 scheme' (n 78) recital 10 to 12, 13.

184 It is irrelevant in this regard that the EU-Turkey Statement cannot be attributed to the EU – at least according to the judgement of the General Court (n 54). Even if the argument was made that the EU-Turkey Statement as such, therefore, does not form part of the Common European Asylum System, this would not be an argument against resettlement forming part of it. This is indeed unquestioned with regard to the return policy under the EU-Turkey Statement, which is implemented by application of the safe third country concept, and which uncontroversially forms part of the Common European Asylum System.

185 See Art 7 para 1 and Art 5 para 3 subpara 1, respectively referring to Art 3 para 2 lit a and d AMIF Regulation; Art 7 EASO Regulation.

186 Even though the GAMM itself is a foreign policy document and advocates for the strategic use of resettlement under the so-called Regional Protection Pro-

ing EU resettlement law must be understood as part of the Common European Asylum System. To be sure, the initiative of establishing 'new Partnership Frameworks' aims at achieving the goals of the European Agenda on Migration through EU external action and conceives resettlement as part of the then envisaged 'compacts' with third States. Nevertheless, resettlement is explicitly understood as part of asylum policy.[187] The Commission's reform proposal of April 2016 accordingly proposes that 'a structured resettlement system' is necessary for 'moving towards a more managed approach to refugee protection in the EU'.[188] The Union Framework Proposal explicitly considers resettlement as 'part of the measures *constituting* the Common European Asylum System' and as an 'essential part' thereof.[189] In the same vein, the European Parliament states: 'A Common European Asylum System must have several safe and legal pathways. Our common asylum system cannot continue to exclusively focus on making it as hard as possible for people fleeing to reach the territory of the European Union. Safe and legal pathways, [...], [are] absolutely vital for a functioning European asylum system. [...] A robust Union Resettlement Framework [...] is one *fundamental part* of such a system [...].[190]

To conclude, the emerging EU resettlement law forms part of the Common European Asylum System.[191] It is firmly integrated into this system both formally, ie, in terms of its legal basis, as well as materially, ie, in

---

grammes, resettlement was already back then defined as 'promoting international protection and enhancing the *external dimension of asylum policy*', see GAMM (n 47) p 17.

187 Asylum policy might then – alongside eg trade policy, development aid, energy, security and digital policy – be considered as providing political leverage to the Union in its external relations, *cf* European Commission, Communication from the Commission to the European Parliament, the European Council, the Council and the European Investment Bank on establishing a new Partnership Framework with third countries under the European Agenda on Migration, 7 June 2016, COM(2016) 385 final, pp 2, 8. This would however not imply that eg asylum policy or digital policy is therefore entirely governed by the rationale of EU foreign policy.

188 European Commission, comprehensive reform proposal of April 2016 (n 59).

189 Union Framework Proposal, p 4 and 6 [emphasis added].

190 European Parliament, Report on the proposal for a regulation of the European Parliament and of the Council establishing a Union Resettlement Framework and amending Regulation (EU) No 516/2014 of the European Parliament and the Council, 19 October 2017 (n 98) 66 [emphasis added].

191 The COM Resettlement Feasibility Study (n 20), vi argued that, due to the complementarity of territorial asylum and resettlement, a 'Common European *Resettlement* System' should be established, which together with the 'Common

terms of its content. The EU institutions have explicitly adopted this view. More specifically, the emerging EU resettlement law is part of the external dimension of the Common European Asylum System.[192]

3.2. Objective I: Providing international protection

In order to understand the objective of the emerging EU resettlement law as part of the Common European Asylum System, it seems useful to begin with analysing the constitutional objective of that system more generally, and then to explore the consequences with regard to resettlement more specifically.[193]

The constitutional objective of the Common European Asylum System becomes apparent from the wording of Art. 78 para 1 TFEU: 'The Union shall develop a common policy on asylum, subsidiary protection and tem-

---

European *Asylum* System' would make up the 'Common European *International Protection* System'. Even though the advantage of this terminology in terms of clarity is obvious, it has not been established. The reason is the inconsistent terminology of the EU constitutional framework itself: Art 78 TFEU refers to a Common European 'Asylum' System with a view to offering 'international protection', at the same time makes clear that 'international protection' at least covers 'refugee status' in the sense of the Geneva Convention and 'subsidiary protection', but then refers to 'asylum' in Art 78 para 2 lit. a TFEU; Art 18 ChFR grants the right to 'asylum', which shall be guaranteed with due respect to the Geneva Convention and in accordance with the treaties.

192 The notion of the 'external dimension' is not clearly defined. The broad definition, which is adopted here, encompasses the 'international dimension' – requiring an external competence of the EU – as well as the 'extraterritorial dimension' – requiring an internal competence of the EU with regard to extraterritorial activities, see L Leboeuf (n 24) 57. In favour of distinguishing the 'international' dimension: M Maes, D Vanheule, J Wouters and M-C Foblets, 'The International Dimension of EU Asylum and Migration Policy' in M Maes, M-C Foblets, and P de Bruycker (n 162) 9. Following the broad definition adopted here, resettlement forms part of the 'external dimension' already because it regulates extraterritorial activities of the EU and its Member States. Resettlement is, however, not necessarily part of the 'international dimension', since even though concluding international agreements can be beneficial to resettlement, resettlement does not presuppose an international treaty.

193 See on this approach in the context of EU asylum law: Opinion of Advocate General Cruz Villalón delivered on 11 July 2013 in the case C-394/12, Abdullahi (n 27) para 40. See in more detail on this approach in the context of EU competition law: R Nazzini, *The Foundations of European Union Competition Law. The Objective and Principles of Article 102* (Oxford University Press, 2011) 107 ff.

porary protection *with a view to offering appropriate status* to any third-country national requiring *international protection* and ensuring compliance with the principle of non-refoulement.'[194] This is in line with the understanding developed by General Advocate Cruz Villalón in his Opinion on the case 'Abdullahi', in which he described the Common European Asylum System as a 'normative system devised by the European Union to enable the fundamental right to asylum to be exercised. That system [is] informed today by recognition of the right enshrined in Article 18 ChFR and the mandate to develop a common policy in this area established in Article 78 para 1 TFEU [...].'[195] The wording, as well as systematic and historical considerations speak in favour of reconsidering whether Art. 78 TFEU and Art. 18 ChFR can indeed be understood as being limited to 'asylum' specifically, or whether these provisions should not rather be understood as referring to 'international protection' in general.[196] For the purpose of this article, however, it is sufficient to conclude that the objective of the Common European Asylum System is 'to provide international protection to third country nationals'. To be sure, identifying the objective of an EU legal system does not mean that the interpretation can be one-sided, or that auxiliary or even conflicting objectives of the same system cannot be taken into account.[197] But, certainly, the fact that a constitutional objective is 'political', in the sense that it is based on certain historically grown

194 Emphasis added. The French, Spanish and Italian versions even more clearly express that the provision of international protection is the 'objective' of the Common European Asylum System (resp. 'visant à', 'destinada a', 'volta a'). From a systematic perspective, it seems that the formulation of the objective should be refined in two regards: On the one hand, it should reflect that the Member States, through this system, commonly comply with their obligations under international refugee and human rights law. On the other hand, it should reflect that Art 78 TFEU must be read in light of Art 18, 19 ChFR. This is in line with the understanding suggested by General Advocate Cruz Villalón (n 27).

195 Opinion of Advocate General Cruz Villalón delivered on 11 July 2013 in the case C-394/12, Abdullahi (n 27193) para 40 [emphasis added].

196 *cf* J Bast, 'Vom subsidiären Schutz zum europäischen Flüchtlingsbegriff' (2018) *Zeitschrift für Ausländerrecht und Ausländerpolitik* 41, 42, 46 who analyses a 'broad European definition of refugeehood' ('erweiterter europäischer Flüchtlingsbegriff') relating to the status of 'international protection'. Remarkably, the UNHCR Resettlement Handbook indeed refers to a 'broad European refugee definition' in the same vein: UNHCR Resettlement Handbook (n 22) Chapter 3.1, 3.4: 'Refugee Status as a Precondition for Resettlement Consideration [...] Eligibility under the Broader Refugee Definition'.

197 R Nazzini (n 193) 133 ff; similarly, T Müller, *Wettbewerb und Unionsverfassung* (Mohr Siebeck, 2014) 135, 164 ff.

ideas, is not an argument against its definition. Quite to the contrary, as has been shown in the context of competition law, this is rather usual.[198]

However, one might wonder whether the EU constitutional objective is limited to the internal dimension of the Common European Asylum System, or whether it indeed also applies to its external dimension. The question arises against the background of international refugee law and the Member States' constitutional traditions, according to which the physical presence in the territory of the concerned State is a precondition for the possibility to seek protection in that State.[199] The apparently underlying concern that the EU can quite clearly not be constitutionally required to provide international protection to the world's refugees regardless of where they are present, does not persist, because the understanding of the objective, as proposed here, does not even imply such a conclusion. It only follows from the constitutional objective that if the EU decides to establish an external dimension, including an extraterritorial dimension, the objective of this dimension is to provide international protection, more specifically and due to the nature of the extraterritorial dimension, to provide legal access to international protection.

The constitutional definition of the objective of the Common European Asylum System entails that the secondary law instruments which constitute that system – hence also the emerging EU resettlement law – must be understood in light of this objective. This follows from the structure of the Treaties: the aim of the Union is enshrined in Art. 3 para 1 TEU,[200] the objectives of the specific areas of EU law are defined in Art. 3 para 2 to 6 TEU respectively, and the objectives of the more specific sub-areas are provided

---

198 R Nazzini (n 193) 107 ff; O Andriychuk, *The Normative Foundations of European Competition Law. Assessing the Goals of Antitrust through the Lens of Legal Philosophy* (Elgar Publishing, 2017) 35 ff; KK Patel and H Schweitzer, *The Historical Foundations of EU Competition Law* (Oxford University Press, 2013).

199 P Endres de Oliveira, 'Legaler Zugang zu internationalem Schutz – zur Gretchenfrage im Flüchtlingsrecht' (2016) 49 *Kritische Justiz* 167; G Noll, 'Seeking Asylum at Embassies: A Right to Enter under International Law?' (2005) 17 *International Journal of Refugee Law* 542.

200 This explicit reference to the aim of the Union is remarkable in comparison to State's constitutions. The reason might be precisely that the EU is not a State: The very existence of the EU and its legal order as normative system does therefore not seem self-evident, and is hence explicitly justified in its constitutional framework by reference to its objective.

for in the respective provisions of the TEU and the TFEU.[201] This structure of objectives and its implications have been analysed in detail in the context of EU competition law.[202] The objective of a certain subsystem of EU law is relevant because 'all [...] provisions which together [...] make up the system [...], must [...] be understood ultimately as [...] instrument[s] operating in the service of that [objective] [...]', as has been explained by Advocate General Cruz Villalón with regard to the Common European Asylum System.[203] This, in turn, has two implications: On the one hand, the judiciary must interpret EU secondary law in line with the relevant objective, by using the derivative method as described above, as confirmed by the European Court of Justice.[204] On the other hand, the EU legislator must design EU secondary law in line with the relevant objective. This follows a fortiori from the former and is indeed explicitly provided for in Art. 3 para 6 TEU in a general manner and in Art. 78 para 2 TFEU specifically with regard to the Common European Asylum System.[205]

To conclude, the emerging EU resettlement law, as part of the Common European Asylum System, serves first and foremost the constitutional objective of that system, namely, to provide international protection to third country nationals, and must therefore be designed and interpreted in light of this objective.

3.3. *Objective II: Complementing territorial asylum procedures*

The understanding that resettlement primarily serves to provide international protection to third country nationals does not as such answer the

---

201 In conjunction with the relevant further provisions: The objective of the area of freedom, security and justice is defined in Art 3 para. 2 TEU, Art 67 TFEU; the objective of the internal market is defined in Art 3 para 2 TEU, Art 26 TFEU; the objective of the economic and monetary union is defined with particular clarity in Art 3 para 4 TEU, Art 119 TFEU; etc.

202 R Nazzini (n 193) at 113 for the identification as sub-system of internal market, and at 119 on the interpretative method. *Cf* European Court of Justice, judgement of 11 Feb 2011, C-52/09, Konkurrensverket gegen TeliaSonera Sverige AB, para 20 ff.

203 Opinion of Advocate General Cruz Villalón delivered on 11 July 2013 in the case C-394/12, Abdullahi (n 27) [emphasis added].

204 European Court of Justice, judgement of 11 Feb 2011, C-52/09, TeliaSonera (n 202) para 20 ff.

205 Art 78 para 2 TFEU explicitly states that the competences are conferred upon the EU 'for the purpose of paragraph 1'.

controversies on the objective of resettlement. In order to assess whether the EU constitutional framework conceives resettlement as complementary to territorial asylum procedures or, rather, as eventually replacing them in the long term, a closer look needs to be taken at the principal constitutional objective of the Common European Asylum System, and at the consequences of the incorporation of international refugee law into that system, in order to assess the constitutional relation between the internal and external dimension of the system.

First, the principal objective of the emerging EU resettlement law speaks in favour of its conceptualisation as complementary to territorial asylum.

As shown above, the emerging EU resettlement law has the principal objective of providing international protection to third country nationals. The EU law on territorial asylum has the same principal objective, as it forms part of the same system. To argue that the emerging EU resettlement law should eventually replace territorial asylum, would thus amount to playing off one element of the same system against another, and thus hinder the achievement of the objective of the system as a whole. Conceptualising both elements as complementary, by contrast, facilitates the achievement of the objective of the system. As the components of the Common European Asylum System serve the objective of that system, or one might even say, as the very existence of these components is justified by the objective of that system, only understanding them as complementary to each other can be reconciled with the principal constitutional objective.

Second, the incorporation of international refugee law into the Common European Asylum System also suggests that resettlement is conceived as complementary to territorial asylum.

Art. 78 para 1 TFEU provides that the 'common policy on asylum, subsidiary protection and temporary protection [...] must be in accordance with the Geneva Convention of 28 July 1951 and the Protocol of 31 January 1967 relating to the status of refugees,[206] and other relevant treaties.' Art. 18 ChFR provides that 'the right to asylum shall be guaranteed with due respect for the rules of the Geneva Convention and in accordance with the Treaty on European Union and the Treaty on the Functioning of the European Union.' It follows therefrom that 'international refugee law in a broad sense' – ie, the Geneva Convention and the relevant human rights

206 1951 Convention and 1967 Protocol Relating to the Status of Refugees [in the following: *Geneva Convention*].

treaties, at least insofar as they are relevant to protection[207] – can be understood as 'international supplementary constitution' of the Common European Asylum System.[208] Therefore, in the following, it will be examined whether international refugee law says anything on the function of resettlement, as this would be of relevance to the definition of the objective of resettlement under the constitutional framework of the Common European Asylum System.

The absence of an international binding framework on resettlement cannot lead to the premature conclusion that international refugee law would be irrelevant to resettlement. Quite to the contrary, it is indeed the cardinal principle of international refugee law, namely the *non-refoulement* principle,[209] which provides guidance on the function of resettlement in relation to territorial asylum. The *non-refoulement* principle requires States to examine an application for protection, which is lodged on the State's territory, at its borders, or anywhere within its jurisdiction.[210] Even though

---

207 In the international law context, protection ensuing from human rights obligations is usually referred to as 'complementary protection', see GS Goodwin-Gil and J McAdam (n 25) 285 ff. The argument can be made that refugee rights should be understood as human rights, see V Chetail: 'Are Refugee Rights Human Rights? An Unorthodox Questioning of the Relations between Refugee Law and Human Rights law' in R Rubio-Marín (ed) *Human Rights and Immigration* (Oxford University Press, 2014) 19 ff. However, at least in the context of the Common European Asylum System, in favour of understanding protection-relevant human rights as refugee rights, see n 196 and more generally: R Alleweldt, 'Preamble to the 1951 Convention' in A Zimmermann (ed) *The 1951 Convention Relating to the Status of Refugees and its 1967 Procotol. A Commentary* (Oxford University Press, 2011) 232.

208 J Bast (n 196) 42: 'völkerrechtliche Nebenverfassung'; R Uerpmann-Witzack, 'The Constitutional Role of International Law' in A von Bogdandy and J Bast (n 24) 177, 178 ff, 210 who for the notion of 'Nebenverfassung' ('supplementary constitution') refers to C Tomuschat, 'Der Verfassungsstaat im Geflecht der internationalen Beziehungen' in *Der Verfassungsstaat im Geflecht der internationalen Beziehungen. Gemeinden und Kreise vor den öffentlichen Aufgaben der Gegenwart. Berichte und Diskussionen auf der Tagung der Vereinigung der Deutschen Staatsrechtslehrer in Basel vom 5. bis 8. Oktober 1977*, 36 (1978) 5, 71 ff.

209 As enshrined in Art 33 para 1 Geneva Convention, on the one hand, and as derived from Art 3 ECHR in particular, on the other hand. The latter follows from the jurisprudence of the ECtHR and has been explicitly codified in Art 19 para 2 ChFR. See W Kälin, M Caroni and L Heim 'Article 33, para 1' in A Zimmermann (n 207) 1334; GS Goodwin-Gil and J McAdam (n 25); UNHCR ExCom, Conclusion No. 65 (1991), (c).

210 This is of course a very simplified explanation of the non-refoulement principle. In detail see: W Kälin, M Caroni and L Heim 'Article 33, para 1' in A Zimmermann (n 207).

only to a very limited extent, the *non-refoulement* principle thus attenuates the 'paradox' of international refugee law, namely that, due to the absence of a general right to enter under international law,[211] a person is required to irregularly cross a border in order to have access to protection.[212]

Indeed, resettlement goes much further in attenuating this paradox, as it provides a legal pathway to protection. At first glance, this seems to favour the argument that 'there should be a preference for resettlement'. However, while the observation that resettlement attenuates the paradox certainly entails that international refugee law is generally in favour of the existence of resettlement as such, no conclusion can be drawn from this observation with regard to the relation between resettlement and territorial asylum. The observation supports neither the 'wait-in-the-line-argument' nor the 'see-saw hypothesis'. This is because those claims would presuppose another argumentative element – namely either that the overall number of persons a country should 'legitimately' accept is stable, or that seeking territorial asylum is 'illegitimate', regardless of whether the option of resettlement is legally and realistically available for the concerned person. As already shown above, neither of these arguments persists. The only scenario in which the argument that 'there should be a preference for resettlement' might entail the 'replacement argument' is a hypothetical scenario in which global resettlement needs would be met by global resettlement capacity – which is, however, far from becoming a reality any time soon.[213]

As resettlement needs actually by far exceed the global resettlement capacity, international refugee law rather suggests that the function of resettlement is to *complement* territorial asylum. The reason is that the understanding of resettlement as eventually 'replacing' asylum in its consequence amounts to an argument aiming to abolish territorial asylum procedures.[214] Abolishing territorial asylum procedures is, however, in contradiction to international refugee law because completely preventing sponta-

211 See, however, on the right to entry under specific circumstances: G Noll (n 199).

212 *cf* P Endres di Oliveira (n 199) 171 ff.

213 In other words: The argument of complementarity of resettlement is convincing as long as resettlement capacity does not meet resettlement needs. Otherwise, the objective of the Geneva Convention, namely, to remedy the situation of refugeehood, would be achieved without the de facto need for territorial asylum procedures. However, as this is far from becoming reality, the above argument persists.

214 Giving preference to resettlement while at the same time reducing territorial asylum proportionally amounts to aiming at reducing territorial asylum to zero. As exemplified by the Australian example, this is actually the practical consequence of the 'replacement approach', *cf* n 106.

neous arrival is not possible without violating the *non-refoulement* principle. Even assuming that prevention of border-crossing could be entirely outsourced to other States,[215] a complete prevention of irregular border-crossing would not be feasible without violating the *non-refoulement* principle.[216] And even if assuming that a complete prevention of spontaneous arrivals was possible without violating the *non-refoulement* principle, one would come to the same conclusion because the 'replacement argument' would then amount to voiding international refugee law of its scope of application.[217] Ascribing a 'replacement function' to resettlement – which in its consequence either aims at abolishing the very foundation of international refugee law or at entirely depriving it of its relevance – can therefore not be reconciled with international refugee law.[218] Accordingly, the incorporation of the international refugee law as 'international supplemen-

215 This would probably neither politically nor practically be feasible in the context of the EU anyways.

216 The Australian example confirms this from an empirical perspective. From a legal perspective: See on the one hand concerning outsourcing processing: G Goodwin-Gil, 'The extraterritorial Processing of Claims to Asylum or Protection: The Legal Responsibilities of States and International Organisations' (2016) 9 *UTS Law Review* 26; see on the other hand concerning outsourcing entry-prevention: N Markard, 'The Right to Leave by Sea: Legal Limits on EU Migration Control by Third Countries' (2016) 27 *The European Journal of International Law* 591. See further: V Moreno-Lax and M Guiffré, 'The Rise of Consensual Containment: From 'Contactless Control' to 'Contactless Responsibility' for Forced Migration Flows' (2017), available online: https://papers.ssrn.com/sol3/papers.cfm?abstract_id=3009331.

217 Already because irregular arrival is a precondition for applying for refugee status under the Geneva Convention.

218 Further, and more specifically, M Savino (n 13) 92 comes to conclusion that Art 31 para 1 Geneva Convention prohibits 'punitive clauses' such as the ones provided for in the emerging EU resettlement law. As the essential purpose of Art 31 para 1 Geneva Convention is to, at a minimalist level, 'remedy' the 'paradox' created by the international refugee law itself, the notion of 'penalty' cannot be confined to 'punishment' or even 'criminal sanctions', but must be interpreted as encompassing even mere procedural disadvantages in a territorial asylum procedure, see J Hathaway, *The Rights of Refugees under International Law* (Cambridge University Press, 2005) 408 ff; however in favour of a more narrow interpretation: G Noll, 'Article 31' A Zimmermann (n 207) 1246 ff. Following the former argument: A fortiori, a denial of legal access to protection due to a prior attempt to irregularly enter the destination country could constitute a violation of Art 31 para 1 Geneva Convention. Nevertheless, two further questions arise: First, whether Art 31 para 1 Geneva Convention is extraterritorially applicable, see on this question R Bank, 'General Provisions. Introduction to Article 11. Refugees at Sea' in A Zimmermann (n 207) 833; and second, whether Art 31

tary constitution' of the Common European Asylum System speaks in favour of the conceptualisation of resettlement as complementary to territorial asylum procedures.

Third, the constitutional framework more generally conceptualises the internal and the external dimensions as complementary parts of the Common European Asylum System, which confirms that resettlement should be understood as complementary to territorial asylum.

As has been argued, Art. 78 para 2 TFEU remains silent on the geographical scope and, hence, covers both the internal and the external dimensions. Yet, the constitutional framework of the Common European Asylum System assumes the existence of its internal dimension as a precondition for the existence of its external dimension. This follows from the existence of Art. 78 para 2 lit. f TFEU defining standards concerning the reception conditions for applicants for international protection, and Art. 78 para 3 TFEU regulating the possible event of Member States being confronted by an 'emergency situation characterised by a sudden inflow of nationals of third countries'. Both provisions would be irrelevant if the Common European Asylum System were limited to its external dimension, which demonstrates that the drafters of the Treaties assumed the existence of the territorial dimension as a precondition for the – optional – existence of the external dimension.[219] This view is indeed confirmed by EU secondary asylum law, which almost exclusively concerns the internal dimension in line with the traditional 'legal access gap'.

To conclude, the constitutional framework of the Common European Asylum System conceives the emerging EU resettlement law as complementary to territorial asylum procedures.

3.4. *Objective III: Sharing international responsibility*

Finally, the function of resettlement with regard to the allocation of responsibility on the international level must be assessed from an EU constitutional perspective. In order to answer whether the constitutional framework conceives resettlement as a tool for ensuring fair sharing of international responsibility or for externalising such responsibility, it is again use-

---

para 1 Geneva Convention applies in such a situation despite its wording requiring that the person must have 'directly entered'. Addressing these questions would go beyond the scope of this article.

219 In a similar vein, see B Kowalczyk (n 21) 147; K Hailbronner and D Thym (n 158) 1039 ff with further references.

ful to analyse the consequences of incorporating international refugee law into the Common European Asylum System.

First, the 'international supplementary constitution' of the Common European Asylum System entails that resettlement serves the objective of ensuring fair sharing of international responsibility.

Even though the Geneva Convention law does not regulate resettlement, it implicitly confirms its existence and defines its purpose as the fair sharing of international responsibility. The Final Act of the Geneva Convention specifically recommends that 'governments continue to receive refugees in their territory and that they act in concert in a true spirit of international cooperation in order that these refugees may find asylum and the possibility of resettlement'.[220] The principle of fair responsibility sharing is indeed accepted more generally,[221] as reflected inter alia in the preamble of the Geneva Convention, which provides that 'the grant of asylum may place unduly heavy burdens on certain countries, and that a satisfactory solution of a problem of which the United Nations has recognised the international scope and nature cannot therefore be achieved without international co-operation'.[222]

Second, the 'international supplementary constitution' also leads to a 'strengthening of the normative quality' of the international policy framework, which in turn stresses the function of resettlement as ensuring responsibility sharing.[223]

The Court of Justice has consistently found that, since EU asylum law must comply with international refugee law, 'documents from the [...] UNHCR are particularly relevant in the light of the role conferred on the UNHCR by the Geneva Convention'.[224] Even though the Court has made this statement with regard to the interpretation of secondary law, the same reasoning applies with regard to the enactment of secondary law. This becomes clear from the argument of the Court itself: The reason for the particular relevance of UNHCR guidelines is derived from the function of the

---

220 Final act of the United Nations Conference of Plenipotentiaries on the Status of Refugees and Stateless Persons (1951), III.D. [emphasis added].

221 R Alleweldt, 'Preamble to the 1951 Convention' A Zimmermann (n 207) 236 ff. See further: D Schmalz, 'The principle of responsibility-sharing in refugee protection. An emerging norm of customary international law' (2019) *Völkerrechtsblog* 6 March 2019.

222 Preamble of the Geneva Convention, recital 4, 5.

223 For the definition of the 'international policy framework' see n 22.

224 European Court of Justice, judgement of 23 May 2019, C-720/18, Mohammed Bilali v Bundesamt für Fremdenwesen und Asyl, para 57 ff. with reference in particular to its judgment of 30 May 2013, C-528/11, Halaf, para 44.

Common European Asylum System as implementing the Geneva Convention.[225] If the requirement of compliance even establishes the necessity of respecting UNHCR guidelines when interpreting secondary law, this must a fortiori hold true when enacting secondary law. In other words, the EU legislator must conceive the objective of resettlement in compliance with the international policy framework.

And the international policy framework clearly states that the function of resettlement is international responsibility sharing. The purpose of resettlement policy is traditionally considered to be threefold: providing protection to refugees, offering a durable solution to refugeehood, and sharing responsibility with host countries.[226] Since 2003, UNHCR has been promoting the 'strategic use' of resettlement, and has further refined this notion since 2009.[227] Even though it seems that the notion of 'strategic use' is prone to being invoked by States as a justification for the use of resettlement in order to externalise responsibility,[228] the international policy framework indeed clearly defines that the notion of 'strategic use' cannot be interpreted in such a manner. According to UNHCR, the strategic use of resettlement means 'the planned use of resettlement in a manner that maximises its benefits, directly or indirectly, other than those received by the refugee being resettled. Those benefits may accrue to other refugees, the hosting State, other States or the international protection regime in general.'[229] UNHCR further underlines that these benefits must consist of

---

225 European Court of Justice, judgement of 23 May 2019, C-720/18, Bilali (n 224), para 53 ff.

226 J van Selm (n 7) 41; UNHCR Resettlement Handbook (n 22) 36 ff. In order to de-politicise resettlement in the aftermath of the Cold War, UNHCR had emphasised its function as protection tool, see UNHCR ExCOM, Conclusion No. 67 (XLII): 'Resettlement as an Instrument of Protection', UN Doc. 12A, A/46/12/Add.1 (1991).

227 The introduction of the notion was an attempt to maintain resettlement at least at a lower level in the context of post-9/11 politics in the US and another 'refugee crisis' in Europe at the beginning of the twenty-first century, see J van Selm, 'Strategic Use of Resettlement. Enhancing Solutions for Greater Protection?' in A Garnier, LL Jubilut and KB Sandvik (n 6) 31 ff.

228 J van Selm (n 227) 31, 38.

229 UNHCR, Working Group on Resettlement, Discussion Paper on the Strategic Use of Resettlement, 3 June 2003, WGR/03/04.Rev 3, available online: https://www.refworld.org/docid/41597a824.html; UNHCR, Working Group on Resettlement, Discussion Paper on the Strategic Use of Resettlement, Geneva, 14 October 2009, available online: https://www.refworld.org/docid/4b8cdcee2.html; UNHCR, Position Paper on the Strategic Use of Resettlement, Annual Tripartite Consultations on Resettlement, Geneva, 4 June 2010 (n 124).

'protection dividends to the rest of the refugee community (for example, through improved access to asylum)'.[230] The notion of 'strategic use' can therefore not be understood as supporting the 'externalisation approach' to resettlement. This is confirmed by the 2018 Global Compact on Refugees, which endorses the 'strategic use' and, at the same time, unequivocally puts an emphasis on the function of resettlement as a tool for international responsibility sharing.[231]

To conclude, the constitutional framework of the Common European Asylum System conceives the objective of the emerging EU resettlement law as ensuring the fair sharing of international responsibility for refugee protection.

Conclusion

EU resettlement law is slowly emerging as a new component of the Common European Asylum System (1). The objective of resettlement is subject to controversial debates. The emerging EU resettlement law recently seems to increasingly reflect the view that resettlement could, in the long term, eventually replace territorial asylum procedures, and that it may be used for the purpose of externalising responsibility for protection to Member States. Such an understanding is, in particular, reflected in resettlement as implemented under the EU-Turkey Statement in an ad hoc manner, and laid down in the form of a model codification in the Union Framework Proposal. However, such a conceptualisation of the objective of resettlement would contradict the international policy framework. The Union Framework Proposal has accordingly been met with fierce criticism (2). The analysis of the objective of the emerging EU resettlement law from an EU constitutional perspective confirms the validity of this criticism.

The emerging EU resettlement law forms part of the Common European Asylum System and is hence subject to its constitutional framework. The rationale of resettlement is thus governed by EU asylum law (3.1), and not by the rationale of EU immigration policy, or even EU foreign policy. Accordingly, the principal objective of the emerging EU resettlement law is to provide international protection to third country nationals (3.2). The constitutional framework further conceives resettlement as complementary to territorial asylum procedures (3.3) and as an instrument ensuring

230 UNHCR (n 18) p 2.
231 2018 Global Compact (n 9) para 90 ff.

fair sharing of international responsibility for refugee protection (3.4). The emerging EU resettlement law should hence be realigned entirely to its constitutional objective.

While the future of the Commission's Union Framework Proposal of 2016 is uncertain, it seems quite likely that the development of the emerging EU resettlement law towards harmonised rules and increasing EU administrative support will continue. In any case, resettlement seems to be in the political focus of the legal access debate on EU level, as shown not least by the regularly recurring proposals to establish extraterritorial processing centres from which resettlement ought to occur.[232] The very objective of resettlement should hence be discussed.

The constitutional framework leaves broad leeway to the EU legislator in designing resettlement schemes. At the same time, however, constitutional law draws a few clear limits. Certainly, an 'Australian version' of resettlement policy would not be compatible with EU constitutional law. Resettlement as an emerging component of the Common European Asylum System is rather to be conceived as an instrument allowing for legal access to international protection in the EU, thereby complementing traditional pathways. At the same time, the emerging EU resettlement law is an opportunity for the EU to assume its share of the international responsibility for refugee protection by providing an appropriate status to those in need of international protection.[233] The emerging EU resettlement law, if entirely realigned with its constitutional framework, thus offers great potential for enhancing refugee protection in the EU.

---

232 See the European Council's Proposal of June 2018 to establish 'Regional Disembarkation Platforms' (n 63).

233 According to UNHCR, 'Figures at a Glance', available online: https://www.unhcr.org/figures-at-a-glance.html (as of Sept 2019), UNHCR, 'Global Trends. Forced Displacement in 2018', available online: https://www.unhcr.org/globaltrends2018/, and UN DESA, 'International Migrant Stock 2019: Wall Chart' (Sept 2019), https://reliefweb.int/organization/un-desa (as of Sept 2019): Out of the approx.70.8 million forcibly displaced people worldwide, approx. 25.9 million are refugees. EU member states together host approx. 3.6 million refugees. Turkey hosts the largest number of refugees worldwide with approx. 3.7 million refugees. While states have recognised with the 2018 Global Compact that 'there is an urgent need for more equitable sharing of the burden and responsibility for hosting and supporting the world's refugees, while taking account of existing contributions and the differing capacities and resources among States', the question what this means and how to operationalise this aspiration requires further discussion.

Chapter 10: EU Initiatives on a European Humanitarian Visa

Eugenia Relaño Pastor[1]

Contents

1. *Introduction*

The last few years have witnessed loss of lives on an unprecedented scale in the Mediterranean and Aegean Seas.[2] The scale of the tragedy has exposed a number of inherent pitfalls in EU's migration and asylum policy and it

---

1 Senior Research Fellow in the Department of Law & Anthropology of the Max Planck Institute for Social Anthropology. The author gratefully acknowledges the assistance of Mr Alvaro Garcia Navarro from the team of the Rapporteur Juan Fernando López Aguilar in providing information that has been used in this chapter. The European Parliament own-initiative report on Humanitarian Visas, authored by Rapporteur Juan Fernando López Aguilar (S&D, Spain), has been used in preparation of this text.

2 3,771 dying in 2015, 5,096 in 2016, 3,139 in 2017 and 2,217 in 2018, see:<https://data2.unhcr.org/en/situations/mediterranean> (accessed 20 March 2019).

has put pressure on the EU asylum system to design legal avenues of entry into the EU for those seeking international protection. In addition to EU resettlement procedures that are applicable to vulnerable refugees, this has not resulted in the introduction of any new procedures in EU law, either in the visa *acquis* or in the borders or asylum *acquis*, to facilitate admission of persons seeking protection in Member States' territory. It has been estimated that 90 % of the persons, subsequently being recognised as refugees or beneficiaries of subsidiary protection, had reached the territory of the Member States irregularly, quite often via life-threatening routes.[3]

The high cost of human lives in the so-called migration crisis of 2015 and the lack of harmonised EU legal framework triggered the European Parliament (EP) to issue an urgent call for the provision of humanitarian visas. In its 2016 *Resolution on the Situation in the Mediterranean and the Need for a Holistic EU Approach to Migration*,[4] the Parliament declared that persons seeking international protection would be allowed to apply for a European humanitarian visa directly at any consulate or embassy of a Member State and that, once granted, such a European humanitarian visa would allow its holder to enter the territory of the Member State which had issued the visa for the sole purpose of lodging an application for international protection in that country.

By a resolution of 11 December 2018,[5] the European Parliament requested that the European Commission (EC) tables, by 31 March 2019, a legislative proposal establishing a European Humanitarian Visa, giving refugees access to the European territory, in effect to the Member State issuing the visa, for the sole purpose of submitting an application for international protection.[6] The European Parliament considered that the legislative act should be adopted in the form of a regulation entitled 'Regulation of the European Parliament and of the Council establishing a Euro-

3 C Hein and M de Donato, *Exploring avenues for protected entry in Europe* (Milan, Italian Council for Refugees, 2012) at 17.

4 EP Res of 12 April 2016 on the situation in the Mediterranean and the need for a holistic EU approach to migration, 2015/2095(INI).

5 EP Res of 11 December 2018 with recommendations to the Commission on Humanitarian Visas, 2018/2271(INL).

6 The legislative initiative report was backed by 429 MEPs, 194 voted against and 41 abstained. See: EP News, *Humanitarian visas to avoid deaths and improve management of refugee flows* (Press Release, 11 December 2019) <http://www.europarl.europa.eu/news/en/press-room/20181205IPR20933/humanitarian-visas-to-avoid-deaths-and-improve-management-of-refugee-flows> (accessed 25 November 2019).

pean Humanitarian Visa'.[7] In March 2019, the Commission's response to the requests of the action taken, or intended to be taken, did not directly tackle a possible legislative proposal on European Humanitarian Visa. According to the EC, its recommendation to Member States about developing enhanced legal pathways for persons in need of international protection of September 2017 has led to the implementation of more than 24,700 resettlement places. Therefore, the focus should be on the regulation establishing a Union Resettlement Framework,[8] particularly as it has the potential of achieving the objective pursued by the Parliament's initiative for a European Humanitarian Visa to increase the overall number of persons in need of international protection admitted by the Member States. The Commission insisted on the unfeasibility of creating a subjective right to request admission and to be admitted or an obligation of the Member States to admit a person in need of international protection.[9]

---

7 The legal basis is Art 77(2)(a) of the Treaty on the Functioning of the European Union (TFEU): '1. The Union shall develop a policy with a view to: (a) ensuring the absence of any controls on persons, whatever their nationality, when crossing internal borders (…)'.

8 According to the UNHCR, resettlement is an international protection tool designed for refugees who cannot return to their countries, even if they have sought protection in another State, where their integration or their safety is at risk. These people can be transferred to another State that has voluntarily agreed to the resettlement programme and has a specified number of available spots. The EU has put considerable efforts into developing a common approach to resettlement with the UNHCR. The EU Resettlement Programme laid down the Union's priorities covering the period from 2009 to 2013, priorities that were revised in 2012. A new funding instrument adopted in 2014, the Asylum, Migration and Integration Fund (Regulation (EU) 516/2014), provides special incentives to resettlement programmes. Later, the Commission submitted a proposal for a Union Resettlement Framework on 13 July 2016. The proposal would complement the current ad hoc multilateral and national resettlement programmes by providing common EU rules on the admission of third-country nationals, procedures of the resettlement process, types of status to be accorded by the Member States, decision-making procedures for the implementation of the framework and the financial support for the Member States' resettlement efforts. On 27 September 2017 the Commission adopted a Recommendation to ensure that resettlement efforts can continue until the operationalisation of the Union Resettlement Framework. According to the Recommendation, Member States should offer at least 50,000 resettlement places to admit by 31 October 2019 to persons in need of international protection from third countries.

9 European Commission, Follow up to the European Parliament non-legislative resolution with recommendations to the Commission on Humanitarian Visas, 2018/2271 (INL) / A8-0423/2018 / P8_TA-PROV(2018)0494.

Furthermore, the EC's statement of March 2019 postpones any further consideration on possible legal pathways to harmonise the Member States' discretionary procedures of humanitarian admissions, as well as to provide effective protection to those asylum seekers who do not fall under the general criteria enshrined in Article 6 Schengen Borders Code (SBC) nor its exceptions. Additionally, it states that in the future, and under the framework of the Union Resettlement Framework, the Commission will evaluate whether additional measures would be needed for admission to the territory of the Member States for persons in need of international protection.[10]

Consequently, resettlements will continue to be the only legal route to international protection in the EU, even if they do not provide primary access to a durable solution, instead helping only those declared refugees. What happened to the Commission's favourable attitude in 2002 towards EU measures on humanitarian visas?[11] Why did the Commission in 2013[12] take a holistic approach to maritime crossings and deaths at sea by exploring new legal channels for safe access to the European Union even as it opposed, later in 2016, the amendments to the Visa Code on humanitarian visas?[13] Which options were on the negotiation table for EU legislation on humanitarian visas? What was the role of the LIBE Committee (Committee on Civil Liberties, Justice and Home Affairs), the European Parliament and the EC in addressing the legal gap in EU law? This chapter aims to provide some clarifications on these questions and shed some light on the twists and turns the responses of the EU institutions have taken on the question of forging safe and legal pathways to access the EU territory for persons seeking international protection.

---

10 Ibid.

11 G Noll, J Fagerlund and S Liebaut, *Study on the Feasibility of Processing Asylum Claims Outside the EU Against the Background of the Common European Asylum System and the Goal of a Common Asylum Procedure* (Danish Centre for Human Rights, Copenhagen, 2002).

12 COM (2013) 869 final, Communication from the Commission to the European Parliament and the Council on the Work of the Task Force Mediterranean. Other actions include security measures such as increased border surveillance, and additional support to the Member States facing higher migratory pressure at 2.

13 See the procedure 2014/0094(COD) on the recast of the Visa Code.

2. *The concept of humanitarian visas within the EU Legal framework*

2.1 *What do we mean by humanitarian visa?*

In 2002, the Danish Centre for Human Rights carried out a study on behalf of the European Commission on the feasibility of processing asylum claims outside the EU.[14] The study examined the practices and legal frameworks on the use of the so-called Protected Entry Procedure (PEP) in select EU Member States and in three non-European States.[15] The study found that there are legal obligations under European Convention on Human Rights (ECHR) that suggest that States

> find themselves obliged to allow access to their territories in exceptional situations. Where such access is denied, claimants may rely on the right to a remedy. These are further reasons supporting the conception and operation of formalized Protected Entry Procedures, which offer a framework for handling such exceptional claims. Protected Entry Procedures would be coherent with the *acquis* as it stands today. Nothing in the present *acquis* curtails the freedom of individual Member States to provide for a Protected Entry Procedure at a unilateral level. Furthermore, there is a Community competence for developing a joint normative framework.[16]

Therefore, humanitarian visas fall in the category of a PEP, which allows

> a non-national to approach the potential host state outside its territory with a claim for asylum or other form of international protection, and to be granted an entry permit in case of a positive response to that claim, be it preliminary or final.[17]

The aim could be that an asylum seeker directly approaches the diplomatic representation of the potential host state outside its territory in order to claim a humanitarian visa, and the eligibility assessment procedure may be conducted extraterritorially by the diplomatic representation of the potential host state. This would entail processing a humanitarian visa applica-

---

14 G. Noll et al. (n10).

15 The above-mentioned study relied on information provided in an earlier study on PEPs, see G. Noll and J Fagerlund, *Safe Avenues to Asylum? The Actual and Potential Role of EU Diplomatic Representations in Processing Asylum Requests* (Copenhagen, The Danish Centre for Human Rights and UNHCR, 2002).

16 G. Noll et al. (n 10) at 4.

17 Ibid. at 3.

tion in-country to identify the degree of protection needed before the third country national reaches the border of the Member State. Hence once a humanitarian visa is issued and the third country national enters the territory of the Member State, he/she may lodge an application for asylum or for any other kind of residence permit.[18] The goals of the humanitarian visas are to (1) provide safe and legal access to territory; (2) secure the physical transfer and legal protection of the bona fide third country national seeking asylum; (3) constitute a legal alternative to irregular migration channels and uncontrolled arrivals; and finally to (4) prevent exploitation, ill treatment, and abuses of victims of human smuggling.

For a long time, UNHCR,[19] IOM,[20] and the FRA[21] have been calling for an urgent response to resolve the issue of protecting persons in need of protection who could not be accommodated through any other available mechanism to enter the EU territory (such as family reunification programmes, work permit or study permit), and have not yet arrived on the territory of a Member State, at the border, or in the transit zone of a Member State.[22] As a result of a lack of EU legal response, protection seekers need to embark upon irregular, dangerous and undignified journeys at a very high risk. Prior to the humanitarian crisis in 2015, the Members States most affected by arrivals by boats were Greece, Italy, Malta and Spain.[23]

2.2. *Humanitarian visas and EU fundamental rights*

The CJEU concluded in *X and X*[24] that visas for asylum-seeking purposes do not fall under the scope of EU law as it stands.[25] The Court arrived at this conclusion when considering the

18 U I Jensen, *Humanitarian Visas: Option or Obligation?* (Brussels, European Parliament, Study for the LIBE Committee, 2014) at 2.

19 A Betts, *Towards a 'soft law' framework for the protection of vulnerable migrants'* (Geneva, UNHCR Research Paper No. 162, 2008).

20 IOM, *Irregular migration and mixed flows: IOM's approach*, MC/INF/297, 19 October (2009).

21 EU Agency for Fundamental Rights (FRA), *Handbook on European law relating to asylum, borders and immigration* (Vienna, 2013).

22 Ibid. at para 1.6.

23 Ibid. at 3 and 10.

24 Case C-638/16 PPU *X and X* [2017] EU:C:2017:173.

25 Ibid. at para 45: 'Since the situation at issue in the main proceedings is not, therefore, governed by EU law, the provisions of the Charter, in particular, Articles 4

purpose of [such] application – so as to reach the external borders of the Member States to subsequently lodge a separate claim for international protection – as 'the defining feature of the situation', thereby implying that, because that purpose differs from the key (policy) objective of the Code -which is 'that of [establishing the procedures and criteria for issuing a] short-term visa' – the situation becomes extraneous to the EU legal order.[26]

However, as it will be discussed later, and as the LIBE Committee pointed out in 2016, there is no legal or rational basis to exclude asylum seekers from the generic group of third country nationals who would qualify for a Schengen visa. There is even less reason to exclude them from the category of 'persons crossing or showing an intention to cross' the external borders of the Member States of the Union to whom admission criteria would apply.[27] This group of 'persons' is included in the Article 77(2) TFEU and is subject to checks when 'crossing external border'. In this situation, European fundamental rights become relevant since fundamental rights govern the internal dimension of EU policies and actions and the external relations with the wider world. Therefore, the Union should observe fundamental rights in everything that the EU or the Member States do 'when they are implementing Union law'.[28] Additionally, any policy made within the Area of Freedom Security and Justice (AFSJ) that is related to policies on border checks, asylum and immigration needs to respect human rights as a matter of EU primary law. The Treaty on the Functioning of the European Union (TFEU) requires the Union to adopt measures regarding asylum in accordance with the 1951 Refugee Convention Relating to the Status of Refugees, particularly, the Union 'shall develop a common policy on asylum ... ensuring compliance with the principle of *non-refoulement*... in accordance with the Geneva Convention...and other relevant treaties'.[29]

---

and 18 thereof, referred to in the questions of the referring court, do not apply to it (...)'.

26 Ibid. at para 47.

27 Art 1 and 2(10) of the Regulation (EU) 2016/399 of the European Parliament and of the Council of 9 March 2016 on a Union Code on the rules governing the movement of persons across borders (Schengen Borders Code) [2016] OJ L 77 and Art 1(2) of the Regulation No 810/2009 of the European Parliament and of the Council of 13 July 2009 establishing a Community Code on Visas (Visa Code) [2009] OJ L 243.

28 Art 51(1) EU Charter of Fundamental Rights (CFR).

29 Art 78 of the TFEU makes provision for the creation of a Common European Asylum system, which respects the obligations placed upon the States under the

The right to asylum and the principle of *non-refoulement* form part of the fundamental rights *acquis* and of the general principles of EU law. Following the Lisbon Treaty, which entered into effect on January 1, 2009, the EU Charter of Fundamental Rights went from being a simple 'declaration' to becoming a legally binding instrument. Article 18 of this Charter includes the right of asylum for the first time within the European scope, and Article 19 of the Charter prohibits returning persons to a State where they are at serious risk of being subjected to death penalty, torture or other inhuman or degrading treatment or punishments. Therefore, Article 4, which states that 'no one shall be subjected to torture or to inhuman or degrading treatment or punishment' is linked to Article 19 (2). Indeed, as the Charter Explanations clarified 'the right in Article 4 (CFR) is the right guaranteed by Article 3 of the ECHR', while Article 19(2) CFR 'incorporates the relevant case-law from the European Court of Human Rights regarding Article 3 of the ECHR'.[30] As the Strasbourg Court reiterated in *Hirsi*, 'protection against the treatment prohibited by Article 3 imposes on States the obligation not to remove any person who, in the receiving country, would run the real risk of being subjected to such treatment'.[31] But this is valid not just in cases of removal. If any action under EU law, such as entry rejection or a visa refusal, could expose refugees or asylum seekers from third countries to ill treatment, Article 3 ECHR and Articles 4 and 19(2) CFR may be infringed.[32] It is important to underscore that there is a 'real risk' of exposing the applicant to irreversible harm (through entry re-

---

Geneva Convention of 1951 and, for such purposes, the following shall be adopted (Art 78): a uniform asylum status for third country nationals valid throughout the entire Union; a uniform subsidiary protection status for third country nationals which, without being granted European asylum, are in need of European protection; a common system for the temporary protection of displaced persons in the case of mass influx; common procedures for granting or withdrawing the uniform asylum or subsidiary protection status; criteria and mechanisms for determining the Member State responsible for examining an application for asylum or subsidiary protection; standards related to the reception conditions of the applicants for asylum or subsidiary protection; the association and the cooperation with third countries for managing the flows of persons who are applying for asylum or subsidiary or temporary protection.

30 See the explanations relating to the Charter of Fundamental Rights [2007] OJ C 303.

31 *Hirsi Jamaa v Italy* (App No 27765/09) ECHR 23 February 2012 at para. 123.

32 See V Moreno-Lax, *The Added Value of EU Legislation on Humanitarian Visas. Legal Aspects* (European Added Value Assessment accompanying the European Parliament's legislative own-initiative own-report, Rapporteur Juan Fernando López Aguilar, PE 621.823, 2018) at 51.

fusal, via visa rejection, or other extraterritorial activity covered by EU law). As Moreno-Lax point outs by quoting AG Mengozzi: 'If the action/omission of the Member State concerned (via entry rejection, visa refusal or anything else) leads to a "real risk" of exposing the applicant to ill treatment, the option contemplated in Article 25 CCV should be understood to turn into an obligation, so as to avoid the risk from materializing'.[33]

3. *Current Regulatory Framework*

European Parliament has already stated that there is sufficient competence under the European Treaties to adopt the humanitarian visas legislation. The legislator could rely on Articles 77, 78 and/or 79 TFEU to this effect. The choice of the most appropriate legal basis must take into account the nature of the content and the aim pursued. Article 77(2)(b) TFEU[34] is one of the legal bases underpinning both the Schengen Borders Code (SBC) and the Community Code of Visas (CCCV) the objectives of which are, respectively, to lay down the 'rules governing border control of persons crossing [or showing "an intention to cross"] the external borders of the Member States of the Union',[35] and to establish 'the procedures and conditions for issuing visas…to any third-country national who must be in possession of (one) when crossing the external borders of the Member States pursuant to (the Visa List Regulation)',[36] which includes the nationals of all refugee-producing countries. As Moreno-Lax points out, Article 77 TFEU could be employed to elaborate on the 'special provisions concerning the right of asylum and to international protection' foreseen in Article 14 SBC, thus allowing for the adoption of uniform arrangements for the regulation of exceptions to the rules on refusal of entry (and pre-entry) contemplated by the Code.[37]

---

33 Ibid. at 52. Case C-638/16 PPU *X and X* [2017] EU:C:2017:93 Opinion of AG Mengozzi at paras 121, 129 and 131.

34 Art 77(1) TFEU: 'The Union shall develop a policy with a view to (…) 2. For the purposes of paragraph 1, the European Parliament and the Council, acting in accordance with the ordinary legislative procedure, shall adopt measures concerning: (b) the checks to which persons crossing external borders are subject'.

35 Art 2(10) SBC.

36 Art 1(1) and (2) CCV.

37 See V Moreno-Lax (n 31) at 55-56. Article 77(2) TFEU provides for measures concerning 'the common policy on visas' The regime constitutes an autonomous system, derogating from the general norms governing visas and border controls on persons, according to both the CJEU and the EU legislator and it eases frontier

The Schengen Borders Code establishes the rules for the control of persons 'without qualification crossing the external frontiers of the Member States of the European Union' and includes in Article 3 two special categories of persons: those enjoying the right of free movement under Union law and the rights of refugees and persons requesting international protection, in particular as regards *non-refoulement*'.[38] According to Article 6(5)(c) SBC now, by way of derogation from the general rule, 'third-country nationals who do not fulfil one or more of the (general entry) conditions… may be authorized by a Member State to enter its territory on humanitarian grounds, on grounds of national interest or because of international obligations…'. In a handbook designed for border guards, referred to as the 'Schengen Handbook', those international obligations were compiled by the Commission, in an effort to spell out the common guidelines, best practices and recommendations on border control. It is relevant to highlight the explicit link between the Schengen Code and the Common European Asylum System (CEAS) legislation in the Schengen Handbook:

> [A]ll applications for international protection…lodged at the border must be examined by Member States in order to assess, on the basis of the criteria laid down in Directive 2011/95/EU of 13 December 2011, whether the applicant qualifies either for refugee status…or for subsidiary protection status […|.[39]

Additionally, a second complementary choice could be the Article 78(2)(g) TFEU, which provides a specific grounding for asylum seekers and foresees that the Union legislator 'shall adopt' measures for a Common European Asylum System (CEAS), including those aimed at 'managing inflows of people applying for (international) protection'. This wording could easily accommodate the situation of asylum seekers attempting to reach the external borders of the Member States to exercise their rights under EU law. Indeed, if we combine Article 78(2)(g) TFEU with Article 14(1) SBC,

---

formalities for 'border residents' with 'legitimate reasons frequently to cross an external border', according to the Preamble of Regulation (EC) No 1931/2006 of 20 December 2006 laying down rules on local border traffic at the external land borders of the Member States and amending the provisions of the Schengen Convention (2006) OJ L 405/1.

38 See also Art 4 SBC.

39 Commission Recommendation establishing a common 'Practical Handbook for Border Guards (Schengen Handbook)' to be used by Member States' competent authorities when carrying out the border control of persons, C(2006), 5186 final, 9 November 2006. Reviewed C (2008) 2976; C(2009) 7376; C(2010) 5559; C(2011) 3918; C(2012) 9330; and C(2015) 3894.

which relates to decisions on the refusal of entry, a legal path for those in need of seeking asylum or international protection could emerge. When taking decisions on the refusal of entry into consideration, Article 14(1) requires that this 'shall be without prejudice to the application of special provisions concerning the right of asylum and to international protection'.[40] The problem is that, although any Member State should ensure that a person who has made an application for international protection has an effective opportunity to lodge it as soon as possible, they may also subordinate the exercise of this right to specific formalities, requiring that applications 'be lodged in person and/or at a designated place' to be valid.[41] Some examples of national practices, particularly from Spain, show that it is left to the domestic law to acknowledge whether there is an obligation under EU Law to provide access to asylum seekers attempting to reach the external border and whether there is a safe place to lodge the application.

For example, the Spanish Asylum Law, Law 12/2009 of 30 October,[42] does not allow applications for asylum to be lodged at diplomatic mission offices but leaves the possibility of facilitating the transfer of the applicant to Spain in the hands of the ambassador if he or she deems that the applicant is in physical danger. The Spanish Ombudsman has stated that denying access to asylum procedures in diplomatic mission offices may impinge upon Spain's international commitments.[43] Consequently, on 19 July

---

40 See the reports by the Fundamental Rights Agency of the EU (FRA): *Fundamental rights at land borders: findings from selected European Union border crossing points* (Vienna, 2014); FRA, Fundamental rights at airports: border checks at five international airports in the European Union (Vienna, 2014); and FRA, Fundamental rights at Europe's southern sea borders (Vienna, 2013) <http://fra.europa.eu/en/project/2011/treatment-third-country-nationals-eus-external-borders-surveying-border-checks-selected/publications> (accessed 25 November 2019).

41 Art 6(2) and (3) Directive 2013/32/EU of the European Parliament and of the Council of 26 June 2013 on common procedures for granting and withdrawing international protection [2013] OJ L180/60.

42 Law 12/2009 of 30 October 2009 governing the right to asylum and subsidiary protection, entered into effect on November 20, 2009. This Law was amended by Law 2/2014 of March 25th, which has added a paragraph to Article 40.1 for the purpose of fully incorporating Article 2(j) of Directive 2011/95/EU of the European Parliament and of the Council of 13 December 2011 on standards for the qualification of third-country nationals or stateless persons as beneficiaries of international protection, for a uniform status for refugees or for persons eligible for subsidiary protection, and for the content of the protection granted [2011] OJ L 337 .

43 See: Defensor del Pueblo, *Asylum in Spain. International Protection and Reception System Resources* (Madrid, June 2016) at 48.

2016, the Spanish Ombudsman issued a recommendation to the Ministry of the Interior to amend the Law 12/2009 of 30 October, in order to introduce the possibility of filing claims for international protection in the diplomatic missions abroad. If that were not possible, the Ombudsman urged the use of the category of humanitarian visa for allowing access to the potential asylum applicant to the country's territory in order to lodge the asylum application in Spain. As the recommendation is still pending, the Ombudsman has argued that it is imperative to regulate visas for humanitarian reasons, so as to allow applicants access to the Spanish territory and to the asylum application procedure in Spain.[44]

Additionally, since 2013, the Ombudsman Institution has warned about the situation of third country nationals in need of international protection but without access to the border control posts of the Autonomous Cities of Ceuta and Melilla.[45] The Ombudsman has always considered Spain's Government to be under the obligation of detecting existing obstacles that prevent persons in need of protection from being able to access the border control posts without putting their lives in jeopardy. Due the Ombudsman's intervention, the Ministry of the Interior, in 2014 and 2015, set up facilities at the border control posts in both Autonomous Communities where applications for international protection were subsequently lodged.[46] Furthermore, many complaints were received by the Spanish

---

44 The Spanish Ombudsman has received complaints revealing this need, which have given rise to the respective interventions. Measures were under way for the granting of visas to Afghani interpreters who had been employed by Spain's Ministry for Defense and who were in an at-risk situation in their country on their contract ending. In the end, the Spanish Embassy in Kabul (Afghanistan) finally granted the visas. In another case, the Spanish Embassy in Ankara (Turkey) did not support a visa being issued for humanitarian reasons for a Syrian minor who had suffered burns on a major portion of his body so that he could come to Spain to officially lodge his application for asylum, even if his immediate family members were in Spain. The suggestion that was taken was for a transfer to Spain of a person who urgently needed to undergo surgery. See: Ibid. and Defensor del Pueblo, Resoluciones 16007048 of 31 May 2016 <https://www.defensordelpueblo.es/resoluciones/impartir-instrucciones-urgentes-para-el-traslado-por-razones-humanitarias-a-espana-de-un-solicitante-de-asilo-enfermo-que-se-encuentra-en-grecia-y-pueda-recibir-el-tratamiento-medico-que-necesita/> (accessed 4 December 2019).

45 See: Defensor del Pueblo, Informe Anual 2014 <https://www.defensordelpueblo.es/informe-anual/informe-anual-2014/> (accessed 25 November 2019).

46 It was found that the persons who were arriving at the border control post experienced a high degree of anxiety as a result of the hardships they had experienced along the way to the border control post. On the one hand, a majority of these

Ombudsman and measures were set into motion with the Administration to verify if Spain's Law Enforcement Forces and Bodies directly at the borders in the cities of Ceuta and Melilla or possibly having intercepted aliens at sea had turned these persons over to the Moroccan police and thereby ignored the possibility that they may be persons in need of international protection.[47]

4. *For a comprehensive approach to humanitarian visas: EU Parliament vs. European Commission and Council*

4.1 *From the Treaty of Amsterdam to the Stockholm Programme*

The 1997 Protocol to the Treaty of Amsterdam incorporated the *Schengen acquis* into the EU framework in 1999. The common list of non-EU countries whose nationals were subject to a visa requirement was a further development of the *Schengen acquis* and was enshrined in Council Regulation (EC) No. 539/2001 of 15 March 2001, listing the third countries whose nationals must be in possession of visas before crossing the external borders and those whose nationals are exempt from that requirement (Visa List Regulation). All the procedures and conditions for issuing Schengen visas were established in the 2010 Visa Code for short stays in and transit through the territories of Member States. Simultaneously, in 1999, the European Council Meeting in Tampere determined the need to create a common asylum system in order to achieve a regime for determining which EU State would be responsible for examining an application for protection, a uniform asylum status, a common procedure for granting or withdrawing the same, and a common temporary protection system.

As mentioned earlier, in 2002, the European Commission asked the Danish Centre for Human Rights to carry out a study on the feasibility of processing asylum claims outside the EU against the backdrop of the common European asylum system and the goal of a common asylum procedure. The Commission agreed to carefully examine the suggestions con-

---

persons were in need of medical care, which the National Police Force officers were not able to identify and make the pertinent referral correctly, and, on the other, unaccompanied minors were usually not taken into account. For an exhaustive analysis, see the annual reports of the Spanish Ombudsman: <https://www.defensordelpueblo.es/en/publications/summaries-of-annual-reports/> (accessed 25 November 2019).

47 Defensor del Pueblo (n 42) at 54.

tained in the study, given the diverse and inconsistent practices in the Member States and argued that since there was a strong need for harmonisation in this area, serious thought should be given

> to the question of access to the territories of Member States for persons in need of international protection and compatibility between stronger protection for these people and respect for the principle of *non-refoulement* on the one hand and measures to combat illegal immigration, trafficking in human beings and external border control measures on the other.[48]

In June 2003, the Commission identified the need of a policy for an orderly and managed arrival of persons in need of international protection in the EU, and it proposed exploring the viability of setting up an EU Regional Task Force to undertake certain functions, such as resettlement and Protected Entry Procedures (PEPs), and gradual harmonisation through a Directive based on best practices.[49] The Commission asked the European Parliament and the European Council to endorse specific elements identified in the Communication, such as managed arrival in the EU, and a legislative instrument on PEPs. At the Thessaloniki European Council held in 2003, the European Council took note of the Commission Communication and invited the Commission to '... explore all parameters in order to ensure more orderly and managed entry in the EU of persons in need of international protection ...'.[50]

Under the EU Italian Presidency, in 2003, at the seminar held in Rome entitled 'Towards more orderly and managed entry in the EU of persons in need of international protection', Member States' representatives discussed the findings of the Danish study. During this seminar, it became clear that with regard to the potential of Protected Entry Procedures (PEPs), 'there is not the same level of common perspective and confidence among Member

48 COM(2003) 152 final, Communication from the Commission to the Council and the European Parliament on the common asylum policy and the Agenda for protection (Second Commission report on the implementation of Communication COM(2000) 755 final of 22 November 2000) at 16.

49 COM(2003) 315 final, Communication from the Commission to the Council and the European Parliament: Towards more accessible, equitable and managed asylum systems at paras. 6.1.2.3, 14 and 16.

50 Presidency Conclusions of the Thessaloniki European Council 19-20 June 2003, Conclusion 26.

States as exists vis-à-vis resettlement'.[51] By contrast, the European Parliament welcomed the concept of PEPs. Due to the lack of common perspective and confidence among Member States with regard to PEPs, the Commission dropped the idea of suggesting a PEP mechanism for the EU, and instead proposed the introduction of EU Resettlement Schemes and EU Regional Protection Programmes.[52]

The Commission did not mention PEPs again until June 2008, when it again reiterated the need of a comprehensive and balanced migration policy to 'ensure access for those in need of protection and ... ensure coherence with other policies that have an impact on international protection, notably: border control, the fight against illegal immigration and return policies'.[53] Based on this consideration, the Commission announced that it would examine a flexible use of the visa regime based on protection considerations, and stated that common action in this area would be needed in order to assure protection and reduce smuggling.[54]

On 15 and 16 October 2008, the Council of the European Union agreed on the European Pact on Migration[55], and the Council made the commitment not only to make border controls more effective but also to strengthen European borders without blocking access to protection systems to those entitled beneficiaries. One year later, prior to the adoption of the *Stockholm Programme*, the Commission issued another Communication in

---

51 COM(2004) 410 final, Communication from the Commission to the Council and the European Parliament on the managed entry in the EU of persons in need of international protection and the enhancement of the protection capacity of the regions of origin: 'Improving access to durable solutions' at para 35.

52 Ibid. at paras 56, 57 and 59.

53 COM(2008) 360 final, Communication from the Commission to the European Parliament, the Council, the European Economic and Social Committee and the Committee of Regions: Policy Plan on Asylum - an integrated approach to protection across the EU at paras 2-4.

54 Ibid. at para 5.2.3.

55 Council of the European Union, 'European Pact on Immigration and Asylum', No 13440/08, ASIM 72, Brussels, 24.09.2008. The Pact is based on five main pillars, which I quote: '(1) to organize legal immigration to take account of the priorities, needs and reception capacities determined by each Member State, and to encourage integration; (2) to control illegal immigration by ensuring that illegal immigrants return to their countries of origin or to a country of transit; (3) to make border controls more effective; (4) to construct a Europe of asylum; and (5) to create a comprehensive partnership with the countries of origin and of transit in order to encourage synergy between migration and development'. See S Bertozzi, *European Pact on Migration and Asylum: a stepping stone towards common European migration policies* (Barcelona, CIDOB, Opinion Migraciones, 2008).

June 2009,[56] emphasising the need to balance security measures with human rights and international protection considerations. For the first time the Commission explicitly referred to humanitarian visas, specifically to the need to establish procedures for PEPs and to issue humanitarian visas:

> In this context new forms of responsibility for protection might be considered. Procedures for protected entry and the issuing of humanitarian visas should be facilitated, including calling on the aid of diplomatic representations or any other structure set up within the framework of a global mobility management strategy.[57]

However, when the European Council adopted the *Stockholm Programme* in December 2009, the Council ignored the convenience of working on humanitarian visas and invited the Commission

> to explore, in that context and where appropriate, new approaches concerning access to asylum procedures targeting main countries of transit, such as protection programmes for particular groups or certain procedures for examination of applications for asylum, in which Member States could participate on a voluntary basis.[58]

4.2. From the Stockholm Programme to the migration crisis

The Action Plan for *Stockholm Programme* provided a roadmap for the implementation of political priorities set out for the Area of justice, freedom and security between 2010 and 2014. The Commission committed itself to take actions to further develop the integrated approach to managing EU's external borders. These include legislative proposals to modify Frontex, the Schengen Borders Code. The Commission also proposed setting up an Entry Exit System (EES) and continuing with visa liberalisation by negotiating Visa Facilitation Agreements with non-EU countries, as well as establishing a common area of protection for asylum seekers through responsibility-sharing among EU countries. The action plan also provides for a strengthened external dimension through cooperation with the United Na-

---

56 COM(2009) 262 final, Communication from the Commission to the European Parliament and the Council: An area of freedom, security and justice serving the citizen.

57 Ibid at para. 5.2.3.

58 *The Stockholm Programme. An Open and Secure Europe serving and protecting citizens* [2011] OJ C 115at para. 6.2.3.

tions High Commissioner for Refugees and through the development of the EU Resettlement Programme as well as new regional protection programmes.[59] In order to develop and implement the *Stockholm Programme*, in a Resolution of April 2014, the European Parliament called on

> the Member States to make use of the current provisions of the Visa Code and the Schengen Borders Code allowing the issuing of humanitarian visas, and to facilitate the provision of temporary shelter for human rights defenders at risk in third countries.[60]

At the time of the 2014 EP Resolution, the tragic events close to the Italian island of Lampedusa, in which more than 366 people died, put back the issue of migration control in the Mediterranean sea at the top of the EU political agenda and triggered the Commission to establish the Task Force Mediterranean. The EC insisted that Parliament should be involved in it[61] and Parliament insisted that since '... EU legislation provides some tools, such as the Visa Code and the Schengen Borders Code, which make it possible to grant humanitarian visas', it was incumbent upon 'the Member States to take measures to enable asylum seekers to access the Union asylum system in a safe and fair manner.'[62] The Task Force Mediterranean set up 38 lines of action and, among other things, asked the Commission to explore guidelines for a common approach to humanitarian permits/visas.

According to the Commission, the recommendations emerging from the work of the Task Force Mediterranean had a very strong operational value, which was extremely relevant for addressing the crisis situation in the Mediterranean, for which reason its content was supposed to be implemented as a matter of priority and urgency.[63] In June 2014, the European Council discussed the guidelines, but did not explicitly endorse the Commission's notion of reinforced legal coordinated approach to humanitarian

59 European Commission, Action plan on the Stockholm Programme <https://eur-lex.europa.eu/legal-content/EN/TXT/?uri=LEGISSUM:jl0036> (accessed 25 November 2019).

60 See: EP Res of 2 April 2014 on the mid-term review of the Stockholm Programme, 2013/2024(INI) at para. 83.

61 European Commission News, *Task Force for the Mediterranean: Actions on migration and asylum* (Brussels, Press Release, 27 May 2014) <https://ec.europa.eu/home-affairs/what-is-new/news/news/2014/20140527_01_en> (accessed 25 November 2019).

62 EP Res of 23 October 2013 on migratory flows in the Mediterranean, with particular attention to the tragic events off Lampedusa, 2013/2827(RSP) at para. 5(G).

63 European Commission, Implementation of the Communication on the Work of the Task Force Mediterranean, SWD(2014) 173 final (22 May 2014).

visas.[64] One month earlier, the Commission had proposed recasting the Visa Code, with an almost exclusive focus on financial and security issues.[65] The Commission did not use this opportunity to introduce substantial amendments to Articles 19 (4) and 25 (1) on humanitarian visas. The Council discussed the Commission's proposal between April 2014 and April 2016[66] and during that period, the European Commission established a comprehensive European Agenda on Migration to address immediate challenges and the EU's responses in the areas of irregular migration, borders, asylum and legal migration.[67] In February 2016, in its communication to the European Parliament and to the Council, the European Commission detailed the implementation of the priority measures within the framework of the European Agenda on Migration. The Commission found that, despite the existence of a feasible system for managing migration, it was failing in its implementation on the ground.[68] The Commission has regularly reported progress made under the European Agenda on Migration and has set out other key actions to be taken.[69]

On the other hand, the LIBE Committee[70] continued to work on the legal gap as part of the review of the Visa Code (2014/0094(COD)), by insert-

---

64 Conclusions of the European Council of 26-27 June 2014.

65 COM(2014) 164 final, European Commission Proposal for a Regulation of the European Parliament and of the Council on the Union Code on Visas (Visa Code) (recast).

66 Art 290 TFEU puts the European Parliament and Council on an equal footing with regard to legislative scrutiny of the Commission's quasi-legislative acts. See: M Kaeding, 'Out of balance? Practical Experience in the European Union with Quasi-Legislative Acts' *in* O. Costa (ed.) *The European Parliament in Times of EU Crisis. Dynamics and Transformations* (London, Palgrave Macmillan, 2019) 161-175 at 163.

67 COM(2015) 245 final, Communication from the commission to the European Parliament, the Council, the European Economic and Social Committee and the Committee of the Regions. A European Agenda on Migration (13 May 2015).

68 COM(2019) 481 final, Communication of the European Parliament Commission to the European Council and to the Council. Management of the refugee crisis, status of the process of carrying out the priority actions in keeping with the European Agenda on Migration (16 October 2019).

69 The latest Communication from the Commission to the European Parliament, the European Council and the Council was on 6 March 2019. See: COM (2019) 126 final, Progress report on the Implementation of the European Agenda on Migration.

70 European Parliament's committees deal with EU legislative proposals by adopting reports, which then are referred to plenary for voting by all Members, and appoint negotiation teams to conduct talks with Council. They adopt non-legis-

ing a number of amendments regarding the creation of a European Humanitarian Visa. The aim of the amendments has been to strengthen the existing provisions by giving a different interpretation of the rather narrow interpretation of humanitarian grounds and international obligations currently in use and by closing some gaps in the Code in order to allow for a more coherent, protection-oriented approach.[71] The text adopted by the LIBE Committee on 15 March 2016 on the creation of a European Humanitarian Visa was as follows:

> (26.a) The possibility to apply for a European humanitarian visa directly at any consulate or embassy of the Member States should be established. The provisions to that end should, however, only become applicable two years after the entry into force of this Regulation, in order to provide the Commission with sufficient time to define the necessary specific conditions and procedures for issuing such visas. When preparing the specific conditions and procedures for issuing such visas, the Commission should conduct an impact assessment. In the event that the Commission proposes a separate legal instrument setting up a European humanitarian visa, it should present a proposal to modify this Regulation before its provisions on a European humanitarian visa become applicable.
> Article 22(5a) Persons seeking international protection may apply for a European humanitarian visa directly at any consulate or embassy of the Member States. Once granted following an assessment, such a humanitarian visa shall allow its holder to enter the territory of the Member State issuing the visa for the sole purpose of lodging in that Member State an application for international protection, as defined in Article 2(a) of Directive 2011/95/EU. The relevant provisions of Title III of this Regulation shall apply with the exception of Articles 11, 13a, 15 and 27.
> The Commission shall be empowered to adopt delegated acts in accordance with Article 48 concerning the specific conditions and procedures for issuing such visas, supplementing or amending Articles 9, 10, 13, and 20 of this Regulation insofar as it is necessary in order to take into consideration the particular circumstances of persons seeking in-

---

lative reports. LIBE is the European Parliament Committee on Civil Liberties, Justice and Home Affairs.

71 Committee on Civil Liberties, Justice and Home Affairs (LIBE), Working Document on humanitarian visas (Rapporteur: Juan Fernando López Aguilar, 2018).

ternational protection and of consulates and embassies of Member States.
Article 18(11a) In the assessment of an application for a European humanitarian visa in accordance with Article 22(5a), only the provisions of paragraphs 4, 9, 10 and 11 of this Article shall apply.
Article 55(3a) Article 22(5a) shall apply from [2 years after the day of entry into force].[72]
Between June and September 2016, while considering LIBE Committee's amendments relating to humanitarian visas, the Council requested further clarification from the European Parliament, arguing, in line with the Commission, that the aim of the Visa Code was not to deal with migration, and the issue had to be examined within the EU Resettlement Framework. The Council discussed the issue further in November 2016 and October 2017. The argument against the amendments for the creation of a European Humanitarian Visa included that (1) the Visa Code was not the appropriate place for such rules as it dealt with short-stay visas; (2) there were other legal pathways, in particular, resettlement; and (3) the amendments risked overburdening consulates.

On 7 March 2017, the Court of Justice of the European Union (CJEU) adopted its judgment in Case C-638/16 PPU *X and X v État belge*, according to which Member States are not required, under EU law, to grant a humanitarian visa to persons wishing to enter their territory with a view to applying for asylum, but they remain free to do so on the basis of their national law. After months of deadlock, with the Council refusing to continue negotiations if these amendments were not withdrawn, in September 2017, Parliament's negotiating team withdrew the amendments in relation to the creation of a European Humanitarian Visa. Instead the LIBE Committee decided to draw up this legislative own-initiative report.[73]

4.3 *The LIBE Committee's legislative own-initiative report*

On 6.12.2017, the Conference of Presidents authorised the request of the LIBE Committee for a legislative own-initiative report on humanitarian visas. According to the rapporteur in charge, Juan Fernando López-Aguilar, EU law as it 'currently stands' could be changed to allow the visas

72 Ibid. at 2-3.
73 Ibid. at 3.

to be issued to such persons. The rapporteur's report was supported by a European Added Value Assessment prepared by the European Parliamentary Research Service.[74]

The rapporteur argued that Parliament should call for a separate instrument in the legislative own-initiative report to be proposed by the Commission due to the fact that the Commission and the Council had repeatedly argued that the Visa Code was not the right instrument.[75] The rapporteur held that Article 78(2)(g) TFEU, which provides for 'partnership and cooperation with third countries for the purpose of managing inflows of people applying for asylum or subsidiary or temporary protection', would permit a sufficient legal basis if combined with Article 77(2)(a) on the common policy on visas and other short-stay residence.[76] Following that, the rapporteur added that it should be possible to apply for such a visa at the consulate or embassy of any Member State, with the Member State granting such a visa subsequently being responsible for the asylum procedure. And it would be up to the applicant to demonstrate that he or she was in need of international protection. The requirements should take into account that such a person was fleeing persecution, ie, could be outside his/her country of residence, lack certain documents, etc. The admissibility and substantive assessment would focus on the question of whether an application is prima facie not manifestly unfounded.[77]

On 4 December 2018, the rapporteur presented a Motion for a European Parliament Resolution with recommendations to the Commission on Humanitarian Visas. The recitals of the new legislative instrument highlighted the need to resolve the paradoxical situation that EU law lacked a provision on how a refugee should actually arrive, owing to which all arrivals take place in an irregular manner. The new legislative instrument will avoid the risk of fragmentation and it will lead the EU to a consistent common policy. The recommendations state that the new instrument should cover third country nationals who are subject to visa requirement

---

74 See European Parliamentary Research Service, *European Added Value Assessment accompanying the European Parliament's legislative own-initiative report*, Rapporteur Juan Fernando López Aguilar, Study by Violeta Moreno-Lax, The Added Value of EU Legislation on Humanitarian Visas- Legal Aspects, EPRS, PE 621.823, July 2018.

75 Committee on Civil Liberties, Justice and Home Affairs (LIBE), Working Document on humanitarian visas, (Rapporteur: Juan Fernando López Aguilar,5.4.2018DT/1150200EN.docx, PE619.272v 02-00) at 5.

76 Ibid.

77 Ibid.

and who are in need of protection against a real risk of being exposed to persecution or serious harm but not covered by any other instrument such as resettlement. The Motion also includes the option of resettlement, but it cannot be the only legal safe pathway, since it addresses only the limited group of already recognised refugees.

The recommendations in the Motion to the EP also cover the conditions and procedures for issuing humanitarian visas, which will be similar to short-stay visas. Accordingly, the visa application should be assessed on a prima facie basis to ensure that applicants have a valid claim of exposure to a real risk of persecution or serious harm. Such an assessment is necessary for the procedure to be credible. The rapporteur is fully aware that important practical preparations need to be undertaken before the new instrument could be implemented. One of the most important steps is to develop an efficient link between visa and asylum procedures in a way that the administrative workflow could function. Finally, some adjustments will be also needed in visa *acquis* and in the asylum *acquis*. Regarding the visa *acquis*, Schengen Borders Code will have to be amended to recognise the humanitarian visa of those arriving at the external border and, in relation to the asylum procedures, any assessment which would have already taken place as part of the visa application should also be taken into account in the asylum procedure, to avoid any unnecessary duplication of efforts.

Unfortunately, to date, the Commission has not submitted any legislative proposal establishing a European Humanitarian Visa and it has focused its attention on Union Resettlement Framework. The Commission changed its position held in 2009,[78] when it specifically referred to the need to establish procedures for PEPs and the issuing of humanitarian visas and affirmed that

> it is not politically feasible to create a subjective right to request admission and to be admitted or an obligation on the Member States to admit a person in need of international protection. Indeed, the Common European Asylum System applies to applications for international protection made in the territory of the Member States and does not cover

78 COM(2009) 262 final, Communication from the Commission to the European Parliament and the Council: An area of freedom, security and justice serving the citizen.

request for diplomatic or territorial asylum submitted to representations of the Member State.[79]

5. *Some concluding observations*

Before December 2018, humanitarian visas were largely discussed in the EU context without any concrete results, although there was always a recognition of the urgency to harmonise an EU-wide intervention to avoid a fragmentation that undermines the existing visa and asylum *acquis*. The current framework as regards the visa *acquis*, on the one side, and the asylum *acquis* on the other, is detrimental to EU values and to EU commitments to fundamental rights. The Charter of Fundamental Rights, in particular the *prohibition of refoulement*, may render the issuance of visas for the purposes of seeking asylum compulsory in certain circumstances. And this obligation must be taken into account alongside legitimate concerns of the respective Member State, considering the significance of such factors as numbers, resource implications, and the workability of the ensuing EU scheme in devising the necessary action.

Since 2016, trilogue or tripartite talks on humanitarian visas between the Parliament, the Council, and the Commission changed the favourable position that the Commission had held towards humanitarian visas in 2009. At the time of writing, in 2019, Europe as a whole seems to be reeling under a more complex reality than the Europe back in 2009. The European Union as such, and particularly some of its Members States, are struggling with an unexpected and uncontrolled response to the arrival of thousands of refugees. Additionally, the fragmentation and the lack of cohesion between different EU policies and programmes, plus the number of initiatives to reform the CEAS proposed by the Commission, and the fact that the EU Member States tend to think about the asylum issue in domestic terms, led to the Commission to be reticent about an EU humanitarian visa scheme that most likely will not be supported for many Members States.

Finally, the Commission has decided to focus on the *EU Resettlement Framework* as part of its efforts to provide viable safe and legal alternatives for those who risk their lives at the hands of criminal smuggling networks

79 European Commission, Follow up to the European Parliament non-legislative resolution with recommendations to the Commission on Humanitarian Visas, 2018/2271 (INL) / A8-0423/2018 / P8_TA-PROV(2018)0494 (1 April 2019).

across the Mediterranean.[80] However, as UNHCR has constantly reiterated, resettlement consists of the selection and transfer of *already-recognised refugees* from a country of first asylum to a third State that agrees to admit them as refugees and grant them permanent residence.[81] Therefore, the main reason for resettlement is the need for 'better' protection of particularly vulnerable refugees who have reached a country of asylum where their situation is precarious or unsafe due to health, security or other reasons. When the Commission presented its proposal for a Regulation setting up a Union Resettlement Framework in 2016, it was probably aware that the *Joint Resettlement Programme* established in 2009 did not work efficiently and the EU Member States' contribution was slow and scarce. Only 10 Member States had established annual schemes with very limited capacity, and, unfortunately, no common planning or coordination mechanism existed at EU level.[82] Nevertheless, the European Commission insisted on launching in 2017 a new resettlement pledging exercise and called on EU Member States to resettle at least 50,000 persons in need of international protection by October 2019. If EU Member States, as expected, have not reacted to a resettlement scheme since 2009,[83] why does the Commission insist on this approach? Declarations, such as 'the Union Resettlement aims to create a more structured, harmonized, and permanent framework for resettlement', have proven to merely be political wishful thinking, with the effect that people smugglers and traffickers have remained undeterred. They have also not prevented persons seeking international protection from risking their lives, or dying, in their attempt to reach the EU territory.

The Commission planned for a comprehensive and balanced migration policy in 2008 and, jointly with the Council, pleaded for a holistic approach to maritime crossings and deaths at sea by exploring new legal channels to safely access the European Union in 2013.[84] Although, in late 2016, both opposed the amendments to the Visa Code, we hope that in the

---

80 The Commission proposal introduces a framework entailing a unified procedure for resettlements to the EU. However, the number of people to be resettled through the framework would be decided upon by individual Member States.

81 UNHCR, *Resettlement Handbook* (Geneva, UNHCR, 2011) at 3.

82 Commission Staff Working Document accompanying the Communication of the Commission on the establishment of a Joint EU Resettlement Programme (Impact Assessment), SEC(2009) 1127 (2 September 2009).

83 Out of 50,000 resettlements to be implemented by the end of October, only 24,700 have been implemented so far.

84 COM (2013) 869 Final, Commission Communication on the work of the Task Force Mediterranean at 2.

next evaluation of the application of the Regulation of the Union Resettlement Framework, the Commission will follow the EP's recommendations and is strongly committed to seeking additional measures towards developing a legal framework for European Humanitarian Visa. The Commission and the Council should enhance effective legal pathways for persons in need of international protection to ensure that Europe stands for responsibility, solidarity and partnership in migration and asylum matters. As the former European Commission President Jean-Claude Juncker said as a candidate to preside over the EC:

> Our common European values and our historic responsibility are my starting point when I think about the future of Europe's migration policy (...) the future of a prosperous continent that will always be open for those in need, but that will also deal with the challenge of migration together, and not to leave some to cope alone.[85]

It is about time we had a forward-looking comprehensive holistic approach, like the one designed in the context of the Task Force Mediterranean, if the European Union is really committed to achieving the Union 's values.

---

85 European Commission, *A Europe that protects our borders and delivers on a comprehensive migration policy* (May 2019) <https://ec.europa.eu/commission/files/europe-protects-our-borders-and-delivers-comprehensive-migration-policy_en> (accessed 25 November 2011).

Conclusion: The Role of the Judge in Controlling the Genuine Enjoyment of the Substance of the Rights

Jean-Yves Carlier[1]

Contents

The issue of migration is a complex one, both in law and in fact. We should avoid a Manichean presentation of a black or white choice between closing or opening borders. The visa is one of many ways to develop 'a renewed global migration governance'. Under EU migration law and policy, there are two paths to using visas as a tool for migration governance. One for the long term, the other for the short term. The long-term path is more a matter of governance, policy and future legislation. The short-term path relates more to the judiciary.

The Long-term Path: Visa Facilitation and Suppression

In the long term, it is possible to shorten the list of third countries whose nationals need a visa to enter the EU. It is not a question of eliminating border controls or even of abolishing visa requirements in one shot. Borders controls are necessary and visa facilitation and suppression is a long term path. It is a step-by-step process, reducing the number of countries whose nationals need a visa and gradually easing the procedures for other countries. There is nothing new here. This is already done. The secondary

1 Professor in the Law Faculty of the Catholic University of Louvain (UCL) and in the Law Faculty of the University of Liège (ULg).

law on visas was among the first texts on migration adopted under EU law (and even EC law). Today, Regulation 2018/1806 provides a list of third countries whose nationals must be in possession of visas or who are exempted from visa requirements to enter the EU. Annex 1 of Regulation 2018/1806 lists the countries whose nationals need a visa. The number of countries has already decreased from 127 countries in 2001 to 104 countries in 2018, ie 23 fewer countries. This is the result of successive adaptations related to EU integration and exemption agreements. Annex 2 shows that 62 countries have their nationals exempted from visa requirements. This is the case in particular for several countries in South and Central America, including Mexico. This is completed and progressively rebuilt by agreements on the facilitation of the issuance of visas signed with various countries (Albania, Macedonia, Armenia, Azerbaijan, Bosnia, Cape Verde, Georgia, Moldova, Montenegro, Russia, Serbia, Ukraine). This is also complemented by Regulation 1931/2006 on local border traffic at the external land borders of the Members States and amending the provisions of the Schengen Convention. This represents a facilitation of the mobility for thousands of people, especially at the Polish borders, including Regulation 1342/2011 amending Regulation 1931/2006 and including the Kaliningrad Oblast and certain Polish administrative districts in the eligible border area. Of course, these are short-stay visas (maximum three months). But this visa policy influences the mobility of people through the development of circular movements, which has direct consequences for migration policy by allowing greater legal mobility and reducing irregular entry.

Gradually, in the very long term, all this could lead to the abolition of short-stay visas and meeting the challenge of what I call the *Suspended Step of the Stork* paradox (le paradoxe du *Pas suspendu de la cigogne*), harkening back to the title of the film directed by Greek filmmaker Theo Angelopoulos (*Το Μετέωρο Βήμα Του Πελαργού*). One of the scenes in this film contains a discussion between a border guard and a man (played by Marcello Mastroianni) who could be a refugee. Both are on the white line of the border between Greece and Albania. They have the possibility to lift a foot over the line without being able to put it down on the other side. This symbolises very well the state of art in international migration law: the right for anyone to leave any country, without having the right to enter the territory of any other country. It is a paradox in a world divided into nation states: how can I leave a State without entering another? This is symbolised by the suspended step of the stork, a migratory bird. The law doctrine explains this paradox (of the suspended step) with national sovereignty. The political scientist explains it because these texts of international law (like art. 12.2 ICCPR) emanate from the time of the Cold War, well known in the history of Germany, with a right to leave challenged by the East and affirmed by the West, but without this right to leave being supplemented by a right of entry. But, intellectually, the question is still there. Migration is emigration and immigration.

On this long-term path, the global governance of migration would not happen so much through visas but rather through the facilitation and suppression of visas. This does not mean the suppression of control. But controls must coexist with comprehensive governance of migration. The Global Compact for safe, orderly and regular migration (GCM) might give an opportunity to build this. In particular, Objective 5 of the GCM to *Enhance availability and flexibility of pathways for regular migration* provides, as action b, to 'facilitate regional and cross-regional labour mobility through international and bilateral cooperation arrangements, such as free movement regimes, visa liberalization or multiple-country visas….'

The Short-term Path: Judicial Control

Along with this long-term evolution, in the short term, it is necessary to examine the extent to which the judiciary has a right of scrutiny on this issue of visas. It is certainly possible at the national level. This volume offers a very interesting set of diverse and topical studies on how the question of humanitarian visa is debated and regulated in different countries. As often in Human Rights, this confirms that the national level remains the first level of protection of fundamental rights.

But what about the European level under the Visa Code? The issue is obviously that of visa applications, called humanitarian visas, which are formally short-stay visas, but with the intention of seeking asylum and thus paving the way for a long stay.

We know that the ECJ considers that such a request does not fall within the scope of the EU law. We know that Advocate General Mengozzi was of a different opinion. The debate is possible. The question is not a question of extraterritoriality. The Visa Code always applies to persons outside of the EU territory. It is not a question of the **territorial** scope of EU law but of its **material** scope. I will not repeat here the legal analysis of the case *X. and X.* Let us simply examine this *X. and X.* case in connection with the EU-Turkey statement in the light of the importance given to the 'intention'. In the EU-Turkey statement case, the General Court (with implicit confirmation of the ECJ) did not at all take into consideration the intention of the parties, which clearly was to create an agreement between the EU and Turkey. Using only an analysis of the format of this statement, the

Court said that it was not an EU Council decision but a decision of the Member States 'réunis en Conseil'. On the contrary, in *X. and X.*, the reasoning of the Court concentrated on the 'intention' of the applicant, saying that even if, formally, the request was a request for a short stay visa, and seen as such by the national authorities, including the national jurisdiction, the ECJ, requalifying the question, said that since the applicant had the intention to ask for refugee status after his arrival in Belgium, the request fell outside the scope of the short-term Visa Code.

Let us think outside this box of 'intention' to examine the material scope of EU law. Let us think from the perspective of the protection of fundamental rights. With regard to free movement within the EU, the Court is increasingly referring to fundamental rights and to the Charter of Fundamental Rights. It does so, in particular, to enter into purely internal situations which, in principle, are beyond its control. The Court did it, in 2017, in the *Chavez-Vilchez* case and again in 2018 in *K.A. et al.*

For this, the Court refers, since 2011, to a notion of *genuine enjoyment of 'the substance of the rights'* of the citizen (*Des Kernbestands der Rechte*). For instance, in *Chavez-Vilchez*, the Court in Grand Chamber held that: 'there are very specific situations in which, despite the fact that secondary law … does not apply (because) the Union citizen concerned has not made use of his freedom of movement, a right of residence must nevertheless be granted to a third-country national who is a family member of that Union citizen … if, as a consequence of refusal of such a right, that citizen would be obliged in practice to leave the territory of the European Union as a whole, thus depriving him of the genuine enjoyment of the substance of the rights conferred by that status.' In other words, *the substance of the rights* is a way of entering within the material scope of EU law to avoid compromising the effectiveness of EU citizenship. And this 'substance of the rights' must be seen in the light of fundamental rights, especially the best interests of the child. In each case, 'It is the duty of the authority to examine an application' without procedural issues preventing it.

What is interesting in this case law is the place given to fundamental rights in purely internal situations. The Charter of Fundamental Rights is no longer only a key to interpreting EU law when the material scope falls within the scope of EU law, but the Charter of Fundamental Right is also a key to entering EU law.

Can the same reasoning based on 'the substance of the right' be held with regard to the right to asylum and the request of humanitarian visa? Some would say no, because it has nothing to do with European citizenship and the rights derived for certain third country nationals as family members and it would be a 'conceptual revolution'. Others would say yes, this parallelism of reasoning is possible if one took into account the competences of the EU in the field of asylum, the reference to the right of asylum in the Charter and 'the substance of the rights' as a general principle. Of course, in the case of humanitarian visas the criterion could not be, as for citizens, the obligation to leave the territory of the EU, but conversely, the obligation to allow entry into the EU territory, because it would otherwise also violate the substance of the rights of the persons concerned.

This is part of a broader question: how much is global free movement of persons linked to citizenship (or how much will it be)? This is also part of the question of how to find a legal concept rather than a discretionary one for this notion of humanitarian visa. Here, with *the substance of the rights* we have a legal concept, which is, for the moment, a work in progress developed by the Court.

In 1942, just before he died, Stefan Zweig wrote in *Die Welt von gestern. Erinnerungen eines Europäers*: 'Wir konnten reisen ohne Paß und Erlaubnisschein, wohin es uns beliebte' (neither passport nor visa was necessary to travel where we wished). Those times are long gone. Maybe, one day, we will say: no visa is necessary to travel where we wish to, mobility is a reality and migration is under control.